Astrology's Secrets to Hot Romance

Astrology's Secrets to  Romance

How to Find True Compatibility and the One Who's Right for You

Phyllis F. Mitz, M.A.

Health Communications, Inc.
Deerfield Beach, Florida

www.hcibooks.com

Library of Congress Cataloging-in-Publication Data

Firak-Mitz, Phyllis
    Astrology's secrets to hot romance : how to find true compatibility and the
one who's right for you / Phyllis F. Mitz.
        p. cm.
    ISBN-13: 978-0-7573-0490-3 (trade paper)
    ISBN-10: 0-7573-0490-7 (trade paper)
    1. Astrology.   2. Love—Miscellanea.   3. Mate selection—Miscellanea.
4. Interpersonal relations—Miscellanea.   I. Title.
BF1729.L6F57 2007
133.5'864677—dc22

                                                                    2006033438

© 2007 Phyllis F. Mitz, M.A.

Publisher: Health Communications, Inc.
                3201 S.W. 15th Street
                Deerfield Beach, FL 33442-8190

Cover design by Andrea Perrine Brower
Inside book design by Lawna Patterson Oldfield and Dawn Von Strolley Grove

Contents

v

Part Two:
Meet Your Match

Acknowledgments

This book is dedicated to my beloved clients. Their open and honest candor about their love lives has taught me volumes about what members of each astrological sign truly want, need, and offer in relationships and the very best ways to love them.

This book is also dedicated to my beloved husband, Richard. He not only keeps my life exciting (true to his Aries Sun Sign), he also shows me, through his love and devotion, how romance and marriage really can get better and better over time—even despite our signs' being so-called incompatible.

Thank you to my dearest friends, Cathy Norman and Susan Guthrie, whose patient "How's the book coming?" queries always supported and encouraged me.

Thank you to my savvy Aquarian editor, Michele Matrisciani, who came into this project with a bang and then shook it up and revolutionized it every step of the way!

Thank you to my publisher, Peter Vegso, who, in true Aquarian fashion, keeps opening doors of opportunity—for me and for countless other authors and readers throughout the world.

To Wendy M., whose Gemini-like request of, "Keep it simple so I can read it quickly" were words I wrote by.

Many thanks to my Cancerian friend and publicist, Kim Weiss, whose nurturing and encouragement championed me and this project through thick and thin.

And thank you to my beloved teachers, John Roger and John Morton, who continually lift, inspire, and liberate me. It's their relationship advice that I consider the most essential. It is: "There is never a good enough reason to withhold your loving." I think that says it all.

Introduction

Whenever you meet people who pique your interest, go ahead and ask, "What's your sign?" It's not only a great pickup line, it's a terrific question. The answer will give you a world of insights about who someone is, what he or she likes, and how to best get along with that person. That's because when it comes time to love, we each act, think, and feel a great deal like the descriptions of our astrological signs. Astrology is an incredible tool for finding and sustaining the kinds of relationships we truly desire. Being familiar with astrology can help you figure out who you should date, how to connect with people or your partner, and ways to keep your love sparked and growing. I wrote this book to provide you with hundreds of secrets for improving relationships of all sorts—from love and romance to family and friendship—and to show you ways to create and maintain the love you seek.

I've been a busy astrologer with a master's degree in counseling for more than twenty-five years. My clients range from celebrities, CEOs, and politicians to doctors, caretakers, office workers, psychologists, and students. No matter who they are or what they've achieved in life, it is their relationships that they ask about most often. Everyone wants to know how to get along better with someone, be it their lover, spouse, boss, sibling, parent, or child. And for good reason—love is what keeps most of us happy, healthy, and fulfilled.

Because everyone wants to love and be loved, I wrote this book to give you the kind of astrological clarity and strategies that can help make your relationships thrive. I've taken much of the guesswork out of astrology by telling you everything you need to know about how to please someone and how to be pleased by them.

In Part One: So Many Signs, So Little Time, I describe what members of each sign are like, including what they want in relationships and how you can give it to them, and what they offer in relationships so you can make them happy by welcoming what they give. And, because romance is so very important, I put a special spotlight on love and sexuality. I describe how each sign acts as a lover, how you can act and dress to attract them, and even what kinds of dates they enjoy. Then, when it's time for making love, I provide some great ideas and advice about that, too.

The good news is that many of the astrological signs are compatible. You'll learn which ones are easiest for you to relate to and how you can make your relationship with them sing even more. Having this information will help you zero in on those people with whom you're most likely to succeed in love.

But the truth is, not all signs of the zodiac enjoy natural compatibility, and some have a really hard time relating to each other. Sometimes they end up being the people who are closest to you. Imagine my surprise when the man I fell deeply in love with turned out to be an Aries, not a sign that my Virgo Sun Sign typically gets along with. Of course that didn't stop me from marrying him (eighteen years ago and counting). I simply put astrology to use. Knowing we're born to express certain traits and that we're not just acting certain ways to drive each other crazy has helped my husband and me to accept and even enjoy the personality differences that may have left us fuming had we not understood each other's astrological tendencies.

The fact that we do occasionally drive each other crazy is another reason I wrote this book. Even the best of relationships have times when someone does something irksome or finds their beloved's behavior annoying. In fact, each sign has its own set of relationship problems. Unlike other astrology books, this book discusses what these challenges are. I provide strategies for overcoming these problems and actions, so you can increase your compatibility. I also show you how you can deal with whatever issues are likely to come up so they don't disrupt the good things you share. Reading this book can help you get along with everyone, from those you adore to those who push all of your buttons.

If someone's astrological sign isn't especially compatible with yours, it doesn't mean a relationship with them can't work. It just means you'll have to make some adjustments. I'll help you understand what those adjustments are and how you can make them. So don't worry if you hook up with someone who is a less compatible sign. This book gives you strategies to get the most out of those relationships!

In Part Two: Meet Your Match, I've compiled a thorough reference like no other you have ever seen in an astrology book. I'll tell you what's good about a relationship with every sign you're curious about: what you'd like about them, what they'd like about you, and the best that can come from your union. But I go further and address the unique challenges you might find with specific signs and, more important, ways they can be worked out. You'll get the full picture of how to build a meaningful connection with almost anyone.

Here's a tip: be sure to read about every sign. That's because each of us is a unique combination of all twelve signs of the zodiac. Surely we behave in relationships the way our Sun Signs describe. But since Venus, our planet of love, and Mars, our planet of sex, can fall in different signs other than our Sun Sign, it's likely that our relationships, tastes, and tendencies display a variety of astrological traits. You're sure to recognize yourself and those you love in quite a few chapters of this book. You'll learn loads of things about yourself, as well as how to find hot romance, true compatibility, and the one who's right for you in romance and all the other relationships you enjoy in your life.

Part One:

So Many Signs,
So Little Time

Chapter One

Aries
(March 21—April 19)

Who They Are

When you have an Aries in your life, you're sure to be excited, challenged, and whisked from one adventure to another. That's because these dynamic creatures are all about living passionately! They love diving headfirst from one pursuit to the next, thrilled by the last one, yet anxious to get on to the next one. Aries are incredibly fast, enthusiastic, and spontaneous—their guts tell them where to go. There is an exuberant trailblazer in every Aries that constantly seeks the new territory, the great challenge, the "never tried before." High-spirited and full of bravado, Aries are by far the happiest when they're initiating a new project or embarking on a new course of interest—including a relationship with you!

Life with an Aries is in a constant state of action, renewal, and adventure. They tirelessly pursue ideas and projects that make life

Aries Is a Fire Sign

🔥 Aries is a Fire Sign, which means that they act a lot like fire: They're excitable, volatile, and explode with bonfires of enthusiasm from little sparks of ideas. And Aries are unpredictable—they jump from idea to interest to relationship with lightning-like speed, all in the name of keeping their passions enflamed. Like fire, Aries can also burn out easily—either from overextension, which they love, or from boredom, which they fear.

interesting and exciting. Same goes for their relationships; never ones to be satisfied with ordinary routines or ideas, Aries will wake you up in the middle of the night to go dancing and take you skydiving for your birthday. So hang on; life with an Aries can be a wild ride!

The essential ingredient for happiness for every Fire Sign, including Aries, is the freedom to explore life's possibilities. Aries absolutely need room to grow and test themselves. They thrive on taking risks that can create magic, a stroke of luck, or a fortunate turn in life. Aries have an aversion to life's being too predictable, safe, and planned out. That lifestyle not only stifles them, it can lead to an unhappy discontent.

Aries' Fire Sign energy gives them a great capacity for leadership. They're imbued with a tremendous urge to initiate new endeavors.

"What's already been done bores Aries, and what's never been done fascinates them to no end."

And Aries are visionaries—they specialize in forging new territories, trying things they (nor anyone else) have ever done before, and always stirring up the proverbial status quo!

Once a project or endeavor is up and running, or if Aries feel they have learned enough from a situation, they're off—starting another project and proving how it can be done in their own, innovative way. If you catch their vision and want to come along, an Aries will welcome you. They love being the heroic leader that makes life zing!

Understanding Aries comes easiest when you understand that their perspective is primarily personal: they are very aware of their personal wants, needs, and desires. In fact, Aries' life lesson is to be true to themselves. Instead of worrying about what others are doing, or even what they want, Aries feel they should live life the way *they* want, when they want to do it. And they expect their needs should be met with immediacy. So when trying to engage Aries' attention toward your ideas or requests, package them in a way so that they're somehow about Aries.

Most Aries approach life as a series of personal missions. Whatever their intentions are, they're *important*. They get a clear vision of what they're after, and they pursue it fearlessly. Whether Aries' mission is winning your heart or choosing the fastest line in the grocery store, their exuberant confidence is rarely distracted with thoughts of failure—they concentrate solely on success!

As Aries themselves will attest—as will anyone who knows one—those born under this sign are incredibly impatient: they want what they want *right now*! Later means forever to Aries, and they will push and drive to satisfy their insistent needs, wants, and curiosity the moment they erupt. It's hard for Aries to wait to fulfill their desires or to let a plan slowly unfold. But encouraging them to do so might help them avoid some unnecessary mistakes.

One terrific way of understanding Aries is remembering that at heart, each one is a conquering hero. They're thrilled and motivated by the idea of doing battle with and vanquishing anything or anyone

Aries Lesson: To Thine Own Self Be True, but Be Patient About It!

⬟ Although Aries are anxious to discover themselves by jumping into life's possibilities, sometimes their impatience can get them involved in some troublesome situations. They are so eager to get into the pool that they dive right into the deep end before even checking to see if there's water! Understandably, patience is a big key for Aries in learning to avoid life's unnecessary pitfalls. If you can help Aries pause just long enough to think things through, you might help them realize their sign's mission: to allow time for their intuitive wisdom to guide them toward their Truest Self's desire. When following that urge, Aries demonstrate their signature ingeniousness and stay on course for what is genuinely best for them. But you'll have to be patient about this—most Aries only learn patience after running headfirst into brick walls time after time.

standing between them and their goals. Aries sense their lives have an important mission, and they're ready, willing, and eager to realize it. Aries act out the conquering hero theme in their relationships. It shows up right away when they make it their mission to do whatever it takes to win your attention, love, and affection. Make yourself a mission worth exploring!

Aries are fierce competitors, as well. True to their zodiac symbol, the Ram, who goes headfirst to claim its territory, Aries' adrenaline rushes when going head-to-head with any challenge they seek or opponent who gets in their way. They love proving to themselves (and everyone else) that they're gallant heroes who'll come out on top.

What Aries Want in Relationships and How You Can Attract One

Aries love mates whose powers and passions match their own. Aries gravitate toward passionate, involved, challenging, and powerful people. If you can inspire them, thrill them, promote them, teach them, or even infuriate them, Aries are interested. So express yourself in a most courageous, inspired manner. Unabashed confidence is what intrigues Aries most. Acting powerfully with genuine self-respect wins their attention and interest.

Aries desire dynamos; no wimps allowed! Aries want to be with mates who are genuinely real and true to themselves. Let your chutzpah and sass show! Are you powerful? Let Aries see it! Sexy? Bring it on! Smart? How smart? Aries like to think they're in the winner's circle, so show your winning self when you're around them!

Forget about clinging or kowtowing to Aries—they won't respect you if you do. The ironic thing about Aries is that with all their jousting to dominate, they aren't interested in "yes people" who jump at their every call. That bores them to tears. They want companions who'll stand up to their Arian energies and show them the kind of power their inner hero can trust and rely on. What hero picks a wimp for a sidekick?

Nevertheless, every Aries usually does have a few impressed groupies tagging along with them in their adventures. "Hey," Aries tell themselves,

Words Aries Love to Hear

"You're the best!"

"You win!"

"You're sexy!"

"Yes, let's do it your way."

"Maybe they'll learn something from the Master—me!" Aries' best friends are either very secure in their own accomplishments or are dedicated fans to whom Aries can be a heroic role model.

Aries want to be at the top of your list. Aries' simplicity asks only that they are the center of your universe, because after all, they are the center of their own universe. They want to know how special they are to you, if not even your absolute favorite person ever! Prize Aries and shower them with compliments—they'll knock themselves out to live up to your good expectations.

Aries want your devoted attention. Aries are rarely the type of companions who readily accept waiting on the back burner while you do something more important. These feisty Rams will simply not be ignored. Never ones to take "no" or even "not now" for an answer, they'll entertain, cajole, and try every angle to call your attention to them. If they can't get your attention by wowing you with bravado, they'll make you deal with their chest-pounding temper. Remember, to an impatient Aries, "later" means "forever." Aries respect that your career and social needs are important, but you must reassure Aries that they're important to you, as well. If you must put them off, let them know how much you value them and anticipate how much fun it will be when you reunite. Then hurry back!

Aries crave constant action and juice in their relationships. In a relationship, Aries want to feel something powerful is being exchanged. If you love an Aries, show it; if you're mad, let them know that, too. Whip up the energy! Cook up activities that surprise Aries, stretch them, and bring out their adventurousness. Aries find what is new to be hopelessly alluring. Present them with new mountains to climb, dragons to slay, and honors to win. Keep their interest sparked by being spontaneous and even outrageous in all you do. Comfortable routines are for other signs.

Aries are exhilarated by "the chase." Aries find great romance and thrill in the pursuit of anything. Give them something about you or life that they can work to win at. Remember that it's the *idea* and the *act* of conquering that's so exciting for Aries. Once they actually win you over, they could become bored and start looking for another chase. So don't give them the impression they've conquered your will and you'll do whatever they want. After all, the idea of winning—at anything—is intoxicating to Aries.

> "Aries aren't interested in 'yes people' who jump at their every call. That bores them to tears."

Aries savor a good competition. Many Aries are thrilled going head-to-head with you to see who's best—at anything. Do they want to win? Oh, yes! But don't just hand success to an Aries. They want to know they've won only if you've played your best. If Aries lose? They'll be back for another round.

Aries crave encouragement for and faith in their abilities. You needn't necessarily be as dynamic or risk-taking as Aries (few people are after all), but they want you to believe in them. Support their inner myth that they are powerful warriors capable of achieving anything they put their minds to. As brazen as Aries act, they nevertheless need and appreciate loads of reassurance. Tell them what's right about their plans, good about their behavior, and smart about their ideas. The amazing thing about an Aries is they do pull off the most amazing stunts, so go ahead and bank on their success!

Aries like gentleness. With their warrior natures, Aries welcome the chance to relax around others, knowing they won't be cut down should they take off their armor. Aries actually glow when they're wooed and admired. As a show of affection, Rams might nuzzle foreheads with you, using their horns for affection, not for fighting. They melt when they're appreciated and acknowledged, and become eager to show what more they can do for their beloved.

What Aries Offer in Relationships

Aries are vigorous in their relationships. If you are able to catch Aries' attention, they will give you *all of it*—at least at first. Aries will consume and penetrate you until they have figured you out. If they like what they see, they will continue to be direct, intense, and attentive. If they don't like what they see? Aries won't waste your time or theirs by stringing you along—they'll be gone in a flash.

Aries bring gusto, intensity, and dynamism to their relationships. Aries will move you with their power and prowess, challenge you with their insights and encouragements, and otherwise make your life extremely exciting. Always looking for what's new and innovative, Aries will treat you to a steady stream of interests and activities that keep you on your toes and discovering things you'd never know existed were it not for Aries' insights and initiation. Needless to say, you will never be bored.

Aries will make you love them, if they want you to. By using their charm, wit, and seduction, Aries will seduce you. When Aries set their sights on you, no one is as compelling. They have an entire arsenal of gifts that attract. And they're not shy about using them.

Aries deliver loads of surprises and newness in their relationships. Everything and anything will be heightened when Aries is around. Their zest for life and love of adventure make whatever you endeavor together fresh and lively. Always looking for the unexpected angle and opportunities to stir energies up, Aries will treat you to adventures galore and unexpected delights. They introduce you to loads of people you've never met (nor have they, but to them no one is a stranger), as well as spark your interest in subjects you've never heard of.

> **Words Aries Love to Say**
> 🦭 "Let's go!"
> "I . . . think, feel, want, desire . . . etc . . ."
> "Let's try something new."
> "Let's stir up a little action around here!"

Aries are unabashedly direct about their intentions. You'll never have to read their minds. "I think you're sexy, and I want to get to know you." "I want your job; how do I get it?" "I want to be your friend; let's get together!" What to do with such direct Arian advances? Run with them! Aries have fantastic instincts, and they're probably right about your potential. Along with that, Aries will pump you up by telling you directly what they like about you. "You're funny! I like that!" or "You're naughty! I'm excited!" And Aries will let you know how to get along with them by telling you what they want to see more of and what they want to see less of as well.

> "You will never be bored with an Aries around."

Aries will give you plenty of autonomy (especially when they know they're number one with you). Aries' natural openness and curiosity create a fertile ground for you to discover new freedom of thought and expression. After all, Aries want their partners to be

exciting, so they encourage you to do exciting things. Instead of holding you to old attitudes, lifestyles, and habits, Aries will applaud as you
change and even find ways to assist in your blossoming.

**Aries will encourage or even *insist* that you develop your confi-
dence and power.** Savvy Aries are able to see straight through to
someone's potential, and they'll help others to develop it *right now.*
Instead of patiently standing by while you talk of dreams, an Aries will
put you on the road to achieving them by making the calls, establishing the connections, or otherwise (gently or sometimes not so gently)
pushing you in the direction you need to go. You can rest assured
you'll never get stuck in a rut when Aries is around.

Aries make you feel sexy. Aries are not only comfortable with their
sexuality, they're downright proud of it! They know how to exude a
compelling animal magnetism that attracts and motivates others—even
while giving a presentation in the boardroom. Aries will show you how
to use your sex appeal as well by applauding your sexy shirt or encouraging you to walk, talk, or move in a way that says "I'm desirable!"

Aries bring a dash of warmth and sweetness to a relationship.
Once you get past Aries' bravado, you'll be exposed to their incredible
tenderness. Aries will touch your heartstrings to make you feel fully
tended to. That Aries neighbor who's gruff and distracted when tending to his yard is also a pussycat who rubs his wife's feet every night.
The Aries boss who's tough as nails? At home she bakes cookies for
the kids down the street. When you are in Aries' trusted inner circle,
they'll extend themselves in countless ways to bring you comfort and
pleasure.

Aries will understand you with deep sincerity and insight. Aries
will say things that show they've been listening to you, watching you,

and most important, learning to know you all along. Their intuition zeros right in on the core of what you're trying to say (often before you know what you're trying to say) and gives you the feeling of being truly heard and

"You'll never get stuck in a rut when Aries is around."

understood by them. Plus, Aries come up with solutions for any problems you report that are so creative and innovative they might initially seem nutty, yet when tried turn out to be ingenious. Aries like being the person you go to when you need counsel or support, provided, of course, you're willing to move on their ideas.

The Aries Lover

As the conquering hero, Aries are naturally spurred on by the idea of winning love. They are invigorated by the chase and thrive on conquering any obstacles that stand in the way of love's promise. Aries make a mission of finding that ideal soul mate with whom they can blend ecstatically and enjoy a true, enduring love. They hunger for a perfected union in which they can devote themselves and serve.

When Aries loves you, they'll put you on a pedestal and do whatever it takes to make you happy. Their inner hero makes your happiness their mission. They'll want to spend quality time with you and connect by talking, telling stories, and showing affection. When they have your undivided attention, they'll make it worth your while by knocking themselves out to be your champion.

Despite their independence and their insistent "I'll do it on my own, my way" approach, Aries are looking for a love they can respect and finally yield to. When they discover the one they can trust enough to become vulnerable to, they let go of the warrior garb and allow themselves to become chivalrously devoted paramours.

> "When Aries loves you, they'll put you on a pedestal and do whatever it takes to make you happy."

Aries adore a swooning, hot, and immediate affair: if Aries is into you, their motto will be, "Why wait until later when I'm attracted to you right now?" Headfirst they launch into winning your attention and admiration. They'll call two seconds after they get your cell phone number, find countless ways to run into you, and send oversized bouquets to your office to put you and all others on notice that they intend to have you. That charming stranger sidling up to your restaurant table for an introduction? An Aries!

And romantic! Whew! Once Aries fall in love, they are devoted, swooning lovers, tireless in their attentiveness and affection for their beloved.

What kind of dates do Aries enjoy?

Take Aries on adventures that get their blood pumping and adrenaline rushing—like a sporting event or an exciting concert. Let them know how impressed you are with them and show them something to be impressed about with you. No need to hide any of your charms: let Aries see them. Aries are also very visual creatures, and they're downright spellbound by beauty. Try wearing something red, and see how the Aries Ram sits up and takes notice. And, since Aries are turned on by confidence, exude an air about yourself that says, "I'm the hottest person in this room!" Let your prowess show.

What are Aries like between the sheets?

One word: passion! Rams consider sexuality one of the most important components of love, and they are enthusiastic, superphysical, give-it-all lovers. So by all means show them how sexy you are and how much you enjoy your sexuality as well as theirs. Beyond wanting lovers who catch their eye, Aries also desire partners they can romance and play with. They take great pleasure in acting on the variety of sensual fantasies both parties conjure up. Aries relish flinging aside inhibitions and letting their lusty animal nature lead by giving and receiving indulgent pleasures (admittedly, with an emphasis on receiving!). And, remember, Aries are also very performance-conscious, so let them know they are the *best lover ever*.

Aries happily allow themselves to be ravished. In fact, the only time they truly do let themselves relax and be "taken over" is in the bedroom. Aries don't mind a little passionate foreplay and teasing innuendos, but true to their impatient nature, they are anxious to "get to the goal line." Too much putting them or their satisfaction off until later can be a deflating turnoff for them.

What turns Aries off?

Aries are turned off when the wind is taken out of their passionate sails: criticism hurts and deflates them, prudishness

> "Keeping your Aries lover applauded, romanced, and surprised with new positions, places, and attitudes keeps their passions and interest high."

disappoints them, and familiar routines bore Aries and prompt their wandering eye. Keep "emotional processing" to a minimum, as well as "let's talk sessions." Aries don't want to talk about love, they want to do it!

Hint: the Aries lover can feel vulnerable—if not jealous—should they suspect your attention is being pulled elsewhere. They may wonder if they are, indeed, enough: Are they a good enough lover? Are they interesting enough? Aries deeply appreciate being reassured that their strength and power are adored and cherished.

Ways Aries Can Drive You Crazy and What to Do About It

*A*s with every other sign, the very traits that make Aries exciting and lovable can also make them frustrating, when taken to extremes.

Aries challenge: Their motto is unabashedly "I, I, Me, Me."

*A*ries act more selfishly than most other signs. They think of themselves first, promote themselves unabashedly, and do exactly what they want to do. There is a very strong "me vibe" in Aries that refuses to be silenced. *Why should it be?* thinks Aries. *This is my life, and I want it my way!*

Aries are famous for calling only when they want something or talking incessantly about themselves, then having to run when it's your time to talk. They'll seem utterly oblivious to your (or others') needs by taking the biggest piece of pie, stealing your girlfriend just for the sport of it, wearing your favorite sweater to a smoky bar, or risking your long-saved nest egg on a get-rich-quick scheme.

Most Aries don't do such things out of maliciousness; they do it out of self-involvement. Aries' apparent selfishness actually comes from their urge to follow their spirit's vision. (Although admittedly, Aries often follow their ego's visions, which they are learning from experience to differentiate from the spirit's.) Every Aries has a destiny that calls them to separate from the pack from time to time and to go off and do things on their own in a way no one else has done or even agrees with, in order to learn to be true to themselves.

What to do?

Don't expect Aries to spend time figuring out your needs; get in touch with them yourself and then vocalize them—over and over, if you need to, in order to get through. When Aries finally hears that you don't want them stealing the biggest piece of pie or risking your retirement fund on a get-rich-quick scheme, they might initially be hurt or baffled that you're not happily going along with their plan. But if you are persistent enough and clear enough in your boundaries, they may eventually come to respect your point of view. In time, Aries might even get a glimpse at the importance of your needs. When that happens they can turn their attention off of themselves and on to considering you.

Aries challenge: The conquering hero may try to conquer you.

Aries are leaders, and that's that. And they're impatient: they just want others to do what they ask of them—quickly and well. Aries' hero's dominance also makes them bossy: if someone puts another idea, goal, or point of view on the table, Aries will simply use their conquering energy to slay it. "No, that's not the way—this way," or "That's your favorite restaurant? I know one that's so much better!" They're not being critical; they simply think they know a better way and want to get to it as quickly as possible.

Aries' dominance occasionally disrupts the peace, if not sparks an all-out war. Their bluntness, aggressiveness, dismissive attitude, or other traits can make them seem incredibly inconsiderate. In fact, Aries usually don't mean to offend you. Aries aren't all that sensitive, nor are they particularly wired to intuit others' needs.

What to do?

If Aries is trying to dominate you or the way you do things, stand up inside. (If you stand up to them in a challenging way, you might elicit a round of head-butting aggression.) When you are confident in your visions, choices, and preferences, state them to Aries in a clear and secure way. They'll respect you and perhaps even back down.

One big motivating factor in getting an Aries to do anything for anyone, including compromise, is this: they adore making others happy. They love being the hero, pulling off the magic, delivering the goods, and making others smile. If you want something from an Aries, make your request directly and clearly, and let them know how happy it would make you if they complied.

Important point: Although Aries are leaders, they can also follow if they fully trust and respect the one who is leading. Aries yearn to find someone they can trust, relax around, and yield to. If Aries witnesses you being effective and admirable, they will be more than willing to support you in a most heroic way.

Aries challenge: Competitiveness

*A*ries' competitiveness can surely make sparks fly. They may compete to prove they're as much anything as you are (except a loser or whiner—they want no part of that). If you're smart, Aries is smarter. If you're rich, Aries is richer (or can be). You're good-looking? Sexy? You're no match for Aries, blessed with a high opinion of their looks and sexual prowess.

Aries love to compete—it can thrill and enliven them like nothing else. And they love to win. Aries can get so revved up while competing that they take a win-at-any-cost stance. In their determination to conquer, Aries become blinded to everything else in life and maintain deadly aim on their goal. Can this elicit their tougher, ever nastier side? If need be. Aries wants to take home the trophy. If you're in their way, they'll do what they can to get you out of it. Truly, it's nothing personal.

Envy can also spark Aries' competitiveness. If they see you have something they want, like attention or riches, Aries might yearn to have it for themselves. That's when they rally for the admiration of your spouse, campaign to get your job, or otherwise win what you have.

Aries' competitiveness is often rooted in insecurity. Beneath Aries' bravado, seeming arrogance, and endless acts of risky chutzpah is a deeply vulnerable ego: What if they're not as original, fabulous, or potent as they seem? Does that mean they aren't lovable? If you get a glimpse of Aries' ordinariness, would you take your love away?

What to do?

*I*f you are uncomfortable with competition or just don't like expending your energy that way, you might be able to sidestep Aries'

"If you are comfortable with competition, then your relationship with Aries can be very stimulating."

challenges by simply not engaging with them. When Aries recognize that you won't go head-to-head with them, they might lose interest and go on to someone or something that will. Or, they'll compete with you anyway, without your paying attention to it. In a way you should be flattered that Aries sees something in you to respect or admire enough to want for themselves.

Sometimes just letting Aries know you love them and don't need proof of their being the best can help quell competitiveness. But don't count on it. The one person Aries is always trying to convince of being the best is usually themselves.

Aries challenge: They go out of their way to seek validation.

Because Aries require validation, if they don't get it from you, they will go elsewhere to get it. This could lead to their making you jealous by having a good flirt, or seeking admiration from others. They feel entitled to amorous attention because it pumps up their ego and reaffirms the fact that they do, indeed, have sex appeal. Most Aries aren't going to act on their flirting and seductions, they just enjoy making the point they could have someone if they wanted to.

What to do?

Keep lavishing regular attention on Aries and applause them and their heroism regularly. Keep yourself interesting to Aries as well by reminding them how desirable you are and how smart Aries is to choose you. Aries love to be right and love it when you compliment their good choices—especially when you're one of them. Underneath all that bravado is a mushy, loving romantic who needs tenderness and reinforcement to go out the next day and champion more causes.

Aries challenge: They have tempers!

Most Aries have fiery tempers and don't feel any need to hide them. They don't fear arguments but relish them. Aries often feel sharpened and invigorated by the energy of a fight and will go head-on until they've won. Should someone thwart them, without a moment's thought that the other person could be hurt, humiliated, or even feel annihilated, Aries go for the jugular. But once the fight is over, it's over—Aries are refreshed and ready to go do a new project, usually unaware or perplexed that their partner might feel hurt or torn apart. They've let it go—why can't you?

What to do?

Many Aries feel that if a partner won't fight with them, they feel robbed of an exciting energy that stirs other passions. Some Aries use anger and reconciling as a way of establishing intimacy. An element of tension, within themselves or with others, is part of every Aries' passion. Since this tension is energy to an Aries, don't try to fix problems or smooth Aries over with a "Just let it go." If Aries creates tension with you, don't take it negatively. They're just trying to shake up the energy a bit. If it's uncomfortable, simply don't take the bait. Let Aries have all the tension they want; you needn't get involved.

> "Aries is an all-or-nothing sign. If the Aries you're dating is still looking elsewhere, forget it. If you don't have *all* of Aries, you have *none* of them. And they expect the same from you."

What else to do should you see Aries' temper stirring? The worst thing you can say is "Don't get mad!" That just triggers them. Instead, say something like, "I can see that you are upset, and I really want to work this out with you but not when you are yelling or acting aggressively." Then step away and give Aries time to have a tantrum on their own or think things through and cool down. Don't give Aries the impression that their anger is wrong. That frustrates them and can spark more anger from their feeling misunderstood or sidelined. Acknowledge Aries' right to feel anger, but don't enable them. Tell them you don't want to relate to it at the moment. That'll give them a dignified way out.

Apologies also work wonders to melt Aries and their anger into a pool of forgiveness. Hearing you say "I'm sorry" disarms Aries' warrior's stance and ignites their admiration for your heroism in coming clean for your part in the argument. That makes Aries all the more enthusiastic to be heroic in turn and to apologize and come clean for their part.

Aries challenge: They hate the status quo and love to upset it.

Aries like to stir things up in life and that includes relationships. The status quo is suffocating for them, and their inner drive to keep reaching new heights means that they are restless when their alliances become too predictable or comfortable. Even if things are going well,

Aries will cook up something they want to try to make things even better. If that means your sex life is great but they want to try something new, they'll expect you to be game. Or, if they want to move to another city to start a new business, they'll expect you and the kids to pack up!

What to do?

If you feel Aries is pushing you or your life together into changes that you want no part of, it's time to negotiate. Try asking Aries what experience they're really after. Sometimes Aries will realize that they simply want to express a new part of themselves or experience what they've already created in a different way. Then they'll see they don't need to throw life into complete chaos just to satisfy that itch.

Other times Aries' instincts for change are for things that are truly right and expansive for them. Letting Aries know you don't want to hold them back, but need certain criterion for your own satisfaction in order to cooperate, helps them look for ways to meet your needs while meeting their own.

Aries challenge: They act first and think later.

Aries' interests are quickly ignited and so is their urge to follow them. They don't feel the need to research matters, study the details, or ask questions—with their confidence and bravado, they figure they'll learn how to do anything as they go.

Sometimes Aries are right—they have been known to pull off incredible feats with their savvy and instincts. That's thrilling for them, indeed. But other times Aries can get themselves into situations that are

> "Aries' restlessness can bring excitement to life, but it can disrupt good things, too, all in the name of keeping Aries from getting bored."

way over their heads or suffer incredible losses because they didn't prepare or think things through. They can even seem downright naive and get conned by others' promises or be so moved by someone's sob stories, they'll risk everything trying to be the heroic savior.

Most Aries can recover from these mishaps. They pick themselves up from failures, dust themselves off, and zestfully begin another risky venture, confident that this one will work. Aries' partners might not be so resilient. They may not view losing their houses, alienating their families, or otherwise creating unstable chaos as a "learning experience." They can resent or even fear Aries' risk-taking and want to put a stop to it.

What to do?

Since Aries can find practical thinking and advice annoying, if not downright deflating, success is all in the delivery. If you respond to an Aries' seemingly over-the-top-nutty ideas with "You've got to be kidding! That will never work!" you are only tempting Aries to drive on to prove you wrong.

It works better if you say, "Love your idea! Now, what are your plans for tackling it?" Then raise the subject that maybe they should learn to sail before they, say, invest in an eighteen-foot yacht to sail around the world. Aries feel hurt when someone doubts them, and that hurt can turn into contempt. Let Aries know you believe in them, even if you're doubting their latest inspirations.

Summary:
Keeping Up with Aries

• Keep in mind that Aries' first motivation is to discover and satisfy themselves, second is to be your hero.

• Be direct, yet gentle with Aries.

• Give Aries plenty of freedom and room to do things "their way."

• When asking for a change of behavior with Aries, don't criticize them or tell them they're wrong. Instead emphasize what they could do more of to make you even happier. And show Aries how they'll benefit, too.

Chapter Two

Taurus
(April 20—May 21)

Who They Are

I f you have a Taurus in your life, you're sure to be in for some treats: treats of pleasures, treats of being provided for, and treats of stability and loyalty. That's because these sensual creatures specialize in creating rich comforts. They want nothing more than to surround themselves and their beloved in an atmosphere of safety and affection. Tauruses are sturdy and practical folks who are driven to build a life of security and comfort. They make good use of everything they've got—including their characteristic determination and tenacity—to ensure that whomever and whatever they care for is well attended to and nurtured.

Life needn't and shouldn't be complicated with Tauruses. They prefer to keep matters simple and effortless. In fact, being content is more desirable to Tauruses than having too many wacky excitements, which can disturb Tauruses' comfy status quo. Instead, Tauruses revel in life's earthier offerings, like the bounties of the luxuries they seek to amass or the pleasures they experience through their senses. Relaxing touches, intoxicating smells, delicious foods, glorious music, and luscious beauty are all gratifying aspects of Tauruses' world.

Tauruses also keep things simple by saying what's on their minds. Why waste energy by cluttering things up with unnecessary fanfare? Tauruses' no-nonsense approach boils issues down to the black and white: something is either good or bad. Someone is either right or wrong. If someone or something isn't worthwhile, Taurus just ignores them. So if a Taurus likes you, you'll (eventually) know it. But if they're unhappy about something you've done, you'll know that too. Tauruses appreciate, even need, the same directness and honesty from you.

Anyone who knows a Taurus also knows how well their zodiac symbol, the Bull, describes them! Like bulls, Tauruses have strong (sometimes stocky) constitutions and patient, steadfast approaches to life. They're powerful, too, and quite determined to get what they want. And, just as bulls love spending leisure time grazing in the field, Tauruses love spending free time lingering at whatever pleases them. They enjoy tending to gardens, watching a

Taurus Is an Earth Sign

🐂 As an Earth Sign, Taurus is imbued with an urge to be reasonable and an ability to be useful and capable. At heart, every Taurus is a cultivator: they love bringing to flourishing life whatever or whomever they value. They'll roll up their sleeves and tirelessly work to make whatever or whomever they seek grow and prosper. They adore and respect companions who do the same.

good movie, or shopping for hours to find the perfect antique. Accompany them on any of these pursuits and they'll enjoy you even more.

And, just as it's nearly impossible to make a bull do anything it doesn't want to do, it's nearly impossible to get a Taurus to do anything they don't want to do. You can push, prod, or beg them, but Tauruses won't budge until they're good and ready. If you should stand in the way of Taurus having what they want, you might meet the pointy horns of Tauruses' obstinate insistence. However, just because Tauruses don't like to be pushed doesn't mean they don't push! Like a bull, once Tauruses set their sight on something, nothing can distract them. What do Tauruses most set their sights on? Values.

First and foremost, Tauruses are concerned with self-value. In fact, one of their sign's life lessons usually involves realizing that they are lovable and "enough" just the way they are. They're also learning that the universe always provides them with what they truly need (but not necessarily with what they want, which is another matter altogether). It's always helpful to encourage Tauruses to direct their wants and desires toward what they already have.

Tauruses also value and deeply desire being loved. Tauruses love to love. In fact, they're ruled by Venus, the planet of love. She provides them with a tremendous desire to give and receive love and affection, in all its shapes and forms. Romantic

> "Romantic love, nurturing love, friendship love—all make life delicious for Taurus."

love, nurturing love, friendship love—all make life delicious for Taurus. Their expression of love is hands-on, physical, and definitely sensual.

Beyond that, Tauruses set their sights on creating security. Most Tauruses seek financial security. They're incredibly interested in knowing that their wallets are full, their bank accounts swelling, and their investments accumulating. Tauruses are famous for their thrifty nature and their knack for getting maximum value for their dollar. Since Tauruses become ruffled (if not downright insecure) if a partner is fiscally irresponsible, they fare best in relationships with partners who demonstrate fiscal wisdom, if not out-and-out savvy.

> "Tauruses fare best in relationships with partners who demonstrate fiscal wisdom, if not out-and-out savvy."

In addition, Tauruses love surrounding themselves with an abundance of wonderful belongings. Although they might worry about their future security, buying a fabulous new luxury item can give them a sense of immediate security. Tauruses love to be indulged and resent it when goodies are withheld or denied. Whatever Tauruses value, be it their car, the rain forest, or both, it's incredibly important to them.

Another key to understanding Taurus is to know that their thoughts and perspective hover mainly around themselves: what *they* want, what *they* need, and what *they* feel. So if you want Tauruses to consider an idea or a request, present it to them in a way that shows how it will impact *them* personally. Tauruses can become overwhelmed should they consider too many people's needs before their own, so don't expect them to (except when it comes to their children). But the beautiful thing about Tauruses is when they do successfully and wisely attend to themselves, they become so full inside, they can't help but give plentifully to others.

What Tauruses Want in Relationships and How You Can Attract One

Tauruses like love to be clearly demonstrated. If you adore Taurus, by all means let them know. They'll think, *Me? You adore me? Oh! Thank you!* Being adored and adoring others back is the elixir of life for Tauruses.

However, although it's music to Tauruses' ears to *hear* about how much you care for them, what they really watch for is how your actions show it. Are you reliably there for them? Spending time with them? Doing what you said you'd do and not disappointing them? Do you treat them with sweetness, kindness, affection, and, most important, consideration? If so, you'll earn your Taurus's trust and interest.

Taurus Lesson: Conquer Worries About Lack by Recognizing Abundance

Despite being very good at providing for themselves, Tauruses can nevertheless suffer from terrible fears of lack. They can worry they might not have enough resources, be it love or money, to fulfill their desire for security. When your Taurus worries that what they have isn't adequate, help them by reminding them of one of their sign's keys to fulfillment: to recognize and then feel grateful for what they already possess. When Tauruses count their blessings and practice gratitude, they are reawakened to their sense of abundance—their surest avenue to happiness and connecting to their spirit. That's when Tauruses can fulfill their mission: to tap into a genuine security of knowing that what they need is always provided. Gratitude also helps Tauruses be more relaxed and poised to take advantage of the future bounties life might send their way. That's fulfilling, indeed.

Tauruses need and expect reliable consistency from their beloved. Tauruses want to feel as if they can depend on a person's affection and attentions. They don't like surprises in life; why should they in relationships? Flirty games or now-you-see-me-now-you-don't tactics are confusing and irritating to Taurus. Are you with them? Then act like you are! In turn, they will be openly and loyally consistent with you.

Words Tauruses Love to Hear

🐂 "You can have anything you want."

"I value you!"

"Let's make ourselves comfortable."

"I'm grateful to you!"

Tauruses prefer a solid circle of familiar and faithful companions. Instead of spreading themselves (and their hearts) too thin, Tauruses are typically devoted to a close circle of tried-and-true companions. Tauruses' affections are strong and deep. They enjoy the safe familiarity of being with those they know and love well. Most Tauruses don't crave the novelty or the unsure stages of meeting new friends—they love enduring, sincere alliances. So instead of trying to get to know their entire neighborhood, most Tauruses value deepening and strengthening the connections they've already established.

Tauruses enjoy simple pleasures. Activities needn't be overly exciting or glamorous to please Tauruses. Spending time relaxing at home with their beloved or just cooking up a good meal and then curling up on the couch can be excitement enough for Tauruses.

Tauruses crave affection. Affection means the world to Tauruses. It is absolutely paramount to them. Tauruses can't live, or can't live well, without it. Touching opens Tauruses' hearts. Affection melts away any of the hard edges they might use to defend themselves from the harsh world and awakens Tauruses' teddy-bear nature in seconds flat. So touch them. Often. They'll love you for it.

Tauruses seek companions who are strong enough to lean upon. Tauruses want to know you have enough integrity and inner strength that they can lean on you. They need to feel that you won't crumble if they butt up against you. And they like to see that you are able to hold to your values and not cave under the pressures of the world or even the pressures of Tauruses' insistence.

Tauruses enjoy a relaxed and genuine partner. More than anything, Tauruses like and feel comfortable around people who can be themselves. They aren't that impressed with fancy images or puffed-up fronts: they see right through them and wonder why people who present them feel they have to act that way. Tauruses want to feel good about who they are and want you to feel good about who you are as well. Forget trying to be something you are not.

Tauruses enjoy being relaxed and genuine around their partners. Tauruses don't want to have to extend themselves to be wittier, better read, more athletic, or anything else that takes undue effort to be with you. They certainly don't want to feel like they have to work to measure up to your expectations in order for you to finally be happy. They want to be comfortable being themselves. Let Tauruses know you like them just the way they are. They'll be eternally grateful.

Tauruses are attracted to those who can help them build security. Tauruses are drawn to companions who have the means or abilities to get them more of what they want out of life. If Tauruses desire a loving home and family life, for example, they might seek someone who can help them create that. Or, if they desire financial prosperity, they'll be drawn to someone who can help make that happen. Most Tauruses are excellent providers themselves but don't want to be alone in this providing; they want to know their companion can help them build the life of their dreams.

Tauruses respect those who are good stewards of finances and other worthy resources. Don't be so flashy or indulgent that Taurus thinks you're living beyond your means. Tauruses cringe at the thought of being with a companion who might threaten or squander assets—especially finances—or who might lead them into financial jeopardy. As much as Tauruses love someone, they also love their security.

Receiving is a big part of Tauruses' delight! Tauruses love presents! Big expensive ones are spectacular, but little, thoughtful ones are impressive as well. Just giving something to Tauruses makes them feel loved and valued and endears you to them. Objects of beauty—like flowers—are always appreciated, but so are useful things they need, like a gift certificate to the hardware store.

Tauruses need patience and time to do things according to their own rhythms. By all means take your time with a Taurus! Don't rush or push them in any way. They move slowly and carefully through life, and like being sure-footed and assured in everything they do, including relationships. Hating to feel pressured, Tauruses will resist if they think you are coercing them to move too quickly toward something they aren't sure about, even if it's a fabulous friendship or a swooning love affair.

Remember this: Tauruses need to be sure in matters of the heart, so they'll rarely act on their first instincts, although they might be quite accurate. They don't want to be fooled by appearances or get sucked in by someone's glamorous front. Don't get impatient with Tauruses' carefully checking you out or seeming hard to get. Give them time to watch you.

What Tauruses Offer in Relationships

Tauruses offer satisfactions galore. When you win the heart of a Taurus, you can expect the attentive, sensual caring that lets you know your needs are satisfied. Tauruses love taking care of whatever it is you might want. Hungry? Taurus will whip up a scrumptious meal. Feeling uptight? How about a foot massage? The wonderful thing about Tauruses is that when they feel safe and secure around you, they'll return the favor by extending themselves so completely and fully, you will have no doubt that they love and cherish you.

> **Words Tauruses Love to Say**
>
> 🐂 "This is mine!"
> "I have plenty!"
> "Let's be patient."
> "Let's just relax."

Tauruses provide an abundance of physical comforts. Because Tauruses are comfort specialists, you can expect them to make your life sensually enjoyable. Maybe they'll fluff up your pillow, touch you softly, or wear a scent you adore, all in the name of putting you at ease. Or they'll share the material gifts with you that make life cozy and luxurious.

Tauruses are reliable and usually show their true colors. Tauruses do what they say they will and rarely pretend they are something they are not. Knowing that in your Taurus friend what you see is what you get can help smooth anxious fears of game-playing, allowing you to rest assured that Taurus is the real thing.

Tauruses are wonderful providers. Tauruses can also bring the kind of comfort that comes from alleviating fears of lack. Afraid of running out of cash? Tauruses make sure their loved ones will be provided for and never go hungry or needy. (Note: Tauruses won't let you

"Tauruses do what they say they will and rarely pretend they are something they are not."

starve, but they won't indulge you either. After all, they are thrifty with themselves and thrifty with others. You'll have what you need, but don't count on excess.) Afraid of being abandoned? Taurus is consistent and there for you. Afraid of life's complexities? Taurus's decisiveness will make it simple for you.

Tauruses lend never-ending support. Tauruses support your building something solid in your life. Be it a thriving business, a gorgeous home, or a fragrant garden, as long as it's a reasonable dream, Tauruses will invest their strengths and know-how—if not their own assets—to help make it a successful reality. Tauruses know how even the biggest of plans come to fruition by putting one foot in front of the other, and they'll take the first steps necessary to help you. And they'll show you how to do it for yourself as well.

Tauruses are happiest, however, when they see that those they have supported eventually learn to support themselves. Tauruses might support a loved one long after they should be on their own, but it pains them to. Nurturing Tauruses are happiest when those they nurture learn how to care for themselves.

Tauruses are not afraid of commitment and give you their undying loyalty. One of the biggest gifts Tauruses offer their valued companions is commitment: once they make up their mind (and heart) that they like you, you will have a devoted companion who is by your side through thick and thin. If Taurus believes in you, they'll demonstrate it with unwavering support. No matter what comes up, Tauruses use their tenacity and strength to plow through it. Tauruses will stick around through the worst of times because they have faith that good times will come again.

Tauruses live for the stability, assurance, and reliability that commitments can bring. They don't bug out when the going gets rough or look over your shoulder to see if someone better has walked into the room. Instead, they invest themselves fully in their relationships. Their loving can and usually does last through distance and time.

Tauruses are levelheaded and help keep their partners calm. Tauruses' steady calm has a way of making life more serene or peaceful. Why run when you can walk? Why push when easy does it better? Maybe life seems less hectic around Tauruses because they try to make it easier. They'll help you to sort out what's genuinely important and what's not. Maybe it's because Tauruses' inner strength communicates, "Don't worry—we can handle anything."

Tauruses are gentle. Tauruses' compassion wants to minimize the suffering and pain of their loved ones. Why be harsh when you can be gentle, or why insistently wrangle for something when a nudge will do the trick? Even when Tauruses get mad, which takes a lot, they usually move to protect themselves rather than to harm the culprit. If Tauruses' anger or insecurity does move them to become harsh or pushy, they resume exuding the sweetness that's inside of them once the issue blows over.

Tauruses will make you laugh with their nutty humor. Usually Tauruses favor physical or even slapstick humor—the sillier the better. If someone takes a spill, dribbles, or wears a funny getup, there'll be Taurus laughing away. Want to get a Taurus to relax and open up? Go have some belly laughs.

The Taurus Lover

*W*hen in love, Tauruses blossom and shine because it gives full rein to their attentive and sensual nature. Tauruses' affection is consistent and their sensuality rich and lingering. Plus, their loyalty and integrity provide an assuredness that their beloved can count on and relax in, knowing that when Taurus commits, it's for sure.

Courtship with a Taurus is an unhurried affair. Love is so very important to them that they don't want to screw up or get hurt. So even if a Taurus is crazy about you, chances are they will still take their time to get to know you, asking themselves questions like, "Can she be trusted?" or "Is he reliable?" After all, Taurus wants to be assured that if they make the investment of their heart, it will not be squandered.

What kind of dates do Tauruses enjoy?

*T*auruses enjoy activities that involve all the senses and enhance their comfort level. How about a romantic picnic (basket brimming with goodies, including desserts and flowers) in a beautiful expanse of nature? Or maybe linger over dinner at a luxurious restaurant, or even at your own home, if it is comfortable and well appointed. Regardless of where you go, make sure you look good and smell luscious. Wear garments that invite Tauruses' touch, maybe something in gorgeous earth shades, like greens or browns. Don't rush to become affectionate with Taurus. But little brushes of your hand and a gentle hug after helping them on with their coat does wonders to open and entice them. It might take Taurus a while to let down their guard and become open to more affection. Let them tell you when they're ready for more. It's worth the wait.

What are Tauruses like between the sheets?

Sex is the end-all, be-all sensual experience for Tauruses, and they want to get as much pleasure from it as they can. So when making love, stick to the Taurus motto: "Don't rush it." Most Tauruses enjoy setting the mood with music, candles, soft sheets, a warm bath, or even a massage. (More practical Tauruses have a "Let's just do it!" approach, but they, too, can be willing to set "the mood" if their partner prefers it.)

Touch is electrifying to Tauruses. Slowly caress them with your fingers, lips, tongue, or anything else your creativity dreams up. Let them drink in your earthy smells and tastes. Keep it natural and instinctive: most Tauruses prefer raw, lusty exchanges that don't involve a lot of thinking. Let your bodies and your desires take the lead.

"When it comes to sex with a Taurus, slow and steady wins the race."

If you want Taurus to try something different in their lovemaking, gently show what you'd like, rather than telling them. When they experience the reward of pleasure one or both of you receive as a result, they'll be more than happy to comply in the future. Taurus is one of the most sexual signs of the zodiac. Tauruses crave the pleasures and the release it offers. So they'll rarely scale down in lovemaking. (When they do, it's a big red flag!) Tauruses want pleasure and they want their beloved to feel pleasure, too.

"In sex, love, and life, Tauruses like to keep it simple."

Ways Tauruses Can Drive You Crazy and What to Do About It

Like every other sign, the very qualities that are so very wonderful about Taurus can also become infuriating, when taken too far.

Taurus challenge: Security can turn into stagnation.

Tauruses' drive for security has been known to cause the occasional challenge to their relationships. They can be so determined to maintain their comfortable (or even uncomfortable!) status quo that they can stubbornly resist change, even if it's for the better. Any suggestion of doing something differently can threaten Tauruses' stability and prompt them to respond with an insistent "No!" For many Tauruses, the prospect of change means the prospect of loss. No matter what they have, it's the known, and that known is worth sustaining. It takes a lot for Taurus to trust that something new (other than a snazzy new material item) could possibly be better. This holds true for any type of change, big or small. Tauruses might resist changing dinnertime as vehemently as they resist moving to another city.

Tauruses can really dig in their heels when resisting, and no amount of asking, reasoning, or pleading can seem to get through. Tauruses often realize they are being stubborn, but they prefer to call it "persistent."

What to do?

If you want change, understand that it's probably going to take some time for Taurus to accept it. It's best if you can provide Taurus with an unfettered explanation about what the change is about and what it is for. Importantly, show Taurus in practical, tangible terms how this change is going to make things better (for them, of course) and what specific benefits will arise from making it. (If they can be written in blood, with a guarantee, all the better.)

"Change does not come easily to Taurus. They hate when you rock the boat."

Forget about pressuring Taurus—that only makes their resistance more firm. Instead, try maintaining a gentle, steady persistence to keep your idea on the table. That'll keep Taurus from ignoring it (which they might try to do) until such a time that Taurus eventually figures out how they can make it work.

Taurus challenge: They want you to "settle down" so they can.

Tauruses' need for stability can make them feel terribly insecure during life's inevitable uncertainties. But a Taurus can also react to your times of uncertainty as well. If you aren't sure about something, or choose to live in a way that doesn't seem to pursue security the way Taurus defines it, they might grow weary of your apparent nebulousness and start to rally for more reasonableness and grounding from you. A Taurus might even pressure you to make up your mind and set down roots, whether you're ready or not, or whether the situation is truly right or not.

What to do?

Remind Taurus that you accept living with times of insecurity or a lack of clear direction as a valuable part of life. If you want to close your thriving business to become a ski instructor, well, it's your life and you want to live it your way. If Taurus is your partner, however, or is affected somehow by your doing something that affects security, like taking a financial risk, you'll need to negotiate with them. Ask Taurus to dig deep and decide what they can live with. Taurus may elect to be a buoy of stability while you bob around in the sea of unknowing. They may show their love for you by providing the kind of support, be it financial or directional, they think you need.

If in the end, Taurus can't bear to be around your choices (or lack of them), they may have to step away from you for a time or leave the relationship altogether. That might be painful for both of you, but it might be the smartest—and in the end the kindest—choice for you both.

Taurus challenge: These bulls are bullishly opinionated!

Tauruses can be stubborn in their ideas and opinions. They may be quite satisfied with how they see the world and refuse to take in new information or consider anything they don't want to consider. This can actually lead to a type of close-mindedness or even prejudice wherein Tauruses might not even be aware that their opinions are objectionable or hurtful to others. Or they may know they are and just not care. Understandably, this can be frustrating to both Tauruses and those they disagree with.

What to do?

When trying to get Taurus to see life in a new way or to consider that something or someone has value, it's always best to do it slowly. Tauruses are wary of others' ideas and don't want to be brainwashed.

They need to quietly gather evidence for themselves. When and if Taurus can find a practical reason to change their mind they will. Forget the "I-told-you-so's," however; those make Taurus more stubborn the next time around.

Taurus challenge: Sometimes, they blow their tops.

One of Tauruses' greatest qualities is their easygoing manner. It takes a mighty lot for them to get thrown off balance, even more for them to get mad. But when Tauruses finally do get fed up enough for their anger to blow, their inner bull bellows, stomps, and snorts!

What to do?

Get out of Tauruses' way and let them express rather than engage in confrontational or painful scenes. When Tauruses are done expressing their anger, they'll do what they can to resume their calm and start to look for ways to iron out their differences with you.

Taurus challenge: They resist, resent, or otherwise keep you out in the cold.

Getting hurt is another matter. Although Tauruses aren't all that sensitive and usually won't demand a lot of "walking on eggshells" from you, they nevertheless have some tender spots. They don't like to get hurt and will go to great lengths to protect themselves. If someone behaves unthoughtfully or seems to devalue them in some way, Tauruses can become hurt and dejected.

A hurt Taurus is a clammed-up Taurus. As a way of protecting themselves, they'll put up a wall and shut out whoever has done the hurtful deed. Tauruses will become uncharacteristically cold and aloof, or perhaps ignore the culprit altogether.

Many Tauruses are consummate grudge-holders as well. Sometimes they can get so used to holding one that they might even forget the specifics of what hurt them in the first place. So don't think, *Oh! She'll just get over it!* A Taurus might not. They can instead be so lost in their hurt or resentment that they might interpret anything one does as an affront and just get more mad.

Tauruses can make matters worse for themselves by refusing to recognize the hoops people are going through to make up with them, or, if they do see them, by dismissing them altogether. Or Tauruses might not give others a chance to come clean with them by refusing to tell the offender what they did to offend them. Tauruses might feel it's too painful or humiliating to reveal what seared them, or they might just believe the offender should figure out for themselves what they did wrong.

Tauruses' cold-shoulder treatment is especially painful to those receiving it because it is so drastically different from the warmth that Taurus is capable of generating. Tauruses can make it hard for others to resolve the hurtful matter because no amount of pleading, reaching out, or apologizing seems to make a difference.

What to do?

Eventually, most Tauruses can be wooed into forgiveness and reopening their hearts. Try touching Taurus and getting them to look into your eyes as you tell them that you're sorry they're feeling hurt and that you want to reconnect. (If you are genuinely sorry about something, by all means tell them that, too.) You may have to be persistent in this and very patient while you wait for Taurus to come around. But when Taurus feels the genuine caring in your concern, they might melt open to you.

A soft touch of affection helps Taurus forgive and forget, but it has to come on their terms. If you reach out too soon, they'll recoil, which means they aren't ready to forgive you yet. Patience and persistence may be necessary. Taurus will forgive and love again, but it might take a while. Tell Taurus they're worth the wait. Keep knocking at their door, and one day it'll open.

Taurus challenge: Their deep thought is, What about me?

Tauruses can seem selfish. And they are. Their needs, wants, and desires need to be acknowledged and fulfilled in order for Tauruses to be comfortable. Part of their life's lesson is finding ways to fulfill themselves. It's Tauruses' job to get to know themselves and be true to themselves. Doing so keeps them happy and poised to give their bounty to others.

However, if Tauruses don't attend to their needs adequately, they can risk feeling used by and resentful of the requests of others. They may believe that they are doing all the giving while no one is providing much of anything to them. In response, Tauruses can become withholding or tyrannically demanding. Although it seems to Taurus as if others aren't giving to them what they should, the trouble might be that Tauruses are not open to receiving or acknowledging what others are trying to give to them.

What to do?

*I*f you feel the wrath of Tauruses' unmet expectations, it might work to sit down with them and ask, point-blank, what they want from you. When that happens, Taurus has the opportunity to make their request, something they might not have done directly or clearly. But something else might happen. Taurus might come to realize that their real issue isn't so much that you aren't providing them with something, but rather that they aren't providing something important for themselves that they need.

Taurus challenge: They can be "withholders"

*S*ince Tauruses are learning about abundance, their challenges usually involve the opposite: feeling some form of lack. Tauruses can suffer from terrible fears that they might not have enough of what they need. They are prone to getting very concerned that something terrible is going to happen and they will lose their security.

This fearfulness can play havoc with Tauruses' relationships, as well. Tauruses might be blind to others' needs as they busily attempt to fulfill their own. Or they might withhold giving to others physically, emotionally, or financially because they don't believe what they give will ever be replenished. Then it can be difficult to relate to Tauruses in a giving and receiving way because Tauruses refuse to give. They may be convinced that one affectionate kindness or one penny can't be given, for fear it might leave the bank empty.

When Tauruses are feeling lack, they can sometimes act as if they love their money or their things more than people. They either spend more time attending to their physical holdings or choosing to nurture and protect their physical assets over their relationships. When Tauruses believe they need physical holdings to measure their value or to ensure their safety in life, they overlook the value of their loving relationships. They'll ignore loved ones while they doggedly try to keep their assets intact.

It can be very painful for Tauruses' companions to watch Tauruses suffer over lack because usually theirs is a needless worry. It's more than likely that Tauruses actually do possess plenty of whatever resources they fear they lack, but they fail to take comfort in them.

What to do?

When Tauruses are worried about lack or any other kind of a survival issue, be it finances or the welfare of their loved ones, they do appreciate reassurance from others. The best kind of reassurance comes in the form of tangible facts. "Here's what we're going to do to help the situation," helps ease a Taurus more than a plain, "Don't worry." Whatever you do, don't dismiss Tauruses' worries as inconsequential.

If you can help Taurus by providing something they need, by all means do so. They will be incredibly grateful to you. But it's likely the most valuable thing you could provide them is your clear insight into the specific ways they already possess what they need. Many times just reminding Tauruses about the ways they have avoided or overcome adversity in the past helps them recognize they are stronger and more resourceful than they imagined.

> "Tauruses' loyalty is certainly one of their greatest assets."

Taurus challenge: Tauruses can be loyal to others undeserving of their loyalty.

Tauruses' loyalty is certainly one of their greatest assets. However, sometimes Tauruses overdo it and remain loyal to someone long past when it's healthy to do so.

Their need for security can prompt them to stick around even when relationships aren't really working. Tauruses might stay in a troubled marriage for the sake of the kids or remain loyal to a family member even if the person has repeatedly taken advantage of them, just to keep the family intact.

Tauruses also might linger in tough relationships because they aren't sure how they would support themselves, materially or emotionally, without them. Unloving relationships are extremely painful for Tauruses, but the thought of leaving can seem even more excruciating. Tauruses loathe and fear the devastation of separation. So they hang in there, trying everything they can conceive of in order to make a relationship work.

What to do?

When Tauruses are 100-percent sure they have tried everything and nothing has worked, they do leave. And then they are gone for good. No amount of begging wins them back. They put up a ten-foot stone fence around their heart, lest they are weakened. So next time you feel exasperated by Tauruses' devotion to someone unworthy, remember even bullish Taurus will know when enough's enough.

Taurus challenge: "Don't push me, but I'll push you!"

As much as Tauruses resist being pushed, they are very good at pushing others. When they want something, they really want it. Tauruses set their sights on their desires and patiently wait for opportunities to open to them.

Tauruses won't forget about a desire, either, even if they act like they do. If they want to marry you, they'll do whatever they need to get you to agree, even if it takes years. If they want a baby, they relentlessly campaign for one. If Taurus wants a new home, you will feel their bullish horns poking you toward the real estate ads every Sunday.

Actually, Tauruses' desires can be so intense they can become quite distracting even to themselves.

What to do?

If you feel Taurus is pushing you into something you don't want to do, be very clear with them that you don't want to do it. Ambiguousness or even diplomacy might not get through to them as well as a plain and simple "No." Be gentle, but firm. No wavering.

Summary:
Troubleshooting with Tauruses

• Remember that Taurus's main motivation is to feel safe and secure.

• Use plenty of patience and gentleness with Taurus.

• Let Tauruses know you value them with actions as well as words.

• When requesting a change of behavior from Taurus, give them plenty of time to warm up to it and accept it. Be sure to show Taurus the benefits they'll receive from doing what you're asking for.

Chapter Three

Gemini
(May 22—June 21)

Who They Are

When you have a Gemini in your life you'll be delightfully entertained, engagingly educated, and intellectually enticed. That's because these witty creatures are incredibly clever and talented, and they love mixing interesting fun into whatever they cook up. Geminis' fascinating stories, madcap adventures, and cast of interesting acquaintances all combine to fill life with unexpected delights. Always seeking to learn something new, their bright and curious minds thrive on exploring new thoughts, subjects, and activities to keep matters fresh and exciting. With their quicksilver wit, Geminis instantly size up situations, and their charm and approachable friendliness attracts instant buddies and fans.

Life with a Gemini is rarely predictable. Their constant thirst for novel experiences and ready eagerness to take chances means life will have plenty of twists and turns that neither you—nor they—expect! After all, Gemini's zodiac symbol is the Twins. True to their nature, most Geminis have at least two, if not more, distinct sides to their personalities. Ask any Gemini if that's true and they'll probably nod their head as if to say, "More than you know!"

Geminis are incredibly flexible with a great thirst for variety. In fact, most Gemini are like quick-change artists—eschewing permanence, they'll change most any and everything on a dime. The more you know them, they more they'll surprise you by changing their minds, appearance, interests, career, and even friends. Being utterly adaptable, with a penchant for mimicking what they admire, Geminis take on whatever traits are necessary to flow with the circumstances or the company they are keeping. They love companions who can do the same.

If matters get predictable? Geminis get restless or snappy, and maybe even disappear, off exploring their next interest.

It's not that Geminis are insincere—it's just that their multifaceted personality feels different from moment to moment. They needn't be consistent to be authentic. They can be all things and everything. However, Geminis rarely show their different sides to the same person. Most of us will only know a portion of our Gemini companion's expression. Others may see a different side of them altogether.

Geminis are chock-full of talents, ideas, and interests. Most are good at and know at least a little about almost everything! Art, music, literature, dance, salesmanship, teaching, language—you name it, from business to massage, Gemini has some talent there.

Because life offers so many interesting choices, it can be truly challenging for Geminis to decide what (or who!) to pursue. They can be successful in so many different endeavors that some have a hard time focusing on just one. Some Geminis resolve this by pursuing one interest with gusto until they feel they've learned enough and then set off to pursue the next fascinating subject. Many Geminis try to pursue all of their interests at the same time!

Commitments to relationships can be difficult for Geminis. Some just don't want to make a commitment and enjoy juggling a few relationships at a time. Other Geminis need to sample a wide range of relationships before they finally choose their special one, finally expressing

> "Geminis are chock-full of talents, ideas, and interests. Most are good at and know at least a little about almost everything!"

a deep loyalty and focus when they do. It's a good idea to find out if your Gemini is interested in commitment, or if they're "still looking." That is, if they can or will tell you. Remember, these folks surprise even themselves with what they end up doing.

Geminis' multiple talents are a big part of what makes them such wonderful, popular, and fascinating companions. Most are entertainers: their storytelling, joke-making, playfulness, and engaging wit make them impossible to ignore.

Simply said, life with a Gemini is fun. (Well, unless Gemini's infamous "Crabby Twin" is surfacing—then watch out! When that happens, you're smartest to just get out of the way and allow time for the "Happy Gemini" to resurface.)

Along with being an entertainer, every Gemini has the heart of a student and a teacher. Life is absolutely fascinating to Geminis and they love learning as much as they can about it, then instructing others about what they experienced. Geminis' curiosity is insatiable: they approach life with a keen eye for what's new and novel and what they can glean from any situation. And they can communicate their discoveries with such clarity and cleverness that even complex subjects can become simple and understandable.

Geminis adore playing the student and teacher in their relationships as well. When playing the student, they'll ask questions, hunt for truths, and try to learn as much as they can about you and your gifts. When playing the teacher, Geminis will instruct you about most anything from the correct way to core an apple to the best strategy for touring Europe. Geminis rarely want to play the guru, however. They don't want the responsibility of living your life for you. And they expect you to give them that same freedom in return.

Geminis are primarily interested in satisfying their own wants and needs, and have a belief that life should be lived according to their own terms. So when making decisions, Geminis generally do what they want to, even if that leads to disappointing, displeasing, or even abandoning others. Sometimes this comes off as innocently childlike. Other times, it's infuriating. But in the end, even if they have a nurturing side, life is about them.

Geminis tend to become attracted to others via their minds or imagi-

Gemini Is an Air Sign

♊ Being an Air Sign gives Gemini a changeable, I-am-here-today-but-I-might-be-gone-tomorrow breezy flow to life. Geminis crave action and movement. And they need loads of breathing room in their lives and in their relationships. Just as it's hard to hold air in your hands, it's hard to hold on to a Gemini. Gemini's Air Sign status also gives them a penchant for taking a more objective, intellectual approach to life over being emotional. They're most at home with concepts and ideas, and have a particular love of words.

nations rather than through overt displays of intense emotions (too heavy!) or even physical seduction (too crude!). Want to intrigue a Gemini? Say something fascinating, surprising, or witty.

What Geminis Want in Relationships and How You Can Attract One

Geminis want to be intellectually captivated. Geminis are most attracted to those who stimulate their minds and imaginations, so let your intelligence and ideas shine! Spark their inquisitiveness by letting them know something interesting about you—not in a bragging or exaggerated way (that's a real turnoff), but in a "Hey! Here's a

Gemini Lesson: Discovering Themselves in Any Pursuit, Rather Than in Every Pursuit

Geminis love discovering themselves by trying their hands at a plethora of interests and activities. But sometimes Geminis' penchant for juggling interests can lead them to become overextended and scattered. Then they're robbed of the kind of meaningful transformation that investing fully in any one interest can provide. If that's happening to your Gemini friend, remind them of their sign's mission: to discover themselves by bringing *all* of who they are to *any* experience, instead of trying to find themselves through *every* experience. When Geminis stay present with what they're doing in the moment, they can become attuned to the fascination they are genuinely searching for: the amazing spirited intelligence that lies within them. That poises Gemini to know how and where to direct their signature creativity so it can blossom into pursuits that are truly meaningful and fulfilling.

Words Geminis Love to Hear

👫 "I've got an excursion planned for us!"

"Tell me more about your thoughts on . . ."

"I've got a surprise for you!"

"Here's some news . . . "

unique twist about me" invitation. Make yourself a good human interest story. Since Geminis can't help but follow their curiosity, show them something to be curious about you.

Geminis adore having to learn about others. Don't let Geminis know everything about you all at once. They need something to think about and love a story to unfold. Geminis enjoy playing a good game of hide-and-seek, and don't mind—in fact, they usually adore—being pleasantly teased. They enjoy the anticipation and wonder of where a relationship is going or discovering something that is not yet revealed, won, or explored about you. So leave Geminis wanting more. If they are interested, they'll be back—even if they live in another state or country.

Geminis are stimulated by lively conversation. Strike up conversations with Geminis, and you'll find they're skilled conversationalists who enjoy nothing more than a spirited exchange of ideas and delightful surprises about what makes someone tic. Don't hide your knowledge—express it, and let Geminis know how interested you are in theirs. Have you read a good book lately? Tell a Gemini what you loved most about it. Seen a good movie? What part had an interesting turn you can analyze along with Gemini?

Geminis need good listeners. Talking is incredibly important to most Geminis: it's not only a way for them to express the many thoughts running around in their head, it's also a way for them to sort out ideas and achieve some objectivity. Heck, talking might even be

Gemini's form of therapy. For that reason, Geminis need and appreciate a companion who will listen to them and be a good sounding board for all they have to express.

And, since Geminis are great word lovers, impress them with your command of the vocabulary or with an invitation to do a word puzzle together. Or tell Gemini that you love them in a language different from their own. That'll make them smile!

"Geminis enjoy playing a good game of hide-and-seek, and don't mind—in fact, they usually adore— being pleasantly teased."

Geminis yearn for adventure. Make life exciting and interesting for Gemini by keeping the activities rolling. Pack up the car for a picnic? Yes! Tickets to the rodeo? Yes! Review your yearly budget? Hey! Where'd Gemini go? Geminis pursue the fun of life and see no reason to shackle themselves to people or activities that bore them. So make everything—including the review of your finances—something that involves intrigue or some laughs.

Geminis want freedom to explore. Geminis want the freedom to chase after their newest interests in life. Anyone who thinks they are going to "tame" a Gemini has another thing coming. Geminis won't be corralled: they will roam with or without their companions' permission or knowledge. So it's better to encourage Geminis to explore the people and the activities they're drawn to. And, although Geminis love companions with similar interests, they don't need them to accompany them on every one of their adventures—many prefer that they do not. Geminis have an assortment of buddies they like to spend time with. Spending time with someone other than you can refresh Geminis and make them appreciate you even more. Just remind

Gemini about the appealing things that are going to happen when they get back!

Geminis need people who keep them moving. Geminis love to travel, so get them in the car or on a plane, and take them somewhere. You'll see them relax and blossom. Geminis love visiting places they've never seen before and trying new things, so a concert or even the neighborhood pet store can be fun for them. Excursions needn't be complex, just different from before.

Geminis like to keep it light and positive. For Geminis, life needn't and shouldn't be a solemn affair—it should be enjoyable. They like companions who keep a positive, "glass is half full" perspective, as well as those who don't weigh them down with heavy responsibilities and concerns. Geminis aren't particularly interested in trying to feel others' pain, and they rarely see the need in digging to discover deep, hidden, ugly truths, whether it's others' or their own.

> "Complaining and whining is a real downer for Gemini. . . . Be positive about life, yourself, and Gemini, too!"

Geminis desire freedom to think their own way. Freedom of thought is paramount to Geminis. So give them plenty of space to think and express what they want. Geminis need to sense that you accept their ideas as valid, even if they are different from yours. Their minds are typically quite open, and they are incredibly eager to learn. Even if you have an opposing opinion to Gemini's, engage in a friendly banter about it. As long as Geminis feel respected for their position, they'll enjoy the mental engagement.

Don't try to forcibly convince Gemini of anything; it's unlikely you'll succeed. Geminis can't tolerate being told how or what to think.

They'll remove themselves immediately, if not by outthinking you or daydreaming you out of their minds, then simply by leaving you.

For Geminis, variety is the spice of life. Geminis crave and need an enormous amount of variety, so be inventive in all you endeavor to do with them. Doing things differently keeps Gemini interested and involved, while comfortable routines only stifle them, bore them to tears, and tempt their wanderings.

Geminis adore others who keep them laughing and entertained. Geminis have terrific senses of humor and love when companions join them in making life comical. Geminis are the first to tell a joke and the first to enjoy and applaud another's. Their sense of theatrics displays good timing and a twist of the unexpected. In many ways Geminis are just like big, smart kids: they want life to be fun and interesting.

What Geminis Offer in Relationships

Geminis bring fun and interest to their relationships. Geminis are witty, actively involved, funny, bright, and curious, and always bring an interesting twist to whatever they are doing. They know just how to make any situation enjoyable and intriguing, and they'll keep you on your toes with their surprises.

Geminis will keep you entertained. Geminis' many talents entertain people time after time. Masters at improvisation, Geminis will always present you with something you didn't count on or plan for. They'll say witty and surprising things, take you to a great obscure movie, or buy you a terrific CD by a band you've never heard of. Just sitting on the couch with a Gemini can be as interesting as a party of five.

Geminis will introduce you to a wider circle full of friends. Geminis will open your world by introducing you to their wide range of friends and acquaintances—or even a few strangers who become friends. Geminis are intensely social and seem to know just about everyone. Rarely jealous or possessive, they'll encourage you to enjoy their friends and vice versa. You'll rarely get bored around a Gemini's close companions—they are all so different! If Geminis see a stranger who seems interesting, they'll strike up a connection and cajole something memorable out of the person.

Words Geminis Love to Say

♊ "I've been thinking . . ."

"This reminds me of a story . . ."

"Let's try it!"

"Let's go somewhere!"

Geminis encourage others to follow their bliss. Rarely possessive or controlling, Geminis give you the same freedom to explore life's possibilities. Do you want to study a year in France? Go do it! Do you want to spend time with friends other than Gemini? Go ahead and enjoy yourself! Geminis will understand your need to spread your wings to learn and grow—in fact, they'll encourage it! They figure it'll only make you even more interesting. And believe me, they'll have plenty to do while you're away.

Geminis strike up excellent conversation. With a Gemini, you'll probably never have to ask, "What are you thinking?" A Gemini is usually more than eager to tell you! Simply said, Geminis are talkers. Exuberantly communicative, Geminis love sparking interesting and meaningful exchanges. Always peppering their talk with, "I recently read" or "I just bumped into someone who told me . . . ," Geminis will keep you engaged and fascinated.

Gemini will keep you abreast of the latest gossip, too. They know how to get the juicy truth out of what's happening in their community, and they do so with great regularity! They're sure to fill you in on all sorts of tidbits about who's doing what with whom, who's going where, and who said what to whom.

> "Geminis are intensely social and seem to know just about everyone."

Geminis will touch you with moments of remarkable understanding. Geminis have a wisely knowing side to them and possess deep insight into what makes people tick. Every once in a while, they'll shoot you a glance that says, "I understand who you truly are, and that's fine and good with me." In doing so, Geminis broadcast a tender nurturing that is intoxicating. Although this side of Gemini may not be as active or obvious as their other, more extroverted sides, a little taste of that can go a long way in creating a warm feeling of intimacy.

The Gemini Lover

The Gemini lover is quite the delightful charmer! Geminis know how to make loving fun. Easy winkers, master flirters, and smooth operators, Geminis make courtship an exciting adventure.

A Gemini lover is rarely easy to catch, however, even when they're very interested. And, if you want to keep Gemini's attention, you'll need to play as hard to get as they are. Geminis love courting. They adore the intoxicating early stage of love in which flirting, leaving cute messages, and then disappearing leads to added interest. Geminis are clever wooers: they tell stories, whisk the hair out of their intended's eyes, and send meaningful "Are you thinking what I am?" glances.

Remember, Geminis fall in love with the brain first. Make them use theirs. They like a challenge of intrigue. Give them something to think about and wonder about you. Tilt your head and say something clever or provoking that they can play over and over in their heads after you leave. Entice Geminis with the lightest of touches, a tease of affection, and then back off a bit. That makes them more interested.

"Easy winkers, master flirters, and smooth operators, Geminis make courtship an exciting adventure."

Avoid heavy scenes of passion or huge bursts of emotion, though. They tend to overwhelm Gemini's intellectual nature and even embarrass them. If you're prone to strong displays of feelings, you might try to hold off until you and Gemini get to know each other better.

Surely pure physical seduction will work to attract Gemini's attention, but without backing it with intellectual intrigue, physical attraction burns out quickly for Gemini.

What kind of dates do Geminis enjoy?

Geminis enjoy active dates that involve a circus of experiences. Take them somewhere they've never been before or do something they've never tried. Geminis like to be entertained, so dates to the theater, concerts, and exciting educational events are always a hit with them. Or appeal to Geminis' love of travel by taking them on a date that "transports" them somehow into new vistas or experiences. Since Geminis are most comfortable in social situations, go ahead and include other people on your date, even some of their friends. Keep your date lively by maintaining a witty conversation that bounces smoothly from one subject to the next. Then, make your next date completely different.

What are Geminis like between the sheets?

Think variety and adventure! Geminis' love of versatility is expressed in their sexuality as it is in everything else. Be creative and inventive, and surprise Gemini with something new every time you make love. After all, Gemini will do the same for you.

Geminis' sexuality is extremely active and breezy as well—they like lots of playfulness and appreciate a companion who's game for anything. Many get turned on with verbal expression before and during lovemaking—so go ahead and tell them what you want to do with them, and what you're doing to them as you're doing it. Experimenting is vitally important to Geminis' sexuality; they want to (and will) try anything, especially if it is new or something they just heard or read about.

> "Geminis like lots of playfulness and appreciate a companion who's game for anything."

Leave Gemini wondering who you will be next! Keep tricks flowing! Try dressing differently or acting out each other's fantasies. That will keep Gemini interested and involved like nothing else can.

What turns Geminis off?

Routines and familiarity turn Geminis off, as do mental dullness or lack of good communication. Crudeness embarrasses them, possessiveness suffocates them, and "heavy feelings" make Geminis want to run for the hills.

Ways Geminis Can Drive You Crazy and What to Do About It

With every sign, the very things that make Gemini so unique and attractive can also have frustrating aspects to them, when taken too far.

Gemini challenge: The dual personality of the Twins can leave your head spinning.

Gemini's changeable nature can truly be confounding—for you and for them! One minute they think, feel, and express one way; the next minute they think, feel, and express another way entirely.

It's true—Geminis are inconsistent. But that's just them being true to themselves. Or should I say that's them being true to *all* of themselves. If one side of a Gemini favors one restaurant today, another side might favor another one tomorrow. Or Gemini might talk endlessly about vacationing in Jamaica in January, but then decide it should be Madrid in March. If Gemini suddenly becomes bored with your favorite friends and wants to go out with another crowd entirely, well, there's no talking them out of it.

What to do?

There's not a lot you can do about Gemini's changing tastes and preferences—they're part of their multifaceted nature. But if you want them to stay focused on your tastes or preferences, invent ways to keep them interesting and fresh. If your heart is set on vacationing in

Jamaica in January, show Gemini how it will be just as exciting as Madrid in March. Sometimes it works to keep corralling Gemini's wandering attentions toward the goals and interests you have; other times you may have to be flexible and go with their whims.

Gemini challenge: Their commitments might be as fleeting as they are.

Gemini's multiplicity also makes it hard for them to commit to long-term agreements or plans. They have a whole dormitory of characters inside of them, wanting expression and desiring different experiences. Usually Geminis' motivation for resisting commitments is a fear they might miss out on something else.

What to do?

If you want a commitment from a Gemini, do your best to pique their curiosity by offering them education or stimulation. And, perhaps most important, show Gemini how any commitment you're asking for can lead to even greater freedoms and adventures than the ones they're leaving behind.

In the end, you can't make a Gemini commit to anything, because many just can't make themselves commit. Either they will or they won't, and sometimes neither you nor Gemini will know for sure what their choice will be. You'll both be surprised to see to what and whom Gemini eventually commits.

Gemini challenge: They resist romantic commitments.

This fear of missing out on other choices can make Gemini reluctant to commit to a relationship. Geminis adore having romance in their lives—but committing to only one person, no matter how fabulous and compatible they might be, ultimately means Gemini might not be able to (openly) pursue that fabulous intoxication of love with another person.

To make commitment matters more challenging, many Geminis hold an ideal of a "perfect mate." That's nearly impossible for a mere mortal to live up to! Nevertheless, Geminis will dart from relationship to relationship, thinking, "No, that's not the right person," "Nope, that wasn't it, either," sometimes for decades. Even if Geminis try to force themselves to commit (usually to keep from hurting the one they're ambivalent about), if it isn't right, something inside of them eventually says, "No. Not yet."

What to do?

If you're waiting for a romantic commitment from a Gemini, keep this in mind: if you sense they're indecisive about you or stringing you along, you're probably right. In most cases, if Gemini doesn't make some form of commitment quickly, they'll never make one at all. If it's been a while and Gemini is still "not sure," then chances are, they'll never be. Don't wait forever for a Gemini.

> "Deep down, many Geminis fear that intimacy and commitment will rob them of their greatest desire: freedom."

Gemini challenge: Are they keeping things light, or just completely shallow?

Some people become annoyed over Geminis' tendency to only skim the surface of matters, complaining that they're superficial. They can be frustrated Geminis will only go so deep or become so introspective, before disconnecting and moving on to the next subject.

Geminis can lose patience with others' intensity or depth. They can become exasperated and demonstrate an edgy distraction should another insist on delving deeper into ideas or feelings that Gemini considers "already covered" or too heavy.

What to do?

Geminis don't necessarily feel the need to inspect life, themselves, or others in a deep way. In fact, Geminis can learn what they need in order to evolve without as much internal processing as others need.

If you feel Gemini is skimming the surface of a topic you'd like to explore more fully, find a way to further engage their curiosity by continually approaching it from a new point of view. Saying something like, "Here's another take on . . ." might keep Gemini's interest more alive.

Gemini challenge: Deep feelings make them skittish.

Geminis feel very little need to delve deeply into feelings—either their own or their partner's. Exhibits of passion and intensity can seem distasteful or suffocating to Gemini. So don't expect them to "share feelings." They might talk about emotions, but it's unlikely

Geminis are going to spend a lot of time expressing them, even when they do feel them.

This cool, distant side to Gemini can be alienating. Their discomfort around feelings can prompt them to respond with a skittish "Now what?" attitude when others express their feelings. Or they can just become numb and ignore them and the person expressing them.

Although Geminis tells themselves they do this to resist being drawn into the undertow of others' emotions and needs, they give the impression that they are discrediting others and their feelings, and ignoring them as well.

What to do?

If Gemini is getting squirmish around, if not resentful of, your feelings or needs, you may need to back off a bit. Perhaps share them with another person altogether.

Or try enticing Gemini's curiosity in your feelings, even your anguish or pain, by sharing with Gemini how when you experience an emotion, you learn something fascinating from it. When you are able to show Geminis how your feelings and troubles are still intriguing and valued aspects of who you are, they may learn from your example how to respect and attend to them.

Gemini challenge: They have an infamous "disappearing act."

Geminis tend to disappear—just drop out of sight—even when things are going well. No visits, no calls, nothing. Companions can wonder "What happened? Was it something I did? Did I say the wrong thing?" Usually it's nothing a companion has done. Geminis just need a change of scenery—a breath of fresh air, so to speak. They'll be back. Just keep living your life.

Sometimes Geminis disappear when they're needed the most. If matters get too intense, too deep, or even too intimate, Geminis might make themselves scarce. And then, when the "heavy situation" blows over, Geminis bounce back like nothing happened. "Hi! Want to go to a movie?"

That's because most Geminis feel awkward when matters get too complex. They can feel confined, uneasy, and scared when too much emotion or crisis is surfacing. Many feel that if someone needs them, it might be too much responsibility. They might not feel up to it or might not *want* to be up to it.

What to do?

Geminis can be very helpful when the going is rough, as long as they don't feel obligated. The free-bird Gemini always needs a way out.

If you want Gemini to stick around during a tough situation or even help you through it, let them know you'd appreciate their help, but aren't dependent on it.

If *you* are having a conflict *with* a Gemini, do not try to force them to come around. The more you pressure, emote, demand, cry, or plead, the more they (sometimes inexplicably even to themselves) feel the need to stay away. What might work better is agreeing on a time frame of distance. Try saying something like "How about if you take twenty-four hours to yourself? Then let's talk about it, okay?" This is your best bet because when emotional or turbulent situations happen, Geminis need to figure out what they think and what they feel. They need time and space to do so. And most usually need to do that on their own. When you allow Gemini their space, it helps them to naturally process the facts and thus express themselves.

Gemini challenge: Their trickster might trick you!

Then there is the infamous trickster side of Gemini—a savvy gamesman who knows how to get the best of whomever he's around. Sometimes this means that your seemingly innocent, first-time poker-playing Gemini friend walks away with everyone's chips at the end of the game. Or Gemini—whose motto is "Imitation is the highest form of flattery"—might flatter you by imitating you, and then take credit for some of your better ideas.

But there can be a naughtier side of the trickster quality of your Gemini "one and only": Gemini might have an additional "one and only" on the other side of town.

Although Geminis have a reputation for being double-crossers and double-agents, this only happens on rare occasions. Geminis usually don't plan to take advantage of people, but sometimes the opportunity is so ripe, they just can't help themselves. When they do, however, it is executed with stunning cleverness.

What to do?

Should you always, therefore, mistrust your Gemini companion, lest they trick you? No! Why bother with a friendship if you'd always be checking over your shoulder? A vast majority of Geminis express their trickster side in playful ways. However, if you sense that something is incongruent, you might look at bit closer at Gemini's behavior. When you confront Gemini about their intentions, you may not get the whole truth: if they are acting the trickster, they'll always have a good excuse. Better do your research on your own. And, just to be safe, only tell Gemini things you wouldn't mind the rest of your community knowing.

> "Just to be safe, only tell Gemini things you wouldn't mind the rest of your community knowing."

Gemini challenge: Their Peter Pan complex can get old.

There is an eternal youthfulness to Gemini that is incredibly enlivening and endearing. But when it's time to do grown-up things, this side of Gemini can let you down. Some Geminis have a fear of the responsibilities and confinements that come with adulthood. Missed dates and dropping the ball on commitments are examples of the childish side of Gemini.

What to do?

Short of trying to police, control, or even parent Gemini, there isn't a lot you can do about their occasional immaturity. But you can be very clear about your boundaries and expectations.

Gemini challenge: They gab and gab and gab . . .

Some Geminis are too talkative for others' tastes. Many can talk all day at work and then spend the entire evening on their cell phones. Conversations needn't be profound or even new for Gemini. Their minds have a "tape recorder" quality that picks up what's been said and runs it over and over. That often results in Geminis saying the same things over and over. Talking is Geminis' way of connecting. But it might also be their way of filling in emotional space.

What to do?

If you are the type who prefers some sweet silences in your companionships, you might need to actually request that of Gemini. Some Geminis understand this and simply strike up a conversation with someone else, or sit down to quietly read. Other Geminis only stop talking when they leave you.

Gemini challenge: They're all talk but no action.

Geminis like to talk about future plans—sometimes more than actually doing them. This can exasperate more practical companions who want to see some results from all that discussion. They don't realize that just talking about a plan is often satisfying enough to Gemini.

What to do?

If you grow weary of listening to Geminis' plans for things that never seem to materialize, tell them you want to hear more about their plans *after* they take the first few steps toward achieving them.

Gemini challenge: They have a crabby side.

Sometimes normally sunny Geminis will become impatient and chop someone's head off with a few well-chosen words. That's their "Crabby Twin" showing up, the side that specializes in bad moods. When that happens, Geminis are irritable and critical, if not worse. This can be confusing, if not crushing, because Geminis can give you the impression that you're boring them to death. Or that they'd rather be with anyone other than you.

What to do?

When Geminis display an ill temper, it's usually smartest to ignore it. Or get out of their way and busy yourself with another task. It might help if you alert Geminis that their attitude is hurtful and that you'd prefer to be treated more kindly.

But unless you enjoy banter or a prickly argument, you'd better not engage with Gemini's ill mood or you might end up arguing about something you needn't. Most of the time, just giving Gemini space will make the "Crabby Twin" stage pass.

Summary:
Taking on the Twins

• Remember Gemini's main motivation is to be stimulated and to learn. Capitalize on that.

• Keep a light, open touch when dealing with Gemini, and give plenty of freedom and options.

• Don't get too heavy.

• When asking Gemini to change behavior, show the interesting possibilities in whatever you're requesting.

Chapter Four

Cancer
(June 22—July 22)

Who They Are

When you have a Cancer in your life you're sure to be nurtured, coddled, and sweetly fussed over. That's because Cancers are tender creatures who specialize in taking care of themselves and indulging whomever they love and cherish. Cancers are deeply emotional and highly sensitive, and they use their instincts to sense the feelings and needs of everyone around them. Although initially Cancers seem quite shy and passive, once they feel safe enough to venture out of their shell and expose their true sweet selves, they blossom into bubbly, determined companions.

Life with a Cancer is rarely lonely or underfed. They're hands-on, up-close, involved companions who love providing sustenance to whomever they're involved with. Many times this sustenance comes literally in the form of food (and lots of it), since most Cancers are great cooks. But beyond great food and a quenched palate, Cancers provide sustenance in the form of emotional support, deep listening, and tender affection.

Being with a Cancer poses a fascinating dichotomy. One minute they're parentlike, exuding a take-charge, wise, and knowing caretaking ability. The next minute, Cancer is childlike, conveying a vulnerable and yielding nature that asks for care from you. Cancers usually want and need to play both roles in their relationships in order to fulfill their sign's potential—which is to develop skills in both giving and receiving nurturing.

When taking the parental role, Cancers might feel compelled to adopt someone who needs help and to work tirelessly to make their life better. When embracing their childlike ways, Cancers find someone who makes them feel safe and takes care of them; they'll listen to that person as they would to a parent. The challenge for every Cancer is to not go overboard in either of these roles, lest they become overly responsible or too dependant.

Cancers live to connect, share feelings, and spend "family time" with those they care for. Don't worry if

Cancer Is a Water Sign

🐟 Cancers' deep emotional nature comes largely as a result of being a Water Sign, which means that they are more likely to go with their feelings and gut when making decisions over practicality. In fact, most Cancers have such powerful and insistent emotions that they can regularly feel overwhelmed by them. As anyone who's been close to a Cancer will attest, Cancer is a moody sign. Depending on the day, hour, or even minute, Cancer can swing from a joyously outgoing silliness to an internal, brooding quiet.

you're not literally family; if Cancer likes you, you'll be welcomed into their home and heart as if you are.

> "Cancers let their feelings run the show."

Don't be fooled by Cancers' tender, even yielding demeanor: they are dynamos (albeit often quiet ones) who have a restless urge to get matters up and going. Cancers especially love stirring up feelings, bringing out emotions, and creating new nurturing connections. Because of this, Cancers—and their emotions—often control the emotional climate of a room. They might do so with great subtlety, but Cancers and their feelings make a huge impact on their relationships and environment.

Cancers have a great need to establish security for themselves and loved ones. They do this in the form of familial stability, financial security, and homemaking. They must be certain that they and their loved ones are safe and cared for.

Cautious Cancers' first question in any situation is, "Is it safe?" Usually this pertains to emotionally safe; Cancers absolutely dread the prospect of getting hurt. Upon meeting a Cancer, you'll see them shyly peering out from their protective shell, assessing whether or not the atmosphere is secure enough for them to emerge. If it is, Cancer pops out and participates in an endearing fashion. But if there's the least bit of tension or threat in the environment, Cancers stay in retreat, waiting for safer times.

Financial security is also extremely important to Cancers. They crave that assured feeling of having the means necessary to care for themselves and their loved ones. Cancers are incredibly resourceful and have a knack for getting maximum value out of a dollar. Because they tend to worry about future rainy days, most Cancers put plenty of cash away in

Cancer Lesson: Quiet Those Nagging Insecurities with Wise Self-Nurturing

🦀 Many born under the sign Cancer experience a deep insecurity regardless of how successful or capable they are in the world. When under the spell of these insecurities, Cancers might worry they don't have enough resources to care for themselves, and believe someone else should support them. Cancers can then be tempted to agree to relationships or situations that aren't really right for them, just in the name of security. That's when you'd be a great friend to remind Cancer of their sign's key mission: to learn to be terrific parents to themselves. When Cancers are as sturdy and wise a caretaker to themselves as they are to those they love, they tap into the genuine empowerment of their spirits. Then Cancer's resourceful confidence is awakened, as is their signature love for themselves and this big family called the world.

drawers, bank accounts, or conservative investments. Money is so important to Cancers that they can be driven to a terrible distraction if they don't think they have enough of it. And it's terribly hard if they are partnered with someone they consider financially irresponsible. Cancers want to know they can trust partners not to squander what they worked so hard to create.

Cancers also seek the security of a home and family life. Every Cancer is about home and family in some way. After all, their zodiac symbol is the Crab—that funny (but capable!) creature who carries its home on its back. Home is Cancers' ultimate sanctuary and they value it more than anything. Cancers make their homes cozy and inviting, stock the fridge with enough food to feed an army, and indulge their kids and furry pets to no end.

If Cancers ask you to their homes, they are inviting you into their inner sanctum. It's there that they are truly relaxed and spontaneous, and definitely in charge. They'll want you to be comfortable when you're there, perfectly attended to and safe. Home is Cancers' retreat. They need time alone there to let go of the pressures of the world. Let them have that time. It centers and refreshes Cancer like nothing else can.

Having and creating a family is another source of security that Cancers deeply desire. Most Cancers' definition of family means children. Children bring out the best in Cancers, as many feel they were born to be parents. But even if it's an unconventional family, like one comprised of good friends or a pet or two, Cancers live for the intimacy, refuge, and day-to-day sweet happenings that a family provides. Many Cancers act as the glue that holds their entire family together. They want the sharing, the harmony, and even the dramas that familiarity promotes.

When dating a Cancer, it's wise early on to bring up the topic of children because it's usually not a negotiable point. Or, if a Cancer already has children, their highest priority will be whether or not you get along with them. Most Cancers will step away from a prospective mate if they don't match their needs for children. Want to appeal to a Cancer? Be good to the ones they love, especially their kids and their mom.

What Cancers Want in Relationships and How You Can Attract One

Cancers seek relationships rich in loving familiarity. Think "happy family" and you'll know what Cancers seek in all relationships.

Cancers want to know they are welcomed, included, and valued. They want to know their companions desire and cherish them, and won't do anything to harm them. Cancers especially enjoy relationships where nurturing abounds and love to be both the caretaker and the care-receiver in relationships.

Cancers deeply desire an emotionally safe atmosphere. Cancers need to feel as if they can open up and express their feelings completely without being judged or rejected. Cancers' emotions are so central to their sense of themselves that they need their companions to acknowledge and validate them in order to feel intimate with them.

Words Cancers Love to Hear

- "You're included."
- "I feel close to you."
- "I love your family/children/home."
- "You and your feelings are important to me."

The need for emotional security is so strong that Cancers don't function well without it. This doesn't necessarily mean that you should be as emotional as Cancers or feel everything as they do. Few can. But Cancers want to know that you, at the very least, accept their feelings and try to understand them as important.

If someone dismisses Cancers' feelings or doesn't share the same feelings or doesn't feel them as deeply, Cancer might interpret that person as disloyal. If that kind of a situation pops up, it's best to say something like, "I love you even if I don't feel what you feel." That helps Cancers sort out the difference between loyalty and being an individual.

Cancers seek deep bonds. Cancers crave the kind of bonding that comes from knowing someone well because this makes them feel connected and bonded. "You are worried about someone?" says Cancer, "Oh! So am I. Let's share our feelings." Again, you needn't feel just as Cancer does. They just need to know that you do, indeed, feel something.

> "If you want to get close to a Cancer, do it by sharing feelings."

Cancers seek loyalty. Cancers will watch companions carefully to make sure they're consistent and dependable. They want to know you'll choose them over others, and that you won't make someone or something more important than them or fail to be their champion.

Cancers need to be assured that they will not be abandoned. Since Cancers deeply fear being abandoned by their companions physically, emotionally, or otherwise, they crave regular reassurance that they won't be. Regularly showing Cancers you are there for them is priceless, indeed. If you're busy, telling Cancer, "I'm distracted right now, but I love you and want to connect with you when I get done," helps them accept your absence without feeling lonely. And, just as a child sometimes wants to know why they are loved, Cancers enjoy your reassurance that they are cared for and considered very special. Remind Cancer about all the things you love about them. They'll return the favor a hundredfold.

Cancers thrive on togetherness. Cancers want to touch and feel and have regular dinners with their beloveds. They are rarely satisfied in relationships that involve distance of any kind. They want you there, under their wings, them under your wings.

Cancers are drawn to those who can provide them security. Cancers' drive for security is so strong that they find those who can help them achieve it very attractive. If you can help Cancer create

> ## Words Cancers Love to Say
>
> 🐟 "I'll take care of you."
> "Are you okay?"
> "I'm feeling . . ."
> "We'd better eat something."

the home, family, or bank account they desire, you might get close to the top of their list!

Cancers yearn to be protected. There is a vulnerable side to Cancer that craves being watched over, parented, guided, and defended. That's often their definition of loving concern, and they'll ask for it from you. Doing so creates a satisfying atmosphere of mutual support between you and Cancer.

What Cancers Offer in Relationships

Cancers offer intimacy. Cancers have a tremendous drive to connect with, be involved with, and to know their beloved. They'll try to climb inside your psyche to discover every single thing about you. Cancers will eagerly listen for your thoughts and experiences about everything from how your day went to what you consider to be your life's purpose.

Cancers feel comfortable going to great depths of feeling themselves, and they'll encourage you to do the same. Their tenderness, perceptiveness, and caring broadcasts, "You're safe with me, so go ahead and reveal *everything*." This creates an atmosphere of closeness and understanding that few other signs can match.

Cancers are compassionate and provide comfort. Cancers feel for everyone and everything, and with their compassion, they reach out to understand and soothe all they consider. They'll rejoice in your wins and cry for your anguish. You'll never need to hide feelings or issues from Cancer—with their empathy, they can sense your struggles and reach out to make them better. They'll even feel closer to you as they do since they cherish the aliveness of connecting with others' joys and sorrows of life.

Perceptive Cancers know when you are distressed and instinctively seek to help. After all, they're in their glory when they are giving and nurturing. Nothing brings out a Cancer's tenderness and resourcefulness like another in need. If times are difficult, Cancer is there. Many Cancers are sought for their counseling, regardless of their profession.

"Cancers bring warm affection to their relationships. Hugging, cuddling, and tender kisses are second nature to Cancer."

Cancers have an incredible knack for providing a home and traditional family atmosphere. In addition to creating a wonderfully comfy home, Cancers also bring the attentiveness, joy, and appreciation that can make most any situation feel like a "family gathering." Cancers remember birthdays, fly across the country for a nephew's graduation, throw their parents wedding anniversary parties, or cook a week's worth of dinners for their neighbor who just had a baby. Holiday time? Of course it's the Cancer's house where the whole gang gathers for a feast of plenty! Do you need to bring anything? Just yourself. Well, an extra dessert is always welcome, if you insist.

Most Cancers contribute financial security to their relationships. Although deep down they prefer being provided for, Cancers' drive for security is so strong they won't sit back and wait for others to provide. They get busy and do it themselves. (Unless someone does provide for them very well—then Cancers most assuredly will sit back and enjoy.) Cancers make sure that they and their loved ones get what they need, even when their budget is quite modest.

Actually, Cancers' resourcefulness and uncanny knack for squeezing value out of the dollar usually helps them create a flourishing quality of life even on the slimmest of budgets. And what if a Cancer's budget is plentiful? Think "thrift" anyway. Cancers just cringe at the thought of wasting money. Perhaps they'll indulge themselves in some areas (usually it involves furnishings or clothing and educating the kids), but in the end, Cancers are protective of their savings account. They aren't about to blow their security.

Cancers keep loved ones safe with fierce protectiveness. Cancers will never stand by while another is hurt or mistreated in any way. If they even get the tiniest whiff of threat, they'll circle the wagons and make sure the ones they care for are tucked away and safe. With an innate sense of defensiveness, Cancers are on a constant lookout for threats. They'll fly out of their shell to put the kibosh on any perpetrator.

Cancers' goofy, silly humor is sure to bring comic relief. Cancers are famous for off-the-cuff funnies that are endearing as well as entertaining. Their childlike side has a wonder and innocence that makes even ordinary moments delightful and fun.

The Cancer Lover

Cancers are tender, private, intimate, and nurturing lovers. And they're so full of surprising moods and expressions that you may feel as if you have many lovers rolled up in one! Sometimes Cancer will be a shy, gentle, dreamy devotee who fluidly yields to your every dictate and need. Other times Cancer is a feisty assertive paramour who enjoys being attended to and indulged.

A Cancer lover will comfort, reassure, and take care of you like few others. They'll strive to make you feel understood and deeply touched. And don't worry about your Cancer lover straying. They understand the meaning of commitment and they cherish having someone to commit to. Even with their feelings being as changeable as the night sky, Cancers' loyalty is as constant as the North Star.

What kind of dates do Cancers enjoy?

Cancers enjoy dates wherein their comfort is enhanced and/or nurturing is involved. Feeding them is always a great idea. Because Cancers are most at home in homes, why not whip up a yummy dinner in your kitchen? (Or order something in for a quiet, intimate evening.) Maybe try a gourmet restaurant where the atmosphere is warm and inviting. Or, better yet, a restaurant that's run by a mama and a papa who come to your table and sing your praises. Going somewhere like a home-improvement show might spark Cancer's imagination about your goals to build a home and family.

Truthfully, you needn't sweat over the right place to take your Cancer date: they're much more interested in how thoughtfully you treat them throughout the date and whether or not you measure up in the "potential partner" department, which they'll know right off the bat.

What should you wear on your date with Cancer? Something soft that invites a cuddle. And go ahead and show your assets, albeit subtly. Cancer females especially love seeing their dates' financial assests. Cancer males especially love curvy figures and are particularly impressed with breasts. Wear something that makes the most of yours, but not so much that the others in the room gawk.

Important hint: if you are dating a Cancer who has children, including them in your plans is extremely important. Show your thoughtfulness by chipping in and helping with arrangements for them to be well cared for and entertained, so your date, their parent, can relax and enjoy you. Or maybe take the kids on a fun outing. And let's not forget Cancer's mom! Find out what kind of date would impress her—and take all three of you there. Along with winning over Mom, you'll win over your Cancer!

What are Cancers like between the sheets?

There is a profound sensitivity to your Cancer lover, enabling them to instinctively anticipate what you want and desire. Cancer women know what makes their partners feel most like men, and they are eager to provide it. Cancer men seem to understand a woman's body so well, you'd wonder if they have been women in their past lives. Perhaps it's not as much about past lives as it is about the Cancer lover's ability to direct their fine-tuned sensitivity toward pleasing their partner.

Turn the lights down low, play some soft music, go to their place or somewhere Cancer would like to be their place, like a luxurious retreat, and let your bodies lead the way. By the way, many Cancers have a passive side that appreciates their lover making the first move. Go ahead and take the lead!

Tender touches, long gazes, and paying special attention to Cancers' tummy are all delicious ways of getting their fires burning. But remember, Cancer is first and foremost seduced by feeling nurtured. The most alluring thing you can do is take care of their emotional needs long before taking care of each other's sexual needs.

What turns Cancers off?

Harshness, insensitivity, and ignoring feelings are all turnoffs to a Cancer. If Cancer doesn't feel coddled and safe with you outside the bedroom, you're not going to be coddled and pleased inside the bedroom.

Ways Cancers Can Drive You Crazy and What to Do About It

As with every sign, the very qualities that make Cancer most appealing can become frustrating if taken to extremes.

Cancer challenge: They're maddeningly moody.

Cancers' moods or moodiness can make relating to them difficult, if not downright exasperating. Cancers can become completely absorbed by their feelings and expect you to cater to those feelings as well. One minute they're happy and open; the next, they're upset and shut down. Sometimes the littlest thing can send them reeling. Hence, there can be a lot of walking on eggshells around Cancers.

What to do?

*F*irst remember that Cancers' emotional moodiness goes with their sign, and it's something Cancers must deal with. Being compassionate about their churning emotions makes you a treasured companion, indeed. That said, you must also remember that Cancers' moods are triggered by them, not you. In that way, you can remain free from believing that you "made Cancer feel" anything by what you did or did not do. Be yourself around Cancer, albeit a kind and gentle version of you, if you want to keep the maximum peace.

Cancer challenge: Their feelings can hold you (and them) hostage.

*S*ometimes Cancers' emotions are so powerful they can feel held hostage by them and become engulfed by what they're feeling. And they respond with tidal waves of reactivity. Problem is, you might feel held hostage to Cancers' feelings as well if you allow them to dictate your activities. You might end up leaving a fun party early because your Cancer doesn't feel connected with anyone, or you may agree to end a valued friendship because Cancer felt hurt by something someone said. You also might find yourself dodging the truth about something you feel for fear Cancer will take it the wrong way.

What to do?

*A*lthough Cancers would love it if you felt every emotion they feel along with them, they'll (begrudgingly) come to understand that's unlikely. But they would nevertheless appreciate your trying to understand their feelings or at the very least respecting them as valid. Never expect Cancer to just "snap out" of a feeling. That's painful and insulting.

But it's also important not to allow Cancers' feelings and reactions to their feelings dictate your life. Reach an understanding with Cancer about how you can each be entitled to your own feelings and choices. Remind them that if your feelings, perceptions, or desires differ from theirs, it doesn't mean you are abandoning, betraying, or dismissing them, you are just taking care of yourself. Although Cancer might be initially skeptical of that type of autonomy, they can end up learning volumes about taking care of themselves.

Cancer challenge: They can be overly sensitive.

Since Cancers tend to take things personally, their feelings are very easily hurt. If someone makes a remark with the least little edge of negativity or sarcasm, Cancers imagine it's because of them. Then they get their famous knot-in-the-tummy and feel terribly hurt and deflated.

Worse, even when there isn't something hurtful in what someone says or does, Cancers may project that there is and become deeply wounded anyway. It can seem like Cancers create rejections or choose offenses even when none were intended. It works the other way around as well: if Cancer suspects they've hurt another's feelings, they might suffer for days.

Cancers' feelings are so real to them that they may not consider that they're not completely accurate. Or Cancers might prolong their painful feelings by resisting confronting the source of their hurt and resolving it, or even verifying that what they thought happened really happened. Therefore, you might be mystified about what's bothering Cancer, even when they are suffering so.

When Cancers are hurt they retreat into their shells and become hard to reach. They sulk, act unhappy, and withdraw from others with a look of blame and disappointment.

What to do?

Reassurance is always welcome to a Cancer with hurt feelings. Saying things like "I didn't mean to be hurtful," or "I'm sure they didn't mean to hurt/forget about/undermine/neglect/insult you" comforts Cancer enough for them to entertain the idea that their hurts might indeed be imagined. Pointing out how most people aren't as sensitive as Cancer helps them to realize that they may be reading too much into another's thoughtlessness. Reminding Cancer how they are loved and adored also puts a welcome salve on the wounds of hurt, too.

Cancer challenge: They're defensive.

Since Cancers are so sensitive and do anticipate hurtful blows, many of them approach uncertain situations with a thick shell of defensiveness. Or instead of being the kind, mushy sweethearts they essentially are, Cancers might stay closemouthed and distant, with-holding all self-expression altogether.

What to do?

If your Cancer is hiding in a shell or suffering from hurt feelings, try wooing them with reassurances and invitations to come out and join and connect with you. Create an atmosphere that helps Cancer feel safe to open up in. Avoid becoming impatient or saying things like, "Now what's the problem?" That usually isn't the best approach for inviting Cancer to be forthcoming. They'll respond much better with a caring "I see you are hurt

> "Tending to feelings will be a big part of your relationship with Cancers."

about something, and I'd really like to hear about it and help make it better—when you're ready, of course." In most cases, that'll eventually bring Cancer around.

Cancer challenge: They're worriers.

Cancers worry a lot. They become anxious over topics such as security, love, and acceptance. Even when Cancers have plenty of everything, they can worry that they might lose what they have. And it's miserable for them. It's not your job to attend to or to fix Cancers' anxieties, since learning to do so for themselves is a big part of their sign's fulfillment. But it sure does help if your Cancer feels the freedom and safety to talk things out with you.

What to do?

Surely you'll win Cancer's heart if you can do something about the matters they worry about—they'll feel tremendous relief as well as an endearing respect for you.

But don't let them get too dependent on your strength. Instead, support Cancer best by supporting their strengths and reminding them that they're full of them. Reminding Cancer of the abundance they do have, the obstacles they have overcome, and all of the ways they regularly demonstrate strength helps Cancer shift their focus away from their worries and back to their confidence.

Cancer challenge: They're self-involved.

Since Cancers' sign is all about learning to take care of themselves and managing their emotions, Cancers are designed to be self-focused. Cancers have a strong sense of "me" and an urgent sense of what they want and need. Without their "selfishness," Cancer wouldn't be as in tune with themselves and their feelings as they need to be in order to grow and evolve. But sometimes it can seem as if Cancers aren't self-focused in an evolving way, but rather in a selfish, self-involved way.

If Cancer is making everything about them, you might need to remind them that you have concerns other than their life, problems, and needs. Doing this good-naturedly helps Cancer realize you can't be there for them all the time, nor should you be. (Even though deep down they wish you would be.)

Unfortunately, sometimes Cancers don't acknowledge their selfish motivations and mask their personal agendas from themselves and others. That's when they might hide behind lots of sacrificing and self-negating behaviors, only to develop a deep resentment that they aren't satisfying themselves. They can employ a manipulative, "I'm doing all this for you" approach, when to you, it seems like they're really doing it all for themselves. And they are. In fact, they're broadcasting an "I've done everything for you, now you should do what I want you to" type of guilty control.

Worse, Cancers can feel like martyrs or use their giving as emotional blackmail against others. They can agree to do something, but then hold others responsible for their happiness in return. Or they can expect you to make sacrifices for them as payback for the sacrifices they have made.

What to do?

When Cancers acknowledge and celebrate their self-involvement, it helps them satisfy their own needs first, which ultimately makes them refreshingly clear and direct with themselves and others. The beautiful thing is when Cancers are satisfied, their kindness quickly overflows, and they get busy helping and nurturing others in getting their needs met. When Cancers are full and self-satisfied, they're better partners because of it.

Be very clear with your Cancer that their nurturing and caretaking are appreciated, but do not indebt you to them. Remind Cancer that if you do something they don't want you to do, or that they consider selfish of you, it's what you choose to do to take care of yourself, not to go against Cancer. Then, encourage Cancer to do what they need to do to take care of themselves.

Cancer challenge: They have a fear of abandonment.

At times Cancers' deep fear of being abandoned can play havoc in their relationships. They die a million deaths imagining they might be left behind or forgotten by someone they love. Cancers might try to possess and control their loved ones in an attempt to prevent them from wandering away. They can easily conjure feelings of being excluded from your life or exhibit jealousy to the point that they imagine that someone is more interesting, enticing, or sexier than them.

What to do?

If you find your Cancer companion becoming possessive or jealous or imagining they are excluded, realize that these feelings are very real to them and are causing them misery. Give Cancer the details of why you want to stay with them and what it is you love about them. Understandably this constant hand-holding can become tiresome for you. It's not your job to make Cancer feel secure, but maintaining compassion for their insecurities and vulnerabilities will make you a stronger couple.

Cancer challenge: They get crabby.

Cancers can get irritable, snappy, and lash out with impatient demands. Sometimes they don't even realize they're acting that way. Other times Cancers know they're being difficult, but believe others should "just deal with them."

What to do?

If Cancers' snappiness bothers you, let them know. Saying something like, "Ouch! That hurt!" alerts Cancer to the fact they have been gruff, and it stings. If their mood persists, give them some space to work their feelings out. Chances are, Cancer won't want you to go and will snap out of their grumpiness pronto. You must do this with loving and caring. If you appear to be abandoning Cancer or discounting their feelings in any way, their mood will go from bad to worse.

What should you do if an argument with a Cancer does erupt? Wear your kid gloves and try to use as much tenderness as you can muster. That's because most Cancers don't recover well from brazen, knock-down-drag-out fights. They can be deeply wounded and sent into hiding in their shells indefinitely. Sidestep heated rages and instead express the deeper feeling underneath your anger. When Cancer understands you're feeling misery or vulnerability, they'll rise to the occasion and start comforting you.

Summary:
Staying Cozy with a Cancer

- **Remember Cancer's bottom-line need is to protect themselves. Let them know you're safe and don't mean to hurt them.**

- **Show respect for Cancer's sensitivity, feelings, and moods.**

- **Draw Cancer out by appealing to their caretaking/ nurturing instincts.**

- **When asking Cancer for a change in behavior, be gentle and soft, and show how it would bring even more security to their life and to your relationship.**

Chapter Five

Leo
(July 23–August 22)

Who They Are

If there's a Leo in your life you're sure to be warmly loved, showered with attention, and endlessly entertained. That's because these dynamic creatures not only specialize in love and romance, they're masters at making life an exciting extravaganza. Leos exude a majestic power that commands respect and wins adoration. Their bighearted generosity thrives on giving appreciation to and receiving appreciation from all, including you. Their upbeat, sunny disposition beams with charisma, and their ability to encourage others inspires affection and loyalty.

Leos partake in expressive pageantry. If something is worth doing, it's worth doing gloriously well and having fun with at the same time. With their flamboyance and exuberant style, Leos tackle life's endeavors in a flourishing way. They are magnetic souls and will seduce you with all their heart, power, creativity, and everything else they've got to win your love. Leos heartily invest themselves in their companions, and they'll desire attentive investment in return. After all, Leos want to be the center of attention and to receive love and applause more than anything else in life.

Leos work hard to earn their center-stage status. Their actions are dramatic, their stories are captivating (if not just a little embellished—for effect!), and their humor is belly-laugh clever. "All of life's a stage" is the Leo life credo. Their intention is to be so captivating that you never need to look elsewhere. In relationships, as in everything else in life, Leos seek to be the shining best.

At heart every Leo is a royal figure. They sense a uniqueness about themselves, even a quality of superiority. Leos love boasting that their zodiac symbol is the Lion. That majestic king of beasts represents them well since Leos feel like lions and even look like lions. (Most sport big hair, powerful eyes, and a king-of-the-jungle swagger.) Leos' impressive air broadcasts, "Yes, I am fabulous, aren't I?" They seek the best in others, but nevertheless consider themselves head and shoulders above the crowd. Always striving to be classy, Leos try to be elegant about their superiority, so as not to make others feel bad. Leos just live life in the most dignified way they can muster. The Royal One within them refuses to stoop to pettiness, stinginess, or small-mindedness, and instead tries to respond to every circumstance in a most magnanimous and uplifting manner.

Leos' royal nature imbues them with a leader's strength, determination, and willful resolution. They call the shots and that's that. With their tremendous self-confidence, Leos believe the way they're doing things is the right (and only) way. And you know what? They're usually correct! Leos have a natural savvy that assesses what will and will not work and how to accomplish projects most capably. And Leos know how to make projects sizzle so others want to be a part of them. Leos can sell anything to anyone. They use their enthusiasm and good taste to polish projects and make them appealing. And since Leos know how to stroke others' egos (since they love their own egos to be stroked), their encouragement brings out others' desires to do their best as well.

"Leos are great motivators and help others naturally tap into their desire and abilities."

With all the creativity Leos possess, you'd think they would be flexible and changeable, but they're not. They actually possess a strong desire for consistency and deep roots. Leos like to have an assuredness about life and relationships, and they'll work hard to establish that. They hang in there with relationships and situations long after others come and go. Leos change, adapt, and reinvent themselves year to year only when and how they see fit. No one pushes Leos into anything. They'll fight to the finish to retain control of all they oversee, especially themselves.

Leos resist being influenced in most matters, that is, except for matters of the heart. Their desire for love is so profound and their value of love is so high that they make huge concessions to keep it alive and thriving. If necessary, most Leos will shift their schedules, if not their entire lives, to meet the needs of a relationship. That's because being successful in love, both romantic and familial, is job one for Leos.

When Leos commit, they do so wholeheartedly. Since they consider losing someone they love a terrible devastation, they devote their considerable determination and go to great lengths to make their relationships work.

Leo Is a Fire Sign

🦁 Leos are fiery, indeed. They're passionate, powerful, and excitable, and possess a demonstrativeness that lets everyone for miles know just how they feel. Leos' fiery nature loves grand possibilities and adventure. They thrive on the challenge of greater accomplishments, the next goal to conquer, and new risks to take. The worst thing that could happen to Leos is no new horizons or surprises—especially in love. If a relationship becomes too humdrum or taken for granted, Leos get sluggish and disinterested. Life and love (perhaps the same thing for Leos) need to keep moving, growing, and expanding.

Like lions, Leos roar. Their fiery temper surely erupts into the occasional, or with some, the not-so-occasional fight. Sparks will fly if Leos feel they are not being treated with the considerate respect they deserve. They'll posture with an indignant: "How dare you? Do you know who you are talking to? I will never stand for that!"

Actually, some Leos become so stimulated by a good fight that there can be problems if their companions won't join them. Leos might feel they're not being engaged enough or being robbed of the intensity they crave. Companions should never worry that a spat with Leos would negate their affection for them. Many view fighting simply as an extension of their passion, a form of attention, a way to make things better. Leos are essentially lovers. They can turn even their biggest fights into a beautiful scene of making up, which, in the end, makes it all worthwhile.

What Leos Want in Relationships and How You Can Attract One

Leos desire others' attentiveness. Leos want to know that they are the most treasured focus of their companions' lives. They want to be treated with the utmost importance and appreciation. Leos want companions to devote loads of time and attention to them, and to consistently demonstrate that they are number one. After all, isn't that how a royal figure should be treated?

Leos seek companions who have integrity and strength. Leos are attracted to others who are as big as they are—or even bigger! Although they like to call the shots and to be the center of attention, Leos don't want to surround themselves with people who seem weaker or lesser.

Leos want to be captivated. Leos are attracted to those who broadcast the same winning energy they do. Want to captivate a Leo? Be

Leo Lesson: To Love Themselves Without Needing the Love of Others

Leos absolutely love to give and receive love. In fact, if they could have it their way, the whole world would love them and they would love everyone back. Many work overtime trying to make that so, trying to be all things to all people, sometimes to the point of exhaustion. That's when you can be a great friend to Leo by reminding them of their sign's mission: to learn to love and respect themselves without needing love, validation, or applause from others. When Leos understand that they can't and really shouldn't please everyone, they are freer to express their genuine royalty: that of their magnificent, bighearted spirits.

influential, compelling, charming, or talented! Leos love the satisfaction that comes from enticing and conquering others who are special and in command. Go ahead and declare your strengths, your resolve, and your successes. Leos will enjoy them, support them, and do whatever they can to help you take them even further. Leos won't envy your accomplishments and prowess—they'll be inspired by them.

> ## Words Leos Love to Hear
>
> 🦁 "You're special!"
> "I love you!"
> "You're the best."
> "You're the most gorgeous person in the world."

Leos demand loyalty and consistency. Leos will expect to be the first and best on your list. They are not charmed by now-you-see-me-now-you-don't behavior. In fact, Leos consider others who cannot commit as oddly weak. Leos go straight for who they want and can't understand others who do not.

> "Leos want partners who can match their royal position."

Leos' enormous pride needs (some say demands) to feel exalted and appreciated. If you behave in a way Leo sees as nonappreciative or worse, dismissive, they may feel humiliated. They expect to be treated like gold. This doesn't mean you shouldn't have a good time socializing when out with others. Leos like to show off their companions and delight when they are popular and well received. But always, no matter what the relationship, Leos expect you to demonstrate how they are your chosen ones.

Flattery gets you everywhere with Leos! They just can't help but purr whenever you notice their wonderfulness. So lay on the compliments. Leos will gratefully accept as many as you care to offer. They'll even make it easy for you by pointing out great things about themselves that you can compliment. And Leos are especially charmed when you notice qualities they hesitate to call attention to, like their compassionate, caring nature.

Leos like to be entertained. With their playful nature, Leos love others who make life fun. They adore being treated to exciting, even glamorous places and activities. (The theater is especially delightful.) Leos will appreciate your taking the time to plan adventures with them.

Leos love generosity in the form of gifts. Although most everyone appreciates receiving a surprise package, no sign adores it as much as Leo. You thought of them! You wrapped it up! You bestowed it upon them! Oh, the wonder of it all! Gifts needn't be extravagant, but they should be worthwhile.

What Leos Offer in Relationships

Leos will shower you with their gigantic love. Leo's intense, exuberant drive to please and be pleased makes them devote the lion's share of their energies to making you happy. Especially in the enticing beginning of a relationship, Leos will do whatever they can to meet even your grandest expectations and needs. They will woo you with guileless charm, entertain, and seduce you all in the name of becoming your dream companion.

Leos will shower you with gifts. Leos love to give gifts as much as they love to receive them. They're specialists at finding just the right present to communicate their high sentiment for you. They adore giving gifts that glitter and impress, and they do it often.

> "Wondering what to give your Leo? Anything shiny should do the trick!"

Leos will open doors for you. Leos are generous in creating opportunities that can promote you, be it through their connections, endowments, or introductions. They love opening doors that could change your life for the better. Leos savor knowing that their efforts helped make you the best you can be.

Remember this: the more you acknowledge Leos for their efforts, the more they'll try to be irresistible and fabulous.

Leos cook up fun activities that make life exciting. No doubt about it: Leo will entertain you. They will orchestrate grand plans, pull the strings, and otherwise manage all concerns in order to ensure that whatever they're planning with you comes off as a raving success. Leos intend to make life delightful, and they do it with flair.

Leos are true to their word. If they say they'll do something, Leos will. They'll try to impress you by not only meeting your expectations, but exceeding them. Leo's expectations for themselves are so high, many times they work like mad to live up to their own expectations by impressing you.

Leos are rock-solid in their commitments. Leos are firm in their devotion. If a Leo deems you worthwhile, they don't waver. Leos are around when life is fun, but they're also reliable when matters get rocky. Their pride keeps them from being seduced away from relationships they value. They're not afraid of conflict or trouble. Instead, they valiantly rise to the occasion to help you resolve them.

Words Leos Love to Say

- 🦁 "They loved me!"
- "I did this really well."
- "You're so great—I love you!"
- "Let's celebrate!"

Leos offer support and encouragement so you, too, can become a fellow royal being. Leos will spot your potential and bolster you so you can attain your majesty. They will give the kinds of advice, encouragement, and assistance that helps you flourish. Since Leos adore being around success, they'll receive great satisfaction in being the one who helps you blossom.

Leos are quite insightful about what you can do versus what might get you in over your head. So if your Leo advises you to do something, you'd be smart to consider it. Many accomplished people got that way because they had a Leo planning their success.

The Leo Lover

*L*eos are Master Romancers: they show their love with bursting drama, exuberant creativity, overflowing enthusiasm, and unbelievable seductiveness. Romance brings out the very best of Leos' hearts and their loving, giving nature. They bask in the attentiveness, the declarations of adoration, and the affection that glorious romance offers.

As anyone who has had the pleasure of being pursued by a Leo will attest, Leos are positively captivating in their creative ways of showing love. Leos unabashedly use every asset they've got to make loving them an exquisite and delightful experience. The heartfelt declarations of how utterly fabulous you are as well as the big, glorious surprises and the countless little thoughtful touches will show you that you mean the world to Leo. Do Leos cherish being treated with the same type of thoughtfulness? You betcha!

"Leos are happiest when carrying on a swooning, dramatic love fest."

What kind of dates do Leos enjoy?

Leos enjoy dates that sizzle, of course! Take them to the theater, a snazzy restaurant, or the hottest club in town. Dress to impress and be generous—with attention, praise, and everything else. (Presenting Leo with a gift is always a nice touch.) Your date needn't be grand to be meaningful to Leo, but they won't shun an extravagant night either.

When dating a Leo, be prepared to be on parade. Leos are very social and want their dates to blend in with and enjoy their friends and business associates as they do. They want their partners to fit nicely into their big social circle and help them climb the ladder of their ambitions. Leos love showing their lovers off and basking in others' admiration that they have won a hot number.

Go ahead and be affectionate—Leo's intimacies aren't as much about privacy and subtle moments as they are about pageantry, demonstrativeness, and letting the whole world know about their grand affair. Your Leo date won't be as interested in discreetly smooching in the back of a dark restaurant as they will be in smooching up front where all can see.

What are Leos like between the sheets?

The Leo lover is a terrifically sexy and sensual lover. Sex is the ultimate in the affection that Leos seek. For Leos, making love has to have gusto, creativity, and true affection. Lovemaking is exuberant and natural for Leo, as they accept their needs and others' needs as part of the drama of love. So lose your inhibitions and be playful! Why not try some creative role-playing and teasing lustiness? Pay special attention to Leo's chests (where their big hearts beat) and/or run your fingers through their hair. Keep the lights on: Leos like to be seen and to see their lovers as well. Be sure to emphasize how much you enjoy their beauty and physicality. Compliment Leos, attend to them, and applaud them; you'll be attended to in return—royally!

What turns Leos off?

Leos are mostly turned off by acts that contradict their being the most important person in your world. Criticism deflates them, being pushed aside hurts and offends them deeply, and prudish, inhibited, or insecure behavior makes their interest wane.

Ways Leos Can Drive You Crazy and What To Do About It

As with every sign, the very qualities that make Leos the most compelling can also be annoying, if taken overboard.

Leo challenge: They're egomaniacs.

Sometimes Leos' royal countenance can overshadow the generous wisdom of their hearts. Said another way, Leos can be egomaniacs. Their urges for domination and attention have been known to cause them to act in an annoyingly arrogant, overbearing way, or even to treat others (and you!) as minions. Leos' strong egos can dominate any conversation they are a part of. No matter what their companions are expressing, Leos might interrupt and share ideas and needs about themselves. The saying "But enough about me—what do *you* think of me?" could be a Leo motto.

Needless to say, Leos' need for the spotlight can be problematic if you are also seeking some time on the stage. They might elbow in, as if to say, "Over here! Listen to what I have to say!" More often than not, Leos are so interesting and magnetic that they do end up stealing the show. This can frustrate others who might feel eclipsed by Leos' dynamo energies.

What to do?

Hold your own around Leos; if you want to express yourself, do so! Don't wait for Leos to back down or step aside for you because chances are you'll wait a long while. But a Leo will respect you if you pipe up and express yourself, especially if you do so with utter confidence! That impresses them. Also saying something like "I want to hear your story, but first, let me tell mine," helps Leo be respectfully attentive.

Leo challenge: They're bossy.

Leos' unwavering self-confidence can make them quite domineering, demanding, and bossy. They bark out orders and expect others to scramble to fulfill them. They'll stubbornly hold on to ideas about how something should be done and dismiss your ideas, even if they are good ones.

Then there's Leos' knack for asking you to do something with an enthusiasm that seems to assume you'd love to do it for them. ("Wouldn't it be *fun* . . . if you babysat my kids?" or ". . . helped me clean my garage?") You might feel that saying no to them would be to rain on their terrific parade.

What to do?

*D*on't take Leos' bossiness personally, and know your boundaries. Don't let Leo seduce you into doing something you don't want to because you fear Leo won't love you if you don't. A Leo's love isn't dependent on your doing what they want you to—it's much stronger than that.

Leo challenge: They're control freaks.

*L*eos have an intense drive to make things happen in the ways they see fit. Their determination to have matters reflect their good taste and superior vision can make it very difficult for Leos to share the reins, much less relinquish them. Their fear is that if they do, matters won't go well. Hence, they have also been known to be control freaks. Leos don't see themselves as control freaks; they see themselves as the most capable people in the room, the ones who should be calling the shots.

When Leos do something, they intend to get it done in the best possible way. If something is their responsibility, Leos do whatever it takes to satisfy their high expectations of themselves, even if that means bossing others around. When Leos are controlling matters (or "leading," as they call it), their focus isn't on you or your feelings, it's on getting their vision materialized. They're concentrating on their goal, and they think you should be, too.

What to do?

If you feel you are on the receiving end of a Leo's probably well-intended, but domineering strategies, pipe up and remind them that you should be treated with more consideration. If they're expecting you to wait on them, define your boundaries by good-naturedly declining. Or let them know that you want to use your skills, abilities, and visions, too. If they work in concert with Leo's plan, show them how they do.

"If you want something done with flair and panache, ask a Leo."

If you have ideas and plans that differ from Leos', ask them for a time-out and discuss with them why you want to stick with them. Leos will stop and listen—and sometimes acquiesce—when ideas and exceptions are fairly presented. Be strong and dignified in your approach to both yourself and Leo. They'll respect that.

Leo challenge: They assume they're in charge.

Leos are likely to appoint themselves in charge of matters. When that happens, they bestow their advice with a "Listen to me, I know what's best" attitude, which can make you feel like saying, "What are my ideas: chopped liver?" Or Leos may use their will to push others aside and take over. Even when Leos are right, their arrogance about it can be infuriating, if not defeating.

What to do?

Avoid bowing down to Leos' demands. Meeting Leos' arrogance with a healthy dose of your own self-esteem not only keeps you balanced, it elicits Leos' interest as well.

Should Leo assume responsibility for something you want to be in charge of, stand up to them and let them know you're in charge. If you challenge a Leo directly, you'll probably be met with loads of resistance or a competitive one-upmanship. Instead, try wooing Leo to your side of the fence by thanking them for their concern and input and telling them their advice is valued, but that you're choosing to do things your way. Giving Leo a little time to absorb the idea

> "When Leos think they're right, they won't easily back down."

that you're in charge also helps. Being dignified and respectful in your delivery will help smooth matters over and garner Leo's pride and respect for you.

Leo challenge: They try to direct your life.

Another way Leos can be controlling (or "helpful," as they call it) is by trying to manage your life and helping you to right the wrongs in what you're doing. Their hope is to save the day for you. Telling Leos that they're butting in will stun them. They're not butting in—that's what nosy people do. Leos' intention is to bestow you with insight that helps you avoid problems and create true success for yourself. Regardless of what it's called, Leos can interfere with your living your life by insisting you listen to their advice, whether you want to or not.

What to do?

What's the best way to handle a Leo's insistent advice? With respect. If you care to hear it, tell them you want to, but that you might not do what they advise. (Note: don't interrupt Leo, or do so carefully.) If you don't want to hear Leo's advice, tell them you appreciate their concerns, but you'd like to figure things out for yourself. As long as Leo doesn't feel dismissed, they'll probably accept your independence. But they'll nevertheless believe you should have done what they told you to do.

Leo challenge: Their need for your attention can wear you out!

Leos' need for attention—their vying for appreciation, compliments, and applause—can occasionally become exhausting. Leos want (some say *need*) a steady diet of attention and acknowledgment. More than any other sign, Leos want their egos to be stroked. If you don't sufficiently attend to Leos in the way they desire, there can be trouble. Your Leo might not possess the type of sensitivity that understands or recognizes when you need a private moment or want some time to yourself. Instead, Leos might interpret your taking care of yourself as neglectful or as a personal affront, and become hurt, which results in sulking or manipulative withdrawal.

What to do?

It isn't your or anyone's responsibility to make Leos feel good about themselves; loving themselves is what their life lessons are all about. But it sure does help when you let Leo down easy. Explaining to Leo that you are busy, distracted, or otherwise need to be elsewhere—but love them anyway—helps Leo feel more secure and accepting of your distractions.

Remember: Leos' egos are very big, but very tender. Beneath Leos' strutting, boasting, and bravado lies a tender side that often fears they may not be as special or as loved as they desperately want to be. Leos' egos are paramount, and they're at their best and most generous when their ego is lovingly supported. When Leos' egos are bruised or squashed, it can be a sorry sight. Their confidence and joie de vivre can shrivel up, and their signature panache becomes deflated. So instead of squelching Leos' ego in order to try to get them to behave differently, redirect it toward what you want: "It would make me so happy if you would . . ."

Leo challenge: Their enthusiasm for love can be overwhelming.

There are times when Leos' greatest asset—their loving way—can be downright overwhelming. Leos can be so excited about the potential of a relationship (be it love, friendship, business, or even a job as your pet sitter), they might push it forward in ways that another might not be ready, willing, or able to accept. In their enthusiasm for what can be, Leos might not understand another's need for more time.

Since Leos get most excited over the prospect of a new love affair, they're most likely to push in the romance department, so much so, that they might forget to check to make sure their intended is as interested as they are. Perhaps Leos will begin with their declarations of love long before their beloved has a chance to catch up or even figure out how they feel. Or they'll shower their intended with so many gifts, praise, and other intense intentions, they become beholden.

Leos have been known to imagine relationships even before they're actually happening. They'll project feelings, amorous intentions, and significant moments that may not have yet taken place. That's because Leos are so desirous and determined to realize the potential of love, it can be hard for them to let it unfold naturally.

What to do?

If you're not ready to jump into a relationship with a Leo as quickly as they are, let them know—firmly but gently. Be clear about your needs and boundaries and communicate them clearly so Leo can hear it. Hinting might not be noticed. Instead, tell Leo what you're feeling directly, but kindly, and then stick to the boundaries that you set. If you are interested in them, but need more time to make promises or decide on next steps, let Leo know in a way that still upholds their dignity.

Summary:
Having a Purr-fect Time with Leos

• Remember that Leo's main motivation is be loved and applauded and capitalize on that.

• Work with Leo's ego instead of against it.

• Uphold Leo's dignity by encouraging more of what you do love about them rather than criticizing or belittling what you don't.

• When requesting a change of behavior from Leo, use patience and diplomacy, and show them how it could win them even more acknowledgment and love.

Chapter Six

Virgo
(August 23—September 22)

Who They Are

If you have a Virgo in your life, you'll find yourself organized, analyzed, and awakened to your greater possibilities. That's because these industrious creatures specialize in creating excellence—in themselves and in everyone and everything around them. Virgos' refined intelligence is always on the hunt for ways to sift out chaos and bring life to order. They love nothing more than knowing they're making a contribution. In fact, Virgo is the sign of service, which they exemplify by jumping in and helping anyone who might need their "fix it" strategy—including you.

Life with a Virgo has a busy and practical "Let's get something accomplished today" gusto. Their productive zeal will prompt you to join them in getting something—anything—done. After all, "Why waste time when there's so much we could improve?"

Virgos are constant observers as well. Never ones to miss a trick (or the fact that the waiter made a mistake), Virgos can be counted on to contribute a steady stream of eagle-eyed assessments and critiques in most any situation. Virgos tend to be quite smart, and they relish companions with whom they can engage in clever repartee wherein ironies and subtleties are noticed and assessed. Virgos usually feel safest broadcasting their practical and logical qualities. But they have a very sweet and tender side, as well. Virgos have special places in their hearts for others who need them because being helpful is one of Virgos' favorite ways to demonstrate love.

Another way Virgos demonstrate love is through work. And they work at absolutely everything. Of course they work at their jobs, but Virgos work at having fun, too. Fun to them can involve cleaning up and creating order, which to them might mean an antiseptically clean space with a classified organization system in place.

Virgos also work at their relationships. Their attitude is "How can I do my best here?" and "What should each of us contribute in order to bring out our relationship's best possibilities?" Then they work to make that a reality. But the "best" that Virgo seeks isn't an over-romanticized idealism, but rather an "Are we best achieving the purpose we've set out to achieve?"

Virgos' perspective tends to be a social one: they consider others' viewpoints and needs along with their own. Virgos also tend to be hierarchical and assess where they stand in relation to those around them. That is, are they more or less important? More or less intelligent? More or less popular? Once they've found their answers, they behave as expected to fulfill that role and expect others to fill their respective roles, too.

Virgos prefer their relationships to be realistic and frank. Why use unnecessary fanfare when the plain truth is just as witty? Ask Virgos a question, and they'll answer you directly and clearly, with their facts in order. Virgos do what they say they will, plus make a dozen extra efforts, just to make sure it passes (theirs, mainly!) inspection.

Virgos' unique ways of expressing their practicality is through their analytical intelligence. Nothing escapes their critical assessment. Their facile minds hone in and inspect even the tiniest details of just about everything: a project, a movie, the way their lover stirs their coffee. God is truly in the details for Virgos!

Does all this attention to details cause Virgos to occasionally miss the proverbial forest for the trees? Yes! A Virgo can walk into a five-star hotel, past the attentive doorman, over the sparkling Italian marble floor, under the exquisite glimmering chandelier, only to focus on a cigarette butt that somehow got lodged in the cracks of the floor. "Someone's been smoking!" Virgo will sniff.

Perfection is what Virgos relentlessly seek, expect, and pursue. They truly believe that if they work hard enough and try their very best that

Virgo Is an Earth Sign

Being an Earth Sign helps shape Virgos' productive personality. Earth energy gives Virgos a practical approach to life. They'll generally choose the reasonable, useful route over the passionate or idealistic routes. Virgos tend to be dependable, grounded, and concrete, and hold attainable goals to build toward. And they like life to be, too. In fact, these attributes are what make Virgos less likely to seek dominating or traditional leadership roles. They are usually most comfortable in the role of "amazing assistant" because it's rewarding to them to knock themselves out helping others to fulfill their roles.

they will ultimately reach perfection. But life is guaranteed to always be a little askew: that's Virgo's torment. Although they intellectually understand that no one's perfect, they try to be anyway.

Many have been misled about why Virgo's zodiac symbol is the Virgin, assuming it suggests Virgos are sexually prudish. Wrong! Instead, Virgo's symbol represents the purity they seek. Virgos love the simplest, most refined, pure expression in all matters. That symbolic Virgin is busy (as Virgos are) separating the wheat from the chaff. Their symbol points to how Virgos act to separate whatever is useful or nourishing from what is not useful. Sifting through the good and the bad, the right and the wrong, is what Virgos do in any situation, project, or relationship they are involved in.

> "Perfection is what Virgos relentlessly seek, expect, and pursue."

At heart most Virgos are healers, yet they can express this gift in countless ways. A good many Virgos are interested in medicine and make a profession of it. Others tend to be "health nuts" who vigorously champion the value of a natural diet, wise use of supplements, and alternative forms of healing. Maybe Virgos' interest in keeping healthy comes as a result of their having a very sensitive constitution; they'll frequently report they have a "touch of this" or a "bout with that." Virgos love diagnosing themselves and their companions, and they are usually good at it, regardless of whether they've had formal training.

Virgos also heal others' emotional troubles. They can't help but notice when someone is suffering, and they'll work to assist them in relieving their pain. But Virgos aren't indulging hand-holders—they expect their subject to do their best to pick themselves up as well.

When Virgos see that someone is trying to improve, they keep involved and support them; however, if Virgos realize that someone isn't making use of their good advice, they give up and move on. Why waste their time when there are so many others who need their help?

Virgos are adept at sizing up what works and what doesn't in various situations. They relish pointing out how matters can become even more efficient. In that way, Virgos tend to be organizational specialists. They do everything with a streamlined efficiency. And Virgos get involved: instead of standing back and barking out orders, Virgos are happiest when rolling up their sleeves and working on the solution themselves.

Virgos are also famous for their literal urge to purify matters by cleaning them. Virgos are always tidying something—their homes, their offices, or their

Virgo Lesson: Forget About Perfectionism; Strive for Excellence Instead

Virgos are undoubtedly awakened to their spirits and to the divine beauty of life by recognizing that life is perfect, just the way it is. But their penchant for faultfinding can make that insight hard to reach. Perfectionism is Virgo's strongest desire and greatest challenge. If your Virgo is caught in a cycle of complaining about what's wrong instead of expressing their characteristic reverence for the magic of life, be a helpful friend. Remind Virgo that their sign's direct route to fulfillment lies in aiming for excellence, which focuses on what's right, versus perfectionism, which focuses on what's wrong. When Virgos practice that subtle, but enormously powerful discernment, they are not only considerably happier, they are better poised to fulfill their mission of applying their signature intelligence and service toward the most uplifting and healing of ends.

neighbor's garage. No job is too big or too small for Virgos' lustful urge for order. They love "getting rid of the junk." Many times they'll do it with a smile, "Tsk-tsk, who left this so messy?"

With Virgos' picky determination to get things done in the most proper way possible, you'd think they'd be stubborn and unyielding, but they're not! They're actually quite flexible and compliant, and have a wonderful ability to adapt to, yield with, and fit in anywhere or with anyone if they want to.

Virgos certainly adapt in their relationships. Most yield so seamlessly and quietly they don't realize they're making concessions. However, there are times when Virgos do realize they're sacrificing and point it out. That's when they will be expecting a favor of equal value to be returned somewhere down the line. Virgos are adaptable, but they aren't doormats. However, they do aim to please others, and when they see a useful way to make that happen, they do it.

What Virgos Want in Relationships and How You Can Attract One

Virgos are attracted to others who are intelligent and interesting. Virgos are most attracted to companions who are bright and informed, people with whom they can share their intelligent wit and observances. With Virgos, say something smart so they know you're thinking! Titillate them by offering ideas that make matters more productive.

Virgos admire those who aspire toward excellence. Virgos have special appreciation for others, who, like themselves, display excellence in what they do. They applaud companions who are reasonable, reliable, and even a touch predictable. Beyond that, Virgos are impressed with talents and abilities, especially if they see someone putting effort or cleverness into developing them. Find a way to subtly display your gifts to Virgo.

Words Virgos Love to Hear

🏹 "You are so intelligent!"
"You did that incredibly well!"
"Thank you for your help."
"You're perfect."

(Hint: Let Virgo be the one to recognize your gifts—bragging only brings out Virgos' desire to point out errors.)

Virgos' favor and attentions are won by class not crass. Virgos' refined tastes gravitate toward those who express a subtle finesse for understated decorum. They adore effortless elegances in people and things. Braggarts, show-offs, and self-important blowhards are difficult for Virgos to endure.

Virgos demand good grooming and cleanliness! Virgos prefer companions to be well groomed and well attired. This doesn't include flashy or trendy types of dressing—that's just too much. Instead, Virgos are usually attracted to natural or quiet beauty, and even pride themselves on discovering qualities in others that most people miss. Present yourself in a way that shows you understand quality: good fit, good fabrics (natural is best), and an appropriate style for who you are. Since many Virgos find perfume smells offensive, avoid them. (They'll comment

"To Virgos, a good idea means nothing unless it's applied. Don't disappoint them by being all talk and no action, screwing up, or dropping the ball."

directly if someone's perfume smells like bug spray.) Instead have that fresh, just-out-of-the-shower scent Virgos love.

Virgos adore and are eternally grateful for companions who appreciate their work. Because Virgos' work is so very important to them, they treasure others who can relate to what they do or even work alongside of them. Shoptalk is the best aphrodisiac of all for Virgos. They will be amazed and deeply appreciative if you assist them on any project they're currently devoted to. Your efforts needn't be huge—the thought of helping them counts. Regardless of whether or not Virgos seem appreciative (sometimes their way of saying "thank you" is to point out what you've missed), assisting them is a mighty good way to bond with them.

Virgos are putty in the hands of those who recognize their efforts. When someone notices Virgos' efforts or acknowledges their job well done, Virgos can't help but melt. "Finally! Someone sees *me!*" Although Virgos treasure being acknowledged for all they do, they are loathe to call attention to themselves and are deeply grateful when someone has the intelligence to recognize their good work.

Virgos are delighted by those who request their help. Another great way to capture Virgos' attention is to request *their* help. Virgos can't resist an opportunity to be of assistance. They're flattered that you think they have something valuable to offer. (In the rare case Virgo turns you down, they'll nevertheless take note of your smart sense to ask them.)

Virgos love encouragement but hate to ask for it. Virgos' penchant for self-criticism can play havoc with their self-confidence and often makes it difficult for them to recognize the value of what they contribute. So be encouraging; your appreciations can do wonders for Virgos' self-esteem!

Virgos appreciate being listened to. Virgos are a communicative sign and appreciate companions who thoughtfully listen to their thoughts, ideas, and concerns. They especially enjoy companions who analyze along with them the details about matters they find so compelling. And, since Virgos are generally superaware of their health, they also treasure companions who will listen to and seriously consider any physical concerns they might experience. "How's your health?" is always a welcome opening line for a conversation with a Virgo.

Virgos respect practicality and disrespect impracticality, and that's that. Virgos work hard to make their lives orderly and don't appreciate it if someone messes it up. If you don't do what Virgos expect of you, neglect to carry through on a promise, or do something in a way that Virgos find illogical, they can become annoyed and disillusioned. If you want to make Virgos happy or get them to respect you, ask them what needs to be done, and then do it—their way.

> ### Words Virgos Love to Say
>
> ✒ "I'm busy working!"
> "I'll help you."
> "I'll do it so it gets done right!"
> "Let's clean this up and get organized."

What Virgos Offer in Relationships

Virgos offer supportive companionship. Masters of subtlety, Virgos rarely declare their fondness for others in over-the-top ways. Instead, Virgos show their affection through countless thoughtful actions. They'll gently take your hand as if to say, "I treasure all that you are." Or they'll cock their heads and shoot a smile that gives their companion the sense they're privy to a very private, intelligent joke.

Virgos' air of refinement keeps matters civilized and life running smoothly. They know the best restaurants, smartest movies, and latest trends, and will keep you informed and up to date on what's posh and what's not. Rarely too emotional or too intellectual, too loud or too quiet, Virgos instead appear just right.

> "Virgos' impeccable taste adds class to their relationships."

Virgos offer thoughtful understanding and insightfulness. Virgos care enough to listen carefully, watch attentively, and try to understand how you work. They enjoy knowing you inside and out and love to point out your little quirks and uniqueness. Virgos will reassure you when you've lost your confidence or make you laugh at something you find intolerable. When Virgos see they've lifted your spirits, a little smile of satisfaction crosses their faces. Mission accomplished.

Virgos offer savvy observances and bright conversation. With eagle eyes, Virgos evaluate their surroundings and provide witty commentaries. Their conversations are intelligent, thoughtful, and peppered with twists of irony and piercing observations. Hating nonsensical small talk, Virgos explore subjects that have meaning and consequence. Their curiosity about all matters, including what makes you tick, makes Virgos perennially interesting and fresh companions.

Virgos express kindness and gentleness. Although they are rarely mushy, Virgos are caring and tender companions. They'll support you and consider your needs, and sometimes make them a higher priority than their own.

Virgos offer their advice and critiques, solicited or otherwise. Virgos love to give "helpful advice," show you what you can do better and how to do it, and diagnose any problems you are experiencing. That's part and parcel of friendship with Virgo. With that said, it's important to note that their penchant for criticism can occasionally sting or their faultfinding might offend, so unless you're thick-skinned, you might find Virgo's "helpfulness" can sometimes hurt your feelings. But Virgo's motivation for pointing out problems or defects is rarely out of maliciousness. Virgo will point out your errors because they want you to live up to your potential. They feel they owe you that.

> "Virgos rarely take their friends and beloved for granted."

Virgos offer constancy and appreciation in their relationships. Once Virgos determine that someone pleases them and assesses that there is a potential for a future together, they commit with relative ease. Virgos rarely take their friends and beloved for granted or consider others to be "lucky to have them." Quite the contrary: since Virgos are quite humble, they tend to feel deeply appreciative when they're included and loved. They demonstrate that appreciation with loyalty, thoughtfulness, and willingness to give their companions whatever they might need.

Virgos have a knack for doing just the right thing. Most Virgos are consummate "givers" and enjoy doing things for you that make your life better. Maybe it's as simple as babysitting your kids so you can have a much-needed night out or researching the best dentist if you need your wisdom teeth removed. "Service is love made manifest" is Virgo's motto!

Virgos often sweat the small stuff; however, they are flexible and accommodating with the big stuff. Although discovering you've put the spoons in the wrong drawer can drive Virgos to distraction, when it's time to move to Germany for your promotion, a Virgo will accept it with an "Okay! Let's get packing!" Virgos rarely want to get in the way of others or make their demands so great that they would endanger their relationships. They'll change if they realize that something they're doing doesn't work for a loved one and would love it if others would do the same for them.

Virgos don't see many things as deal breakers. It takes a huge difference or a lot of fights for Virgos to decide that someone they love is just not worth the effort. Once someone has won their heart, Virgos apply their industriousness to making it work, even if that means a lot of bending and shifting.

The Virgo Lover

Romantic love is rare for Virgos. With such a discerning nature, they don't find very many people interesting enough to capture their attention let alone their whole hearts. But when Virgos finally fall in love, they are committed and work hard at making it a success.

When considering the Virgo lover think subtlety, gentleness, and refinement. Virgos have a way of extending a quiet, yet endearing appreciation for their beloved. It's as if they say, "I've looked all over the world, and you, my precious one, are the most perfect jewel of all!" They treat their lover with respect and an esteemed deference. Virgos gracefully, willingly become their beloved's humble servants ready to make any wish their command. (You would think they were a geisha in a past life, what with their intuition about what would please you and their devotion to satisfying it.) Virgos use their cleverness and attention to detail to make their romances intriguing.

It can take a bit of effort to win Virgos over. They have to sort out whether or not they like you, if they feel comfortable around you, and if you can fit into their schedules. That can take a while. Beyond that, Virgos find so many more frogs than princes that it's hard for them to believe they've stumbled upon someone they truly like! Virgos don't suffer fools gladly and want to be with someone who is worth their while. Show them that you are.

What kind of dates do Virgos enjoy?

Virgos enjoy dates that have finesse. Take them to a quiet, pristine atmosphere that allows for easy conversation. Since Virgos appreciate enriching themselves, a day at the museum or a night at a classical concert should be a hit. (If there is an informative lecture beforehand, by all means, attend that too!) It's not so much about what you do with your Virgo date—it's how you act while you're on it. Flashing around cash or exerting one's self with over-the-top attempts at winning affections rarely impresses Virgos. Rather, Virgos are wooed by classy, appropriate, genuine behavior that has an understated elegance and consideration to it. Although renting a stretch limo might be fun for some signs, Virgos appreciate it more if you spend that cash on something reasonable and bring your own car. But vacuum it first.

Virgos have an aversion to seeming too soft. Although they may be impressed with or even weak in the knees about their dates, they feel more comfortable expressing themselves in a low-key way. So if your Virgo date seems subdued, don't automatically assume it's because they don't like you. It might be quite the contrary—they might be quite taken with you but don't want to seem too vulnerable. How can you tell the difference? Ask Virgo on another date.

What are Virgos like between the sheets?

Lovemaking is where Virgos can surprise most everyone, including themselves! Remember that pesky reputation for prudishness their astrological symbol, the Virgin, alludes to? Well, here's the thing: sexuality is so special and meaningful to Virgos, they won't squander it with just anyone. When they find just the right person and have just the right circumstances, Virgos really open up and love. While some Virgos are sexually adventurous and enjoy many sexual partners, they nevertheless still withhold truly opening up until their beloved comes along. What are the right circumstances? An appropriate time and place, privacy, and everyone scrubbed and smelling fresh.

All those requisites fulfilled, Virgos become quite the affectionate lovers, exchanging their aloofness for attentiveness and eagerness to please. They'll hone in on their lover's every need, wanting to do a good job of pleasing them thoroughly. Virgos have an unusually gentle, even healing touch that can make loving magical and transformative. They'll work to discover the tiniest of details that pleasure their lover and fulfill them. Although Virgos don't care for overtly barbaric activities or show-off posturing, they do have their own type of earthy lustiness that is rich and captivating. But only that special one will ever receive it.

Keep it natural with Virgo. No need for props, toys, or anything else that distracts from the business of lovemaking. Pure and simple satisfies Virgo the most.

> "Virgos' have an unusually gentle, even healing touch that can make loving magical and transformative."

What turns Virgos off?

Bad hygiene really turns Virgos off, as does crude or uncouth behaviors or words. Ignorance or lack of curiosity annoys Virgos to no end. Too much exuberance or flamboyance makes Virgos cringe, but behaving too passively or spacey invites them to dismiss you.

Ways Virgos Can Drive You Crazy and What to Do About It

As with every sign, the very qualities that make Virgo interesting can also drive others nuts if allowed to run rampant.

Virgo challenge: Their "critical analysis" is just plain critical.

Virgos are famous for taking their exuberant keenness for problem-finding way too far. They can seem to persistently harp on what's wrong, what should be done differently, and ways you and others should be improving. It isn't so much of a "glass is half empty" pessimism, rather a "this glass is dirty—and it has a defect!" kind of perfectionism.

Virgos can be supercritical of their relationships, as well. Instead of expressing gratitude or appreciation for the love they share with others, Virgos can instead focus on what they think is wrong in their relationship. Beloveds can wonder of Virgo, "Do they even like me? Or enjoy our relationship?" even when Virgo is crazy about them.

Virgos' complaints can be deflating for anyone who's trying to enjoy spending time with them. And their focus on what's wrong can come off as negative and put a damper on the fun.

What to do?

If you feel Virgo is going overboard with criticisms or assessments of what's wrong, ask them for their assessments of what's right. Saying something like, "What do you like about this?" or "What does work here?" alerts Virgo that you'd like some positive comments and energy from them. Asking Virgo, "What do you love about me?" or "What do you appreciate about our relalationship?" not only reminds Virgo that you'd like some appreciation, it might also help Virgo realize how much they do value you!

Big hint: always redirect Virgo's focus respectfully, kindly, and acceptingly. If you dismiss Virgo with a "Now what are you complaining about?"or "Can't you find something positive to say?" attitude, they'll increase the volume of faultfinding, just to prove their point. Virgos don't mind being nudged toward a positive focus as long as they don't feel they're being criticized for not doing so in the first place.

For your own peace of mind, keep in mind that Virgos consider it their job to point out what's wrong—that's why they do it so zealously. Although they would love it if you rushed to remedy all those problems they zealously point out, Virgos don't truly expect that. Most times it's enough for Virgos to simply point out the problem. But a Virgo will appreciate it if you acknowledge their observations. "Yes, that glass is dirty, isn't it?" is satisfying. If you go a step further and acknowledge

their discerning taste, they'll feel wonderfully validated.

*Virgo challenge: Their best or
your best isn't good enough.*

Although Virgos' insistent drive for per-
fection can lead them to excellence in their endeavors, it can also frustrate them and everyone around them to no end. Expecting an
often-elusive perfection can undercut Virgo's self-confidence, as well as
anyone else's who's searching for Virgo's (sometimes) rarely given
approval. Virgos can be incredibly tough critics who overlook whatever's
good in life only to see what isn't measuring up. That's when Virgos for-
feit their positive get-up-and-go nature for crabby complaining.

Virgos themselves tend to suffer from a deep sense of inadequacy as
a result of their perfectionism. They rarely measure up to their impos-
sibly high standards. Although they might be the brightest, most
accomplished member of a group, Virgo can nevertheless feel they are
somehow lacking. Even when their considerable gifts bring them acco-
lades, Virgos might become nervously concerned they won't measure
up to the next challenge they'll face. Virgos' perfectionism and self-
criticism can be heartbreaking for those who love them. It's hard to
watch them be so hard on themselves.

What to do?

If you should find your Virgo falling into the black hole of perfectionism or criticism, or if they're hyperfocused on a flawed detail and
missing the big picture, try this: first remind Virgo that seeking

perfection is an action they choose, not a mandate for living. Then good-naturedly request their intellectual honesty: challenge them to find as many good things about themselves, others, or situations, as they find wrong. Their busy mind will get right on it. The exercise can work wonders to pop Virgo's brain into focusing on the rightness of their life as well as reawakening their hopefulness and self-esteem. That makes you refreshing to be around, too.

If you feel Virgo's perfectionism is expecting too much of you and/or missing the goodness or rightness of what you're expressing, by all means let them know about it. If your standards aren't as high or as strict as Virgo's, tell them they're not and that you are perfectly okay and accepting of yourself. If you want more acknowledgment, tell Virgo that too. Help get that ball rolling by confidently listing some things that you appreciate about yourself, that you think you've done well, and that you believe you should be applauded for. Virgo might be initially taken aback by your self-congratulations, but they'll hear you loud and clear. Later, they'll not only be more forthcoming with their acknowledgments, they may also learn from your example how to recognize when you, they, and life itself is good and that's enough.

If your Virgo companion is tormenting themselves with their perfectionism, show your appreciation for them in all they are and all they do. They'll think, "Really? You think that was good?" and become relaxed and reassured, if even for just a moment.

Virgo challenge: They're consummate critics.

Virgos often take it upon themselves to critique others, whether they're asked to do that or not. A Virgo might come right out and tell you that you look more tired than you used to and that you should consider vitamins, hint that your home would be more appealing if you cleaned it more, or notice that your social schedule is distracting you from your rebellious teen's cries for attention.

Instead of wondering if their "feedback" might be hard to receive or even be insulting, Virgos believe they've done others a favor. *No need to thank me,* Virgos think to themselves. *All in a day's work.* Although Virgos seem negative, they don't feel negative. They figure they owe you their astute observations as part and parcel of a friendship.

What to do?

If you don't care for Virgo's "helpful criticisms," tell them so. Saying something direct like, "I like doing things the way I'm doing them, thankyouverymuch" is generally all the hint Virgo needs that their comments are not welcome. *Oh, well,* Virgo will think, *You'd be better off if you would listen to me,* but they'll do their best to keep their ideas for improvement to themselves.

Virgos generally have the heart of a servant. Telling them, "Critical comments don't assist me as much as positive or reassuring ones do" might also teach Virgo how you like to be treated.

Virgo challenge: They can dish it out, but can't take it.

Virgos' exuberance for criticism is rarely a two-way street. They can be extremely sensitive and reactive when it's their turn to receive criticism. Virgos can feel terribly crushed after even the tiniest of corrections. That probably stems from their being so hard on themselves—they've probably already suspected whatever faults you might point out.

What to do?

If you care for Virgo and truly want to bring out their best, deliver your feedback with plenty of gentleness and consideration (even jokingly) and be sure to include what Virgo *did* do right. But don't baby them. That's insulting.

Virgo challenge: They're married to their work.

Sure Virgos love to work, but there are times when it seems they think their jobs are more important than their relationships. Virgo can get so wrapped up in projects that their beloved can feel sidelined, waiting for Virgo to give them some attention. In fact, the biggest competitor in anyone's relationship with Virgo isn't an exotic stranger, it's Virgo's job. Every night, millions of Virgos' companions the world over are eating dinners alone while Virgos work late.

What to do?

It's a good idea to be independent and have interests of your own to pursue until Virgo finally does come home (exhausted, but satisfied). Here's another helpful hint: if you want to spend more time with Virgo, literally book time with them. When you are part of their schedule, they'll make being with you a priority.

Virgo challenge: They're industrious and want everyone else to be, too.

Virgos' work ethic is great, but when they expect others to be as industrious as they are, it can be exasperating. Virgos can become resentful when others don't work as hard as they do or if they aren't doing as good of a job. Virgos might then broadcast a huffy "I'm the only one doing any work around here!" vibe.

What to do?

If Virgo is complaining about your work ethics or strategies, remind them that your goals are different from theirs. Use the same strategy when Virgo claims you're not doing something right. Invite Virgo to help or give you credit for what you are managing to get done. If all this is done in the spirit of understanding and kindness toward Virgo, they will catch on and back off. Virgos know they are fussier than others; however, they do feel hurt when their need for order and productivity is simply dismissed.

Virgo challenge: They mask their feelings.

Emotions, especially gushy or vulnerable ones, can be awkward for many Virgos. Feelings can seem messy, embarrassing, or even weak to them. Plus, Virgos might fear being inadequate in dealing with emotions and consequently try not to acknowledge their own or others'! That's why Virgos sometimes appear aloof and stoic, even when there's a tidal wave of feelings churning inside them. (But don't assume Virgos are experiencing churning tidal waves of emotions; they may not be.)

What to do?

While Virgos may seem cold, hard, and unfeeling, they most likely aren't—they just don't know the appropriate way to express themselves. When emotions are rising—yours or Virgo's—you may need to take the lead in dealing with them. Approaching matters factually might help. Ask Virgo something like, "Can you identify what it is you feel?" But don't try to get Virgo to express a feeling—they might feel put on the spot or even resent you for it.

If you want Virgo to be more accepting or acknowledging of your feelings, let them know that, too. Tell them you respect your feelings and what they point to, and that you choose to express emotions as an act of self-care and health. However, don't hold out hope for indulgence—Virgo will listen to you, but will rarely coddle you. In Virgo's world, coddling is for babies, not capable adults. Virgos are tender and healing, but they refuse to do anything that even hints at supporting a weakness.

Virgo challenge: They have a militant love of order.

In their love of order and reasonableness, Virgos have been known to pressure others to behave in an orderly, "reasonable" way as they do. Virgos get nervous around someone whose behavior is out of the ordinary. They'll roll their eyes around someone who's effusively expressive, sniff disdainfully about others' eccentricities, and/or tsk-tsk around another who's taking too many risks. Virgos become unglued altogether around people who show it all, gamble it all, or otherwise go to "inappropriate" extremes. Worse, Virgos are completely exasperated by others who are spacey, forgetful, or just plain old "not trying": to keep up or be the best they can be.

Does that make Virgo seem persnickety? To some yes. To others, including Virgo, it's appropriate and classy.

What to do?

Although Virgos can occasionally feel exhilarated with companions who demonstrate wild or over-the-top risk-taking qualities, or a certain level of "quirkiness," it eventually just gets to be too much for their nerves. If they can't corral a companion's behavior to better match their own rhythms and rules, Virgos will eventually tell themselves, "Who has time for this unhealthy behavior?" and leave.

Virgo challenge: Their independence seems aloof.

Many Virgos have a self-sufficient independence that can create feelings of distance with those around them. Sometimes they simply seem less available or not as emotionally involved as some companions might prefer. Other times Virgos just insist on doing things their own way or on their own.

Although Virgos aren't rebellious or loners, they do possess a side that is reserved and private. Partners of Virgos might interpret this as being secretive or holding out for someone better. That's usually not the case for Virgo. The truth is there is something about each Virgo that is reserved for them and only them. And they guard this place as they would a sacred treasure.

What to do?

Giving Virgo space works wonders to make them more comfortable and able to reconnect with you. You have to accept the part of them that remains an independent, occasionally aloof mystery. If there is something about Virgo that you want to know more about, ask them. They may not realize you're as interested in them as you are. Virgos generally aren't secretive, just self-contained. Asking them about themselves can help draw them out, reveal their mysteries, and bring them closer to you.

Summary:
Living Harmoniously with a Virgo

• Recognize Virgo's main motivation is to help, not hurt. Capitalize on that.

• Create an atmosphere where everyone recognizes and values each other's contributions.

• Remind Virgo that there are many ways to do something "right."

• When seeking a change of behavior from Virgo, keep criticisms to a minimum, and focus on what they have done well and *then* what you want more of.

Chapter Seven

Libra
(September 23—October 22)

Who They Are

I f you have a Libra in your life, you'll surely be charmed, enchanted, and delightfully engaged. That's because these elegant creatures thrive on attracting and pleasing others, and they do so in a most gracious manner. Libras specialize in relationships: to them, love makes the world go round. They come equipped with an armful of talents to help create the meaningful alliances they seek: first, they wow you with a gorgeous smile, and then they engage you with their sparkling intellects. "After all," says Libra, "if something is worth doing, it is worth doing attractively, don't you agree?"

Libras are remarkably attuned to the refined offerings of life. They enjoy surrounding themselves and their beloved in an atmosphere of harmony and splendor, in both their physical worlds and in their interactions. Libras use their wit and well-weighed insights to keep

> "Libras specialize
> in relationships—
> to them, it's what makes
> the world go round."

things lively and interesting, always ready for friendly discourse or debate on one of the many subjects they are knowledgeable about.

Libras are born initiators with a strong drive to make things happen—especially relationships. They're the first ones to introduce themselves to a stranger and are terrific bridge-builders dedicated to spotting potential for successful interactions.

Relationships are so very central to Libras' identities; they completely shine in the company of others. Their pursuit of fairness keeps them constantly attuned to the balance of their social interactions. Is everyone included, considered, and being treated fairly? If not, Libras will remedy matters. Always poised and appropriate, Libras work their magic with decorum, trying not to ruffle even the slightest feather and attempting to keep everyone happy.

Libras seek harmony in every endeavor. They knock themselves out making favorable impressions, keeping others satisfied, and displaying actions that are in accordance with "good form." Libras will bend and adjust the presentation of their needs and views to maintain a flowing connectedness with others.

Libras' need to create pleasing relationships is reinforced by their appreciation of aesthetic beauty and harmony in their environments. If something isn't right, just beautify it! Libras absolutely thrive on beauty; some claim that they *need* it in order to feel right. Predictably, many Libras are artists, but even if they're not, they possess a true gift for finding just the right colors and arrangement of things to create environments rich in design. Balance is essential to Libras: every object must relate well to every other object.

Balance in environment and harmony in friendship often play a major role in Libras' ability to create peace among people. Most every Libra is a peacemaker at heart. They are convinced that with enough understanding and effort, everyone, regardless of their

> "Libras' peacemaking ability makes them excellent mediators."

differences, can come together in a cordial, cooperative way. Libras do what it takes to make sure matters between others are as equitable as possible. This is so instinctive in Libras that many times they soothe angers, settle differences, and set up truces without even knowing how they pulled it off.

Libras' peacemaking skills can be challenged, however, when it's *they* who face differences with others. Libras desire harmony and want to be liked and approved of so desperately that they might exact peace with someone at great cost to themselves. Most Libras dread conflict, thinking it has no place in a relationship, or worse, that it can put an end to one. In those cases, Libras might be incessant people-pleasers, compromising

Libra Is an Air Sign

♎ As an Air Sign, Libras are intellectual and are more at home with thoughts and ideas than with feelings. Libras' Air Sign qualities give them a breezy and changeable nature that needs lots of room to breathe. Although they certainly love and need to spend time with companions, Libras also love and need their space away from them as well. Libras can feel "penned in" if they don't have the freedom to pursue their individual interests or if someone starts to squeeze them with too much emotion or neediness.

their own needs and desires, in order to not "rock the boat."

But that doesn't work, or work for long, for Libras. Remember, Libras aren't doormats; they are actually quite determined. But despite wanting what they want, Libras want everyone else to get what they want. If someone doesn't agree with them, Libras can second-guess themselves, thinking maybe the other's point of view is more valid. Or, worse, Libras can believe that rallying for their desires can make them appear unappealingly selfish, thinking, *Who would love me if I'm acting selfishly?*

Libras' unique expression of their Air Sign quality gives them a tendency to evaluate and assess—everything. Just as their zodiac symbol, the Scales, illustrates, Libras weigh all matters great and small to find just the right balance, perspective, and answers to all of life's questions. Libras don't see life from one point of view; they see it from every point of view.

This weighing back and forth of things big and small is Libras' strategy for identifying the best choice and avoiding the wrong choice. Once Libras do make up their mind about something, it's done! They've come to their conclusion. They are right! And they'll tell you why.

What Libras Want in Relationships and How You Can Attract One

Libras prefer companions with whom they make a good team. Libras enjoy that special dynamic wherein they feel they really click with someone. They love when it's easy to agree with their companions, to do things together, and to communicate without awkwardness or effort. Make Libra see how the two of you are good partners or good teammates. That'll make them happy to be involved with you.

Libras love companionship. To Libras, every relationship is a primary relationship—it's involved and engaged. So maintain your relationship with Libras by including them in your life. Of course they'd expect to accompany you during your important life transactions, but Libras even enjoy accompanying you on everyday errands. Togetherness is good for Libras, no matter where you go.

Libras want you to be "in a relationship" with them. Libras want to sense that you are always aware of them, considering them and including them. It bugs them, for instance, if you talk to someone else on the phone while they're in the room or make plans without consulting them. It really hurts Libras when you don't call when you should. Don't give Libras the feeling that you've forgotten about them. Although they don't need to be with you constantly and actually

Libra Lesson: The Peace They Seek Is Inside of Themselves

♎ Libras' spirits soar when they're surrounded by peace and harmony. So much so that they can believe that any conflict is bad and wrong and become intensely unhappy if the least little disharmony is bubbling around them or even in the world. That's when you'd be a great friend to remind Libra of their sign's mission: to discover how the peace they seek is always present—*inside of themselves*. When Libras quit waiting for their world to be perfectly harmonious in order to be happy, and instead tap into their personal equanimity, they are happier and more fulfilled. It also poises Libra to tap into their signature calm, empowered wisdom that knows just how to make the uplifting and balancing impact on others they seek.

Words Libras Love to Hear

♎ "You are so attractive!"

"Everyone loves you!"

"You're included."

"We," "Us," and "Let's."

prefer to be alone much of the time, Libras still want to be assured that they have a partnership with you and that they can count on your being there for them when they want to connect.

Remember that it's stressful and confusing for Libras when companions aren't available to them or when they insist on doing their own thing. So, if you can't or don't choose to include Libra in something you're doing, at least let them know you're thinking of them.

Libras appreciate companions with panache. Be charming!! Libras are smitten by those who have a sense of style and finesse, so keep yours well honed and displayed when around them. Don't be too bland, as it's boring. Don't be heavy-handed, as it's a real turnoff. Forget about being rude or crude—that'll make a Libra cringe or even turn away. What to do instead? Be appropriate for the situation and behave as the classy, composed, and charming person you are.

"To Libra, every relationship is a primary relationship— it's involved and engaged."

Libras like companions who take pride in their appearance. Libras can't help but notice someone who's gorgeous, so, if you are good-looking, flaunt it! Being well dressed is always an eye-catcher for Libras. Beauty is an advantage in Libras' book. But it's only an advantage. If you can't back up your attractiveness with stimulating conversation, Libra will prefer to look, but not touch.

Libras seek out intellectual stimulation. Engage in lively, witty, or otherwise fascinating conversation with Libras. If you're bright, show Libra! If you are informed, then communicate what you know. Don't be too worried about finding interesting things to talk about with Libras because they'll come up with plenty of topics to share with you. Usually they'll start the conversation with an inquiry of "What do you think about?" on a subject they suspect interests you. They'll listen attentively, looking you in the eye, nodding their heads to show they're with you. Then it's your turn to reach out and ask Libras about their thoughts, as well. That's because although they are eager to express their points of view, Libras might be too polite to just butt in. When you query about their thoughts? Oh! That sort of give and take is heaven!

Libras respond to those who keep their emotions in check. Forget about dramatic outbursts of feelings or gushing emotions—they can make Libras feel awkward. Remember these folks are intellectual and objective, and prefer their companions to be as well. If you become overwhelmed by your feelings, Libras suspect you've lost your balance and control, which is uncomfortable for them. Too much emotion riles Libras' sense of logic. Anger and jealousy are downright unattractive to them. Nor do they appreciate others who act like insensitive robots; that's unnatural and unappealing. Libras prefer a balance in everything, including how others express themselves.

Libras are socially conscious and mesh well with others who are, too. Libras respect companions who are as fair and as considerate of others as they are. They also respect companions who take action on social issues that they believe in. So if you do volunteer work or if you're active politically, let Libras know about it. Libras will zero in and interview you to find out what you think, who you know, and how you feel about everything else in that part of your world. Try to find points of consensus with Libra. They like it when you share their values.

It's thrilling for Libras to connect with someone with whom they have a "meeting of the minds." If Libras don't agree with you about something, they'll attempt to convince you to change your mind (albeit with charm). They'll even enjoy a hearty banter up to a point, hoping that you both might gain a new perspective. But it's always nice if you can find something to agree on.

Can moral or ethical differences be deal breakers between Libras and their friends? Not as long as there are open doors of communication and consideration on both sides. But if matters become polarized or blinding angers flair, Libras may find what they consider as another's lack of insight too much to bear. So leave Libras smiling by finding points of consensus that bring you together.

What Libras Offer in Relationships

Libras offer true partnership. Libras excel in creating a union of equals. They'll let you know you are a valued and integral part of their lives. Libras are very supportive to the ones they love, wanting to make sure that they do their part in helping others live well. Rarely ones to put you on the back burner while they go about the duties of their lives, Libras instead make their relationships job one. Libras will invite you to go along with them in all they do, enjoying your company. Perhaps more than any other sign, Libras love to operate as a duo even if it's just while shopping for tomatoes.

Libras are generous in compliments and endearing words. When Libras adore you, they'll show you in all kinds of thoughtful words and deeds. They're generous in their attention and affection, and enjoy making you feel like a million bucks.

Libras are magnetic. Libras treasure being liked and loved, so they earn it by being as appealing and entertaining as possible. Always thinking of witty things to say and charming stories to tell, Libras' creativity and expression are rewards for your attention.

Libras also do their best to look and smell good and to have good manners. Although there is something proper about Libras, they rarely come off as snooty or prissy. Instead, most Libras come off as incredibly elegant and suave.

Libras aim to please. Libras know how to ingratiate themselves to others and will enchant you, even when cleaning out the garage. Take a Libra on a night on the town and heads will turn with admiration. Libras love it when others find them and you, their companion, attractive. Will a popular Libra stray? Rarely. Libras think in "we" mode: Did they like us? Did they find us charming? So in social situations, a Libra partner will laugh graciously at your joke, even if they've heard it a hundred times. Would they love the same from you? Absolutely.

Libras bring good taste to their relationships. Libras will introduce you to

> ## Words Libras Love to Say
>
> ♎ "I like you!"
> "Tell me more about you . . ."
> "I love how well we get along."
> "This is what I'd like, if you don't mind."

> "Libras love to operate as a duo. One-on-one relationships are their specialty."

excellent music, surround you with incredible art, and offer you books they think you will appreciate. A Libra friend will kindly offer you valuable advice on how to dress (telling you honestly if your new lipstick truly suits you) or what furniture would most make your living room pop. Although Libras see how anything can be made more appealing almost immediately, most will not offer unsolicited advice. But they love when you ask them what they think.

Libras offer well-weighed advice. Libras will listen attentively to your concerns and do their best to help you find solutions to any problem you may be dealing with. They'll help you weigh the pros and cons of any decision you are making in order to find the best solution. Then, when you make up your mind about something, Libras back you up. After all, that's what a good partner does.

The Libra Lover

Talk about getting swept off your feet—the Libra lover will sweep you off your feet like no other! Romance is what Libras live for and what they devote themselves to wholeheartedly. They are masterful at amorous love and use everything they've got to make it a beautiful success.

> "Libras will change their entire world to make love fit."

Libra lovers set out to enchant and seduce you with elegance and charm. They'll go to great lengths to create a romantic scene, but they'll do so subtly, so as not to seem off-balance, even when they are nearly falling over in love.

What kind of dates do Libras enjoy?

When preparing for a date with Libra, it's important to first look your best, smell your best, and wear your most flattering colors and most refined ensemble. Libras notice the little things, like the fact that you've had a manicure or that you're wearing cashmere socks. *Nice touch,* they'll think. Second, be on time, but never early. Do compliment Libras on their attractiveness, paying attention to how wonderfully the color they're wearing brings out their beautiful eyes. "Oh! You noticed!"

Then, whisk Libras off to somewhere tasteful and gorgeous. Dinner overlooking the city is a great idea, or how about a concert or an art show? Have a good CD playing as you drive through the most attractive part of town. Show Libras your good taste by pointing out lovely things along the way, maybe interesting architecture or a well-planned garden. Most important, talk to Libras about what interests them and what interests you as well.

Since Libras place importance on the back-and-forth in conversation, don't expect them to spend too much time talking about themselves without trying to redirect the talk to "What about you?" Go ahead and share. If you've read something compelling, tell Libras about it and why it moved you. Then, when it's Libras' turn to talk again, find out why they are moved about things. Be sure to point out where you share ideas and interests in common. That'll be heaven for a Libra.

What are Libras like between the sheets?

When it's time for lovemaking, you're in for a treat. Libras aim to be the most pleasing of lovers, and they have a way of casting a spellbinding effect on their beloved. Always preferring a soft touch to ripping clothes off, Libras enjoy an ease in their affections. Remember to bring beauty into the scene: bring out your most gorgeous sheets, scented candles, and best music. Be sure to woo Libra visually, perhaps by wearing something gorgeous and begging for touch, like silky lingerie and intoxicating perfume.

Lovemaking for Libra is the ultimate in communion, so be sure to look them in the eyes to reinforce your connection. Libras will do the same for you. After all, they want to make sure they are giving and taking pleasures with equal indulgence.

Remember: Libras seek balance in all matters, including romance and sex. Be neither too aggressive nor too passive. Be expressive of your feelings, but don't go overboard. Be available, but not so much so that a Libra doesn't feel a need to woo and win you. After all, Libras like to work a little to win someone's attention. Let them work for yours.

What turns Libras off?

Behaving in a way that's gruff violates Libras' tasteful sensibility, and being too crude makes them cringe. Dressing sloppy or appearing unkempt (in an uncool way) disappoints Libras who think you should try harder to be attractive. Being extreme at anything (with the exception of being too beautiful) turns Libra away pronto.

Ways Libras Can Drive You Crazy and What to Do About It

As with every sign, the very qualities that make Libra most unique and interesting can also be what drives others crazy, if taken too far.

Libra challenge: Their scales can teeter.

Libras' seemingly endless process of evaluation often results in indecisiveness. They can get so caught up in weighing matters back and forth (and up and down and sideways) that no decision can be made!

Libras' indecisiveness about matters great and small can really keep you hanging. In their attempt to figure out the best decision, they may move rapidly from "Yes, let's do it!" to "No, let's not!" So, for example, when deciding whether to vacation in Greece or Italy . . . first you're going to Greece, then you're going to Italy, then you're back to Greece again. Then, it's *which* part of Greece?

What to do?

One effective way to help Libras make up their minds is to agree with them. For example, say you've already made your plans to vacation in Greece, when Libra begins to wonder if Italy would be better. If you protest, saying the tickets are already bought and the hotel is already booked, Libra could become more convinced that Italy is better. So try saying, "Sure, Italy sounds good." Within minutes, Libra will swing back to the original plan, and argue that Greece is better. After all, the tickets are bought and the room is booked. There, they've convinced themselves. Done.

Using reverse psychology—arguing for one point when you'd like the opposite—is another great strategy for helping Libras make up their mind. Since a Libra can't help but evaluate every side of a choice, stake your claim on the side you don't want so Libra will argue the side you do.

Yet another way to help Libra make a decision is to tell them what your decision is. Sometimes it's easier for Libras to make up their minds when they know what others want. That narrows down the vast field of possibilities and provides Libras with something to weigh their decisions against.

Libra challenge: They hold unrealistic expectations of relationships—they want everything to be just perfect.

Libras' indecisiveness can make it hard for them to commit to relationships and especially to marriage. They want to commit and know they need to commit, yet it's such an incredibly important and monumental decision to them that they don't want to make a mistake. Libras can love someone very deeply, yet, if they think the relationship is missing something, they nevertheless fear they might not have the right person.

That's because Libras hold idealistic expectations of relationships; they want everything to be just perfect. They believe their partners should be able to fulfill most every need, match them on most every interest, and be able to harmonize with them in most every way. When they don't, Libra may wonder if they should hold out and wait for someone who can: but since they do love the one they're with, they don't want to let them go. But maybe they should because this might not be the best choice. But on the other hand, perhaps if they get to know their partner better, things would evolve. But then they haven't by now . . . and so on. Meanwhile, Libra's partner is left waiting and hoping. Are they going to commit or not?

What to do?

If your Libra is struggling over whether or not to commit to a partnership with you, marriage or otherwise, help them decide by doing something drastic: leave Libra alone. When Libras are left without companionship, they feel stranded. Their concerns about the relationship will most likely evaporate in lieu of their memories of how much they enjoyed you. Your absence can work wonders for the confused Libra, helping them realize that you are perfect and that they can't live without you.

Libra challenge: They try to keep the peace at any cost.

Most Libras are so uncomfortable with conflict they do whatever they can to avoid it. They often believe they would be less lovable if they did something that displeased others, so they knock themselves out to keep everyone happy. But sometimes Libras' attempts to keep the peace can result in more confusion and frustration than if they would have just come out and said what was bothering them in the first place.

One way Libras avoid conflict is by being passive and indirect. They'll even sidestep the truth, just to avoid an ominous conversation. Libras are famous for sugarcoating their point of view to soften their blow or burying their heads in the sand and avoiding the issue altogether.

Libras often say "yes" when they really mean "no" (or more likely "maybe"), all in hopes of keeping their companions happy. But if they're agreeing to something they really don't want to do, they might show their displeasure by becoming passively aggressive. That's when they'll sabotage plans or even pick a fight about something totally unrelated to what's really bothering them. Later they'll say, "You made me do such and such," when the truth is they were trying to keep the peace by making themselves do it.

If Libras do bring up a contentious point, they can make it sound like it's your fault that there is trouble. For example, Libras won't outright declare, "I don't want to spend Christmas at your mother's house," but rather try, "Don't you think you'd be happier if we just spent Christmas here at home?" It's called passing the buck. Libras aren't consciously trying to be manipulative when circling a truth or attempting to get someone else to be responsible for problems. They're just trying to keep things "nice" and agreeable.

What to do?

*I*t really helps Libras and their relationships when Libras are reassured that they won't lose love if they are honest about their feelings and needs. When Libra is assured that you won't bail on them during times of disharmony, it's an enormous relief. Libra thinks, *You would love me even if I don't want to go to your mother's for Christmas? Wow! That's precious!*

When Libras are struggling with their need to please both themselves and others, remind them that it's okay to please themselves first and then please others second. Encourage your Libra to make the choices that keep them in harmony with themselves. If that means rocking the boat with others, so be it. Being fair means being fair to themselves first. There is no fair without honestly facing and expressing what is really going on inside of them.

Libra challenge: Disagreements ruffle their feathers.

It's true that Libras like to be right. Well, don't we all? But Libras like to be the kind of right wherein others agree with them. When that doesn't happen and a partner continues to see things differently than Libra, it can get uncomfortable. Should you disagree with Libra, you'll have a vigorous debate on your hands! (But, please, let's keep it civilized. There's no need to raise your voice, and certainly no yelling. "Don't lose our composure, dear.")

What to do?

Ease matters by putting it back into the context of the relationship: "*We* seem to disagree on that, don't *we*? Let's agree to disagree." There. You're still in accord. Peace.

Libra challenge: Their "pleasantness" can seem emotionally superficial.

Libras' style of keeping matters gracious can sometimes lead them to resist tense or painful situations, or appear to be glossing over deeper feelings altogether. Sometimes Libras do this by changing unsavory subjects to more pleasant topics. Or they might avoid discussing darker truths about themselves or others. This avoidance can lead to lack of communication about what's going on in the mind of your Libra, which can cause you to become suspicious that they lack depth or that they want to spray air freshener over life's trials to make everything seem "just fine."

What to do?

Libras are emotional, sensitive, and compassionate, but they believe that painful feelings are, well, painful. Libras don't want to linger in anguish for long and prefer demonstrating objectivity; they prefer that their companions do so as well. If someone doesn't snap out of uncomfortable feelings, Libras might become uncomfortable and distance themselves.

If you feel Libra is glossing over a painful issue or feeling you've brought up, or that Libra appears to be distancing themselves, explain to them that you are comfortable with your emotions and that you intend to go right on experiencing and expressing your feelings because you want to. Remind Libra that if you are crying, grieving, or even hating, you are all right. That helps Libra understand that you haven't truly lost control and you are aware of the route you are taking for yourself. *Hmmm. In that case, then,* thinks Libra, *maybe I'll join you for a bit with my own feelings.*

Libra challenge: They need to please others and expect you to please them, too.

Libras' need to maintain a sense of decorum and image of graciousness is essential to their identity and motivation. Problems might arise when they pressure you to please others and maintain that nice decorum as well. So whereas you don't like attending fund-raisers, Libra might insist you go along because others expect it. Or, if you don't want to stop by the new neighbors and introduce yourself, Libra will dismiss that and march you up to the neighbors' front door.

Companions of Libras often report feeling held hostage to Libras' need to be liked or to being pressured into doing things they truly don't want to. Not to mention doing so under Libras' watchful eye of style: "You're not really wearing that, are you?"

What to do?

If you feel pressured by Libra to do something just to please others, you may need to let them know *you* don't need to please others. Ouch! That might not go over well, at least not at first. Libras are so driven to make a good impression that your refusal to join them in their pleasing campaigns can seem like a complete act of abandonment. So let your Libra understand you don't value pleasing others as much as they do, and that you fully accept that about yourself. But also point out that you appreciate their need to make others happy and to go ahead and do what they think they need to do. This is a very sensitive issue for Libras, one of great consequence to their egos, so be respectful about it and never dismiss it as a weakness. Your Libra will be very disappointed that you won't cooperate with them, but they will work to see your point.

The good news is Libra might take your cue of independence and learn to say no to others' expectations more often. After all, Libras who break free from their need to win others' approval are truly liberated.

Libra challenge: They are eternally searching for that perfect beauty.

Libras' sense of beauty is so developed that if something isn't perfectly beautiful, it can really irk them. For some, if something isn't *just* right, it's wrong. Whereas other family members can live in a kitchen that's painted the "wrong" color green, it can drive Libra to miserable distraction.

What to do?

You can resist a Libras' attempts to make their environment perfect, but usually it's to no avail. They'll rally until it is. While you might find it indulgent to drive back to the house so Libra can change outfits, they believe it to be a way of keeping themselves happy and healthy. Just do it and get it over with.

Libra challenge: They can be lazy.

Although Libras can be quite the dynamos when they want something, if something doesn't matter to them, they can just seem to drift away. Libras don't want to overexert themselves or try too hard to achieve something that isn't important to them; they're perfectly happy just relaxing while others knock themselves out getting chores done or climbing the ladders of ambition.

What to do?

How do you motivate Libra? Show them what they'll get out of satisfying your requests. Libras want to know they'll gain something from their efforts. Entice them with the benefits and satisfactions they'll receive, even if it's simply making someone happy. Another great way to motivate Libra is to mention who else is doing what you want them to do and how Libra might enjoy relating to them as they participate.

But in the end, if Libra wants to relax for a while, they'll find a way to. "Honey, you go ahead and paper-train the puppy, okay? You're so much better at it than I am," is one gracious way Libra begs off from a distasteful activity. But since Libras are fair, negotiating is always available. "Okay, I train Whiskers, but you take him to the vet on Tuesday." *Darn!* Libra thinks, *You got me! But fair is fair.* "Honey, I'd love to."

Summary:
Loving Those Libras

- Appreciate that Libra's main motivation is to keep matters harmonious and gracious.

- Show Libra you're considering their needs by dressing, acting, and communicating in as pleasing a manner as possible.

- Talk out problems in a levelheaded way, keeping emotions smooth and even.

- When requesting a change in behavior from Libra, let them see how it's fair and equitable, and how it will make you happy. Show Libra, too, what you are willing to concede.

Chapter Eight

Scorpio
(October 23–November 22)

Who They Are

If you have a Scorpio in your life, you're sure to be compelled, captivated, and transformed in some significant way. That's because these intense creatures dive to great depths within themselves and everyone they're drawn to. Scorpio is one of the most powerful signs of the zodiac, which makes them not only fascinating, but also hard to resist. They possess passionate desires, deep emotions, and seductive sexuality. Scorpios also possess sharp, savvy minds that easily size up situations—and you—in seconds flat. Scorpios exude a natural confidence and magnetism that commands respect. Although they use their powers to accomplish most anything they desire, Scorpios enjoy using them most to bring out possibilities and potentials, including in their relationships.

Life with a Scorpio is as intense as they are. They love to pursue and satisfy their desires and live a life of consequence. Scorpios seek to make a significant impact in the world around them and do so by solving mysteries, exposing hidden meanings, and penetrating and altering matters to their very core. They will want you to join them as they dive deeply and fully into whatever or whoever interests them and let their passions and desires consume them.

Scorpios want to impact you, too. Most likely they'll do so by compelling you to *feel* something—be it your passion, ideals, or unresolved issues. Nothing about you (or anyone else in their orbit) escapes Scorpios' penetrating analysis. They'll let you know they're watching and understanding you like no one has ever before. Scorpios can touch you in such a profound way you may be forever changed. They'll entice you with their mysterious charisma, stun you with their insightful revelations, and then make you laugh with their sarcasm.

Scorpio Is a Water Sign

🐚 When getting to know a Scorpio, keep in mind Scorpio is a Water Sign, which gives them an intensely sensitive and emotional nature. Scorpios tend to rely on their feelings and instincts even more than their sharp intellects when making decisions or evaluating situations.

Scorpios experience the gamut of emotions. They'll feel joyous loving, tender compassion, seething jealousy, even hatred—perhaps all in one day. However, usually Scorpios mask these feelings with a cool, neutral exterior until they feel safe enough to express them.

Why do Scorpios hide their feelings? Partly because they're extremely private (and secretive) and don't want people knowing anything about them they don't want known. This talent keeps Scorpios from feeling vulnerable. If someone gains access to their feelings, Scorpios suspect their feelings might be used against them.

Scorpios absolutely dread being hurt, or worse, humiliated. That's because despite their considerable power, Scorpios are also very sensitive. They prefer to be liked by others, but at the very least, they expect to be respected. When that doesn't happen, or doesn't happen the way Scorpios expect it should, it can tear them up inside.

> "If offended, Scorpio will react calmly and coolly, even if a hurricane is raging inside of them."

Scorpios are legendary for their inner strength. In fact, Scorpios have remarkable endurance and tenacity; once they decide to do something, nothing can get in their way, and they will finish what they started, *Even if it kills me,* they think.

There's an all-or-nothing quality about Scorpios' intentions. If they don't intend to invest their all in something or someone, they usually don't want to be involved at all and just prefer to go away.

Scorpios need stability. They seek deep roots with others and consistent routines in life. Many Scorpios find change unsettling if not unbearable. In an attempt to avoid the dreaded, unwanted change, Scorpios can exert great effort to control matters so surprises can't creep in. But therein lies the great paradox of being a Scorpio: although they desire stability and predictability, they're actually "transformers" at heart. Scorpios just can't help imagining what *can be.* When Scorpios spot unrealized potential, unexplored possibilities, and underused resources, they feel an irresistible urge to develop them. That's when Scorpio pushes buttons and confronts others, even creates a crisis in order to shake up what's stagnant or undeveloped.

As gifted transformers, the act of improving something is the highest form of Scorpio's creative expression. They live to do it.

Most Scorpios try to resolve their dual urges for stability and transformation by seeking to manage and control matters so they change and transform the way they see fit. This gives them a sense of security and protects them from being vulnerable.

Scorpios are masterful at solving problems and mysteries. The obvious is boring to them because whatever is hidden is fascinating! They'll look past smiles and backslapping to sniff out secret agendas. When working on projects, Scorpios zero in on what's faulty or weak, and then insistently lobby for it to be remedied. The same goes for relationships; they address head on what needs to be acknowledged or healed, and rally to alter it. Sometimes Scorpios' observations are hard to accept, but they're usually right on.

Those who think Scorpios' focus on problems is a negative trait are mistaken. It's not: Scorpios are built for probing, and they pride themselves on their ability to identify what doesn't work. They love others who appreciate their sharp contributions.

"Scorpio welcomes the challenge of a good mystery."

Scorpios also love others with whom they can stir up emotional scenes and passions. They feed on the drama of emotions, so they often pull strings to elicit them in others, even if that means igniting a little negative drama. Some Scorpios enjoy stirring up a fight just for the release of energy or perhaps for the closeness of the makeup sex. Or Scorpios might create antagonistic drama so they can whip up aggravation and gossip. This can be exciting to both Scorpios and their partners alike because there's a lot of energy available when everyone's emotions are flared.

One thing is certain: each Scorpio is complex in their own unique way, which explains why there's not one, but three zodiac symbols to illustrate them—the Scorpion, the Eagle, and the Phoenix.

Scorpios' traditional symbol, the Scorpion, depicts their infamous tendency to sting—or get revenge on—those who don't please them and even sometimes on those who do!

Scorpios' revenge needn't be immediate, however. They can wait in delicious anticipation for the exact right time and situation in which to deliver their deadly sting. And it's potent: with their psychological insights, Scorpios know just what to say or do that will deliver the greatest debilitating impact.

The Eagle depicts Scorpios' capacity to rise above a situation or to evaluate it with objectivity. It also symbolizes Scorpios' ability to rise above their lower nature, which might prompt them to seduce and manipulate for their selfish gain, and instead choose to do what's best for the greater good. When Scorpios are acting as their Eagle self, they can affect and move others in remarkable ways. In fact, working toward doing what's the highest good for all is Scorpios' way to achieve empowerment and transformation.

Scorpio is also symbolized by the Phoenix, a bird that crashes into fire and burns only to resurrect out of the ashes into something more glorious. This is indicative of Scorpios' penchant for "crashing and burning." Scorpios are known for going to extremes and exhausting themselves physically or emotionally. Sometimes they obsess so intensely they can no longer think straight or feel so strongly they're overcome. Crashing and burning is extremely painful for Scorpios. And it's painful for others who watch them experience it, as well.

But true to their Phoenix nature, it's when Scorpios feel they've "hit rock bottom" or are even somehow "dying" that true transformation can take place. When Scorpios finally "give up," they can discover their most essentially precious and powerful truth: that who they truly are can never be destroyed. This reawakens Scorpios' passion for life and for love.

Interestingly, Scorpios' attraction toward life-or-death experiences leads them to take part in others' transformations as well. When others are having a crisis, Scorpios rise to the occasion and become their best. They whip out their problem-solving skills and start to find ways to redeem matters.

But Scorpios rarely rescue others; they hold a strong conviction that people should learn from their mistakes. Scorpios also believe that people usually deserve whatever comes to them. But Scorpio will lend a very strong hand for others to pull themselves up, and they are glad to do so.

What symbol does your Scorpio companion live by? Most likely all three. Perhaps more than any other sign, Scorpios are in a constant state of choosing how to direct and use their powerful energies, and they learn volumes about themselves by experiencing the consequences of their choices.

Scorpios have a need to impact many people's lives in some significant way in order to feel fulfilled. In fact, a big part of Scorpios' identity is shaped by the role they play in their larger community. When Scorpios know they're doing their best to contribute to something greater than themselves, they not only respect themselves, they can feel as if the Force, so to speak, is with them.

Scorpio Lesson: To Recognize the Potential for Light in All That Darkness

🦂 Scorpios' piercing intelligence loves to deeply analyze matters to discover what is not working or is unfulfilled. But sometimes Scorpios' gift for spotting troubles goes into hyperdrive and problems are all they can see. Then they can develop a brooding suspicion that everything is bad and nothing is right, and a dark cloud of cynicism shades their normal empowered stance. When that happens, life gets miserable for Scorpios and for those closest to them, as well. If that is happening with your scorpio be a good friend to them and suggest that being seeped in problems actually poises them to demonstrate their sign's mission: to transform what's dark and wrong, within themselves or their world, into something that's usable and valuable. (Do this respectfully and patiently, however; don't expect Scorpio to "snap out" of any worries.) When Scorpios direct their considerable powers (and hearts—that's a big key, too!) toward turning even big problems into something uplifting, their intelligence focuses on possibilities rather than defeats. Then Scorpios' spirits soar as they demonstrate their signature empowered resourcefulness that knows just how to transform troubles into avenues of redemption and Light.

What Scorpios Want in Relationships and How You Can Attract One

Scorpios prefer to surround themselves with a few trusted intimate companions. Although Scorpios desire to affect many others, they only want to be intimate with a few, well-chosen companions. Scorpios are extremely selective about who they include in their lives and usually take their time to evaluate people before befriending

Words Scorpios Love to Hear

🦂 "Your power is intoxicating!"
"Here's a secret I've never revealed to anyone . . ."
"No one has ever affected me this way."
"What should I do?"

them. Be patient in getting to know Scorpio. Initially they'll want to study your intention: What do you want from them? What will you give? Can you be trusted? Few pass Scorpios' rigorous tests, but if you do, you'll be treated to a tremendous depth of intimacy and attentive caring. Show Scorpio you can be trusted to be true, honest, and thoughtful about them, their feelings, and their space.

Scorpios need to feel something potent is being exchanged. Scorpios want to feel something powerful is happening between them and others, some type of rich exchange. A strong sexual vibe between you and Scorpio is by far the best way to capture their attention. So is creating a powerful emotional connection, an intriguing mental stimulation, or a spiritual alliance that makes Scorpios sense you have something rare and special. Scorpios need to feel they can "lock on" to something in another. Look into Scorpios' eyes with all you've got. They'll be moved by your willingness to reveal yourself, which prompts them to reveal themselves to you.

Scorpios want to be compelled. You must pique Scorpios' interest by either exuding some sort of power or mystery, or by doing something that intrigues them. Use your prowess to move Scorpios by arousing their sexuality, igniting their emotions, stimulating their minds, or capturing their imaginations about how satisfying it'll be when they conquer you. Make Scorpios hungry to discover more about what makes you tick by giving them the impression that your power and energy are unique and can somehow enrich their lives.

Scorpios seek others who exude complexity or an interesting inner life. Scorpios have great substance of character, and they want to be with others of substance as well. Giving Scorpios hints about the treasures that lie deep within your character appeals to their fascination with solving mysteries.

Power is intoxicating to Scorpios! Financial power, social power, and political power command Scorpios' attention. They love the sensation and fruits of power, as well as the energizing high that power brings. If you wield power over others or possess a mastery over something, reveal it to Scorpios slowly and subtly (never boastfully), so Scorpios become intrigued. Respect yourself, express yourself genuinely, and resist caving in to others' expectations. That said, Scorpios might see more power in you than you do and enjoy helping you to develop it.

Scorpios seek deep intimacy. Scorpios thrive in relationships wherein everything is inspected, talked about, and hashed over, down to the tiniest detail. Scorpios want to know their chosen companions extremely well and be known deeply by them (on their terms, when they're ready, of course). They expect their loved ones to invest time with them and to be attentive to them. Scorpios like to get to the meat of the matter; otherwise, why waste your breath?

Scorpios demand genuineness, warts and all. Tell it like it is. To Scorpios, being genuine doesn't mean making nice or always emphasizing how good matters are. Scorpios' complexity seeks and accepts the dark in others. They're suspicious or even turned off by people who insist things are always "fine." Scorpio thinks, *You've got to be kidding* *me—no one is* that *happy. They must be out of touch.* And off they go.

Scorpios want in on the "juice" of who you are. What kind of juice? Passions, of course. If you have a strong charge about something, either positive or negative, tell Scorpio about it. Let Scorpios know what you aspire to, what you desire. But keep it real, and avoid getting heady, abstract, or emotionless; Scorpios want to ride your feelings and emotions along with your dreams.

Scorpios need to know they are central in your life. When you are with a Scorpio, they want you to act like you are. They want your attention, consideration, and sensitivity aimed in their direction. Scorpios want and need to be able to count on you to be there for them through thick and thin or else they'll feel insecure.

Scorpios expect loyalty in their relationships. To Scorpios, loyalty means standing by them no matter what and never betraying them in word, deed, or thought. It also means being consistent, doing what you say you will, and being there when you say you'll be. It also means keeping the secrets they divulge to you and never, ever siding with someone else over them.

Scorpios expect you to be sensitive to their moods. A sea of feelings, emotions, and energies regularly churn through Scorpios. Sometimes Scorpios' moods are open and easygoing. Other times, they're irritable and feel constricted, and don't want company. Respect that. Scorpios need time to themselves to gather their wits. So ask your Scorpio companion if it's a good time to talk or to make love. They'll tell you honestly whether they're available. If not, leave Scorpio alone.

Scorpios welcome a mystery and a challenge. One sure way to capture Scorpios' attention is by being mysterious. Scorpios love nothing more than getting someone to reveal themselves, and they don't mind the challenge of making that happen. If it doesn't take much to figure someone out, Scorpios usually dismiss them as superficial and uninteresting. Give Scorpios a persistent sense that there is more to you than meets the eye. Don't reveal everything about you too quickly, especially in the early stages of a relationship. Scorpios will want to stick around and try to discover you, if you present yourself as a challenge. Although Scorpios usually dismiss others who play "now you see me now you don't" games as superficially uninteresting, they can become attracted to someone who is a bit hard to read and hard to catch. They relish the challenge of finally conquering their heart and winning them over.

Remember, however, that Scorpios recognize others' manipulative strategies and refuse to play along. So avoid game-playing, being coy, saying what you don't mean, or not doing what you say. Otherwise, Scorpios might find such actions tiresome and point their stingers in your direction and beat you at your own game.

Scorpios crave gentleness. Always on the lookout, Scorpios treasure companions with whom they can feel safe enough to let down their guard and be themselves around. Scorpios treasure tender moments, ones of such softness that even the most precious of feelings and sacred thoughts can be expressed.

Scorpios adore subtlety in their relationships. Why be blaring when you can be sublime? Scorpios love quiet, yet thoughtful kindnesses, favors, and private glances that communicate a special knowing between you and them. They also adore companions who share their penchant for noticing what others miss.

Scorpios give and receive affection. Scorpios love the sensuality and connectedness of touches and hugs and kisses. In fact, Scorpios don't live or live well without regular physical gestures. But use your radar to check if the moment is right. Scorpios will cringe if someone approaches them when they aren't ready. Try gliding in to see if your Scorpio welcomes you. If Scorpio's receptive, there will be an exchange of warmth that makes it worth your while!

What Scorpios Offer in Relationships

Scorpios will attract, touch, and affect you deeply. Scorpios love creating meaningful and intense connections with those they choose to have in their lives. Chances are, you'll never be the same once you bask in the beam of Scorpio's love or attention. Scorpios exude something that can deeply touch your psyche and that makes it impossible to ignore or deny them.

Scorpios' attention makes you feel fully observed and understood. Scorpios pay attention to their companions with the intention of truly knowing about them. They study others in order to solve the mystery of who they might be. Scorpios communicate, be it verbally, emotionally, or physically, "I know you."

Scorpios are specialists at creating deep intimacy. When Scorpios care for someone, they do so all the way. Their love runs very deep. Scorpios immerse themselves fully into their alliances and let companions know they're completely there for them. Scorpios treasure their loved ones and invest whatever they've got to make their relationships work.

Scorpios extend empathy to their companions. Scorpios use their sensitive feelers to pick up even the most subtle moods, needs, and feelings of their companions and respond to them in kind. They open the door to the most intimate kind of sharing by becoming so lusciously soft, so deliciously tender, so vulnerable themselves, that others can tap into that same yielding place. Intimate exchanges with Scorpios can be so exquisitely rich and profound that no other companion can seem to compare.

> ## Words Scorpios Love to Say
>
> 🦂 "Let's keep this a secret between us."
> "Let's look at this more deeply."
> "I care for you, which is why I'm pointing out your problems and mistakes."
> "I'm suspicious, and I'm going to get to the bottom of it."

The important thing to remember about Scorpios is they want to be a part of all of your feelings and moods. There's no need to hide painful emotions or difficult issues from Scorpios. They won't run from your problems. Go ahead and call Scorpio when the going gets rough or when it seems like there are insurmountable odds to succeeding at something. Sure enough, they'll find a way to work things out.

Scorpios will stimulate you intellectually. With the same potent intensity Scorpio will understand you emotionally, they will stimulate you intellectually. Scorpios are extremely savvy and astute, and they'll zero in on what you have to say with a probing analysis and deep attentiveness.

Scorpios offer insightful counsel. Scorpios can be counted on to give useful, profound solutions to issues you may be having. But keep this in mind: when a Scorpio is answering you truthfully, you might not always like their answer. Scorpios feel they owe others the benefit of their insights, so they'll let you know what's not right as keenly as what is. Occasionally Scorpios will hold their tongues if they don't think you can handle the truth or the power of their insights. But that's not Scorpio's idea of real intimacy; deep down they feel insincere. They may feel they let an opportunity to help you slip away.

Scorpios are fierce protectors. Scorpios protect both their relationships and the people in them with ferocious attentiveness. They circle the wagons and ensure no one takes one little step to threaten or harm anyone they care about. If they could, many Scorpios would take the pain from others or even lie down on the tracks and get run over by a train instead of stand by and watch a beloved get hurt. Scorpios often create an enclosed circle of "It's you and me against the world" that creates a sense of protection and safety.

Scorpios keep their connections strong. Scorpios tend to the relationships and intimacies they care about, and keep them alive and poignant. Even when overwhelmed with other commitments and promises, which they often are, Scorpios keep their fingers on the pulse of their relationships. If something is going awry, they're there to deal with it. Scorpios won't let their companions wander off. Scorpios know the meaning of quality time and can zero in and connect with their beloved in seconds flat.

Scorpios are loyal. Scorpios demonstrate their allegiance to their beloved in a way that claims, "I would walk through fire for you!" If they love you, or deem you worthy, they will stand by you, regardless of how hard, catastrophic, or boring your life becomes. Even if Scorpios disagree with you about something, they will defend you from another's criticism or attack.

Scorpios are committed to long-term relationships. Once Scorpios commit, they are in—hook, line, and sinker! Scorpios are generally in their relationships for the long haul and usually work to overcome big differences in order to save relationships they value.

Occasionally Scorpios find it unbearable to be around someone they have a beef with and will step away until it's less painful to them. But as long as they haven't been betrayed or humiliated, chances are Scorpios will help that relationship rise out of the ashes of disagreements, disappointments, or simply disinterest to start anew.

Scorpios share their special gift of transformation. If you are involved with a Scorpio, you'll inevitably be changed in some significant way. Scorpios' ability to spot unrealized potential is especially astute when it comes to those they love. They'll push you to realize your potential, whether you feel ready to or not! Scorpios are famous for opening the kinds of doors, giving the kind of advice, or making the kinds of introductions that can change a person's entire destiny.

Scorpios offer terrific wit. Although most Scorpios feel quite serious, there is a side to them that is brilliantly funny. Scorpios' humor is sophisticated and ironic, usually loaded with sarcasm that's rooted in their shrewd observations. Do Scorpios want you to make them laugh? Oh, yes! They appreciate the relief!

The Scorpio Lover

Scorpios' rich sexuality and urge for intimacy thrives when they have a lover to devote themselves to and share with. Scorpios love savoring the lusty desires, sensual pleasures, and heady passions that courtship stirs inside them. And they are masterful at igniting the same in their partners.

Chemistry and physical attraction are extremely important to Scorpio; it's imperative that they like both what they see and what they feel with a lover. They'll pursue someone who stirs desire in them, entices them, or even holds some sort of mystery or power that they relish. Scorpios are intensely desirous and lusty. Give them something in yourself to desire and lust after.

Seduction is the elixir of life for Scorpio, and sexual seduction is its highest form. Never rush a Scorpio's pleasure by making it too easy for them to capture you. Allow them to draw you ever closer, bit by bit. As they do, reveal to Scorpio how they're stirring you. And, if it's so, tell Scorpio they're touching you like no one has before.

What kind of dates do Scorpios enjoy?

Scorpios enjoy dates that are seductive, romantic, and where intimacies are shared. They prefer private atmospheres that allow them to hold their date's attention and work their alluring magic with no interference. Scorpios like a sexy and relaxed mood, and to feel they are in control.

Why not take Scorpio to an out-of-the-way, quiet, dark restaurant and sit at a table way in the back? Then later, how about a romantic little club where you can cuddle in a private booth while listening to music that puts you "in the mood"?

What are Scorpios like between the sheets?

When it's time for making love, you'll discover why Scorpios have a reputation for being the world's greatest lovers! Scorpios have an instinctive mastery over sexuality's many expressions. They're at home with the ultraintimacy of sexuality: the intensity, the depth, and the complete union sexuality offers. They know what they're doing.

When seducing Scorpio, remember that to them, sexuality is as much about the energy exchange and the desire that stirs between partners as it is about the act of sex itself. Don't shortchange Scorpio on the intoxicating energies of seduction they crave. Scorpio thrives on sexual tension, innuen-

"Scorpios have a reputation for being the world's greatest lovers."

dos, and the deep lasting looks that say, "Later, you'll be *so* satisfied!"

With Scorpio, emit sexual energies long before you ever hit the bedroom. But be subtle about it. Scorpios love knowing that you are sharing something powerful and wonderful while the rest of the world is just going on with its business. Scorpios enjoy drawing out the act of lovemaking, as well. Enticing, tempting, getting close to climax, and then holding off just a bit to intensify pleasures pleases Scorpio.

Scorpios savor giving and receiving all sorts of erotic affections and relish making love to your entire body, from head to toe. Scorpios won't hesitate to use everything they've got, including their tongues, to explore even your more hidden erotic zones and appreciate it when you do the same. In fact, most Scorpios take special delight in oral sex and celebrate partners who show talent and enthusiasm for that lovemaking act.

Since Scorpios love unveiling mysteries, make yourself as appealing as possible as you unveil. Silky, sexy, even naughty lingerie are thrilling to Scorpio, who'll love viewing you in various stages of undress. Even more important than how you look is what you exude. Take your time. Sexuality is a big deal for Scorpios. Brew something magical, powerful, and intoxicating between you.

What turns Scorpios off?

When sexual tensions and attractions wane, so does Scorpio's interest. If Scorpio decides someone is superficial or not that smart, they're gone. "All talk no action" people frustrate Scorpio as do those who are overly mental with not enough passion to keep Scorpio juiced up. Should someone betray or humiliate Scorpio, even by accident? They've had it.

Ways Scorpios Can Drive You Crazy and What to Do About It

As with every sign, the very qualities that make Scorpios appealing and unique can also make them frustrating, when taken too far.

Scorpio challenge: They sting.

It's true: Scorpios sting. They take direct aim and say or do exactly what deflates, embarrasses, or otherwise wounds a person to the very core. Sometimes Scorpios' stings are delivered with such precision, even wit, that it takes people hours, even days, to realize they've been cut to shreds. But make no mistake: they will feel it.

Scorpios' stings also come in the form of using others to get what they want. Or perhaps a rumor gets started, or a hurtful suggestion made. Where'd it come from? Scorpio—who's somewhere in the background, quietly watching the fireworks they've lit.

Scorpios can be deadly when they want to be. What makes them want to be? Being threatened, of course! Scorpios' nature is both very sensitive and very territorial. They loathe being hurt, undermined, or betrayed. Even worse is being humiliated—that's a fate akin to being annihilated. Scorpios ferociously protect themselves from the possibility of any of those acts. If they even suspect someone doesn't have their best interest at heart, they'll go on the defensive, and do what they can to remove them from their orbit.

Scorpios protect their territory with the same watchful gusto as they protect themselves. And their territory is most everything: their relationships, the people in their relationships, their possessions, their livelihood, even their ideals are all part of Scorpio's domain. If anyone exudes even the tiniest threat over Scorpios' sphere of influence, they'll enact a cleverly placed tactic to take them out.

What to do?

How can you keep a Scorpio from stinging you? You might not be able to. Short of acting like a saint, you're likely to eventually do something objectionable and thereby receive "the sting." Scorpios just tend to be quite guarded, so no matter what your actions or intentions, there might be times when Scorpios interpret you as threatening. So give a Scorpio plenty of time to develop a trust in you.

When Scorpio reacts to something, try to have compassion. Don't take it personally. When the air clears, let them know, "That hurt, and I didn't deserve it. And here's why." Scorpios know they're tough. When calmed down and objective, most Scorpios realize when they've been needlessly mean. They'll do what they can to make it up to you, which can be very precious.

Scorpio challenge: They're possessive.

Scorpios are possessive. They want and expect their companions to be true blue. *You're mine!* they think. And when you are a Scorpio's, you should be no one else's. Possessiveness leads to one of Scorpio's greatest demons: jealously. Scorpios can be racked with jealousy! It's torture for them. They die a million deaths when imagining someone important to them might be aligning with someone else. The thought of losing someone they care for is so dreadful to Scorpios, they believe it might devastate, humiliate, or even kill them. So Scorpios stay on the lookout for betraying attractions.

Occasionally Scorpios imagine attractions and betrayal where they don't exist. Scorpio might dismiss others' claims of innocence and go right on believing there is trouble. They'll grill their companions with interrogations like, "What did you mean when you said this? What were you after when you did that?"

What to do?

When Scorpio is feeling jealous, give them loads of reassurance. They need to hear that they are the one you love, adore, and are committed to. But words alone might not do the trick. You'll have to show Scorpio that you are loyal, even if it means severing a relationship with someone else altogether. Encourage Scorpio to heal their insecure, jealous feelings by digging deep and remembering and claiming what an entirely lovable and desirable companion they are.

Scorpio challenge: They have a sneaky side.

There is a side to Scorpios that can be sneaky or dishonest. They can deftly hide the truth about what they're doing or feeling, or what their true intentions are. Some Scorpios have felt let down

> "Even though Scorpios are suspicious of others' motivations, they are one thousand times more seductive and likely to conjure lusty thoughts about others than their partners will ever be!"

by others freaking out or judging them as bad or wrong after they've revealed themselves, so they'll use deceit to protect themselves and their relationships.

What to do?

If you sense something is amiss, say something like, "Something feels off here, do you have any idea what that might be?" That puts Scorpio on notice that you are alert to something fishy. It also gives them a chance to come clean, if they need or want to. Scorpios respect that, even though they may also resent it. In time, you might find out what Scorpio is hiding.

Another way to way to maintain truth between you and Scorpio is to demonstrate that you can handle their truth, even if it's tough. When Scorpio knows you are strong enough to love them no matter what, they will deeply appreciate being able to be honest with you.

Scorpio challenge: It's hard to tell if they're brilliant strategists or control freaks.

There is the side of Scorpios that they call "strategic," while others call it "controlling" or "manipulative." Scorpios have very definite ideas of what they want to happen, how people should behave, and how the environment around them should be run. And they are confident about these ideas. Scorpios learn very early in life that few others are as clever as they are, so they assume they should guide matters. Do Scorpios reveal their plans? Rarely! Instead, they quietly and patiently pull strings, make innuendos, and use their insight to motivate others to get them to do exactly what they want.

Among Scorpios' arsenal of control strategies is their ability to use sex appeal to manipulate others to get what they want. Sometimes Scorpios seduce others just to see if they can. They might make sport of someone's heart. Seduce a friend's spouse? If they're not a good friend, yes. Seduce the boss for a raise? Perhaps. Seduce someone to get them to reveal a secret? That's easy!

Then, when Scorpios get what they want, the game is over and Scorpios are gone. Sure that's a sting. But sometimes the seduction is so sweet, it's worth it.

What to do?

How do you keep a Scorpio from controlling you? By knowing what you want and being in touch with what's right for you. That way you won't be as open to Scorpio's seductive tactics. They'll respect you for it, even if they don't like it. Although there might be genuine loving behind Scorpio's seduction, there can be other motivations as well. Listen to your own instincts about where Scorpio's enticements are leading you. Is it toward intimacy and truthfulness? Or does it sway from that somehow? You may need to put on the brakes of your own responsiveness or lust toward Scorpio to get some objectivity about what's right for you.

Scorpio challenge: They'll hold sex over you.

Scorpios may use sexual teases or build sexual energies by tempting their partner, but withhold the act of love until they get something they want. This works because sex with Scorpio is so luscious, partners might be driven to distraction when Scorpios won't put out.

What to do?

If your Scorpio lover is using sex to manipulate you, stop allowing it. Perhaps remind Scorpio (and yourself!) that sexuality is a sacred union and the powerful glue that holds your romance together. It shouldn't be used as leverage. Encourage Scorpio to put aside your differences when you enter the bedroom and partake of the bonding sexuality offers. If Scorpio genuinely cares for you, they'll see the wisdom in that request and stop trying to use sex as a bargaining tool.

Scorpio challenge: They want to exchange deep feelings, whether you want to or not.

Scorpios thrive on tapping into deep and powerful feelings with those they're close to. But some partners might not want to, don't need to, or can't dive into the introspective depths Scorpios revel in. This can frustrate them and Scorpios to no end.

What to do?

If you feel Scorpio is pressuring you to express something you don't care to, emotionally or otherwise, tell them you are aware of what they want of you but choose not to go there. If Scorpio persists on certain emotional exchanges that you're not comfortable with, or even claims there's something wrong with you when you won't explore feelings they think you should, you may have to ask them (and yourself) to make this choice: either they accept you and your emotional nature as it is or let go of the relationship. Whew! That's tough! But it brings out what's really valued in the relationship pretty quickly.

Ending a relationship is excruciatingly painful for Scorpios, because they invest themselves so fully into them. They hate to let go of anyone they have found (or suspected they would find) something special with. And they hate to be defeated as well, which is how they might interpret broken relationships.

Scorpio challenge: They're obsessive.

Scorpios' penchant for probing analysis can sometimes go overboard and make them extremely critical or even obsessive. Scorpios' minds tend to lock on to things and run them over and over in a way that drives them to distraction. This could be about matters great or small, but they obsess all the same.

What to do?

If you feel Scorpio's obsessing is getting in the way of having a satisfying conversation with them or even in the way of your relationship in general, tell them. Maybe they'll attempt to snap out of it.

Other times, you'll have to tell Scorpio that you just can't have one more conversation that revolves around said topic or their insistent view of that topic. At least in that way you can excuse yourself from Scorpio's mental tempest.

Summary:
How to Snatch a Scorpio

- Remember their main motivation is to exert a powerful impact on their world. Support them in doing so.

- Create powerful chemistry with a Scorpio by matching their intensity sexually, physically, emotionally, or mentally.

- Communicate that you respect Scorpio's feelings, boundaries, moods, ideas, and privacy, both verbally and nonverbally.

- When requesting a change of behavior from Scorpio, use plenty of patience and consideration. Encourage them to explore with you how troublesome situations can be transformed into something improved.

Chapter Nine

Sagittarius
(November 23—December 22)

Who They Are

Wh

When you have a Sagittarius in your life, you'll surely be inspired, awakened, and motivated to reach for great things. That's because these extroverted creatures specialize in creating adventure and meaning for themselves and everyone around them. Sagittarians' philosophical nature sets them on a hero's journey of discovering whatever's good and meaningful about life. They're at their best when life is exciting and spontaneous with plenty of new thrills to seek. Sagittarians' wit and charm—not to mention salesmanship— inspires others and convinces them to go along with Sags' many ideas and schemes. Sagittarians' jovial and generous nature attests to their optimistic belief that the glass is not only half full—it's overflowing!

Life with a Sagittarius is a steady stream of escapades. Packed and ready to go anywhere in seconds flat, Sagittarians treat their

> "Sagittarians' ease in finding the bright side of matters keeps them perpetually fun and interesting."

companions to adventures galore. These can be trips to far-off lands, the great outdoors, or just your backyard. No matter where you go or what you do, Sagittarius makes it exciting by finding ideas and things to explore and discover. Even a trip to the mall can feel like a safari.

Being a Fire Sign makes Sagittarians unpredictable. You (or they) never know exactly what's going to happen next—and Sags love it that way! Sagittarians thrive on taking risks, and they do so continually. Want to hold Sag's interest? Keep the surprises coming!

Sagittarius Is a Fire Sign

🐾 Sag is as excitable and volatile as fire. Even tiny sparks of ideas are fueled by Sag's passion and explode into bonfires. They enmesh themselves in various and wide-ranging interests and approach life with unquenchable curiosity and enthusiasm. They'll help you to feel it, too.

Sagittarians are extremely confident and get a thrill out of stretching their limits. With their courage and faith in life, they're quick to discount failure and instead trust that Lady Luck will bring them fortunate surprises. And she does! Sagittarians are one of the luckiest signs of the zodiac. Perhaps they truly are born under a lucky star. But it's more likely that Sags *make* their luck by looking for the goodness or the opportunity in every situation.

Sagittarians love to keep stimulated by going to extremes. Life has got to be interesting! However, sometimes they burn out by overextending themselves. Their huge appetite for life can lead them to the brink of physical, emotional, and financial exhaustion. But that's a good kind of burnout for Sag. *Okay, so I overdid it. It was worth it,* they think.

Sagittarians fear matters becoming too predictable or boring. They wilt when life is too stable.

Freedom is the foundation to Sagittarians' happiness. They need to have a sense that they are free to do and think whatever they want, whenever they want. Sagittarians feel entitled, even ordained, to lead exactly the kind of life they choose for themselves. Restraints or bending to the expectations of others can be unbearable to them. Anyone who thinks they can tame a Sagittarius or get one to settle down to any routine or (gasp!) other people's rules may be deluding themselves. In the end, Sagittarians do what they want to do and justify it as they do.

> "Freedom is the foundation of Sagittarians' happiness."

Sagittarians' nature is flexible and changeable as well and thrives on variety. They can easily blend into many different types of situations and relationships and do so regularly. If Sagittarians should spot a greater potential elsewhere, they'll likely go for it—even if it means letting go of their current job, home, or relationships to grab it.

The essential drive for Sagittarius is to find meaning in life. In fact, Sagittarians are philosophers at heart: they're driven to discover some higher purpose in life. Sagittarians seek to be uplifted and inspired by everything they do and everyone they know. And they want to uplift and inspire others as well, which they do so easily with their sunny dispositions and belief in life.

Sagittarians' philosophy usually includes a grand sense of themselves and the sense that their life is an important mission. That mission might involve a religious or spiritual practice, an educational pursuit, or simply an outdoor trek that awakens Sag to the magnificence of the wild.

As much as Sagittarians' inner philosopher gives them a love of learning about life, it also gives them a joy of teaching about the many subjects they find of interest. They excel at spirited debates (some say lectures) about why something is right, wrong, or otherwise. Few can match Sagittarians' eloquence or wit: they punctuate their points with entertaining tangents and winks of endearments that make you adore them, if not totally agree with them. Sagittarians are brilliant thinkers and loquacious orators. Salesmanship comes easily to them—their expression brims with excitement and enthusiasm.

Do Sagittarians always have their facts straight? Not exactly. They don't tether themselves to the confines of reality as it is—they grasp what can be and believe it as if it were true. Exaggeration is the spice that makes any idea or story even more exciting. And excitement is what it's all about, isn't it? If you get the feeling that your Sag companion is embellishing or otherwise going a bit over the top, understand that that's all part of the show.

Sagittarians' astrological symbol describes much about their essential nature and motivation. It's a centaur, a creature that's half horse, half man, who's aiming a drawn bow and arrow toward the heavens. The horse body of the centaur represents the earthy, lusty, instinctive side of Sagittarians' nature—the side that gives them a tremendous love of sensory pleasures. Eat, drink, and be merry is one important aspect of Sagittarians' philosophy. (Even if, for some Sags, that means eating vegan and drinking healthy fruit juices.)

The human part of the centaur represents Sagittarians' higher nature, which enjoys refined aspects of life's offerings. The bow aimed at the heavens exemplifies Sagittarians' ambitions to live according to high principles.

Can Sagittarians always live up to the high principles they profess? Of course not, but Sags sure do like to *attempt* to live up to their higher aspirations. And they respect others who attempt to do the same.

Most Sagittarians are social and gregarious beings. They need to feel they are part of a group or community in order to be fulfilled. Sagittarians tend to have one or two very close companions, a few good friends, and then loads of associates. A trip to the local grocery store can be a steady stream of "Hey! How are you?" and "You look *great* today!" toward the many friends and strangers in Sags' life.

Sagittarius Lesson: Everything About Life Is Meaningful

Sagittarians are some of the happiest people of the zodiac and most inclined to feel connected to their spirits and to the majesty of life—especially when they believe they are pursuing something meaningful. But if Sagittarians feel they have nothing promising to look forward to or that their life is "just ordinary" with nothing spectacular going on, their inspiration fizzles and they become dejected. Then Sagittarians can get a defeated sense of "Why bother?" and lose their signature joie de vivre. If your Sagittarius is struggling with dejection, remind them of a key to fulfilling their sign's mission: to look for the good and the meaningful in all of life's experiences, including ordinary, confined, or even (gasp!) dark ones. When Sagittarians remember that all of life's situations are fodder for growth and upliftment, they are poised to demonstrate their highest calling: to celebrate the good, even the Divine in every situation.

What Sagittarians Want in Relationships and How You Can Attract One

Sagittarians want others to enrich them, excite them, and inspire them. Since Sagittarians enjoy exploring interests and passions in life, they gravitate toward others who can join them in their pursuit.

> ### Words Sagittarians Love to Hear
>
> ❧ "You make me feel exhilarated!"
> "You are *such* an inspiration to me!"
> "Your ideas awaken me."
> "Let's do something daring or amusing!"

Depending on what rings your Sag's bells, sharing philosophies, knowledge, hobbies, or opinions can be very satisfying. Sags love chumming up with those who profess similar ideas or who can awaken them to even better ones. So let Sagittarians in on the interesting things that you do and the abilities you have that might make their life more interesting.

Sagittarians enjoy trusted sidekicks who are up for a good adventure. Sagittarians aren't ones to sit around watching TV—they want to do something! They treasure partners who jump in and live life with the same gusto and adventure as they do. Sagittarians seek special friends with whom they can "pal around with"—those who are comfortable to be around and who regularly say, "Yes! Let's go!" Show Sag how you can be the trusted sidekick who accompanies them on their many adventures.

Sagittarians are attracted to optimistic personalities. Sagittarians like being with others who share their upbeat dispositions. Why take life too seriously when it's supposed to be a celebration? Sagittarians are not known for plunging into deep emotional waters. They feel, but they prefer to feel *good*. Most Sagittarians work hard to snap out of difficult or negative emotions. They don't see

> "Sagittarians want to let their hair down and laugh it up."

value in spending time languishing in dark emotions and usually don't. So be sure to show your enthusiasm for life when you're around your Sag friend, and keep discussion of worries and fears to a minimum.

Sagittarians need freedom to think and say what they choose. It's absolutely vital for Sagittarians to feel they can speak freely with their companions. If you're companion to a Sag, they want you to respect their thoughts, even if you disagree with them. They'd rather know you have a different point of view than have you appease them by agreeing.

Sagittarians have to roam and explore to feel whole. Sagittarians gravitate toward companions who give them loads of space to explore. Let them wander. They'll come home, wagging their tails behind them.

Sagittarians are attracted to others who are independent and self-reliant. Sags don't feel comfortable with people who lean or rely on them or need them too much. They favor companions who have interests and abilities of their own that they can enjoy with or without Sagittarius. You needn't include them in everything you do; go out and find something interesting to bring to the relationship!

Since Sagittarians need to be challenged and kept on their toes, you needn't be consistent or predictable, either. In fact, the more surprises, the better!

Jealousy and possessiveness have no place in Sagittarians' relationships. A Sag wants you to think well enough of yourself that you don't deter them with bouts of insecurity. If Sagittarius is with you, it's because they want to be. Want to get rid of Sag? Leash them. Want to keep a Sag? Give them full rein.

Sagittarians crave intelligence and education. Companions who make Sagittarians think deeply or who can further their knowledge of a subject are enticing, indeed. Someone who makes a Sag smile is great, too. Good, stimulating conversation is one of life's great pleasures for Sagittarius. So captivate Sagittarius's mind: if you are an expert about something or have a current passion about a certain subject, let Sag know. They'll love to be around you when you're lively and involved.

"Sagittarians admire those who are true to themselves."

Sagittarians prefer those who stoke their hopefulness. Sagittarians feed on hope and the great expectation that something good is right around the corner. They love uplifting messages and talks of bright futures. Avoid becoming too pessimistic or worried about matters. Sags don't see opportunity for expansion or promise in cynicism.

Sagittarians value authenticity. Forget pretending to be something you are not. Sagittarians detest phonies and posers, whom they spot instantly. Just be confident. Sag will respect you for it.

Sagittarians love a bright student. As interested as Sagittarians are in people who can teach them something, they are also interested in those whom they can teach. Sagittarians get a kick out of seeing the light of recognition coming into someone's eyes or feeling that they have made a positive impact on someone.

What Sagittarians Offer in Relationships

Sags bring excitement to their relationships. Sagittarians make life interesting, meaningful, and promising. Their enthusiasm brings exuberance to whatever activities they engage in, be it a trip to the Far East or a trek to the corner store for milk. In short, Sagittarians are fun to be around.

Sagittarians will inspire you. Sagittarians will stir you, awaken you, and otherwise get you out of your seat and involved in life. Sagittarius will prompt you to think more deeply about yourself and life because they enjoy talking about matters of consequence. "How do you imagine God?" "What about your work do you love the most?" "If you could travel to anywhere in the world, where would you go?" "Why?"

> ## Words Sagittarians Love to Say
>
> 🐎 "Here's what I think . . ."
> "This is good!"
> "Let's have an adventure!"
> "I'm learning something from this."

Your Sagittarian companion will encourage you to follow your inspirations as well. "If you dream of going into business for yourself, do it!" Sag will encourage, "You only live once!" They'll refuse to listen to your limits and objections and instead insist you can do what you want to.

Sagittarians offer robust, bighearted, loving affection. When Sagittarius likes you, they'll let you know openly. Sagittarians approach the objects of their affection with big smiles, open hearts, and acceptance. "You're so great!" comes easily from them. They get so filled up with love and excitement about who you are, you can't help but believe you're as wonderful as they say!

Sagittarians are cheerleaders and champions. When Sagittarians see the value of your hopes and dreams, they'll do their darnedest to help you realize them. They bolster your confidence, believe in you all the way, and help you believe in yourself. "Go for it!" they'll tell you, whether it's getting your Ph.D. or simply wearing that sexy dress to your class reunion. Sagittarians can pull off astounding stunts to help you achieve whatever you desire as well.

Sagittarians can teach fascinating things. Sagittarians also bring interesting facts and observations to their relationships. They'll engage you for hours talking about ideas and possibilities. Sagittarians can contribute little-known facts, insightful suggestions, and funny quips to add to any conversation.

Sagittarians are entertaining. Sagittarians adore the spotlight and have a way of holding court for you and your friends. Their ability to find the humor in any circumstance (whether others do or not) and their famous penchant for storytelling will hold you captivated for hours. Everything in their life is fair game when storytelling is concerned. Sure, they'll spice up the facts to make them more interesting—why not? Life is all a matter of perception, and Sagittarians' perceptions are larger than life.

Sagittarians make great audiences. Sagittarians love to be entertained, too, and make great audiences. They'll throw their heads back and laugh at your jokes (even if they don't get them) and nod with interest as you tell them about your adventures, mentally taking them with you.

Sagittarians bring levity to their relationships. Sagittarians loathe heavy scenes and those who make mountains out of molehills. Instead they want their lives and their relationships to be about enjoyment.

They'll give you the benefit of the doubt, won't sweat the small stuff (probably because they don't even notice it), and keep a positive focus. Even if matters do get difficult or contentious, Sagittarians usually approach it with a "We can work this out" attitude rather than a "Something terrible is happening" attitude. They believe the positive can outweigh the negative, so why not just keep focusing on the positive?

"Sagittarians'
motto:
'Don't sweat
the small stuff!'"

Sagittarians will shower you with their boundless generosity. Sagittarians freely give of their time, ideas, and money. "Why not?" they figure. Their confidence gives them a sense of plenty—so they can afford to give—sometimes lavishly.

Sagittarians offer great counsel. Sagittarians have a knack for turning what seems bad into a possibility for good. Their forte is showing you how you don't have a problem but an *opportunity*. Sags' positive attitude can help you laugh at yourself and your dilemma, as well as recognize that everything is fine. Beyond that, Sags are masterful at suggesting clever solutions or presenting insights that can spark inspiration in you. One great asset Sagittarians have is an ability to be cavalier—they don't let things get them too down. They can show you how to do the same.

The Sagittarian Lover

The Sagittarian lover is extremely passionate, full of excitement, and, of course, brimming with adventure. Sagittarians love all the fireworks of romance and the glorious hopefulness of courtship.

When Sagittarians fall in love, they go all the way. They become spellbound and intoxicated, and desire to consume their beloved to the very core. Never ones to subtly demonstrate their affections, Sagittarians make loving an all-out extravaganza.

And talk about being on a pedestal! Sagittarians see you for the god or goddess you are, because after all, they would never be captured by someone ordinary! You'll be the most brilliant, or the most beautiful, or the most enticing person on earth to them. Sagittarians are full of compliments, declarations of devotion, thoughtful gestures, and chivalrous actions that'll make you swirl with excitement.

> "When Sagittarians fall in love, they go all the way."

Should you eventually slip off that pedestal? Do what Sag would do: laugh it off. With a sheepish smile on your face say something like, "Oops—no one is perfect—not even me! But I'm lovable nevertheless, aren't I?" They'll be happy to accept your honest shortcomings, especially when you do.

But remember even in romance, Sagittarians need a good chase. Don't be all that easy to capture. Sagittarians thrive on the challenge of winning your love. Even if they have you with "Hello," keep their interest sparked by letting them work for you a bit.

However, even when Sagittarius might be acting as if commitment is right around the corner, it might not be the case. Sags protect their independence and can become quite skittish if there is too much emphasis on commitment. When pressed, they might back up, hands in air, and protest, "Now wait a minute! Why fix something that isn't broken?" They might even disappear for a while. (If that happens, get busy with your own life; they'll be back if they're genuinely interested.)

Since beauty and finesse stuns most Sagittarians, be sure to look your best when around them. Got legs? Show 'em! Got boots? Wear 'em! High-heeled boots, cowboy boots, and even hiking boots—Sagittarians can't resist them. The sporty types of Sagittarians may find you most attractive while muddy from head to toe after an exhilarating day of rock climbing. Find out how your Sag finds you most attractive and go for it.

> "Be independent and passionate about your life, and you'll nab yourself a Sag lover."

What kind of dates do Sagittarians enjoy?

Take a Sag on an adventure of some sort! Try going on a hike or to a sporting event or a concert, especially if getting there involves some sort of trip. Keep things playful and upbeat. Sagittarians love gazing into their beloved's eyes, but enjoy it more when hanging from a bungee cord. Be humorous and show Sagittarius what a good "buddy" you are. Keep your wit and interesting conversation rolling by letting Sagittarius tell you about their dreams and ideals, and let them know what yours are as well.

What are Sagittarians like between the sheets?

When it's time for making love, let loose! Sagittarians give of themselves fully, enthusiastically, and zestfully, and appreciate receiving the same kind of affection in return. They need variety and adventure in lovemaking as much as they do in any other endeavor, so be spontaneous and creative. Turn up the music! Swing from the chandeliers! Open the windows! Or better yet, make love outside! Sags are extremely physical and lusty; let them see all of you! Spice things up by springing something unexpected on Sag; a new place, position, or attitude keeps your Sag enthralled and coming back for more.

Sagittarians flirt shamelessly and admire others openly. That's part of their life-is-a-party style. Even when they are gloriously, drunkenly in love, they're still likely to check out the hottie walking by or keep sharing compliments with everyone around, including your best friend. That doesn't mean your Sag doesn't love you. Just be very, very confident in yourself, and avoid allowing jealousy to sour the good vibes between you. Sags need the freedom to express and enjoy. Jealousy feels like confinement to them. Sagittarians expect you to be so confident that you're not threatened by their playful fun with others. Remember it's you they have on that pedestal.

What turns Sagittarians off?

Any type of clinging or possessive behavior turns Sagittarius off, as does trying to corral them in any way. Routines suffocate them and inspire them to wander. Too much emotional processing bores Sagittarians to tears, and talking about problems brings them down.

Ways Sagittarians Can Drive You Crazy and What to Do About It

As with every sign, some of the traits that make Sagittarius so fascinating and fun can also turn irritating when taken to extremes.

Sagittarius challenge: They're pontificating know-it-alls.

Sometimes Sagittarians' urge to show the way can become downright annoying. Sure they adore awakening others by teaching them something of meaning and value, but when they get on a roll about something, Sagittarians get so consumed they might not realize they're completely hogging the conversation. Or maybe they realize it, but don't care, because what they have to say is *extremely important*. Others can fume with resentment, waiting to get a word in edgewise, but Sag might just talk right over them.

Sagittarians' verboseness can move into outright pontificating and lecturing. They can be so sure their opinions are right that they give others the impression that their ideas don't amount to much. Sagittarians can disqualify others' points in seconds flat. While Sagittarians don't mean to make others feel dismissed or dejected, that's often the result. Unfortunately, Sags can't resist letting others know what they know. Besides, Sagittarians usually believe they're being helpful.

What to do?

If you find that Sagittarius is overrunning your conversation or taking over the lectern, find a way to jump in. Let Sag know it's your time to talk, and that it's their time to listen, lest they get up and leave when you start to speak. This will awaken them to the fact that you have something to say and that they've been insensitive. They'll respect you for your courageousness and may even remember to offer you the floor next time. But don't count on it. Sagittarius is a very talkative sign, and they tend to push past limits regularly. Make sure to set yours firmly. Saying something like, "With all due respect, I would like to offer another way to look at this subject," can also prompt Sagittarius to listen.

Sagittarius challenge: They're commitment phobes.

Commitment is a squeamish subject for Sag and a painful one for anyone who's trying to get a commitment from one. Sagittarians cherish their freedom and independence so much so that they can fear a commitment to anything—a deadline, a certain plan, let alone a lifelong agreement. Since confinement is a fate akin to death for Sagittarians, they may be reluctant to make a commitment. Many a Sagittarian is a confirmed bachelor or bachelorette and relishes being so.

What to do?

When trying to help a Sagittarius make a commitment, emphasize the possibilities it holds. A Sag might be so focused on what they'll lose they might not recognize what they'll gain. Help Sag by showing them how a commitment might open a new avenue of experience, growth, and revelation. Let them know about the adventures you'll be sharing in your relationship. Encourage them to consider how instead of losing themselves, they might actually realize more of their potential through being loved by you. And be even freer.

Big hint: be prepared with some good examples of people your Sag admires who have flourished via commitment. That's because they'll be armed with tons of examples of others who have not.

Sagittarius challenge: They have seemingly unquenchable wanderlust.

Sagittarians frequently become antsy and itchy for new vistas and want to travel, make a change, or create some excitement to get their juices flowing. They have a tendency to believe the grass is greener elsewhere, so they want to go there.

What to do?

If it's a temporary restlessness your Sag is feeling, encourage them to take a road trip. Sagittarians love to wander and always come back refreshed and renewed. But if their restlessness is more pervasive than that, encourage them to try to find ways to make what they're doing more interesting. Assist Sag by asking what essential experience they're looking to achieve. And then challenge them to create that feeling or experience right where they are.

Sometimes it's best if Sagittarians do bolt off and find what they are looking for. After all, they need to be true to the voice of their inner calling. But before they do, Sagittarius would be smart to evaluate *what* voice is calling them and for what reason. Do they believe there are more possibilities for growth elsewhere? Look again! Maybe they could learn more by sticking around and trying a different approach to what they're already doing.

Sagittarius challenge: They crave freedom.

Sagittarians adore their freedom so much that they can become sour, constricted, or even depressed when life or their relationships

"When Sagittarians believe
they are learning something,
they can happily
withstand most any circumstance,
even confinement."

don't allow for the autonomy they crave. Sagittarians may even start to wonder if they should change everything, including their relationship, in order to get relief from a crushing sense of confinement.

What to do?

*I*f your Sagittarius is feeling confined, challenge them to find inner freedom. Remind Sag that their happiness shouldn't be held hostage to outer circumstances, but that they should learn to find expansion and meaning in themselves no matter what's going on around them.

Sagittarius challenge: They gloss over the negative.

*S*agittarians' tendency to gloss over what's bad or negative can cause problems in their relationships. Whereas some find this admirable, others, especially those who consider themselves realists, find this trait suspect. They can object when Sagittarians wax philosophical or shrug off problems or issues.

What to do?

*S*agittarians just don't seem to process life like most other signs. Although they are certainly capable of feeling things deeply, many choose not to or work to uplift themselves as quickly as possible when they do feel down. It's likely Sagittarians don't need to feel the entire gamut of emotions in order to understand themselves or to grow into the person they were meant to be. You might have to take Sagittarians' optimism as genuinely authentic. They really do believe that tomorrow will be a better day, and oftentimes it is.

Sagittarius challenge: They expect others to gloss over their problems, too.

Since Sagittarians are insistently optimistic and can easily snap themselves out of painful or negative feelings, they often think everyone else could and should as well. Or they seem clueless about others' feelings altogether. Sagittarians have been known to dismiss others' pain with an "Oh, get over it!" attitude, sometimes not realizing they are being insensitive. Sagittarians might think that others are being dramatic or indulgent if they are hurt or upset for (what Sags think) a prolonged period of time. "Come on! You can't miss your old boyfriend that much! Just find another one!" is Sag's way of comforting a grieving friend.

What to do?

If you find Sag runs roughshod over your feelings, let them know. Most likely, they'll be surprised and possibly confused, maybe even a bit defensive. But then, they'll reach for a greater understanding of you and be your champion the way you'd like them to be. Just don't expect Sagittarius to join you in your feelings or have a good cry with you. That's probably asking too much. Sags don't want to be that vulnerable or that down.

You might have to educate your Sag companion about the nature of your feelings. Explain that you can't or you won't just let something go or laugh it off. Let them know that your feelings bring a certain valued texture and understanding to life that you aren't willing to miss by closing them off.

Sagittarius challenge: They use optimism to justify whatever they do.

Sagittarians' positive focus often allows them to justify whatever they do. They can build a defensive block and refuse to accept the feedback that they might be in error in any way. "No—this is why I did what I did . . ." and so on. Taken to extremes, Sags' ability to justify allows them to try to get away with some pretty objectionable behavior because they always have a good excuse.

What to do?

To request a correction from a justified Sagittarian, listen to their reasoning and acknowledge it. Then ask them to listen to your reasoning in return and acknowledge it. Tell them they don't need to concede a thing, just to hear you out. That way your Sag doesn't think you are trying to blame them or insinuate anything. When you don't make them wrong, they don't need to prove they're right. Present problems as simply a variance in perception. Or present it as the fact that you're both simply expressing a variance in perception. That might make Sagittarius more receptive to hearing and considering what you have to say.

Sagittarius challenge: They have fiery tempers.

When disagreements arise, Sagittarians' fiery temperaments can take hold. Then they'll let you and everyone for miles know how they feel! Sagittarians yell, pace, pound on tables, and declare, "I've had it!" Lectures might come pouring out as Sagittarius "educates" you about why *you* were in the wrong. If you engage with Sags while they're in such a state, chances are you won't win. Their anger combined with their debating skills equip them with quick comebacks for anything you can dish out. Some Sags find a good fight stimulating and invigorating. That's good if you do, too.

What to do?

If you don't find fighting with Sagittarius exhilarating, try backing off while Sag blows off steam. Then, when the smoke clears, ask to talk things out. Be honest about your feelings and take personal responsibility for your part. When you do this, Sagittarius will be putty in your hands. They relish honesty and personal responsibility and your doing so will encourage them to do so in return. When Sags are able to see why you are doing or asking something and how it genuinely reflects your integrity or beliefs, they'll better understand and cooperate with you, even if they disagree or take exception with it.

Sagittarius challenge: Their risk taking is too risky.

Although Sagittarians thrive on taking risks, they can sometimes go way too far. If you're the type that shudders at the idea of investing your retirement savings on a get-rich-quick scheme or signing up for extreme skiing before you've mastered the bunny slopes, Sags can push you to your limits. When they're enthused about something, very little can stop them.

What to do?

If you don't want to go along with Sagittarian's schemes, don't just drop hints or subtle innuendos. Be direct and say something like, "I don't want to invest my money in that scheme," or "No—I'm not skiing down that mountain with you." They'll shrug and think it's your loss and go on with their plans.

What if you are married or otherwise partnered to a Sagittarius and their wild risks would legally, financially, or in others ways threaten your security? That's when you still need to declare directly, "Stop!" and negotiate with your Sagittarian. Since they may consider you a stick-in-the-mud, you might need to concede a bit, just to stay partnered. But if something is really important to you, let your Sag know why, and how they would benefit or even grow by trying things your way. Sagittarians use their salesmanship to sell their ideas, but they're willing to be sold on others' ideas as well. Don't apologize for not wanting to go along with their plans; instead, sell them the upside of yours.

Sagittarius challenge: They tell tall tales.

Telling big tales is part of Sags' charm and expression. It can also be part of their conning you out of your lunch if you aren't aware enough to ask the right questions. Sagittarians love to see what they can get away with. It's a way of flexing their inspirational muscles.

What to do?

Sagittarians love to spice up their stories with an exaggeration or two. Should they report that they saw twenty coyotes trotting right by their campsite, chances are there were only three. If it's twenty coyotes for entertainment purposes, so be it. They'd love it if you were a good sport about it.

Sagittarius challenge: They're self-righteous.

Sagittarians can become so confident in their philosophy, religion, or even political affiliation they might believe it's the *only* way anyone should go. That's when their "inspiration" zooms past pleasant idealism into holier-than-thou fanaticism. Then Sagittarians can become impossible to talk to about anything other than their narrow focus of beliefs. That can be frustrating and painful for anyone who is trying to relate to and love Sags.

What to do?

If you find that Sagittarius's righteous beliefs are causing a gulf in your relationship, try expressing your concern. Tell them you value them too much to let differences in opinion get in the way of the other good things you share. You could say, "In respect for our loving relationship, let's make this a subject we don't talk about." Find the subjects and activities you and Sag can agree on, and then respectfully leave the subjects you disagree about out of the relationship. Most of the time, Sag's wisdom will recognize the opportunity in your request, and they'll work to find ways to connect. But other times, Sag will choose to be true to their ideals over the relationships. You'll have to deal with them on their terms or let them go.

Sagittarius challenge: They feel thwarted by practicality.

Sagittarians need hope and fantasy to keep their enthusiasm alive. If someone continually douses their dreams, Sagittarians can feel deflated, if not depressed. As a defense, they'll tell themselves the other simply has no vision and then be tempted to dismiss them or bolt from the relationship.

What to do?

One way you can get your Sagittarian to respect your practical point of view is to entice them to consider your realistic ideas, perspective, and *another* kind of intelligence. Then Sagittarius might be interested enough to at least consider that your ideas have some value, even if they don't want to go along with them.

Summary: Staying Tight with Sagittarius

• Remember that Sag's main motivation is to learn and explore and capitalize on that.

• Give Sag plenty of freedom and choices.

• Keep the respect and communication flowing.

• When requesting a change of behavior from Sagittarius, emphasize the upside of the situation and what can be learned from doing so.

Chapter Ten

Capricorn
(December 22/23—January 20)

Who They Are

When you have a Capricorn in your life, you're sure to be challenged, guided, and encouraged to meet your potential. That's because these ambitious creatures are all about achievement, and they enjoy supporting you toward a path of success, too! Setting their sights on nothing less than the pinnacle, Capricorns are a rare combination of visionary, strategic planner, and political boss: they're incredibly capable of making their big dreams materialize and assume tremendous responsibilities in life. Don't be tricked by their cautious, sometimes stoic disposition, though; if you look and listen closely, you'll notice Capricorn's well-developed funny bone and sense

> "Capricorns are convinced that they should earn—and then grab—the brass ring."

Capricorn Is an Earth Sign

🔖 Capricorns' realistic, usually conservative personality is partially due to their being an Earth Sign, which gives them a practical, can-do sensibility that helps them naturally grasp how to make their life work.

of irony that brings humor to most situations.

Capricorns' astrological symbol, the Mountain Goat, deftly climbs over rocky terrain to reach the very peak of the mountain, and Capricorns make the same climb with determination and confidence, step-by-step, inch-by-inch, toward their goals.

That's because Capricorns aspire to become important members of their world. Their ambitions include being respected and admired by others. In fact, most Capricorns are intensely interested in prestige and status, official positions of authority, and the titles that accompany them. Believing in the value of hard work, Capricorns will go to great lengths to earn their status through exceeding the expectations of others.

"Being unproductive can drive Capricorn nuts."

Capricorns are characteristically cautious, though, and they don't expect life to be easy. And for some, it isn't. Perhaps this is because Capricorns' fate regularly presents them with hard challenges. Or maybe Capricorns *make* their lives hard by pressuring themselves with responsibilities and high expectations. Whatever the case, it works for most Capricorns, who eventually achieve what they desire—be it a significant station in life, your heart, or both!

Whether it's businesses, governments, organizations, or architecture, Capricorns are builders at heart. They relish creating something that supports them and their community. Most Capricorns enjoy wielding power and managing big-picture situations, and can be perfectionists, demanding that even the tiniest details be meticulously addressed. Everything they do elicits quality, functionality, and refinement. Why clutter up something when simplicity is so very elegant? If you want to catch a Capricorn's eye, perform tasks with function and simple elegance.

Capricorns' discipline is legendary. They'll make a plan and then stick to it, no matter what. In fact, many Capricorns delay the pleasurable gratifications of life, from playtime to marriage, until they have met the other goals they've set for themselves, and they respect others who show this same type of self-discipline as well.

Eager to assume responsibilities, Capricorns are confident in their abilities to get things done

Capricorn Lesson: To Use Discipline to Become the Person *They* Admire

Capricorns are famous for using their signature discipline to achieve respect and admiration—especially from those they admire. But sometimes they can be so concerned with impressing others, Capricorns can devote their lives to winning others' approval rather than doing what truly satisfies them. If your Capricorn is getting caught in that trap, encourage them to evaluate what is really motivating them. Do they respect and enjoy what they're doing? Do they like who they're becoming? In that way, you remind Capricorn that the key to their sign's happiness lies in their using discipline to follow the callings of their inner authority, rather than caving to the demands of the world's authority. In doing so, Capricorns tap into the power of their incredibly wise and capable spirits, which leads them to achieving their highest mission: to create genuine success by building a life they enjoy, respect, and are truly satisfied by.

right. They're happiest and most secure when they are the ones calling the shots, leading themselves and others toward a worthwhile goal.

What Capricorns Want in Relationships and How You Can Attract One

Capricorns need time to warm up to you. Relationships are extremely important to Capricorns and integral to their happiness. But they're not easy creatures to win over! Capricorns tend to be a bit shy and cautious, not to mention selective about when and to whom they open their hearts. Give Capricorn time to warm up to you and be patient with the hoops they put you through to evaluate if you are right for them.

Capricorns are drawn to sincerity, patience, and consistency, and can initially be suspicious of friendly gestures, wondering why others are being nice to them. Let Capricorn see through your actions that you have their best interests at heart. "Slow and steady wins the race" with Capricorn.

Capricorns seek authenticity. Capricorns gravitate toward companions who have substance, intelligence, and something to which their own practical natures relate. They're attracted to mates who exude the type of integrity and inner power that demonstrate they can be relied upon through thick and thin. Show Capricorn that you possess a depth of character and honorability they can count on—that you're true not only to your word, but to yourself as well. Be authentic, realistic, and respectable around Capricorn.

Honesty is an essential ingredient in creating an atmosphere of trust and respect with Capricorns. They might be savvy about the ways of the world and politics but can feel vulnerable and cautious when it comes to love and friendship. Who to trust is a big concern. Capricorns want to feel assured you're being straight with them and not pulling any punches.

> **Words Capricorns Love to Hear**
>
> ♟ "I respect you!"
> "Your contribution is important!"
> "I admire all you have achieved—good job!"
> "You are important to me!"

Capricorns like straight talk. Capricorns consider bluntness to be a trustworthy quality. Dressing up the truth or diluting it implies Capricorn can't take it. Just speak plainly. Give them the facts without a lot of unnecessary flourishes. Even if you tell Capricorn something they don't like to hear, they'll respect the courage it took for you to tell them. Then they can trust you to be authentic and appreciate your being a voice of truth in their life.

Capricorns demand dependability. If you say you are going to do something, do it, and do it well. If you don't, Capricorn will not only feel let down, they may also be insulted that you didn't think enough of them to follow through. Furthermore, if you say you are going to meet them somewhere at 8:00 PM, don't be fashionably late. Capricorns rarely consider tardiness charming.

Excuses don't go over well with Capricorns, either. They don't let themselves get away with excuses, so why should they indulge others'? Of course Capricorns are open to a change in plans, but they want to be advised and consulted on that change.

Capricorns' relationships require loyalty. Capricorns are intensely sensitive to the politics and alliances of social situations and expect members of their camp to behave with utter allegiance to them. Even a little betrayal can humiliate Capricorns so deeply that they'll find it hard to forgive or trust. Put yourself on the line for Capricorn, and they'll do the same for you.

Capricorns enjoy relationships with a purpose. Capricorns like spending time with people who can help them achieve something purposeful. That could be anything from creating a wonderful family together, engaging in a successful business endeavor, or working shoulder to shoulder on a worthwhile cause. Show Capricorn how being with you can help them achieve something they value.

Capricorns admire other high achievers. Capricorns love companions who share their high expectations, impeccable taste, and exacting standards of excellence. They see themselves as high performers and enjoy surrounding themselves with others who strive for high quality as well. Let Capricorn in on ways you've acquired the best of the best or reached (or intend to reach) the top of some mountain.

Capricorns adore tastefulness and genuineness. Although Capricorns accept the reality that many people have reasons for putting on false fronts or for acting superficially glamorous, they're rarely fooled or impressed by them. In fact, flashy, look-good-on-the-surface types disappoint and bore them. If you want to get to know your Capricorn, be genuine to them (they'll know if you're faking), and they'll open up to you.

Capricorns are impressed by worthy accomplishments and positions of power. Capricorns are famous for befriending those at the top of their profession or assimilating into prestigious circles. They especially adore companions who have overcome insurmountable odds and have gone on to meet success. After all, they see themselves as doing the same. To impress Capricorn, be sure to mention (never boastfully) if you're "important" in some way or to anyone. Watch their ears prick up. They will tingle at the thought that they are with someone significant.

Capricorns deeply appreciate being recognized. Being applauded for their efforts is the elixir of life for Capricorns, but they are too classy or subtle to call attention to themselves. Make Capricorn feel special by noticing what they've invested their time and effort in and complimenting it. They will get the "warm fuzzies" because you have the intelligence and wit to spot the value of what they do.

Warning: empty compliments will get you nowhere, so be sincere! If Capricorn even suspects you're patronizing them or trying to butter them up, they'll resent it.

Capricorns like demonstrations of love. It may be cliché, but "actions speak louder than words" could be Capricorns' motto. Endear yourself to Capricorn by doing something thoughtful and kind for them. Pick up their dry cleaning on days they're too busy, or take the time to cook their favorite meal. Your simplest acts of kindness will let Capricorn know you are concerned about their well-being. They will surely be humbled. "Me? You did that for me? Oh, my, I don't know what to say." And they might not say anything. But their heart has melted, and you have just scored major brownie points.

Capricorns seek tenderness and nurturing. Since Capricorns usually possess enough ambition and accomplishment for two (if not twenty) people, they often seek companions who offer a soft spot to land on after a hard day's toil. Capricorns place high value on being loved and cared for unconditionally, and find it richly rewarding to be with someone who is capable of extending sweetness and kindness toward them. In fact, many Capricorns crave outright nurturing but have no idea how to elicit it. So (slowly at first, don't overwhelm them!) extend the affection, thoughtfulness, and pampering that makes Capricorn feel cared for and nourished (but not babied) by you. They'll keep coming back for more.

Capricorns delight in mentorship. Capricorns adore taking someone with potential under their wings and guiding them along. They receive tremendous satisfaction in watching apprentices blossom.

Capricorns also relish being a respected authority figure. Want to ingratiate yourself to a Capricorn? Approach them as an expert and ask their advice about how you can achieve something. Then, do it. Capricorns enjoy being able to give someone good advice and seeing it put into action.

Capricorns prefer companions who garner admiration. Capricorns' taste for prestige gives them a fondness for company who they can show off in some way to create an air of "important by association." Be at your best when accompanying Capricorn, and extend yourself to make a worthwhile "approval winning" contribution to the situation. Capricorn will glow with pride and be anxious to show you off in other arenas. Bottom line: Capricorn wants to feel proud of you.

Capricorns find comfort in companions who can bring a bit of spontaneity to a situation. Sometimes Capricorns' serious demeanor can intimidate others and cause them to clam up around them. That bewilders Capricorns. Don't let a Capricorn's carefulness make you uptight. Being relaxed around Capricorn helps them be more relaxed around you. Capricorns also appreciate the breath of fresh air spontaneity provides. And they adore someone who makes them laugh. Tell Capricorn a good joke or make an intelligent observation filled with irony, and you'll have them in the palm of your hand. Capricorns work hard, but when it's playtime, they play hard, too. Win over a Capricorn by helping them cut loose when they need to.

What Capricorns Offer in Relationships

Capricorns are genuine and loyal friends for life. Once they're convinced of your loyalty and decide to invest in your relationship, Capricorns' loyalty doesn't waver. They value their chosen companions and, in times of need and trouble, stand by them and stand up for them. Capricorns work hard to make their relationships as successful as the rest of their endeavors. They show how they value their relationships by sharing time, devotion, and interest that says, "You are important to me."

Capricorns will support you, no matter what. When a Capricorn cares for you, they want the best for you. Generally, you'll hear from your Capricorn friend, "Are you okay?" "Is everything working the way it should?" "Is there anything I can do to help you?" A Capricorn wants to be there for you in a supportive, helpful way.

> ## Words Capricorns Love to Say
>
> 🛏 "I expect the best."
> "Let's be cautious."
> "Here's the plan . . ."
> "Let's achieve even more."

Capricorns will guide you toward your potential and purpose. Capricorns love being the guiding hero who contributes to others' successes. If you need something, Capricorn will use what they have to help open doors. Of course they won't do it *for* you—Capricorns believe in empowering, not enabling, their loved ones, so show that you are willing to take their advice and accomplish things for yourself.

Capricorns are known for tough love. In a paternal way, Capricorns will try to advise others and help them toward their potential. For example, instead of just sitting back and listening about your hopes and dreams, Capricorn will nudge you to get started—and perhaps even show you how. They'll identify what you're capable of and expect you to reach for it.

A Capricorn will also try to help you succeed in life by refusing to indulge your weaknesses—they feel they owe you that. Capricorn won't encourage you to take nutty risks or to invest yourself in endeavors that have slim chances of working out. But they will offer you excellent ideas about what would work and show you ways to achieve them.

Capricorns will keep their commitments to you. Capricorns take their commitments and promises seriously and don't make them hastily. They'll take their time to consider and measure their agreements to ensure they'll be able to come through. So when Capricorn gives you their word, they won't renege.

Capricorns make good on their commitments because they like planning and tend to be uncomfortable when things are left dangling.

"Once Capricorn's heart is given, they're true. When they're your friend, they're your friend for life."

Capricorns can be sweet and tender. The closer you get to Capricorn, the more you'll be on the receiving end of their tenderness. When Capricorns trust someone, they expose their soft side through thoughtful gestures and concern.

When you've reached this stage of acceptance, you'll be able to expose yourself—warts and all—and Capricorn will respond with an all-encompassing acceptance. As a matter of fact, letting Capricorn know about the challenges you've had in your life can help them trust and understand you more.

Capricorns love to give affection (when the time is right) and have a wonderful soft touch that can soothe and heal. The seemingly tough Mountain Goat has a sweet side that will melt your best defenses. They'll curl up with you and tend to your deepest needs.

Capricorns expose you to the finer things in life. When you're close to a Capricorn, you may be treated to the fruits of the luxurious world they have earned for themselves. Brushing elbows with important people, partaking in privileges that come with success, and enjoying objects of abundance are all great perks of accompanying Capricorn in their achievement-filled life.

Will Capricorn indulge you with their riches or lavish you with their luxuries? Probably not. They believe that each person should work for their own success and thereby become empowered by finding it. Capricorn will share their wealth with you—until it gets to the point they believe you'd be "spoiled" by it. They'll have no part in that.

Capricorns will treat you to their playful humor. Although Capricorns reveal their darkly delicious ironic, sarcastic humor to most anyone who seems to "get it," it takes a while for them to let down their guard and expose something rare to others: Capricorns' silly, buoyant playfulness. Their humor will flow, and your sides will split from laughter. Although life can be serious to Capricorns, it also presents loads of fodder for jokes. They admire people who get their sense of humor.

> "The tough Mountain Goat also has a sweet side, which they reveal when they finally trust you."

The Capricorn Lover

Capricorns pursue love the same way they pursue every other important endeavor—with determination, planning, and confidence they'll succeed. Although it might take a while for Capricorn's heart to awaken, when their interest is finally piqued, they'll stop at nothing to win your love and attention. Capricorn will pull out all the stops to impress you, entice you, and convince you that they are the only one for you.

Capricorns savor the companionship and the rare intimacy romantic love offers, and when they genuinely love someone, they treat them with deep consideration. Romance with Capricorn is a steady stream of subtle adoration and kindness. You won't find your Capricorn shouting from the mountaintop that they love you, but you will be wooed by their deeds of quiet affection: sideways glances, stolen kisses, and private nuances that let you know there is something special between the two of you. You'll be amazed how this ordinarily cautious, practical character turns teddy-bear soft as they connect with you.

You might initially win Capricorn's attention by being someone they can admire. But admiration alone does not elicit true love from Capricorn—there must be more to you than your success. Capricorns need to feel safe to be themselves around their mates. So show Capricorn how you genuinely like and appreciate their true nature—that's what they're really after.

Capricorns appreciate smart appearances and refinement. Wear clothing that is classic, well thought out, and event appropriate. Maybe something in subtle earth tones made with soft, natural fabric that invites a touch. Whatever you do, don't dress too sexy or outrageous— the flamboyance can embarrass the stoic Capricorn. Worse, it could lead them to thinking you're easy—a definite turnoff for ambitious Capricorn. Make them know that you are a challenge not to be won by just anyone.

What kind of dates do Capricorns enjoy?

Since Capricorn likes to be impressed, use your influence to get tickets to a sold-out play that's all the rave, or take them to a newly reviewed (and four-star!) restaurant with a waiting list.

While on your date, take your time with Capricorn and allow them to relax and warm up to you. Tell them about projects you're working on and perhaps ask their advice about them. Be sure to ask Capricorn about their past achievements, current projects, or future goals—that will put them at ease. If you genuinely respect Capricorn, by all means let them know.

Listen to Capricorn intently. Show them you're bright and savvy enough to participate in their world. But remember: while Capricorns are pleased to be admired for all they have accomplished, they treasure being admired for who they genuinely are. Let Capricorn know you really "see" and like the person behind all those achievements. Go ahead and genuinely flatter Capricorn, but steer clear of gushy patronizing.

What are Capricorns like between the sheets?

When it's time for making love, be prepared for your senses to awaken. Capricorn lovers reveal an exquisite sensuality they may not show at any other time. In fact, Capricorns are quite sexual creatures and truly enjoy physical love. But first things first: go somewhere private—Capricorns don't go for public displays of affection.

Behind closed doors Capricorn's motto is "Anything goes!" Touching, kissing, caressing, and exploring are all parts of Capricorn's sensual repertoire. For most Capricorns, the earthier the better; they love the tastes and textures of the human body, and like taking in all the pleasures it offers. Let Capricorn smell you, feel you, taste you. Why hurry? Make it last. Lovemaking is extremely important to your Capricorn, and they like it to be a lingering, sensual affair.

What turns Capricorns off?

Forget about smooching in public or playful scenes of affection while dining out. Capricorns don't mind a little emotional foreplay, but shun publicly showing it.

They also shun neediness, inappropriate expressions, and overt gushiness. Yuk.

Ways Capricorns Can Drive You Crazy and What to Do About It

Every sign has certain qualities, that, when taken to extremes, gets in the way of their relationships.

Capricorn challenge: Their penchant for "management" makes them control freaks.

Although Capricorns are aggressive movers and shakers, they tend to only want to be involved in situations that *they* are moving and shaking. If they can't manage a situation to flow in the manner they see fit, Capricorns are prone to digging in their heels and resisting it.

Yep, Capricorns are controlling. Control is the cornerstone of their sense of security, sure-footedness, and even their sanity! Capricorns thrive on their drive to control themselves, their routines, and their environment, thinking it's a respectable discipline. Trouble is, Capricorn might try to "manage" you, too, in ways great and small. You could find them dictating the type of clothes you wear, and even the career path you should follow.

Funny thing is, Capricorn's control really isn't about you—it's about them. Since they have a specific plan for how their life should be and you're part of their life, Capricorn feels it's perfectly reasonable to manage you so you fit into their scheme of things. Never mind the fact that you don't want Capricorn deciding what your favorite sport should be or what type of books you should read.

What to do?

If you feel Capricorn is overmanaging you or your life, thank them for their great advice, but let them know that *you* respect your choices and *you* prefer to be the manager of your life. Since Capricorn will worry you're making a mistake by not following their guidance, point to the practicality of your ideas to underscore your authority. If your life is intertwined with Capricorn's, show them how your plans and activities can work to bring them more of what they want, too. Be patient with Capricorn and allow them time to thoroughly consider and warm up to your ideas.

Remember, too, that whenever you suggest a "course correction" to a Capricorn, always use respect. Otherwise, they'll suspect you're controlling or criticizing them, which will distract them from hearing your concerns.

Capricorn challenge: They're nonstop drill sergeants.

Capricorns' ability to make plans and use discipline to see them through is an integral part of their nature. Yet, at times, they can seem like drill sergeants who don't ever take a break. Instead of being sensitive to your needs and preferences, Capricorn might instead stay focused on what needs to be done, the right way, and right now! When they're in that mood, Capricorn barks out orders, dismisses the input of others, or, if others are in the way, dismisses *them!*

But the fact is, Capricorns hold incredibly high standards for themselves, so naturally they project those onto others. Capricorns don't coddle themselves or let themselves get away with excuses or distractions from their goals, so why should they allow others to? So even when it's Saturday morning and time to relax at the beach, Capricorn can make packing up and driving there a chore: "No fooling around! Let's get to the beach, *then* we can have fun!"

What to do?

If you are on the receiving end of Capricorn's not-so-fun regimen, you might gently remind them that (to you) *getting* to the goal is just as important as reaching the goal. (Unless Capricorn is your boss.

READER/CUSTOMER CARE SURVEY

We care about your opinions! Please take a moment to fill out our online Reader Survey at **http://survey.hcibooks.com.**
As a **"THANK YOU"** you will receive a **VALUABLE INSTANT COUPON** towards future book purchases
as well as a **SPECIAL GIFT** available only online! Or, you may mail this card back to us.

(PLEASE PRINT IN ALL CAPS)

First Name _____ MI. _____ Last Name _____

Address _____ City _____

State _____ Zip _____ Email _____

1. Gender
☐ Female   ☐ Male

2. Age
☐ 8 or younger
☐ 9-12   ☐ 13-16
☐ 17-20   ☐ 21-30
☐ 31+

3. Did you receive this book as a gift?
☐ Yes   ☐ No

4. Annual Household Income
☐ under $25,000
☐ $25,000 - $34,999
☐ $35,000 - $49,999
☐ $50,000 - $74,999
☐ over $75,000

5. What are the ages of the children living in your house?
☐ 0 - 14   ☐ 15+

6. Marital Status
☐ Single
☐ Married
☐ Divorced
☐ Widowed

7. How did you find out about the book?
(please choose one)
☐ Recommendation
☐ Store Display
☐ Online
☐ Catalog/Mailing
☐ Interview/Review

8. Where do you usually buy books?
(please choose one)
☐ Bookstore
☐ Online
☐ Book Club/Mail Order
☐ Price Club (Sam's Club, Costco's, etc.)
☐ Retail Store (Target, Wal-Mart, etc.)

9. What subject do you enjoy reading about the most?
(please choose one)
☐ Parenting/Family
☐ Relationships
☐ Recovery/Addictions
☐ Health/Nutrition
☐ Christianity
☐ Spirituality/Inspiration
☐ Business Self-help
☐ Women's Issues
☐ Sports

10. What attracts you most to a book?
(please choose one)
☐ Title
☐ Cover Design
☐ Author
☐ Content

TAPE IN MIDDLE; DO NOT STAPLE

BUSINESS REPLY MAIL
FIRST-CLASS MAIL PERMIT NO 45 DEERFIELD BEACH, FL

POSTAGE WILL BE PAID BY ADDRESSEE

Health Communications, Inc.
3201 SW 15th Street
Deerfield Beach FL 33442-9875

FOLD HERE

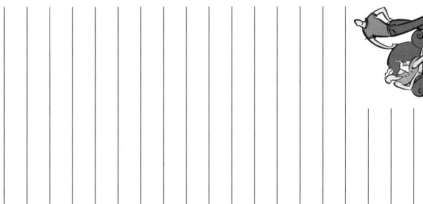

Comments

Then, you're better off getting with the program.) Capricorns occasionally need a little reminding that living life pleasurably is just as important as checking things off of the proverbial checklist.

Another way to help Capricorn become more at ease is to encourage them to evaluate whether they are in a balanced place. When Capricorns shift into overdrive, they're not only tough and harsh with others, they're wound up inside. Respectfully suggesting that perhaps they take a moment to step back and gain some objectivity might help them realize they've been pushing too hard.

Capricorn challenge: They're cautiously guarded.

Many Capricorns maintain a guarded demeanor. They're slow to open up to others or to situations that they haven't determined safe or acceptable. Capricorns don't assume the best is going to happen, nor do they assume the best in others. In fact, it's usually quite the opposite: Capricorns are constantly waiting for the other shoe to drop and anticipating that they'll probably be let down in one way or another. Does that make Capricorns pessimistic or realistic? Your call.

Capricorns absolutely, positively *dread* being hurt. They don't want the devastation or the humiliation of having their feelings tromped on, their affections rebuffed, or their trust betrayed. So don't do it. Whatever you think you will gain from hurting a Capricorn, the price you'll have to pay will be greater.

What to do?

Capricorn learns to trust others by seeing that they won't harm or betray them. Let Capricorn witness your sincerity in deed as well as word. Show them you can be depended upon. Humor can really help Capricorn to let down their guard, as does pointing out things you have in common. Be patient, be yourself, and Capricorn will come around.

Capricorn challenge: They "stoically" ignore feelings.

Capricorns often have a stoic nature and tend to underplay their emotions or refuse to express them altogether. Some Capricorns even consider feelings as unhelpful, frivolous, or (worse!) an avenue of unwanted vulnerability.

When Capricorn is feeling threatened by their vulnerability, they tend to ignore not only their feelings, but yours as well! This emotional suppression can build a wall between Capricorns and those they love because it discourages the type of warmth and understanding cultivated through emotional exchanges. It can also leave Capricorns' companions feeling lonely and isolated. Capricorns might feel lonely and isolated, too, but choose to stay that way rather than risk vulnerability.

This is why when someone shows emotion, Capricorns can seem, at best, a little uncomfortable and, at worst, downright judgmental. To Capricorns, the more emotional someone becomes, the more needy that person seems to be, thus provoking the distant and reserved Capricorn response. Needless to say, in these cases, Capricorns come off as uncaring and hard-hearted, and can hurt the other person terribly.

From the Capricorn point of view, they're stepping away because they're being reasonable and resisting being pulled under. They see nothing wrong with refusing to attend to someone whose emotions are running the show: "They're just being impractical."

What to do?

*T*ry showing Capricorn why your feelings are important. Let Capricorn know that you value what it is you feel and that you would like them to value it as well. Try to give Capricorn practical reasons for taking your feelings into account. And, if it's the case, tell them how you find it perfectly reasonable to factor feelings into your decision making, regardless of whether they seem practical or not. When you respect your own feelings, Capricorn might be more likely to do so in turn. But for your own sake, you might want to cultivate other relationships where your emotional expressions and needs are readily accepted and understood so as to fill in the gaps that Capricorn's stoicism might leave.

Capricorn challenge: They get stuck in stuffy ruts.

*A*lthough Capricorn's organized, structuring tendency can bring much-needed stability to relationships, other times it can bring a stuffy staleness. Many a partner of Capricorns complain of feeling bored or thwarted by Capricorns' insistence that life continue on with well-rehearsed regimens.

What to do?

*I*f you want more variety, change, or simply spontaneity in your life with Capricorn, remember it's all in your presentation. Make your case patiently and gently, with an eye toward why it would be advantageous or useful for Capricorn to go along with your request. That'll help them be more open to considering it.

If Capricorn won't agree, try exploring new things yourself and

232 Part One: So Many Signs, So Little Time

showing Capricorn the benefits of what you're trying. Your Capricorn is watching, even if they're pretending they aren't.

Capricorn challenge: They're ambitious.

One of Capricorns' most outstanding qualities is their ambition, but it can also interfere with their relationships. They can be so utterly determined to reach that high station in life that they let their relationships suffer. More than any other sign, Capricorns are known for keeping intimate relationships at bay until they have accomplished certain goals. They either feel relationships are not as important as their worldly ambitions, or they don't want the distraction of love. (What's ironic is that deep down, most Capricorns want to achieve success in all parts of their lives because that's what they believe will make them more lovable.)

If you're in a relationship with a Capricorn who's still climbing to the top, you may find that they put you off or put you low on their priority list. They might expect you to get on with your life pretty much solo while they work toward bringing home the trophy that will improve both of your lives. They might not want to spend time doing the little things with you that make companionship satisfying, and this can make life with Capricorn lonely.

> "More than any other sign, Capricorns are known for keeping intimate relationships at bay until they have accomplished certain goals."

What to do?

*B*ecause Capricorn doesn't intend to put you off, bring it to their attention that they are spending less quality time with you—they might not realize they've put you on the back burner and may be flattered that you want them around more. But if Capricorn is wrapped up in a project, don't take it personally if they tell you it's impossible for them to meet your needs.

If that happens, negotiate. First, tell Capricorn that you understand the importance of what they're doing and that you want them to succeed. Then ask for some ideas about how they can find some time to spend with you. Make it worth Capricorn's while. Chances are they're so stressed they'll be incredibly relieved to find that time with you is a rewarding respite. Or make plans for what you'll do when Capricorn finally finishes the project. Then get on with your own independent projects. Sure Capricorn likes to be supported. But sometimes supporting them means living your own life as well.

Capricorn challenge: They use anything to get ahead—even you.

*W*arning! There is a ruthlessness to Capricorn's ambitions that allows them to use people to get ahead or to cut ties to them if they can't keep up with them. Ouch! But it's something to keep in mind when connecting to Capricorn. Use your instincts to assess whether Capricorn likes you for you or likes you for what they think associating with you will win them.

The funny thing is that many Capricorns suffer from suspicions that others are intent on using them. Perhaps that's because they've had that happen to them, or perhaps they're projecting their own ambitious intentions on others. That said, many a Capricorn will initially befriend someone who can help them meet their goals, only to grow deeply fond of the person and form a lifelong alliance.

What to do?

*H*ow can you tell what Capricorns' true intentions are? Look into Capricorn's eyes as they talk with you. Are they soft and unguarded? Do they reveal themselves to you? If so, they value you.

Capricorn challenge: They're prone to melancholy.

*T*here is usually something about every Capricorn that seems a little sad, disappointed, or depressed. Capricorn is a sober sign—life does seem to take its toll on the Mountain Goat. Either Capricorns feel too much weight and pressure from their responsibilities or their expectations have not been met, both of which leave them feeling down.

And Capricorns worry! They worry about things that could possibly happen to them, their loved ones, their source of security, or even the world, and to Capricorn, it can seem like life is filled with bleak possibilities.

What to do?

*W*hen your Capricorn is in a dark mood, do your best to extend patience and understanding toward them. Resist any temptation to try to just snap them out of it or expect they should resolve their concerns by thinking happy thoughts. They won't. If you dismiss their worries and see them as simply negative (rather than recognizing *they* see themselves as concerned), they might dismiss you as unrealistic.

Instead, let your Capricorn know you understand they're concerned about things and that you're there for them if they want to talk things out.

Sometimes it's helpful to remind Capricorn that worrying about things they aren't truly responsible for—like other people's problems—isn't very productive or practical.

When trying to connect with a melancholy Capricorn, sharing your own worries lets them know you can empathize with them. Concrete solutions are always welcome. They'll think it over. Understand Capricorn, but don't try to rescue them. They're too proud for that.

Summary:
Cohabitating with a Capricorn

• Remember Capricorn's main motivation is to win admiration and prestige. Do what you can to support their goals.

• Always take a pragmatic, undramatic approach to working things out with Capricorn, and show respect for their ideas and requests.

• Show Capricorn how your ideas and requests have practicality and usefulness.

• When requesting a change of behavior from Capricorn, be very patient. Show them in sincere and factual ways how their satisfying you can bring important benefits or help them satisfy even more of their ambitions.

Chapter Eleven

Aquarius
(January 21—February 18)

Who They Are

I f you have an Aquarian in your life, you are sure to be awakened, electrified, and continually wowed! That's because these unique creatures specialize in bringing an unexpected twist to whatever they do—including their relationships. Aquarians are pure individualists. They feel a need, perhaps even a calling, to express themselves in ways that distinguish them from everyone else. Aquarians are free-spirited and enigmatic; just when you think you understand them, they will shift and present a new opinion, interest, or alliance that gives them another color altogether. Because they adore others who do the same, Aquarius will encourage you to listen to your own drummer as well.

Life is rarely ordinary around Aquarians—they keep it fascinating by introducing a wide assortment of surprising, progressive, and even wild experiences in hopes of realizing life's greater possibilities. In fact,

Aquarians are known for their zany nature and unique magnetism that attracts unusual events and people to them, even when they aren't trying to. You might not be able to put your finger on exactly why, but life seems to sizzle more when your Aquarian companion is around. Just sit back and enjoy the ride! They do.

Paradoxically, as much as Aquarians adore the unusual and unpredictable, they also crave consistency and are driven to establish roots and stability. Aquarians want and need things and people they can depend upon. There is a solid strength to Aquarians wherein they hold true to their values, commitments, and relationships, even as their lives take unexpected turns. Even Aquarians' passionate search for whatever's new is rooted in their urge to create a life for themselves and others that is as functional as possible. Their revolutionary tendencies are not about overturning matters (although that's often the result); they're just trying to create a better, more secure, world—for everyone.

Aquarians are strong and determined beings; once they make up their minds about something, that's it. If they intend to do something, nothing can veer them off course. On they'll push, stubbornly bulldozing any resistances they meet, in order to accomplish goals.

Aquarians' astrological symbol explains much about their humanitarian nature. It's the Water Bearer: a being kneeling over and pouring life-sustaining water from a vessel. That symbol depicts Aquarians' humanitarian urge to do something that supports their community in some life-enhancing way. Aquarians possess a particularly

"The identity of Aquarians is largely shaped by the role they play in their world."

global perspective: they are deeply concerned about the world they live in.

Aquarians think in a broad "us" context. They aren't just interested in getting ahead—they want every member of the world to get ahead. They don't mind making personal sacrifices in order to benefit the greater whole—in fact, they want to. Nothing makes an Aquarian happier than knowing they are making an important contribution to a worthwhile cause. They would appreciate it if you made one, too.

Aquarians work to detach themselves from their emotions and passions, which might steer them wrong, in order to follow the most objective, pure truth possible. The benefit in this is that Aquarians are usually as bright as can be, and their logic usually involves compassion and a humanitarian bent.

Aquarians refuse to accept that life has to have limitations, divisiveness, or especially inhumanity. Aquarians' idealism usually focuses on the possibilities of progress and evolution; they have great faith in human beings becoming an advanced race worth being proud of. They seek to put aside

Aquarius Is an Air Sign

Aquarians are Air Signs, which means they typically take a mental approach to life: they favor their ideas and thoughts over their emotions when assessing life or making decisions. Aquarians place high value on objective thinking and strive to be logical folks. Even if their feelings prompt them to do differently, they will act according to how their ideals expect that they "should" act.

"Aquarians' unique expression of their Air Sign quality is idealism. They tend to elevate their thinking—about anything—to a big picture of what's possible."

their personal preferences (or even a personal life) in order to serve a greater glory. Intolerance and prejudice are especially unacceptable to them. Instead of believing one person or group is more important or special than any other person or group, Aquarians believe everyone is special and important in their own right. (They believe the opposite as well: to Aquarians, no one is so special or important that they should be singled out or exalted.) The Aquarian dream: that the world acts as one big rainbow coalition.

"Most Aquarians are a combination of logical scientist and intuitive visionary."

Aquarians find it easy to entertain abstract thoughts and concepts, and enjoy thinking outside the proverbial box. Instead of being satisfied with the status quo, Aquarians constantly seek to add to or contradict what's already been proven, accomplished, or accepted as truth.

If fact, many Aquarians are inventors at heart. They love tinkering and experimenting in order to discover innovations that improve life. There can be an ingenious or even a mad-scientist quality to your Aquarian friend who pushes the envelope of whatever they're involved in. However, as unconventional as Aquarians are, they see themselves as pragmatists. They want to come up with ideas that improve this world, hopefully in a way that benefits others. If their attempts are unfruitful, Aquarians are satisfied that at least they tried.

What Aquarians Want in Relationships and How You Can Attract One

First and foremost, Aquarians desire friendship. Friendship is so central to Aquarians' ideal of love that they seek it in most every type of relationship. Aquarians savor knowing that they can say or do anything around their companions and be respected for who they truly are. Listen to your Aquarian friend, and demonstrate understanding and appreciation for their individuality. If they find you attractive, they will surely do the same for you!

Aquarians are drawn to uniqueness. Aquarians are attracted to people who express something

> ## Words Aquarians Love to Hear
>
> 🐾 "You are so unique."
> "I love your individuality!"
> "I appreciate the contribution you're making to our group/ community/world."
> "Your ideas are so fascinating to me—tell me more about them."

new, something novel, or something that they haven't seen before. They relish individuality and are enticed by those who are free thinkers or behave in an unexpected manner. Aquarians are disinterested, if not bored, by those who fit into the box of what's typically considered conventional. If you can break away from the pack and be or do something different, creative, or even shocking, Aquarius will consider you worth investigating further. Surprise Aquarius and make them sit up and notice that you aren't just an ordinary person.

Aquarians need to feel connected. Most Aquarians operate on such

Aquarius Lesson: To Avoid (Fed-Up) Intolerance with Unconditional Positive Regard

🜄 Aquarians pride themselves on being tolerant and inclusive, and they are most awakened to their loving spirits in doing so. But ironically, Aquarians can sometimes become extremely intolerant of those who don't see life the way they do or act in the humanitarian way they see necessary. When that happens, Aquarians can become disappointed in people, even bitter. If your Aquarius is struggling with unmet expectations of others, remind them of a key to their sign's happiness: to use unconditional positive regard for every person. When Aquarians strive to respect each individual's unique way and time of evolving, they become more tolerant and appreciative of others' expression. That's when Aquarians are poised to express their highest mission: universal love for humanity in all of its shapes and forms.

a unique wavelength that at times they can feel quite different from the majority of humanity. Therefore, they especially appreciate others who can share their ideas, activities, and visions. If you can join Aquarius in some of their many causes, they will feel a kinship. Share your visions with your Aquarian friend—they'll feel closer to you for doing so.

Aquarians prefer open-mindedness. Aquarians pride themselves on their humanitarian ability to respect and support differences between people. They get a kick out of seeing the variety of ways in which people can express themselves. Aquarians prefer to surround themselves with others who take the same tolerant stance. Demonstrating a broad acceptance and enjoyment of others will open Aquarius's heart and respect for you.

Aquarians want and expect plenty of freedom in their rela-

tionships. Being ruled by Uranus, the radical planet of freedom and individuality, makes Aquarians extremely independent. They want to know that they can come and go as they please without worrying they'll hurt or disappoint their companions. To Aquarians, freedom means the absence of being possessed in any manner. Clinging to Aquarians or being jealous of them is a real turnoff. No leaning or expecting Aquarius to complete you in any way. Aquarians want to be with someone who is complete in and of themselves.

Whatever you do, don't try to set limits on your Aquarian companion. Stipulations about what they can and can't do irk them. Chances are that your Aquarian has friends and/or interests that are as important to them as you are, and these might occasionally compete with your time together. Aquarians firmly believe they should do what they want to do. If you would like to spend more time with your Aquarian friend, you might accompany them on some of their many endeavors. But if you do so just to keep an eye on them instead of being truly interested in what you and they are doing, Aquarius will sense it and resent it. What should you do instead? Get busy doing something you truly enjoy. Then, when it's time to get together, you'll have even more to talk about.

Aquarians enjoy and prefer intelligent companions with whom they can think freely and easily share ideas and opinions. Aquarians savor lobbing ideas back and forth, and having their insights considered. If someone dismisses an Aquarian's ideas, they might lose their attention. When dealing with this sign, keep an atmosphere of openness wherein all ideas are fodder for lively discussion and consideration. Aquarians agree with the concept that there are no absolute rights and wrongs because to them everyone is a unique individual with individual thoughts, insights, perceptions, and opinions. Because of this open-minded approach to others, Aquarians know how to keep communication flowing. And having a flowing, intellectual, interesting conversation from which an Aquarian can grow is the Aquarian's ideal way to spend time.

Aquarians are attracted to stars. Aquarians are often drawn to companions who capture the spotlight. Unions between Aquarians and over-the-top expressive companions can be terrifically rewarding. Aquarians enjoy the way an entertaining companion spices life up. (You'll see the Aquarius sitting back, just watching their mate and smiling.) They can also appreciate the social doors their dramatic friends open.

What Aquarians Offer in Relationships

Aquarians offer undying friendship. Aquarians bring to relationships the very thing they most want to receive from them: friendship. Aquarians value the people they love perhaps more than anything else in life. And they show it. They are loyal and appreciative friends who strive to be excellent companions. As free-spirited as these folks are, they are rock-solid in their chosen relationships. Aquarians understand what it takes to create and sustain friendships, and they willingly do so.

But because no one is truly a stranger to Aquarians, they're sure to welcome new friends into their orbit. Why not include everyone? The more the merrier!

Aquarians respect your independence. Aquarians are happy to be included in your life. They'll tend to take you on your terms. If you are busy, Aquarians appreciate the time you make for them. If you have other interests that don't include them, they are happy for you and want to hear about them. As long as you are an interesting companion while you are around, Aquarius will be content to be involved with you in whatever manner works for you.

> ## Words Aquarians Love to Say
>
> 🜍 "Let's approach this logically."
> "Why not try something different?"
> "Why try to be like everyone else when you can be yourself?"

Aquarians add excitement and adventure to your life. Aquarians have fun-loving personalities and are game to accompany you in interesting activities. They thrive on concocting new schemes and discovering new territories to explore. You'll meet more people through your Aquarian companion than you ever would on your own—and more unusual kinds of people at that. Or, if you are doing something ordinary, an Aquarian will use their quirky inventiveness to make it extraordinary.

Aquarians offer unabashed support and encouragement. Among the precious things about an Aquarian's companionship is their wholehearted acceptance and encouragement of your being you. They'll want you to be the best person you are capable of being, and they'll encourage you to act in a way that shows your individuality. Aquarius will accept your quirky ways, honor your preferences, and won't try to change you. Aquarians are loathe to think they could put pressure on you to do something that isn't right for you—or worse— get in the way of your expressing your true self. Even when Aquarius holds strong opinions about what you should do (which they often do), they nevertheless try to express a respectful regard for whatever you choose to do, and without judgment.

Aquarians enter into relationships free of envy. Aquarians' belief

"Aquarians don't like high-maintenance relationships, and they don't want to be high maintenance themselves."

that everyone is equally important and equally special translates to their preference to have balanced, equal alliances free from competitiveness or chest-pounding bragging. It's unlikely that an Aquarius would go toe-to-toe with you in order to discover who's top dog. And they'll rarely try to steal the scene from you in an attempt to capture the attention for themselves. Rather, Aquarians focus on what they can contribute. They want to be the type of companion with whom people can relax and be themselves.

Aquarians possess great listening skills. Aquarians are terrific listeners. They are always intrigued by what others might come up with next. When you've piqued an Aquarian's interest, you'll see them raise one eyebrow, as if to say, "Hmmm." You needn't put on airs around Aquarius (as a matter of fact, don't. They can spot a phony a mile away and really hate it!), nor do you need to hide anything.

Unless they believe you're creating problems for dramatic excitement (Aquarians tend to give up on those folks), Aquarians will set aside what they're doing to hear your dilemma. They will evaluate your issue logically and factually, and then do their best to advise you thoughtfully. Chances are an Aquarius will come up with a solution that is so inventive that you would have never considered it on your own.

Aquarians' vision will help you see things you normally wouldn't. Aquarians bring a unique "awakening effect" to their companions. They are on a constant search for new liberating ideas and approaches, and they love nothing more than delivering them to their friends' doorsteps. Your visionary Aquarian friend has a finger on the pulse of the world. They'll be the first to let you in on a new fad, an emerging entertainer, or ideas that the rest of the world will eventually be talking about. Aquarians are on the cutting edge of life, and they can help you to be, too.

Aquarians will awaken you. Aquarius will awaken you by not letting you get stuck in limiting ways. They'll say what needs to be said (objectively, of course, without any accusatory drama) in order to jolt you out of doing something that isn't in your best interest. Aquarians value honesty over coddling someone's feelings. If an Aquarius observes you're off track, they'll tell you about it, even if it might be hard for you to hear. If you have gifts or opportunities that you aren't using as well as you could, they'll identify them and encourage you to bring them out.

The Aquarian Lover

As impersonal and "buddy-oriented" as Aquarians can be, when they're in love, a unique intimacy and softness spring out of them, which communicates, "You are special and sacred to me." But, nevertheless, Aquarians are wired differently than most people in that friendship is their ultimate bottom line. Aquarians need to feel a sense of friendship with someone even more than the typical swooning, passionate, intoxicating effects of romantic love. Friendship is the elixir of life to Aquarians, and they want it from their beloved as much as they want it from their busboy.

There are two types of Aquarian lover: those who want intimacy and commitment and pursue it, and those who don't and run from it. Most Aquarians do desire a special someone and are capable of being intensely focused and loyal when they find that person. They enjoy the tenderness, intimacy, and sharing of their deep soul with another deep soul. Although it might take them a while to make one, these Aquarians have no problem with commitments—when they make a commitment, they stick to it.

Other types of Aquarians might tell themselves they want to find a special someone, but it seems they never do. Perhaps they are too idealistic about love and no one ever manages to measure up. Perhaps it's because they fear that love would ask things of them that would smother their individuality. In order to remedy the ambivalence, these Aquarians regularly become smitten with those who are unavailable or just out of reach. And if they do become available? Suddenly Aquarius is gone.

What kinds of dates do Aquarians enjoy?

Aquarians enjoy dates in which you do something out of the ordinary, of course! Take Aquarius to somewhere unexpected, like a concert of experimental music or a social gathering of unique people. Since most Aquarians are happiest when surrounded by their many friends or a sea of strangers, instead of private affairs, invite them to activities they can share with their buddies or where they can be elbow to elbow with humanity in general. (Then, when they're "peopled out," Aquarius will be more ready and comfortable to share time alone with you.) Keep the conversation alive by asking them what they've seen lately that has amazed them.

Remember this: always give your Aquarian lots of room to operate.

Let them see that you enjoy being with them, but allow them plenty of freedom to express their social side and mingle with others if they want. Since Aquarians are attracted to whatever's different, dress in a way that stands out or broadcasts that you are distinctive. Aquarians admire lovers who show they are their own person, so be your genuine self. As long as you keep the surprising activities and interesting ideas flowing, your Aquarian will stay interested.

What are Aquarians like between the sheets?

You're in for a (perhaps unexpected) treat! The rare intimacy that sexuality offers is very sacred to Aquarians, and they express a tenderness and caring that you might not see them express in most other situations. Although they might be logical, even detached in everyday life, most Aquarians are usually attentive and involved lovers in the bedroom. They very much want to please their partners by meeting their every need, whatever they may be.

As with every other area of Aquarian's lives, they like to experiment! New positions and new places are exciting to them, as is something that has a degree of unconventionality to it. They'll be game for whatever novel approach you suggest, so keep their interests high by suggesting them, or better yet, doing them! Aquarians adore inventiveness in their lovemaking as much as any other worthwhile endeavor.

While Aquarians are game for a lot, they find public displays of affection and clinging, needy possessiveness to be uncomfortable and embarrassing. To them, affection is a private affair.

Remember, Aquarians are seduced through their minds: stimulating conversation is always the first step to great sex. Then, take that a step further with some talk of titillations to come. Although pure physical attraction might get Aquarian's attention for a moment, unless you capture their mental curiosity, it won't hold them.

What turns Aquarians off?

Any type of clinging or possessiveness turns Aquarius off, as does too much emotionality. Trying to fit Aquarius into routines stifles them, and expecting them to fit into any mold sends them running for freer grounds.

Ways Aquarians Can Drive You Crazy and What to Do About It

Like every other sign of the zodiac, some of the qualities that make Aquarius fascinating can also make them frustrating, if taken to extremes.

Aquarius challenge: Free bird—insistently, defiantly so!

Aquarians have to be their own person—that's for sure. Freedom is not only their keyword; it's their lifestyle! They expect it, even demand it as a prerequisite for participating in relationships. But some Aquarians are so insistent on maintaining their freedom that the thought of making a commitment to anything, whether it's a lunch date or a relationship, can seem overwhelmingly confining to them. Sometimes Aquarians just don't want their choices limited. Other times Aquarians resist commitments because they fear their wings would be clipped. Then, instead of being the solid, reliable friends or lovers they're capable of being, Aquarians act in a frustratingly flighty and undependable way. Now you see them, now you don't.

When Aquarians are ambivalent about committing to relationships, they put out confusing signals. If you're available, Aquarius is suddenly busy or utterly absent. Then, when you're distracted, Aquarius is right there, campaigning for attention, wanting to make plans. It will seem like they want a connection with you until they have it. Then they don't want it anymore.

This behavior can be confusing to the Aquarian as well. They might believe they want closeness or a confirmed relationship, but something inside of them becomes skittishly resistant! The truth is, Aquarians want to be included and want to be loved. Moreover, they absolutely dread, even fear, being rejected. (If someone does reject an Aquarian, it might ignite an impassioned drive in them to win the person back—even if it means taking extreme actions.) But, ironically, Aquarians reject others who are available to them.

What to do?

Some Aquarians are just free birds, and choose to live their lives without the shackles of commitment. But most others eventually come around to forming lasting connections. How can you help your Aquarian to do so?

Find a way to communicate to your Aquarian that they are free to be themselves in your presence. The more they see that you won't judge them for being themselves, they'll realize a relationship with you won't rob them of their individuality. Better yet, if you're the type that accepts or wants unconventionality in your relationships, let your Aquarian know what you have in mind. More than any other sign, Aquarians like to relate to others in nontraditional ways.

If it's truly okay with you, let your Aquarian understand that they are free to do as they please. If they believe you won't begrudge their other interests or, importantly, their other friends (that's a must!), they will realize that they won't have to sacrifice their freedom to be with you. That's critical for the Aquarius.

If something your Aquarian does makes you feel uncomfortable, unhappy, or as if you're taking the backseat in the relationship, try negotiation. Let them know what else you'd prefer and the reasons for your preferences. If they can understand your logic, it might help them concede. If they don't, you might be out of luck—Aquarians refuse to be controlled in any way. They expect to be accepted on their terms. But Aquarians like to see themselves as accepting others on their terms as well. Show them where both of your terms meet.

Aquarius challenge: They fear you'll see them as "just" ordinary.

Here's a little-known secret about why Aquarians tend to be hesitant to allow anyone to get too close to them: they're deeply fearful that, if someone really gets to know them, they might be revealed as just ordinary folk. That's a fate worse than death to Aquarians! If they become exposed as just a regular, normal human being, they worry they won't be worthwhile, much less lovable. You might think that's silly, and your Aquarian might consciously think that's silly, too, but it might be a factor in their distant nature nevertheless.

What to do?

Find a way to let your Aquarian friend know that you treasure and respect their "ordinariness" as much as you do their zaniness.

Aquarius challenge: Their personalities are too quirky to connect with.

There is a definite quirky side to every Aquarian, but some are quirkier than others. More than a few Aquarians feel they don't fit in very well at all—like "strangers in a strange land." Some Aquarians enjoy the distinction of not fitting in. Others find it lonely. Most Aquarians are somewhere in between.

Aquarians like to use their unconventionality to not only declare their uniqueness, but to protect their freedom as well. But occasionally they can become so zealous about it that others can find it hard to relate. Aquarians can intentionally exaggerate differences they have with others for effect: they enjoy shocking people and keeping them on their toes. Standing out and making statements that declare "I'm different" is a frequent and comfortable stance for an Aquarian to take. *If it puts others off, so be it,* Aquarians figure. *At least I've made them think.*

But sometimes Aquarians take things too far and wind up feeling isolated, different, and terribly alone because of their individuality. They may feel they're in the wrong group, city, or even world, one with no one they can relate to, and that can be painful.

What to do?

If an Aquarian close to you complains of feeling isolated, alienated, or separate from others, you might encourage them to evaluate whether they are overemphasizing their individuality while underemphasizing their concern or love for other people. If so, remind Aquarius that the best use of their individuality is when they contribute to and inspire humanity, rather than staying separate. Encourage your Aquarian friend to find ways to join in and participate with others, even if and when they don't have everything in common.

Aquarius challenge: They're equal-opportunity rebels.

*A*quarians are rebellious by nature. They thrive on challenging a limiting status quo of any kind. In fact, Aquarians are equal-opportunity rebels: they rebel against people, groups, organizations, or governments in order to end injustices or push through a better idea. They'll rally against even the tiniest misuse of power and take a stand to try to get others to do the same.

What to do?

If you are in a relationship with an Aquarian, they might rebel against any limits or expectations you try to put on them. So do yourself a favor, and try not to. Or, if you must, bring your Aquarian in on it. Explain to them why you want or expect something of them. Let them see your logic. More important, help them (and yourself!) to understand how everyone, not just you, can benefit. Appeal to Aquarius's sense of justice and urge to do what's best for all.

Aquarius challenge: They like to play the role of the "should" police.

One of the great ironies of Aquarians is that, despite the fact they are freedom lovers and freedom advocates, they can also be quite controlling! Usually that takes the form of becoming stubbornly strict (even militaristic!) in their expectations of what others *should* do in order to be acceptable.

The challenging thing about Aquarians is they never want to acknowledge they are being controlling at all. They tell themselves they are doing the right thing, and others should be doing (their idea of) the right thing, too. they see themselves as championing the cause of something or someone other than themselves, rather than seeing themselves as controlling.

Aquarians are so willing to put their lives on the line for their ideals, they can be stunned, not to mention very disappointed, when others don't. Therein lies their challenge: they judge others for acting purely for personal gain, considering them selfish and stunted. They become a forceful voice of dissent and defiance, or become out-and-out rebellious toward their opposition. Taking a stand is an empowered position for Aquarius. But becoming intolerant of others and their ways puts Aquarians into judgmental separation from others.

What to do?

If you find your Aquarian sinking into intolerance, or simply becoming disillusioned by others, encourage them to remember that everyone evolves at different rates. Helping Aquarians view life as a big experiment, wherein every human is living according to their unique

> "When Aquarians
> exercise tolerance,
> they can relax and
> return to their
> characteristic gift:
> unconditional loving
> of all."

consciousness and truths, helps them approach differences among people as evidence they are learning and growing in their own way. Others may not be able to act in the expansive, idealistic way Aquarian sees as right. Nor perhaps should they.

If you find you are on the receiving end of an Aquarian's control, judgment, or intolerance, you might let them know you feel they're impinging on your individual freedom to think and choose. "I am right for me—and I'd like you to respect that," is an approach Aquarians might consider.

Aquarius challenge: Aquarians always need to be "right"!

Adhering to their sense of truth and values is one of the most admirable traits of Aquarians. But Aquarians' smug belief that they are "right" can also be one of their most infuriating traits. They stubbornly take a position and reject outright any difference posed by others. They may even arrogantly believe they are more intelligent, insightful, or evolved than others.

Do Aquarians hold their tongues when they disagree with others? Nope. They are extremely opinionated and feel compelled to let others know the truth as they see it. Some Aquarians might have learned diplomacy, but that doesn't for one minute mean they are giving up their point of view.

What to do?

It takes a lot to get Aquarius to change their mind. A lot of what? Depending on the Aquarian, a lot of facts, a lot of compassion, or a lot of proof. Present your point as a new idea to be considered. Aquarians like to see themselves as open-minded, so capitalize on that. Instead of getting into a who's-right-and-who's-wrong discussion (which can intensify their stubborn resolve), use a "Hey—let's explore how we can both be right" approach. Then use facts, examples, and logic to communicate your point. Will Aquarius change their mind? Maybe—if the facts are sufficient. Always use a respectful attitude and try to keep emotional dramas to a minimum. *Just because you're hysterical doesn't make you right,* Aquarians say to themselves. Leave them to think it over. Forget about trying to argue with an Aquarian—that just makes them more resistant.

Aquarius challenge: You can't tell if they're calm, cool, and collected or just plain callous.

*A*quarians adhere so much to their logical stance that they can seem to discount feelings—their own, as well as others'. Simply put, most Aquarians aren't comfortable around gushing scenes of emotion. It can be truly off-putting to them. They might interpret someone letting their emotions loose as the person's being illogical (at best) or losing control (at worst). When feelings are flowing, Aquarians don't know what to do. They certainly aren't going to join in and express their own! Most become even more detached and logical in hopes the other gets a grip.

> "When Aquarians are singled out as special or celebrated, they can behave oddly uncomfortable or aloof with that type of personal attention."

Aquarians' adherence to their detached logic can make them seem aloof or even downright cold. Others might interpret this as Aquarius not caring for them or not feeling strongly about what's going on. This can be hurtful or alienating for those who want and need to connect emotionally with an Aquarius. They may believe that Aquarius is dismissing them because they are dismissing their emotions.

But that's usually not the case; instead, it's most likely just the opposite. Aquarians feel very deeply for others, but they don't believe that getting emotional about it adds as much value as coolly evaluating the situation. Aquarians want to be as clear as possible, and not let their emotions get in the way of finding what's really right. They'll try to keep themselves a bit above situations and exercise detachment in order to gain objectivity.

What to do?

When relating to Aquarius, remember that they probably value the clarity of logic over the messiness of emotions. Moreover, they value the impersonal overview of a situation more than the intimate personal view. That can be disheartening for those who want their Aquarian companions to feel their pain or empathize with their dilemmas. Aquarians are compassionate, but they show it through their ideas and actions, not feelings. So instead of waiting for your Aquarian friend to show their concern by having a good cry with you, learn to recognize the show of affection that comes through their thoughtful, albeit objective offerings.

The same goes for being treated as "special." Aquarius can grow weary of a companion's need to be singled out or to be the center of attention. They can lose patience, not to mention respect, for people who always try to make themselves special cases or who demand a lot of maintenance. Even when Aquarians themselves are singled out as special or celebrated, they can behave oddly uncomfortable or aloof with that kind of personal attention.

Sometimes that can translate to even your closest Aquarian beloved's treating you the same as they would a stranger. Don't take it personally—it's just their being their global Aquarian self.

If you are having a hard time connecting emotionally to an Aquarian, address it with them. Chances are they'll be surprised to discover that you find their aloof manner objectionable. (After all, Aquarians work at it, thinking it's the best approach they can take.) Tell them you'd like to see more of their feelings. If they can, they'll oblige you. But if an Aquarian claims they can't be more emotional, forget insisting they do. They won't. You may just have to understand that they just don't want to express their feelings like you do, but that they care for you nevertheless.

You might also try advising Aquarius that you see value in your (and others'—including Aquarius's) emotional expression, and that you would appreciate it they could, too. When Aquarians seek to appreciate people's feelings as an integral part of their individuality, they can respect that others' emotional approaches are as valid as their own, even if they often do things that oppose Aquarian's "good sense."

Oftentimes Aquarian's alliances with highly emotional folks can become frustrating and annoying to both parties. Sometimes it's easier to just give up and move on than to try to change Aquarius's emotional nature or their companions' emotional nature.

Summary:
Amazing Your Aquarian

- Remember Aquarius is idealistic with a strong motivation to contribute something important to their community.

- Be clear and factual in your communication with Aquarius.

- Let Aquarius see you respect their individuality and freedom.

- When asking for a change in behavior from Aquarius, don't push or insist that they do things your way. Instead, give Aquarius plenty of leeway to satisfy your requests in their own way.

Chapter Twelve

Pisces
(February 19–March 20)

Who They Are

If you have a Pisces in your life you're sure to feel enchanted, empathized with, and encouraged to dream. That's because these romantic creatures have an urge to merge and create a unifying connection with everyone around them—including you! Pisces possess vivid imaginations and love considering the wondrous possibilities of every situation. With their spiritual natures, they yearn to feel a part of the greater whole and encourage others to feel it, too. Pisces' highly attuned sensitivity, combined with their love of helping others, makes them especially compassionate and giving companions. There's something otherworldly about your Pisces friends—nothing is ordinary to them, or, if it is, they make it extraordinary. Why live in a black-and-white world when there are so many colors to enjoy?

Life with a Pisces is a unique combination of soothing peacefulness

> "With a Pisces around, magic is in the air."

and dramatic excitements. One minute they're blissfully flowing along, emanating a vibe that everything is perfect, just as it is. The next minute Pisces stir up a little excitement or even dilemmas that elude easy resolutions. Pisces adore the passion plays of life! Instead of running from intense emotions and situations, they'll jump right in and join you in your feelings, wins, or conundrums.

Pisces believes in all things fantastic. And somehow, with them, life always is.

Pisces Is a Water Sign

Pisces is a Water Sign, which means they're quite emotional and sensitive. Most rely on their feelings over their intellects or even what's practical. Want to appeal to a Pisces? Communicate with feelings and passions they can tune into. And treat them with tenderness, as their feelings can be easily and deeply hurt. Pisces' main expression of their water energy is empathy and compassion. They love using their sensitivity and intuition to reach into others' psyches to think, feel, or experience what they do.

There's an "Old Soul" quality about Pisces—they seem to be able to understand and empathize with most everyone. You needn't try to hide anything from them—your pains and sufferings are just as interesting, maybe more so to Pisces, as your strengths and wins. "I feel your pain" is a Pisces motto.

Pisces' astrological symbol, two fish swimming in opposite directions, describes much about their complex nature. Pisces possess a duality wherein they feel pulled toward opposite urges concurrently. Some Pisces experience this as a need to indulge themselves in worldly offerings, yet pursue a spiritual life as well. Other Pisces feel a duality of ambitions—they'll lead one type of lifestyle and career while wondering if another would be more satisfying. At times, Pisces' duality can show up in their committing to one relationship while fantasizing about another.

Pisces' penchant for "swimming in two directions" can make it hard to figure them out. But it's hard for Pisces to figure *themselves* out, as well! Decisions and commitments can be rough for them. They think, *Why put limits around choices when there are so many possibilities? After all, won't they all lead to the same place in the end?*

Another factor that contributes to Pisces' complexity is their changeable nature. Pisces thrive when there's plenty of change and variety in their lives, and they enjoy spontaneous situations over orderly predictability. Pisces's egos and identities are very fluid and penetrable, which makes them seem chameleonlike. They have an unusual knack for identifying with both everything and nothing at all. Sound odd? Try being a Pisces!

Pisces' adaptability allows them to satisfy their spiritual urge of seeing the beauty and magic behind most things and people—even if they are as different as night and day. In fact, Pisces are mystics at heart: they look past the appearances of ordinary life, seeking the mystery of what's happening. They have an otherworldly essence: at times Pisces can be with you, yet seem to be somewhere else as well.

One way Pisces express their spiritual nature is through selfless service. They cherish the expansive feeling that comes from losing themselves in devotion to others. Pisces go to great lengths to rescue or redeem someone or something they think needs help, donating their time and resources to making matters better. This can be deeply fulfilling for Pisces: the more they let go of their own needs or preferences in

Pisces Lesson: Serving Their Own Spirit

✒ Pisces' spirits soar when they make the kind of sacrifices that lead to assisting others. But sometimes they can go overboard. Pisces' urge to help can be so compelling that they risk neglecting their own needs or the needs of their relationships in order to assist others. But that's not the kind of self-sacrifice that genuinely enlightens Pisces—it's just plain not taking care of themselves. Worse, it can lead to martyrdom. If that's happening with your Pisces, be a good friend and remind them that a key to their sign's happiness is realizing that true fulfillment comes from serving their own spirit. By taking excellent care of themselves and their own needs, Pisces become strong, stable, and clear. That's when Pisces are best poised to use their compassion to uplift and redeem themselves and all they meet.

order to assist others, the more they tap into strengths and qualities they never knew they had.

Pisces' self-sacrifice also comes from their "global identity" or need to make a significant contribution to their greater community in order to be personally fulfilled. Pisces' sense of "us" is usually greater than their sense of "I." As much as they want to feel safe and sound, they want everyone else to as well.

Pisces also express their mysticism through creativity. They regularly lose themselves in their imaginations, conjuring up alternative realities and possibilities for themselves and others. Pisces fantasize about people, other lives, ways things could look differently, and ways life could be different, just for the experience of fantasizing. In fact, Pisces are so impressionable and their imaginations are so vivid that they can sometimes fail to discern actual reality from what they are dreaming.

Look into Pisces' eyes and you'll often see them in a far-off place, dreaming.

Spirituality, drifting into fantasies, creativity, and service can be as much of a relief from the harsh realities of life as an avenue for Pisces' experiencing something more profound. Pisces certainly appreciate companions who help them step out of the ordinary, humdrum (if not painful) aspects of life into the more magical, impressive ones. You can lead them, or you can let them be your guide into something that's out of this world.

> ### Words Pisces Love to Hear
>
> ❧ "I feel a deep connection with you!"
> "You are spellbinding!"
> "I appreciate your depth and caring!"
> "I need your help."

What Pisces Want in Relationships and How You Can Attract One

Pisces want to feel a compelling connection with others. Pisces gravitate toward others with whom they sense a powerful exchange of something strong, deep, and meaningful. They want to feel that they are connecting so fully, so deeply, that they can lose themselves (and vice versa) in a wondrous union.

Pisces desire a "merging" kind of intimacy. Pisces don't seek "You-be-you-and-I'll-be-me" individuality in their relationships; they consider merging as the highest form of connectedness. They love melding their personal boundaries with another—even if it's in the boardroom! Pisces thrive on magical symmetry and want their companions to let go and feel it, too.

Pisces seek companions who are emotionally available, open, and safe. Pisces are in heaven when surrounded by others who let their guard down and reveal to them their soft and tender vulnerabilities. When that happens, Pisces will swim in to further the connection: Do you feel happy about something? Pisces will celebrate with you. Do you feel sad? They'll feel sad along with you.

Pisces love to be around exciting, successful people. Pisces want companions they can look up to or admire. They enjoy others' confident energy and successes. It's an honor for Pisces to participate in their companion's achievements and bask in their glories along with them. Plus, strong and adept companions reassure Pisces by bringing them an appreciated security.

> "Tell a Pisces what's on your mind, and they'll be sure to listen."

Pisces value those who come to them when they are troubled. Pisces understand pain. In fact, many believe that pain is the common denominator of the human experience. When you reveal the cross you're bearing to Pisces, they can better understand your humanity and feel even closer to you. Since Pisces like to feel they have something they can contribute, find a way for Pisces to help you. That'll make them feel needed.

Pisces are especially drawn to those who fascinate them. Pisces adore artists, dreamers, and visionaries. They thrive on the dramas, inventiveness, and surprising ideas that creative companions can elicit. If you have an interest in art, dance, or music, let Pisces know. Do you have unusual friends? Bring Pisces to your circle, and they'll blend right in.

Pisces appreciate encouragement and acknowledgment.

Although Pisces easily spot others' gifts and goodness, it's often difficult for them to be objective about themselves or to recognize the value of their contributions. This can result in insecurity in Pisces or a sense that they aren't measuring up somehow. When you reassure Pisces—perhaps by telling them why you love them so much or what they're doing that is so helpful or impressive to you—they're deeply touched and grateful.

> ## Words Pisces Love to Say
>
> 🐟 "We have a deep connection."
> "I feel your pain."
> "There is magic between us."
> "I'll rescue you."

Pisces are attracted to the mystery of someone who's emotionally unavailable, even stoic. Although Pisces generally thrive in relationships where emotions are easily shared, sometimes they can be drawn to the mysteries of someone who keeps their emotions locked inside. They may be curious about what lies beneath someone's stoic nature and want to discover their hidden secrets. Or they may sense something has been hurt in them and would love to heal and liberate them. Many a tough, wounded creature has a Pisces to thank for redeeming their hearts and wooing them out of their shell. In turn, a companion's stoicism can help Pisces develop a healthy distance from their feelings and passions.

Pisces treasure people with whom they can escape. Pisces love the feeling of escaping the boundaries of ordinary life. Many like to escape around water, or yearn for the release of a partying atmosphere. Other Pisces escape through art or music and gravitate toward others who enjoy them with the same abandon they do. Most Pisces don't need a formal setting to escape, however. Just create an atmosphere where they can feel they're getting away from it all—even if it's in front of the TV.

Pisces are also attracted to those they can rely on. Pisces can find everyday life daunting, if not simply annoying, and appreciate a partner who can be relied on to be reasonable and practical through thick and thin. This type of union helps Pisces relax, thanks to the security and solidity their practical partner provides. Pisces, in turn, can bring texture to a pragmatic companion's life and treat them to experiences they would have never explored without Pisces.

What Pisces Offer in Relationships

Pisces offer intimacy. Since Pisces love connecting with others in meaningful, even spiritual ways, they'll invest much, if not all, of themselves to make that happen. They'll release their boundaries, preferences, and point of views, and expose much of who they are so they can fully engage in a relationship.

Pisces expose their vulnerability in order to better connect. So they can connect with others, Pisces will open up and reveal whatever's inside, from their greatest joys to their deepest wounds—and they'll invite you to do the same. Pisces know how to create an inviting atmosphere that communicates, "You're safe with me." Pisces will reach out to you with a most caring touch and look at you with gentle, soft eyes as if to say, "I understand you and I feel for all you are going through."

Pisces have the ability to see things about you that even you can't see. Pisces will use their sensitivity to pick up on the depth and complexity of who you truly are. Their compassion and empathy not only give them insights into people's natures, they give them insights into why people do what they do.

Pisces seek to be tolerant, understanding companions. Another beauty of Pisces is they usually accept most anything others dish out.

> "Pisces have an amazing knack for making you feel good about yourself."

Pisces tolerate things that most people find annoying, just letting it slide right off their backs. "Oh that?" Pisces will say, "I don't let that get to me."

Pisces will believe you're doing the best you can—and that it is *enough*. Instead of believing that you should be trying harder to be perfect, Pisces will usually appreciate what you have done and who you have become. That kind of acceptance and support is priceless.

Pisces will be easily impressed and fascinated by you. Most Pisces tend to be impressed with others' abilities and accomplishments. When Pisces direct their admiration toward you, it can make you feel like a million bucks! They'll enjoy supporting you and helping you feel good about yourself. Pisces will laugh at your jokes and see the genius in your efforts, no matter how ordinary you might think they are.

Pisces offer an enticing sweetness. Pisces are not only disarmingly kind and gentle, they also ooze a sweetness that is downright enchanting! Plus, they exude a type of harmlessness that makes them feel safe to be around. Even when Pisces has tough feedback or bad news for you, they won't clobber you with it; they'll try to deliver it as gently and thoughtfully as they can to avoid hurting your feelings.

Pisces tend to be forgiving. Pisces are generally pretty darn good at letting go of others' trespasses. Maybe it's because they understand

> "Pisces want connectedness more than anything else in their relationships."

why people do what they do, or maybe because it's painful for them to feel separation between them and others. Or it might even be that Pisces isn't even sure someone has done them wrong. Pisces want connectedness more than anything else in their relationships. So when love is offered, forgiveness is easy.

Pisces take the high road in order to keep relationships afloat and happy. Pisces are typically easygoing companions who just aren't that driven to get their way, be right, or even defend themselves. They want to be included, more than anything. They'll yield their preferences, points of view, or ideas to accompany others in theirs. Even if a Pisces is very good at something, they'll allow someone else to try it their way, if that's what they want. As long as you can do it together, it's worth a try. In fact, Pisces rarely take bows or expect adulation for all the cool things they bring to their relationships. They might even forget they were the ones that brought the changes to the table! Pisces are more "connectors" than competitors.

Pisces offer support and empathy. Pisces don't stand on the sidelines of your life; they jump in and become as enmeshed and involved in it as you are. A Pisces friend will stay up all night worrying about your sick child or canvas the neighborhood to find your lost cat. Even if Pisces can't figure out how to fix your problem, they will certainly feel for you as you navigate through it.

Pisces' romanticism will make your life romantic, too. Spend five minutes with Pisces and you'll realize what essentially romantic creatures they are. Their rose-colored glasses imbue a dreamy quality to whatever you're doing together, even if it's balancing the budget. Pisces seek the romance of life: they'll be spellbound as they sit with you and watch the sun set. They'll cry at the movies (or even a tender commercial) with you.

Pisces offer a spiritual calmness. Pisces aren't as invested in this world or as pressured by its demands as other signs. Instead, their flowing stance dissolves demands and makes time float away. With their spiritual quality, Pisces know how to let problems go and appreciate the mystery of life, and they can help you do the same.

The Pisces Lover

*P*isces is the original and the shameless hopeless romantic! Nothing captivates them more than romantic love. After all, what better way to merge with someone than through beating hearts? When love is in the air, Pisces' gentle caring, attentiveness, tender compassion, and yielding sexuality all blossom and flourish. Romantic love is what Pisces most love sacrificing themselves to, and they devote themselves to their lover hook, line, and sinker!

Fantasies play a huge part in Pisces' romantic relationships, as they love losing themselves in dreams and anticipations about the magic that will unfold when they and their beloved meet in ecstatic union.

"Pisces don't mind pining for someone who's out of reach or somehow unavailable, even if it makes them heartsick. Suffering in the name of love is an honor to Pisces, and often intensifies devotion even more."

So give Pisces something to fantasize about. Instead of revealing all of yourself at once, let Pisces unwrap you with their own senses and intuitions. Pisces love the thrill of getting to know their lover in intimate ways never before explored.

Fantasizing about romance is so central to Pisces' nature that they spend as much time fantasizing about relationships that aren't happening as much as ones that are. In fact, Pisces have been known to carry on entire love affairs in their imaginations! They can see someone at a bus stop, start wondering what it would be like to be with them, and by the end of the day have the wedding completely planned.

If you are in a real-life relationship with Pisces, you'll likely be on the receiving end of their rich fantasies. Why not use that to your advantage and give them some positive things to fantasize about? A thought-ful note, a little gift slipped under their door, a look across the room that says, "I want you!" You don't need to be that elaborate—Pisces will fill in the details.

> "Pisces are known to be champion kissers."

Since Pisces love being the heroic rescuer, you might woo their heart by giving them something about you they could rescue. Let Pisces know how much you need them to save the day for you and how much you appreciate them as they do it. Helping you out of a dilemma is a perfect aphrodisiac for Pisces.

What kind of dates do Pisces enjoy?

Pisces enjoy enchanting escapes! Take Pisces to a captivating spot that inspires their imagination. Going somewhere around water is always a good idea. The ocean is the best, but a lake will do, or even a restaurant with a waterfall. Keep the lights down low (all the better for conjuring fantasies) and have some romantic music playing in the background. Cozy spots work best to make Pisces feel special and intimate. Depending on your Pisces' sensibilities, a little nectar of the gods (wine) might be just the thing that makes your moment complete. Wear something soft and fluffy, perhaps in quiet blues or sea greens. Remember that the place you take Pisces isn't as important as the connection you make with them.

What are Pisces like between the sheets?

When it's time for making love, Pisces' urge to merge is at its finest! Pisces are incredibly tender, attentive, facile lovers who are widely revered as champion kissers. Pisces know how to use lingering touches as a way of awakening pleasure centers in their beloved. There's often a passive quality about Pisces that appreciates your taking the lead. Fluff up the pillows, and wear something exquisitely romantic—even make it a little naughty. Ask Pisces what they fantasize about and do it, and they'll do the same in return.

What turns Pisces off?

Any type of gruffness hurts Pisces' sensitive feelings as do harsh words or actions. Too much emphasis on practicality or even "reality" bores Pisces and makes them run for more imaginative hills.

Ways Pisces Can Drive You Crazy and What to Do About It

$\mathcal{A}$s with every sign, some of Pisces' most endearing qualities can become frustrating if taken to extremes.

Pisces challenge: Sometimes they need a reality check.

$\mathcal{P}$isces can seem lost in a world of their own, one very different from yours. And they are. Pisces love indulging in their fantasies, but they can become so involved in what they are imagining is going on, or what should be going on, or what's probably going on somewhere else, they forget to pay attention to what is actually going on around them.

This dreaminess can skew their reality to the point they become convinced what's imagined is real, and they overlook the facts about what is truly taking place.

Needless to say, this can interfere with true intimacy. Pisces' pre-occupation with their own thoughts and feelings can keep them from participating fully with what's happening with you. Or Pisces can be so convinced they know what you feel or think that they might not bother to pay attention to what you actually do.

What to do?

One way to get a Pisces to notice the difference between what they're imagining and what actually is: ask, "Yes, but is it happening right now?" That way you don't discredit Pisces' dreams or discourage their imagination. You simply invite them to look at whether it is a current scenario.

Sometimes, however, Pisces just prefer their alternate reality and don't see the need or want to leave it. Companions of Pisces may need to learn to accept that Pisces just doesn't need or want to see life as they do.

And, because Pisces' boundaries tend to be so open and fluid, they might not realize if yours are not. Lovingly telling Pisces what you're open to and what you aren't will help Pisces understand you, respect your boundaries, and give you what you need.

Pisces challenge: Their feelings can go overboard and take you over, too.

Pisces can sometimes become so engulfed by the tidal waves of their own emotions that they lose sight of everything and everyone around them. They might lose interest in participating with those around them, and their signature compassion gives way to a self-involved focus that makes others feel isolated. It's easy for others to feel pulled under by them as well. Pisces might expect that their partners join them in their feelings and dilemmas as an act of loyalty.

Pisces can seem to make issues harder by hanging on too long to the pains or hurts of life, reliving them over and over, or perpetuating them by refusing to resolve the problem. This can frustrate companions and cause them to feel like they are being held hostage to Pisces' feelings and emotional dramas.

What to do?

How can you help a Pisces swim out from the undertow of overwhelming feelings? First, ask them if they want out. For some Pisces, being overpowered by feelings is not only acceptable, it's an enjoyable escape. But if Pisces' feelings are blocking you from relating to them, tell them. Remind them that you want to be a part of their world, and you want them to be a part of your world as well.

If you don't want to join Pisces in their feelings, let them know you understand how they feel, but that you choose to be the kind of friend who helps by remaining objective. (Pisces might not like that, but when they see you truly do care for them, even if you aren't crying along with them, they'll understand.) Then, go about your life. Maybe check in from time to time, but let Pisces work it out. When Pisces sees you are doing something interesting, they'll come around and join you.

No one else is responsible for helping Pisces come to terms with their feelings and hurts, just Pisces. Still, there is a way for you to help: let Pisces know you understand they're experiencing something difficult, and you want them to do what they need to do to take care of themselves.

Whatever you do, don't discredit Pisces' feelings by demanding they resolve them according to your time line. They might act like they're resolved, but inside Pisces is still suffering. Instead, let them know you honor their process. They'll treasure your understanding.

Pisces challenge: They can be excessively empathetic.

With their sensitivity, Pisces are often highly attuned to the harshness, disappointments, and cruelty in the world, and they can become deeply hurt over others' suffering. Whereas Pisces' companions might see this as overly dramatic or needless, Pisces do not. Their sense of connectedness means that if one is suffering in this world, then they are, too.

What to do?

*I*t helps if you encourage Pisces to consider that others' pain and difficult circumstances might be what they need to grow and develop in life or that there might be an important learning opportunity in their circumstances. Encourage Pisces to imagine what that could be.

Pisces challenge: They feel they're "the victim."

*O*ne of Pisces' greatest challenges is their sense of victimization. Pisces have a tendency to feel bullied by life. With their trademark sensitivity, they can interpret others' behavior as maltreatment, regardless of whether or not it was intended. Pisces' tendency to interpret themselves as victims can be so ingrained they may not recognize how they create, promote, or allow it. They don't realize that by refusing to stand up for themselves or by failing to maintain healthy boundaries, they are actually sacrificing themselves in a way that creates a victim-like dynamic.

Pisces might even believe that being the victim or sacrificing to the point of martyrdom makes them a good person, even a more spiritual person. Many a Pisces has taken the hit for something, allowed themselves to be blamed, or simply let others walk all over them because they felt like they were strong enough to endure it. This can be hard to watch in a Pisces you adore.

What to do?

*I*f your Pisces friend is feeling victimized by you or anyone else, talk it out. First acknowledge that Pisces does feel victimized. Ask what happened that was so painful. Try to empathize with how that could have hurt Pisces. Just being heard and understood might work wonders to help Pisces heal.

Even if you believe that Pisces is creating this themselves, it's smarter not to jump to the "You are bringing this on yourself" approach. You might lose Pisces if you do. Pisces might initially resist taking responsibility for their feelings, and instead believe you're trying to control them or discrediting their experience. Giving Pisces time to talk their feelings through helps them be more open to exploring their own role in creating this victim status.

Pisces challenge: They can have addictive tendencies.

There are times when Pisces just wants to escape it all and get lost in something greater than ordinary life offers. But if they don't find healthy ways to do so, drugs and alcohol can seem like attractive avenues toward finding the relief and magic they crave. Many Pisces' sensitivities gives them a propensity toward addiction.

What to do?

If you believe Pisces is escaping through drugs, alcohol, or any type of addictive behavior (even service), be very clear with them that it's not acceptable in your relationship. And perhaps remind Pisces that it's not going to take them to the place they're truly searching for. Instead, assist Pisces by pointing to the kinds of escape that help them access their inner spirit: a creative, spiritual, or service avenue that uplifts them. Show Pisces by your own example how amazing the uplifting, life-enhancing forms of escape can be.

Pisces challenge: They're expert deniers.

Denial—or refusing to acknowledge something is happening—can be another way Pisces escape unpleasant realities. Whereas some Pisces jump feetfirst into life's churning feelings, other Pisces do whatever they can to avoid them. They don't want to feel the pain that might come from dealing with challenging situations, so they don't.

What to do?

If you find your Pisces' denial interfering with your relationship, gently encourage Pisces to see whatever it is you think they're ignoring. Many times the best way to do this is to elicit compassion. When Pisces realizes their behavior is hurting you, they may be much more prone to listening to your concerns.

Pisces challenge: Their heads are in the clouds.

Since Pisces only have one foot in this world, they might not consider the demands and time lines of this world as important as you do. Many Pisces approach commitments as possibilities, not "must-do's." They believe that life is unpredictable, and they should take advantage of the surprising opportunities that pop up.

So even if Pisces did agree to be ready for a date at 7:00, if someone calls with interesting news, they want to be able to explore it with that person, even if it means they're not ready until 7:30. Or they'll forget to show up for a dinner date because they got lost listening to a beautiful piece of music. *That should be okay,* Pisces thinks. Needless to say, this can seem incredibly irresponsible to those who expect Pisces to stick to their commitments and do what they say they will.

What to do?

If you want Pisces to fulfill commitments with you, be clear about your expectations. It's always helpful to let Pisces know *why* something is important to you, too. And better yet, how they'd make you happy by doing what you expect of them. But in the end, you might have to give your Pisces a wider range of room to satisfy agreements than you do anyone else in your life. Pisces just don't believe that life should be lived according to any prescribed regimen.

Pisces challenge: They're elusive.

*D*espite being capable of deep, enchanting intimacy, there's also something about Pisces that eludes discovery. Many a companion of Pisces confides that they don't really know their Pisces, that they remain a mystery somehow. Maybe that's because Pisces are a mystery to themselves.

What to do?

*L*et's face it: there is something enigmatic about intimacy with a Pisces; one minute, they are intensely, completely yours, and the next minute, they're not. Relax: they'll be back.

Pisces challenge: They sugarcoat things at your expense.

*P*isces might tell you what you want to hear, even if they don't believe it themselves. Or they'll promise you something with little intention of fulfilling it. Usually it's to avoid disappointing or hurting you. Pisces figure if they appease you in that moment, it will be enough. They aren't thinking about the ruckus it might cause when they don't carry through.

What to do?

When trying to nail things down with Pisces, it's a good idea to try to get to the bottom of what Pisces really intend. Sometimes Pisces themselves are genuinely fuzzy about what they really intend to do while other times they struggle with ambivalent feelings that prevent them from being sure. A Pisces might not want to admit their true thoughts or feelings to you for fear you might judge them for it, or for fear they might hurt you. It's part of their escape routine.

Try assisting Pisces by creating a safe space for them to both figure it out and to tell you what they decide. Do they really want to become engaged? Do they truly intend to finish this project this Wednesday? If it's true, tell them you are willing to accept whatever they're willing to commit to. If Pisces believes that you are open to hearing the truth without judging them or having a meltdown, they might be more willing to be forthcoming about what they're really willing to do.

Pisces challenge: They enjoy a good dilemma.

Perhaps more than any other sign, Pisces have a knack for getting involved in conundrums. These can be difficult or even painful for Pisces and for you if the disaster is also affecting your life. But these situations can also be deliciously exciting for Pisces as well.

What to do?

*I*f you don't want to get caught in Pisces' dilemmas, step away when you see them coming. Let Pisces sail through the windstorms of their predicaments while you just get on with your life. Don't try to rescue Pisces, even if they ask you to. That will rob them from learning a lot about themselves and life.

Pisces challenge: They're gullible.

*A*lthough Pisces are wise and insightful, they have a gullible side as well. They can be taken in by a sob story or become mesmerized by someone's fish tales. Companions of Pisces might be stunned by some of the ways Pisces let themselves be tricked. Even if someone lies to them or takes advantage of them, the excitement of the ride may be worth the price Pisces has to pay.

What to do?

*Y*ou might encourage Pisces to be more careful and to strengthen their boundaries. Maybe they will, maybe they won't. There is only so much you can or should do. Let Pisces live and learn for themselves.

Summary:
Pairing Up with Pisces

• Understand Pisces' main motivation is to tap into imaginative worlds and fantastic feelings. Create the kind of magic connection Pisces crave.

• Be gentle and caring, and create a safe space for Pisces.

• By respecting their sensitivity and their (changing) emotions, you'll help Pisces open up to you.

• When seeking a change of behavior from Pisces, emphasize how happy you would be if they did so, and how it might make their world even more interesting.

Part Two:

Meet Your
Match

How Do the Signs Match Up?

This part reveals everything you need to know about how *your* astrological sign gets along with other astrological signs of the zodiac. Find out what you'll like about each other and how you can expect your relationship to flow.

To make it quick and easy to find if someone's sign is right for you, I've developed an easy-to-follow rating system:

At-a-Glance Compatibility Key

♥♥♥♥—exceptional compatibility: lots of chemistry, inspiring connections, and wonderful, fun-filled times

♥♥♥—above-average compatibility: delightful, communicative, friendly, and easy

♥♥—average compatibility: equal amounts of good times and challenges

♥—less than compatible: more annoying challenges than good times, takes (loads of) effort, but can be an interesting match

How Aries Match Up

The Aries / Aries Relationship ♥♥

A pair of Aries makes a terrifically dynamic duo—especially when they cooperate! Aries love the challenge and adventure of being with a powerful companion, so the excitement another Aries delivers can be downright spellbinding. Aries revel in one another's up-front intentions, bask in each other's gutsy willingness to take risks, and are captivated by their mutual overt sexuality. They instigate each other to continually seek new adventures and ideas, and spark each other to be the best they can be. "Let's do it!" is their relationship motto.

Being the same sign gives Aries advantageous insights into keeping each other interested and happy. They know how important action, novelty, and freedom are to their relationships. They also understand that, regardless of their confident exteriors, Aries companions also crave tenderness, reassurance, and a constant flow of affection. Aries smartly soothe the stings of each other's life's hurts by bringing up new adventures rather than deflating "I-told-you-so's."

Romance between two Aries is one spark-flying, sexually adventurous, explosive fighting—with awesome makeup sex—extravaganza. Each ravages the other with as much gusto and creativity as they can muster, relishing how their passions are more than matched and returned.

Possible Aries/Aries Challenges

As with all same-sign relationships, Aries can be too similar to get along. Their respective need to feel empowered by calling the shots and controlling matters can prompt explosive fights. Plus, since Aries believe they should get their way and are quite determined to do so, both can become annoyed with the other's vying for leadership.

When Aries don't trust that their partners have their best interest at heart, they can resist conceding anything, big or small, for fear it makes them seem weak. The result? A stubborn standoff. Says Aries One, "Why do you always think of yourself first?" Responds Aries Two, "Because you are always thinking of yourself first! Why don't you think of me first for a change?" Responds Aries One, "I'll think of you first after you consider me first!"

Aries' competitiveness can also get the best of their relationship. A win/lose challenge can be ignited wherein both Aries try to establish themselves as the winner, rather than as a giving or harmonious partner. At times Aries' fiery temperaments barrel into warring energies and powerful confrontations. Although Aries desperately need to be treated tenderly, they may find it hard to be tender if they feel challenged. Worse, Aries might block themselves from giving or receiving when they feel angry and resentful.

Aries can also encourage each other to become overextended if neither is willing to take a conservative, disciplined stance. Their impatient natures might egg each other on to jump into too many projects without either partner thinking matters all the way through.

Romantic problems can arise over Aries' jealousy and possessiveness. Both love to flirt and have plenty of freedom to explore, but expect their partner to be utterly devoted. Or, if each Aries suspects the other is selfish, they won't award their juiciest lovemaking prizes.

Advice for the Aries/Aries Relationship

Aries get along best when each feels potent and valued for their contribution. Identifying areas in which each Aries gets to be the respected leader works wonders to keep both happy and empowered. Plus, acting as one another's champion rather than competitor strengthens Aries' connections and solidifies trust. When both Aries admire each other, they are more encouraged to be their supportive and generous selves.

Along with encouraging each other's energy and power, Aries foster greater intimacy when they share gentleness and understanding.

Romantic problems can better be resolved when Aries replace their warring armor with loving amour and use affectionate sexuality to please and connect with their partners. Showing one another and the world that each other is number one keeps their trust and lusty passions burning high.

The Aries/Taurus Relationship ♥♥

*A*ries and Tauruses can enjoy a sensual and enjoyable relationship, especially when they adjust to each other's pace. They bond through their pursuit of the "good life" and all the lusty satisfactions that entails. Even their differences can prove complementary: Tauruses count on Aries to keep life moving with the swift adventurousness they themselves are too conservative to initiate, while Aries count on Tauruses to stabilize matters with the grounded sensibility they are too restless to pursue. Together they make a strong and productive pair who attain the dreams and desires that satisfy them and provide support and enjoyment to those they love.

Aries are soothed by Tauruses' calm demeanor and comforted by their steady reliability. They admire Tauruses' patience and feel assured by their loyalty. Tauruses' practical advice can build Aries' self-esteem as well as their bank accounts.

Tauruses are impressed with Aries' positive enthusiasm and enjoy their exciting energies. Aries' confidence increases Tauruses' security, and their moxie encourages Tauruses to take more risks. Aries awaken Tauruses' self-understanding and even their spirituality.

Romance between Aries and Tauruses is a captivating push-pull of the seductions and teases that both love and adore. Aries find Tauruses' luscious sensuality beguiling, while Tauruses are enthralled by Aries' powerful sexuality. Lovemaking is intimate and affectionate, as each instinctively knows how to satisfy the other's desires.

Possible Aries/Taurus Challenges

*A*lthough Aries and Tauruses are both passionate about their desires, what they desire and how they express passions causes friction between them. Whereas Aries are passionate about adventure and thrive on taking risks and initiating new endeavors, Tauruses are passionate about security and the comfortable status quo. Aries can dismiss Tauruses as stuck in the mud, while Tauruses write Aries off as impetuous dreamers. When each accuses the other as being (annoyingly) selfish, the impatient ram and stubborn bull lock horns.

Aries' drive to stir up something "new" gets derailed by Tauruses' conservatism. Tauruses' slow pace and thriftiness makes Aries want to scream with frustration, as does their concern over personal comfort and safety.

With their drive for stability, Tauruses resent Aries' constant rallying for change and (seemingly ill-conceived) innovative ideas. Plus, Aries are just too fast for Tauruses' tastes, and their tempers intimidate and hurt them.

Romantic problems arise when Aries and Tauruses believe the other is selfishly more concerned with pleasing themselves than each other. Aries' flirting makes Tauruses insecure, while Tauruses' materialism makes Aries suspicious they love their stuff more than them.

Advice for the Aries/Taurus Relationship

*A*ries and Tauruses get along best when they capitalize on each other's passions and desires. When Aries respect rather than override

Tauruses' careful pace and practical outlook, they'll not only relate better to Tauruses, they may learn to avoid jumping into matters unprepared and attain even more success. When Tauruses consider (rather than deny) the genuine possibilities in Aries' visions, they not only connect better with Aries, they may learn to capitalize on the opportunities life and Aries offer them.

Aries get the most out of Tauruses when they are patient and reliable. Understanding that building security *is* Tauruses' definition of excitement helps Aries look for secure successes that excite them both. Plus, Aries entice Tauruses by showing them how their own ideas and projects will yield Tauruses more of what they desire.

Tauruses appeal most to Aries by being lively and adventurous. When they understand that risky innovations *are* Aries' definition of security, they'll understand why giving them latitude to play and risk is so important. Tauruses entice Aries by showing interest in their ideas.

Romantic problems can better be resolved when Aries and Tauruses show attentive consideration of each other's needs. Affection, softness, and vulnerability keep both feeling loved and ignites their chemistry, which eclipses differences and reignites passions.

The Aries / Gemini Relationship ♥♥♥

*A*ries and Geminis can enjoy an exciting and delightful relationship that's full of friendship, laughter, and adventures. They bond through their high-energy enthusiasm for investigating new projects and their knack for keeping life fresh and interesting. Communication comes easily between Aries and Geminis. Their restless, freedom-loving, boredom-phobic natures keep their partners on their toes. Together they pursue the creative projects that satisfy them and captivate their wide social circle.

Aries' enthusiasms are fanned by Geminis' curiosity and brilliance. Aries especially adore that, like themselves, Geminis are ready for any adventure at any time and make most situations interesting. Geminis' many moods and expressions fascinate Aries, who think, *That's you right now? Okay! Let's run with it.*

Geminis adore Aries' magnetic exuberance and thrive on their gutsy initiative. Never knowing what Aries will pull next keeps Geminis' interests piqued. They love being able to say anything to Aries and have it understood, if not capitalized on. Aries are fascinating friends to Geminis, whose confidence reminds them the world is their oyster.

Romance between Aries and Geminis is exciting and daring as each provides a challenge, inventiveness, and playfulness that ignites the other's interest. Lovemaking is sometimes deeply sensual, other times breezy, but always affectionate and satisfying.

Possible Aries/Gemini Challenges

Although they are basically compatible, some differences between Aries and Geminis can cause problems. Aries are hotly passionate, instinctive, and love to compete and dominate. Geminis have a breezy refinement and take an intellectual approach to life. Aries can consider Geminis' detachment as lacking juice or fire, while Geminis can consider Aries' intensity too crude.

Geminis can be overwhelmed by Aries' passions, both physically and emotionally. Their combative all-or-nothing drives and their overt sexuality can seem unsavory to Geminis. Aries' favorite subject, themselves, can bore Geminis, who wish Aries would consider a wider range of topics.

Aries get frustrated by Geminis' hard-to-control independence, and Geminis' intellectualism leaves Aries feeling alone with their passions.

Sometimes Aries' and Geminis' youthfulness can overly indulge each other's irresponsibility. Emotional growth can be delayed if both ignore the uncomfortable feelings or situations that lead to maturity.

Romantic problems arise if Geminis consider Aries obsessed with sex and/or not communicative enough, or if Aries feel Geminis are more in love with their thoughts than they are with them. And since both are big flirts, jealousies can arise as each "circulates." Or, if each gets too independent, lovemaking can become a distant memory for both.

Advice for the Aries/Gemini Relationship

Aries and Geminis get along best when they capitalize on their natural friendship and relinquish any attempt to control one another.

Aries are smart to encourage Geminis to take personal time and give them occasional breaks from their intensity. Using dominating "I'm right!" strategies rarely convince Geminis of anything. Instead, Aries invite Geminis' cooperation by enticing Geminis' interest in what they'll learn and letting Geminis do things their own way.

Geminis get the most out of Aries by letting them know how important they are to them. Instead of bolting if Aries' energies get overwhelming, Geminis can build Aries' trust by letting them know they're still interested but need Aries to turn it down a notch or two. Geminis ignite Aries' interests in their ideas and projects when they show them how exciting they'll be, and how Aries will be tackling something no one else yet has.

Romantic problems can better be resolved if Aries provide the witty conversation that turns on Geminis, and Geminis sustain the sexual attentiveness that turns on Aries. When each makes it clear the other is number one, flirting becomes a nonissue, and lovemaking remains joyful and intimate.

The Aries/Cancer Relationship ♥♥

Aries and Cancers can enjoy a tender, yet dynamic relationship, especially when they make allowances for their different degrees of sensitivity. They can bond through their love of whipping up action, their pursuit of abundance, and their urge to satisfy personal desires. Even their differences can be complimentary: Cancers count on Aries' willingness to initiate things they themselves are hesitant to pursue, while Aries count on Cancers to show the kindness and nurturing they might feel but are uncomfortable expressing. Together they make a creative and adaptable pair who climb new mountains, then settle in and make them a home for themselves and the others they love and support.

Aries are nurtured by Cancers' tenderness and restored by their understanding. Aries respect how Cancers' tenacity and practicality ensures that life is safe (and paid for). Cancers' emotional depth awakens Aries to their deeper feelings.

Cancers are impressed with Aries' power and thrilled by their gutsy confidence. Cancers learn from Aries' self-assurance to be more brazen and direct. Aries not only open doors of opportunity for Cancers, they push them through.

Romance sings as Aries are the heroes of Cancers' fantasies, and Cancers are the adoring companions for whom Aries' trophies are worth winning. Lovemaking alternates from fiery lustiness to soothing tenderness.

Possible Aries / Cancer Challenges

Although Aries and Cancers are dynamic creatures, how they express their dynamism can cause sparks. Cancers are dynamic about nurturing and protecting, while Aries dynamically initiate and conquer. Cancers are emotional and sensitive, while Aries are bold and aggressive. Aries can consider Cancers overly protective crybabies, while Cancers dismiss Aries as insensitive barbarians. Plus, both expect to get their own way and can see the other as selfish.

Aries resent when conservative Cancers refuse to take risks that make life interesting. They're frustrated that Cancers put the kibosh on adventures or possibilities. Aries resent Cancers' reactive moodiness, thinking, *C'mon, Cancer, your sensitivity ruins all the fun!*

Cancers find Aries' hyperenergy and intensity overbearing, and want to retreat when faced with such rambunctious behavior. Cancers fear Aries' directness, and worse, their tempers, finding it extremely difficult to recover from their fiery confrontations. Aries' extravagance threatens Cancers' security, who think, *Aries risk too much and plan too little.*

Romantic problems arise when Aries forget the tender intimacies

Cancers need, or Cancers withhold the sexual daring Aries need. When Aries feel suffocated by Cancers' clingy control, or when Cancers feel scorched by Aries' temper or rebellion, lovemaking loses its spark.

Advice for the Aries/Cancer Relationship

Aries and Cancers relate best when they work with, not against, their differences. When Cancers consider how Aries' innovative ideas could make things better, they'll not only get along better with Aries, they might discover the satisfaction that taking their own risks provides. When Aries acknowledge Cancers' emotional and financial security considerations as valid, they'll not only appeal more to Cancers, they might discover how to better manage their own assets.

Aries appeal most to Cancers when they are gentle and thoughtful. Being respectful of their sensitivity and even revealing their own (gasp!) vulnerability opens Cancers' trust. Toning down their directness or enthusiasm helps Cancers to feel safer. Aries entice Cancers to go along with their ideas and projects by showing Cancers how they or those they love benefit by them.

Cancers are most attractive to Aries when they are more confident and expressive, even more adventurous. Cancers spark Aries' interest in their ideas and projects by showing them how innovative they are or how heroic Aries will be by helping. If Aries' temper surges, Cancers are smart to assert that they care, yet choose to step away from being on the receiving end of their furnace blasts. Both will respect that.

Romantic problems can be resolved when Aries extend the affection, patience, and loyalty Cancers need, and Cancers show the admiration, sexuality, and applause Aries need. Then their chemistry overrides differences and helps sparkling courtship resume.

The Aries / Leo Relationship ♥♥♥♥

*A*ries and Leos can enjoy a wonderfully powerful and energized relationship that's full of excitement and pizzazz. They ignite one another's leadership and confidence, and invigorate each other's sex appeal! Whatever Aries and Leos create, it's sure to be glamorous and rich in possibilities. They make terrific audiences for one another as they stoke the flames of each other's charisma through applause and laughter. Together, Aries and Leo are so attractive and compelling that others can't help but want to be a part of their world!

Aries respect Leos' dignity and rely on their strength for encouraging direction. They bask in Leos' bighearted attentiveness and delight in their entertaining flamboyance. Aries appreciate how Leos not only envision their ideas but work to make them a reality. Plus, Leos' discipline impresses Aries, who count on them to organize and pull off the biggest of plans.

Leos love the exciting ride Aries take them on. They adore Aries' compelling self-assurance and applaud their courageous heroism. Leos love that Aries are powerful enough to stand shoulder to shoulder with them, and exude enough savvy and innovation to capitalize on the attention and opportunities they create.

Romance between Leos and Aries is a fireworks display of the dramatic attentions, passions, and sexuality that consumes them both. Lovemaking is intense as each knows they have met their erotic match.

Possible Aries/Leo Challenges

Although Aries and Leos spark one another's excitement, their differences can easily explode into anger and resentment.

Since both are powerful leaders, neither is about to be dominated by the other. A fierce competitiveness arises over control or for the position of Top Dog. Or, if one feels the other isn't providing the proper applause or attention, roaring and posturing ensue.

Aries get frustrated by Leos' determined drive to secure things the way they see fit, especially when it's at the expense of the exciting risks Aries want to take. Aries resent how Leos stubbornly dismiss their suggestions or take sole credit for success they contributed to. Aries think, *How can I be the hero when Leos think they are?*

Leos resent Aries' restless urge to initiate new things, as it threatens their status quo. Aries' impatience irks Leos, as does their leaping into matters before thinking them through. They think, *Aries would be more successful if they'd just listen to my advice!*

Romantic problems arise if Aries neglect the attentiveness Leos need, or Leos forget the reassurance Aries need. When one or both fail to make the other feel fabulous or exalted, lovemaking is replaced by anger, then sulking and displeasure.

Advice for the Aries/Leo Relationship

Aries and Leos get along best by showering one another with attention and encouragement and harnessing their powers into projects big enough for the both of them.

When Aries value Leos' strategic advice, they'll not only better ingratiate themselves to Leos, they may enjoy being more successful. When Leos give Aries rein to do things their own way, they not only win their heroic support, they may gain some unexpected wins.

Aries appeal most to Leos by being confident yet reliable companions. Leos are attracted to Aries' power, but need to see their consistency and loyalty to trust them. Aries entice Leos' interest in their projects and ideas by showing Leos how glamorous they'll be or by asking for, then respecting, their help.

Leos best capture Aries' heart by being adventurous and flexible and by recognizing Aries' leadership. Aries love Leos' organizational strengths but hate feeling controlled by them. Leos ignite Aries' interest and cooperation when they show Aries how daring they are, or how Aries will be an impressive hero by tackling big projects.

Romantic problems can more easily be resolved when each showers the other with sincere attentiveness and admiration—and keeps the sexual fires burning. When Aries know they're Leos' favorites, and Leos feel exalted by Aries, lovemaking stays fiery.

The Aries / Virgo Relationship ♥

*A*ries and Virgos can enjoy a unique and creative relationship, especially when they understand they're nothing alike. They bond through their urge to make worthwhile contributions, their pursuit of intriguing subjects, and their love of taking part in situations of consequence. Even their differences can prove complementary: Aries are grateful that Virgos attend to the details they're sticklers for but hate tending to themselves, while Virgos appreciate how Aries' initiative stirs the excitement they love but are too proper to create. They make a dynamic and intelligent pair and innovatively tackle the important projects that satisfy them and inspire others.

Aries are enthralled by Virgos' keen intelligence and respectful of their refined class. They rely on Virgos' practical insights to help them avoid booby traps and realize their ambitions. Aries adore how Virgos are devoted supporters who let them handle the big picture while rarely stealing their thunder.

Virgos are impressed by Aries' innovative abilities and their confidence. Aries' enthusiastic encouragement gives Virgos confidence and pushes them through doors of opportunity they may be too humble to open for themselves. Aries are relentlessly exciting to Virgos, who find them deliciously impossible to analyze.

Romantically, Aries and Virgos make an unexpected, but interesting match. Virgos' intelligence challenges Aries, and their soft touch brings a sweet, even healing effect. Aries' confidence beguiles Virgos, and their sexual fire ignites a passion they're surprised exists.

Possible Aries/Virgo Challenges

Aries and Virgos are different in so many ways, it can be hard for them to get along. While Aries are bold, have big hearts, and love to push their limits, Virgos are careful, love dealing in details, and shun activities they don't excel in. Aries can dismiss Virgos as bothersome complainers, while Virgos write off Aries as clueless blowhards.

Aries can become stymied by Virgos' obsession with details, and their optimism can be squashed by Virgos' criticism. Virgos' insistence on doing things "perfectly" dampens Aries' spirits, and their focus on problems instead of what's working annoys Aries to no end.

Virgos can find Aries brutish and dismiss their dominating stance as rambunctious posturing. Virgos wish Aries would think things through more and boast less. Plus, Aries' rebuffing of Virgos' attempts to rein them in leaves Virgos feeling ineffective and unable to keep up.

Romantic problems arise when Aries lose amorous steam over Virgos' properness, or Virgos feel violated by Aries' impatient rushing to the finish. When Aries find Virgos too prudish or Virgos find Aries too lusty, each can lose interest.

Advice for the Aries/Virgo Relationship

It's best if Aries and Virgos capitalize on their gifts. When Aries recognize value in Virgos' analysis, they'll not only appeal more to Virgos, they might discover the insight their own analysis brings. If Virgos consider the actual possibilities of Aries' risky ideas, they'll not only appeal more to Aries, they might gain confidence in their own risk-taking. Loads of adjusting is necessary between them, but clever innovations can come as a result.

Aries get the most out of Virgos when they tone down their enthusiasm and show more patience and practicality. Virgos like Aries' exciting leadership but hate feeling out of control when it's too fast or impetuous. Aries entice Virgos by showing their reasonableness or asking for Virgos' help.

Virgos appeal most to Aries when they're confident and good sports. When they understand that it's Aries' job to stir things up to get them running, they better enjoy Aries' interesting ride. Virgos entice Aries by showing them how exiting or innovative they are, then letting Aries tackle problems their own way.

Romantic problems can better be resolved when each generously adapts to each other's tastes. When Aries are more thoughtfully refined and Virgos are more spontaneously lusty, lovemaking reminds them why they got together in the first place.

The Aries / Libra Relationship ♥♥

Aries and Libras can enjoy a fascinating relationship that's rich in the rewards and delights that come from the classic Mars/Venus (aggressive/harmonious) dynamic. They bond through their social interests, love of creativity, and stunning personal chemistry. Even their differences can prove compelling: Aries show the assertive, conquering, competitive traits Libras admire but feel uncomfortable expressing, while Libras express the peacemaking, beautifying, balancing qualities Aries respect but are too aggressive to show. Together they make an attractive and dynamic pair, one that initiates the excitements that satisfy them and entertains and inspires the many they include in their interesting social circle.

Aries are intoxicated by Libras' gracefulness and fascinated by their keen intelligence. Libras' compliments flatter Aries, while their soothing calm disarms their warrior stance. Libras' support makes Aries feel like a million bucks, even as they concede to Libras' every wish.

Libras are in awe of Aries' raw power and heroism. They're impressed with Aries' unabashed boldness and their ability to do and say outrageous and important things. Libras thrive on Aries' optimism and continual instigation of fun and excitement, and they appreciate how Aries give them courage to reach beyond their already-proven limits.

Romance between Aries and Libras is something to behold: Aries swoon, act heroically and watch beautiful Libras with admiration, while Libras, calmly accepting such attention, gasp at Aries' prowess and continually flirt to let Aries know they're desired.

Possible Aries/Libra Challenges

The qualities that most attract Aries and Libras can also drive them apart. Libras' need for peace gets disrupted by Aries' warriorlike strategies, while Aries' need for exuberant competition is thwarted by Libras' attempts to keep life fair. Aries fume that Libras care more about what others think than they do about them, while Libras dismiss Aries as selfish bullies.

Libras want Aries to be less brazen and quit disturbing others—mainly them. They cringe when Aries insult, challenge, or dismiss others and wish they would be more tactful. Libras crave more intellectual exploration of subjects Aries find dull, like the arts or moral issues. They think, *C'mon Aries, use a little finesse and think about something other than your own desires once in a while!*

Aries find Libras' concern about whether or not someone is going to like them frustratingly baffling. Unlike Libras, Aries' definition of fair is when they dominate and everyone else follows. Libras' indirectness infuriates Aries, who wish they'd say directly what they think and feel. Plus, Aries grow weary of Libras' indecisiveness: "Just make a decision!"

Romantic problems arise when Aries' inconsiderateness makes Libras lose amorous feelings, or if Aries lose their patience with Libras considering others more than them. When Aries are too aggressive or Libras are too indirect, the fireworks of their lovemaking fizzle out.

Advice for the Aries / Libra Relationship

Aries and Libras relate best when they use their opposite drives to complement, not compete with each other. When Aries respect the value of Libras' peacekeeping they'll not only be more appealing to Libras, they might learn how diplomacy helps them win even more in life. If Libras accept that Aries' directness has its own charm, they'll not only enjoy Aries more, they might also discover how asserting themselves can enhance, rather than deter, intimacies with others.

Aries keep Libras happiest when they display an effort to be charming and are kind around them. Toning down their warring antics, or curbing their outrageousness so they don't ruffle as many feathers within Libras' orbit, helps Libras relax and trust them. Showing Libras how their ideas and leadership promote Libras' wants and desires encourages Libras to support Aries.

Libras are smarter to support and applaud Aries, rather than attempt to polish them. When they let Aries be themselves, Libras will be surprised at how their undeniable charisma ends up winning hearts and friendships. Libras entice Aries' interest in their ideas and projects when they tell them how heroic they'll be by doing so.

Romantic problems can be soothed over when Aries use calm and consideration, and Libras cut back on insisting Aries do things their way. When Libras act as the gracious foil to Aries' power, their mutual chemistry develops into a sustainable passion.

The Aries / Scorpio Relationship ♥

Aries and Scorpios can enjoy one raw, powerful, and intense relationship, especially when they forget trying to control each other. Both are ruled by passionate Mars and can bond through the traits it gives them: their strong drives, urges to dominate, and sexual intensity attract each to the other. Even their differences can prove compelling: Aries love how Scorpios expose insights they don't have the patience to find themselves, while Scorpios admire how Aries display a frank openness they themselves are hesitant to reveal. Together they make a dynamic and magnetic pair, one that succeeds at astounding projects and in stirring up admiration in the many they attract.

Aries are captivated by Scorpios' power and sexuality and want to plunge into their mysterious depths. They admire how insightful Scorpios recognize opportunities like they do, yet also bring a patient, strategic savvy and stealthlike determination.

Scorpios' curiosity is piqued by Aries' overt power, intentions, and sexuality. They're impressed by Aries' fearlessness and admire their expressive moxie. Scorpios appreciate the expansiveness of Aries' positive enthusiasm and adore the excitements they bring to life. Scorpios see Aries as wild cards of potential they would love to develop.

Romance is hot and heavy as Aries deliver the intense sexual charge and Scorpios deliver an enticing, spellbinding seductiveness. Their strong personalities provide the challenge that keeps each attentive and makes for lovemaking full of wild fits of passion.

Possible Aries/Scorpio Challenges

Although Aries and Scorpios both possess intense passions, the ways they express them can provoke frustrations. Aries quickly move into interests, learn a little, and then move out. Scorpios move more cautiously and deeply, penetrating interests to the core. Aries seethe with impatience over Scorpios' analysis, thinking they're obsessing over inconsequential details or needless worries. Scorpios can dismiss Aries as too superficial to be interesting or too impulsive to trust.

Aries can become deflated over Scorpios' love of instigating and investigating problems. With their need to see life promisingly, they have little sympathy for Scorpios' complexity and emotional turmoil. Scorpios' stubborn resolve to not change a thing unless they choose to makes versatility-loving Aries want to scream.

Scorpios resent Aries' disruptive rallies for innovation and cringe with dismay that they don't look before they leap. Scorpios aren't impressed with Aries' chest-pounding assertions of greatness and refuse to support their childish self-absorption.

Romantic problems can arise if Aries' flirting with others humiliates Scorpios, or Scorpios prompt Aries' insecurity by making them jealous. When Aries pressure Scorpios to hurry to the explosive climax, or Scorpios resist Aries by insisting on lingering seductiveness, lovemaking turns frustrating for both.

Advice for the Aries/Scorpio Relationship

Aries and Scorpios get along best when they show loyalty and respect for each other's power and strategies. When Aries see the wisdom of Scorpios' planning for and anticipation of problems, they'll not only win Scorpios' respect, they might employ such thoughtfulness and find more success. If Scorpios acknowledge Aries' gutsy instincts as possibly brilliant, they'll not only get along better with Aries, they may discover the thrilling opportunities their own spontaneity offers.

Aries appeal most to Scorpios by using patience and deliberation. Instead of expecting Scorpios to think more positively, Aries are wiser to address Scorpios' concerns. Showing them specific ways their ideas and projects can work may help elicit Scorpios' interest and cooperation, as does giving them a sense of control by inviting and considering their input.

Scorpios get the most out of Aries by being adventurous, open, and encouraging. Understanding that Aries need to experience everything to learn, including failure, keeps Scorpios from trying to protect Aries from screwing up. Setting boundaries of what they can and cannot risk, and allowing Aries freedom to experiment with the rest, keeps Aries happy, interested, and cooperative.

Romantic problems can better be resolved when Aries show loyalty and patient seductiveness to Scorpios, and Scorpios show admiration and zesty sexual enthusiasm to Aries. That'll allow their unabashed lustiness and sexual chemistry to soar.

The Aries / Sagittarius Relationship ♥♥♥♥

Aries and Sagittarians can enjoy an outstanding mutual-admiration relationship, replete with fun, exploration, and excitement galore! They bond through their adventurous temperaments and a shared urge to fend off dreaded boredom by living life to its fullest. Aries and Sagittarians respect one another's need for freedom and encourage each other to grow. They agree that life should be fun and that their wishes should be indulged. Why suffer? Life is too full of amazing possibilities and special surprises.

Aries adore Sagittarians' largess and expansive natures, and are thrilled to join their many expeditions. Sagittarians' confidence reassures Aries and their approval keeps them strong and happy. Sagittarians' philosophical nature prompts Aries to consider the broader purpose of their lives and to make meaningful choices.

Sagittarians enjoy Aries' forthrightness and celebrate their passion and confidence. They relish Aries' penchant for spotting what's innovative and their knack for opening doors. Sagittarians also appreciate Aries' ability to capture their visions and run with them.

Romance between Aries and Sagittarians is passionately sexual one minute, playfully adventurous the next. Both act as the other's adoring sidekick and are independent enough to keep them captivated and involved. Lovemaking is exciting, enthralling, and satiating, as neither sees any need for inhibitions.

Possible Aries/Saggittarius Challenges

Although Aries and Sagittarians usually inspire each other's admiration, their differences can ignite immense annoyance. Sometimes it's their independence that's troublesome: if one even suspects the other is trying to control them or emerge as the dominating leader, fur flies. Or, each can get so wrapped up in their own interests or perspectives, they forget to connect or cooperate. Plus, if Aries' and Sagittarians' positive natures go overboard, and neither wants to bring up troubles, difficult issues can be left unresolved.

Aries' and Sagittarians' different philosophies can also spark problems. Aries define a purposeful life as doing what they want. They have little need to explain or justify their motivations, and they become insulted when Sagittarians insinuate they should. Sagittarians, however, need to feel they are pursuing a greater meaning. They like to present inspired reasons for their actions and feel disappointed when Aries won't agree on the same.

Aries get bored with Sagittarians' waxing philosophical and don't buy Sagittarians' declarations that their ideals are God's truth. They lose interest when Sagittarians' conversations get too theoretical or if they take themselves too seriously.

Sagittarians feel frustrated when Aries keep their insights too superficial and refuse to look at life's deeper implications. They wish that Aries would forget about themselves for a moment and consider the bigger picture. They also wonder why Aries makes everything a battle.

Romantic problems arise if Aries and Sagittarians resist making a commitment or if they define it in different ways. If Sagittarians don't make Aries feel important by exalting them to number one status, or if Aries' possessiveness makes Sags feel corralled, the wild gusto in their lovemaking turns tame.

Advice for the Aries/Sagittarius Relationship

The surest way Aries and Sagittarians keep each other perennially interested and happy is by remaining their authentic selves. When they stick to making life fun and demonstrating a mutual championship, they keep each other's hearts singing.

If Aries become impatient with Sagittarians' intellectualizing, instead of dismissing them with a yawn, they might let Sagittarians know they prefer discovering deep truths for themselves. Sags love Aries spicing things up with their gut-level take on life. Some things Aries say from the heart are tremendous inspirations for Sagittarians.

If Sagittarians should find their Aries companions too self-involved or inconsiderate, they're better off withholding judgmental attitudes and realizing that Aries' philosophy involves discovering themselves from moment to moment. Accepting that Aries don't need to aspire to anything more than they do helps Sagittarians relax and enjoy them.

Romantic problems get resolved when Aries and Sagittarians keep up their admiration, encouragement, and expression of love. Tending to their sexual fires and setting limits to flirting keeps both reassured and happy.

The Aries/Capricorn Relationship ♥♥

Aries and Capricorns can enjoy a fascinating and powerful relationship—especially when they cooperate with each other's leadership strategies. Both are powerful initiators who can bond through their drive for power and love of doing important things. Even their differences can prove complementary: Aries count on Capricorns to attend to the practical protocols they see as necessary but get bored doing, while Capricorns count on Aries to create the new activities they are too traditional to instigate. Together they make a strong and ambitious pair, one that builds impressive successes that satisfy them and win admiration from many.

Aries admire Capricorns' discipline and are impressed with how they see goals to completion. Aries respect Capricorns' accomplishments and learn from their vast, practical knowledge. Aries find Capricorns steady and sincere advisors who help them define and cultivate their abilities, professional or otherwise.

Capricorns are captivated by Aries' spirited leadership and fascinated by their brazen ways of pulling things off. They're moved by Aries' enthusiasm and refreshed by their directness. Capricorns love that, like themselves, Aries are big thinkers who offer confidence and encouragement.

Romance between Aries and Capricorns is unexpected yet sexy, as both take pride in being outstanding lovers. Aries bring lusty adventurousness while Capricorns deliver earthy sensuality.

Possible Aries/Capricorn Challenges

Control issues are likely to arise from Aries and Capricorns having such different leadership styles. Aries will and do try anything, especially if it involves risk. Capricorns are much more careful and do things the proper way. Aries think, "Take a chance!" Capricorns say, "Let's make a plan."

Capricorns' cautiousness drives impatient Aries crazy! Their discouragement of risks as too impulsive dampens Aries' spirits. Aries become deflated over Capricorns' stoicism and find it coldly self-denying when Capricorns delay pleasures until after tasks are accomplished. Aries grow restless with Capricorns' conservative regimens, thinking, "Why does everything have to be so organized?"

Capricorns wish that Aries were less impetuous and would just calm down. Aries' jumping unprepared into matters unnerves Capricorns and prompts them to consider Aries loose cannons they can't take seriously. Capricorns resist Aries' impulsiveness, believing they'll have to clean up after Aries' mishaps.

Romance can get dicey if Aries insist on spontaneity, while Capricorns insist on a proper time and place for affection. When Aries find Capricorns too inhibited or Capricorns find Aries too raw, or if each thinks the other is selfish about getting their needs met, love-making becomes cold and mechanical.

Advice for the Aries/Capricorn Relationship

Aries and Capricorns get along best when they show admiration for one another's power and strategies. When Aries recognize how Capricorns' careful planning wins trophies, they'll appreciate Capricorns more and perhaps even adapt their strategies to create even more success. If Capricorns acknowledge the ingeniousness of Aries' risks in reaching new status and territories, they'll not only appreciate Aries more, they might discover the opportunities their own spontaneity creates.

Aries appeal most to Capricorns by being practical. Accepting that

Capricorns' heroism is expressed through seriousness and caution helps Aries quit trying to loosen them up and to recognize the gallantry of their perspective. Slowly building Capricorns' trust is suggested, as is sharing with them facts or, better still, a plan.

Capricorns get the most out of Aries when they are flexible and adventurous. Releasing expectations that Aries should be reliable or mature helps Capricorns accept that Aries' idea of respectable accomplishment is keeping life edgy and moving. Enticing Aries with a "Let's make this exciting" or "I'd love your input!" encourages Aries' interest more than emphasizing duties.

Romantic problems can better be resolved if Aries honor Capricorns' sense of appropriateness, and Capricorns indulge Aries' need for inappropriateness in courtship and lovemaking. When each shows flexibility, trust builds and hearts open.

The Aries / Aquarius Relationship ♥♥♥

Aries and Aquarians can enjoy a truly stimulating and engaging relationship as they are kindred spirits in many ways: each is fiercely independent and decidedly individualistic, and neither sees any reason to live life conventionally. They bond by being each other's champions in reaching new heights of innovation of thought, expression, or lifestyle. Communication flows easily as each applauds the other's fresh ideas. Aries and Aquarians make an outstanding, sparkling pair, one that investigates the progressive subjects that satisfy them and contributes groundbreaking ideas to their wide social circle.

Aries applaud Aquarians' uniqueness and are thrilled by their visionary thinking. They enjoy being surprised by Aquarians' unpredictable antics and find their independence a refreshing challenge. Aquarians make natural friends to Aries, who assist them in realizing dreams or introducing them to fortunate alliances.

Aquarians are wowed by Aries' outrageous style and love being part of their excitement. Aquarians admire Aries' fortitude, appreciating how they honor their gut instincts rather than being shackled by others' opinions. They also love how Aries not only understand their ideas but run with them.

Romance between Aries and Aquarians alternates between being steamily sexual one minute and playfully friendly the next. Their independent natures keep their mutual interest engaged and their love-making spontaneous and creative.

Possible Aries/Aquarius Challenges

Although Aries and Aquarians are both visionaries, what their visions involve can cause friction. Aries' visions are focused on what they can personally achieve, while Aquarians' visions are focused on global possibilities. Aries might feel envious of Aquarians' devotion to causes, thinking they're more important to Aquarians than they are. Aquarians can find Aries too self-involved and want them to consider the bigger picture.

Passionate Aries can feel lonely around objective Aquarians or abandoned by their aloofness. They long for Aquarians to single them out as special, which rarely happens. Aries wish Aquarians would use their instincts more and mental theories less. Aquarians' logical resistance of jealousy, anger, or other feelings leaves Aries thinking, *How can I connect with Aquarians if I can't get a rise out of them?*

Aquarians find Aries' passions overly intense and their tempers off-putting. Aries' conquering hero tendencies seem unrefined to Aquarians, who prefer intellectual conversations over swashbuckling action. Aries' refusal to value researched facts over their own instincts leaves Aquarians wondering, *Can't they have an educated thought?*

Romantic problems can arise from Aries needing a constant sexy dynamic, while Aquarians prefer breaks from amorous exchanges. If Aries resent being treated more like friends than lovers or Aquarians rebel from Aries' possessiveness, lovemaking becomes distant.

Advice for the Aries / Aquarius Relationship

Aries and Aquarians stay happiest by nurturing their natural friendship and forgetting about control of any kind. When Aries acknowledge the value of Aquarians' causes, they'll not only relate better to Aquarians, they might become inspired to make worthy contributions of their own. If Aquarians see value in Aries' promoting themselves first, as well as their fighting for principles, they'll not only appeal more to Aries, they may discover that taking care of themselves is empowering and that one person can make a difference.

Aries get the most out of Aquarians when they are logical and socially conscious. Interpreting Aquarians' objectivity as their expression of passion helps Aries feel less lonely and more interested in the clarity it offers. Aquarians are more open to Aries' ideas when Aries don't push them, but rather present them factually and neutrally, and enlist their unique practicality.

Aquarians bring out the best in Aries when they are flexible and pas-sionate. Instead of expecting Aries to be more global, Aquarians might notice how their personal motivations end up working to resolve big-ger matters. Aquarians elicit more of Aries' heroic cooperation when they fortify Aries through applause and personal acknowledgment.

Romantic issues are better resolved when Aries allow space for Aquarians' amorous breaks and friendships, and Aquarians remind Aries that they're special and remain emotionally available to them. When both establish camaraderie and trust, sexual intimacy is easy and delightful.

The Aries/Pisces Relationship ♥♥

Aries and Pisces can enjoy an inventive and unique relationship, especially when they accept how different they are. They can bond through their urge to make life romantic and extraordinary. Even their differences can prove complementary: Pisces count on Aries' assertiveness to conquer life and promote their dreams, while Aries count on Pisces' compassionate, imaginative gentleness to bring a sense of calm or spiritual perspective. Together they make a dynamic, yet caring pair, one that explores the interesting subjects that satisfy them and offers unique perspectives to the many they love.

Aries' warrior stance is empowered by Pisces' yielding support and soothed by Pisces' kindness. Aries' imaginations are stoked by Pisces' creativity and enlivened by their wondrous fantasies. Aries find Pisces understanding counselors whose wisdom helps them direct their heroic strengths.

Pisces are captivated by Aries' raw energy and bravado. They love Aries' unpredictability and relish the excitement of Aries' wild antics. Aries encourage Pisces to develop more of their own abilities and to grow by asking for what they truly desire.

Romance between Aries and Pisces is a swooning delight. Pisces love being hopelessly beguiled by Aries' raw sexuality and enjoy surrendering to their powerful command. Pisces' sensuality transports Aries to another galaxy. Lovemaking is passionate and creative as neither holds anything back.

Possible Aries/Pisces Challenges

Although Aries and Pisces are zodiac neighbors, their differences can make them feel universes apart. Aries like to stand out and love being the winner. Pisces' malleability loves merging with others and enjoys surrendering to serve the greater whole. Aries' youthfulness approaches everything like it's new and exciting, while Pisces' feel like an "old soul" who's already seen it all.

Aries can consider Pisces' emotions as too gushy and their fantasies as cop-outs. They mistake Pisces' gentleness as weakness and feel unchallenged. Aries cringe when Pisces take on others' pain and suffering, thinking it's needless martyrdom.

Pisces are overwhelmed by Aries' intensity and hurt by their combative stance. They wish Aries would be more considerate of others' feelings. Pisces are mystified about why Aries make everything a contest, and consider Aries' self-promotion unevolved.

Romantic issues arise if Aries are too aggressive or rough for Pisces' gentler romantic tastes, or Pisces are too passive for Aries' dynamic ones. If Pisces feel Aries are selfish about getting their needs met, or if Aries feel eclipsed by Pisces' emotional indulgences, lovemaking becomes scarce.

Advice for the Aries / Pisces Relationship

*A*ries and Pisces fare best by valuing the other's dispositions. When Aries respect how Pisces' self-yielding strategy leads to an even more empowered self, they'll not only respect Pisces more, they might discover the rewards their own sacrificing offers. If Pisces acknowledge that Aries' driving self-interest is a worthy avenue of spiritual discovery, they'll not only like Aries more, they may learn how taking care of themselves makes them a more effective caretaker of others.

Aries appeal most to Pisces when they are gentle and caring. Instead of expecting Pisces to show the kind of dynamism they do, Aries might look to see how their imaginative ways create enchanting dynamics all their own. Aries entice Pisces' cooperation by showing Pisces how helpful or needed they'll be, which ignites Pisces' heroism.

Pisces get along best with Aries when they're assertive and alert. Understanding that Aries are designed to compel, not comfort, others helps Pisces learn to develop their own empowered resourcefulness. When Pisces use their compassion to look past Aries' rambunctious natures, they'll discover the sweet soul underneath.

Romantic problems are better resolved when Aries maintain a sweet tenderness and consider Pisces' feelings, and when Pisces show a lusty attentiveness that makes Aries feel important. When Aries are more yielding and Pisces are more aggressive, their lovemaking becomes the wondrous connection both dream of.

How Tauruses Match Up

The Taurus/Aries Relationship

See The Aries/Taurus Relationship on page 290.

The Taurus/Taurus Relationship ♥♥

Two Tauruses can enjoy a wonderfully supportive relationship that's rich in comfort and understanding, especially when they keep growing. They bond through their pursuit of security, zest for acquiring valued things, and enjoyment of sensual pleasures. Whatever Tauruses do together they'll enjoy, even when their industrious natures work very hard at it! They make a reliable, productive pair, one that builds tangible successes that satisfy them and provide practical, yet gentle, support for all they love and nurture.

Tauruses love in each other what they like most about themselves:

serene kindness, practicality, loyalty, and goofy humor. Tauruses know how much they hate to be pushed or overly challenged, so they create a comfortable, patient atmosphere for one another. They agree on setting routines and boundaries that keep unexpected surprises from threatening their reliable status quo. Tauruses also agree that life should be full of earthy delights and they pursue them together, endlessly.

Romance between Tauruses is never hurried, always sensual. Each extends the enticing delights and lingering seductions that make courtship pleasurable and comfortable. Sexuality is natural and loyal as each loves giving and receiving the luscious, attentive affection their sign specializes in.

Possible Taurus/Taurus Challenges

As with all same-sign relationships, Tauruses can be too alike to get along or to keep each other interested. Sometimes, just their hesitancy over making the first move keeps them apart. Other times, Tauruses' head-butting stubbornness makes things rough.

A contest of wills can develop over which Tauruses' needs, wants, or fears should be honored. Each holds out for getting what they want and deflects the other's requests. Worse, if they suspect the other is acting inconsiderately or selfishly, Tauruses respond by digging in their heels.

In the name of staying secure, Tauruses can put off the life-enhancing adventures and changes that encourage growth. One bull might say, "Hey, I hear there's greener grass over in the next pasture, let's go get it." But the other responds, "What? And leave this pasture that we know so well?" "You're right: this field *has* been good to us."

Tauruses can so fear that change of any kind will result in loss that they keep their life together in a "safe" standstill. Or, if one Taurus does want change, the other's resistance to it can prompt resentment. Sometimes both Tauruses want change, but neither has the gumption to initiate it.

Making up after disagreements can also be slow between Tauruses. If one or both believes it's a sign of weakness to give in or apologize, or resists forgiving and forgetting for fear it might open them to being hurt again, resentment can fester.

Romantic troubles can arise if one or both Tauruses feel they're not receiving the affection or support they deserve or find it difficult to forgive hurts. When resentment or withholding takes the place of trusting affection, lovemaking becomes distant and lonely.

Advice for the Taurus/Taurus Relationship

A Taurus/Taurus relationship flourishes when each remains open and flexible. Broadcasting a clear "I value you!" message also helps, as does demonstrating genuine effort to satisfy each other's desires.

Changes might have to come slowly between two Tauruses in order for each to maintain their sense of sure-footedness. But introducing new ideas with patience and understanding works best, as does showing all the practical, tangible ways plans or new ideas can work and make things better. Clarifying and honoring Tauruses' limits of what they can and cannot risk also helps each feel more open to trying new things.

Kind words and gestures also keep Tauruses happy and cooperative. If appropriate, affection is a terrific comfort and motivator. Gratitude? Invaluable. When each Taurus feels and expresses their appreciation for the other, both stay aware of the value of the relationship.

Romance problems between Tauruses are most easily resolved when attentive affection, kindness, and sexual generosity is kept flowing. When they know how much they're loved and desired, Tauruses move mountains to overcome problems.

The Taurus/Gemini Relationship ♥♥

Tauruses and Geminis can enjoy an engaging and adoring relationship, especially when they accept their different styles of seeking fulfillment. They bond through their love of living life for "now" and their drives to satisfy personal desires. Even their differences can prove complementary: Tauruses count on Geminis' flexible adventurousness to stir up excitements they are too careful to create, while Geminis rely on Tauruses' solid reliability to handle the practical concerns they find too boring to attend to. They make a youthful and instinctive pair, one that creates the innovative projects that satisfy them while entertaining and supporting the many they love.

Tauruses admire Geminis' freewheeling breeziness and respect their brilliance. They love how Geminis keep life spicy by opening new doors and even pushing them through the doors. Geminis' wit tickles Tauruses' funny bone, and their encouragement builds Tauruses' self-esteem and other important resources.

Geminis respect Tauruses' stick-to-itiveness, and become captivated by their sensuality. They love how Tauruses' admiration inspires them while their loyal consistency grounds them. When life gets too complex, Tauruses' practical wisdom reassures Geminis and makes their world simpler again.

Romance between Tauruses and Geminis is as playful and sensual as teenagers. Each offers the enticing seductions and nuanced affection that keeps courtship lively. Lovemaking is special and full of surprises.

Possible Taurus/Gemini Challenges

Although Tauruses and Geminis both enjoy pursuing personal desires, what they desire and how they pursue it can spark friction.

Tauruses desire a life that's solid and predictable while Geminis desire a life of variety and adventures. Tauruses get annoyed by the risks, inconsistencies, and even the intellectualizations Geminis adore, wishing Gemini would just settle down and accomplish something useful. Geminis feel limited by the routines, precautions, and security Tauruses enjoy and wish Tauruses would break free and do something surprising.

Tauruses dismiss Geminis' flitting from one interest to another as flighty and see their risk taking as irresponsible. Geminis' spontaneity and changeable nature unnerves Tauruses, who value steadiness over novelty any day. Tauruses get suspicious over Geminis' wanderings. Plus, Tauruses aren't impressed with the ideas Geminis incessantly talk of but do nothing about.

Geminis get bored with Tauruses' consistent ways and resent that they won't make a move until they're good and ready, which seems like forever! Tauruses' black-and-white thinking seems too narrow, making Geminis wish they'd be more curious and inventive. Geminis resist being tethered to their practical demands.

Romantic problems arise if Tauruses feel threatened by Geminis' wanderings or ambivalence over commitment, or if Geminis feel limited by Tauruses' slower pace or demands for a commitment. When Geminis' inventive and intellectual sexual tastes clash with Tauruses' earthier ones, lovemaking becomes frustrating.

Advice for the Taurus/Gemini Relationship

Tauruses and Geminis get along best when they capitalize on each other's gifts and strategies. When Tauruses value Geminis as innovative "idea people," they'll not only appreciate Geminis more, they might appreciate the pleasures their own spontaneity and inventiveness provide. When Geminis take interest in Tauruses' practical perspective, they'll not only be more fascinated, they might discover the rewards stability and productivity bring.

Tauruses appeal most to Geminis when they're curious and flexible. Understanding that Geminis' idea of security is having plenty of options helps Tauruses understand Geminis' restless wanderings. Tauruses needn't try everything Geminis do, but giving Geminis freedom to roam and explore keeps Geminis happier and more cooperative with the practical requests Tauruses make of them.

Geminis get the most out of Tauruses when they're practical and patient with them. Geminis entice Tauruses' cooperation with their ideas and plans by presenting them with ways they can work. Matching their words with concrete actions and keeping agreements also helps Tauruses understand and trust Geminis more.

Romantic problems can better be resolved when Geminis show Tauruses they're loyal and focused on pleasing them, and Tauruses show

Geminis surprises and adventures. When Tauruses talk a little more and Geminis talk a little less, their sexuality remains steamy and satisfying.

The Taurus / Cancer Relationship ♥♥♥

Tauruses and Cancers can enjoy an incredibly comfortable, secure, and rewarding relationship wherein both feel supported and appreciated. They bond through their urge for safety and security, love of satisfying personal desires, and enjoyment of simple and luxurious pleasures. Their easy communication makes each feel understood and valued. Together these snuggly creatures pursue the personal indulgences that satisfy them and provide comfort and support for all they love.

Tauruses relish Cancers' fussy nurturing and adore their bubbly, sometimes kooky personalities. They count on Cancers' emotional support and ability to provide a cozy atmosphere. In Cancers, Tauruses have supportive confidants who value security as they do, yet encourage them to keep reaching for more.

Cancers admire Tauruses' strength and relish their practical, can-do approach to life. They relax in the guarantees of Tauruses' loyalty and determination. Cancers adore accompanying Tauruses in their sensual activities and possessions, feeling deliciously safe under the warm blanket of their reliability.

Romance is affectionate and luscious as Tauruses and Cancers genuinely enjoy each other's personality, sensuality, and loyalty. Touching, caressing, and sexuality are natural and easy in this relationship.

Possible Taurus/Cancer Challenges

*A*lthough Tauruses' and Cancers' similarities usually unify them, sometimes they work to pull them apart.

Since Cancers and Tauruses believe their needs should be met and their strategies for security followed, conflicts can develop when each wants different things or seeks security in different ways. Both might cling tenaciously to their own desires while complaining the other is behaving selfishly. A resistant withholding can take place wherein no one gives an inch unless they get what they want first.

Tauruses' and Cancers' penchant for worrying about security can also get the best of them. Fears over lack—of money, love, or anything else—can prompt them to resist making changes that lead to growth. This keeps them locked in limiting patterns or situations.

Plus, Cancers' emotions are intense and immediate, and they expect Tauruses to acknowledge and understand them. But Tauruses' emotions are more balanced. They can dismiss Cancers' need for emotional exploration and hunker down to doing what's practical.

Cancers get hurt that Tauruses are unfeeling or uncaring when they don't indulge their feelings or claim they lack depth. Sometimes they intensify their emotions to get a rise out of Tauruses, who shut down in response.

Tauruses can become frustrated around Cancers' insistent emotional promptings, claiming they are being childish or manipulative. They wish that Cancers would just attend to their own feelings and leave them be.

Romantic problems arise if either suspects the other is withholding the love or attention they deserve. When each responds with an "I don't need you either," stubbornness and aloofness takes the place of affection.

Advice for the Taurus/Cancer Relationship

Tauruses and Cancers get along best when each remains respectful and supportive of the other's security and emotional needs, and gives and receives in equal measure. Plus, adding a dash of risky initiative keeps life exciting.

Tauruses appeal most to Cancers by staying flexible and emotionally available. They needn't join in all of Cancers' feelings, but it helps if they consider what their emotions are pointing to. That not only elicits more of Cancers' trust and intimacy, it might awaken Tauruses to the wisdom their own emotions provide. That interests Cancers even more.

Cancers are most attractive to Tauruses when they keep their emotions fairly even or express them in a way in which Tauruses can practically respond. When Cancers demonstrate tangible attempts to support Tauruses, Tauruses are more open, flexible, and willing to indulge Cancers.

Romantic differences between Tauruses and Cancers are most easily resolved when kindness, affection, and caring are kept flowing, no matter what. When each is assured the other loves and cherishes them, they're more willing to move mountains to please the other.

The Taurus / Leo Relationship ♥♥

Tauruses and Leos can enjoy a dynamic relationship that's exciting, yet stable, especially when they remain flexible. They can bond through their strong drives, love of luxurious pleasures, and urges to build something of value. Even their differences can prove complementary: Tauruses count on Leos' flamboyant enthusiasm to create the excitement they love but are too conservative to generate, while Leos count on Tauruses' practical realism to provide the groundedness they respect but are too flashy to attend to. Their determinations make them an unstoppable force, one that creates successes and provides stability for the many they love.

Tauruses are thrilled with Leos' fiery dynamism yet assured by their bighearted loyalty. They love that, like themselves, Leos also strive for consistency, yet bring panache to make things glamorous. Tauruses love basking in Leos' adoration and use Leos' savvy fortitude to gain confidence to pursue their own ambitions.

Leos relish Tauruses' consistency and support and admire their rocklike strength. They respect how Tauruses don't wilt in the presence of their powers and feel freer to express themselves as a result. Leos rely on Tauruses' practical advice, which steers them toward success but rarely steals their spotlight.

Romance between Tauruses and Leos is sensual and powerful with tidal-wave-like dramas. Each provides the attentive seductions, sexual intensity, and loyalty the other needs to feel loved and desired. Lovemaking is lusty and luscious as each relishes giving and receiving maximum pleasure.

Possible Taurus/Leo Challenges

*A*lthough Tauruses' and Leos' strengths spark attraction, they can also ignite exasperating clashes of will. Often it's over risk taking: Leos' fiery temperament prompts them to stay challenged by pushing past their established limits, while Tauruses prefer to leave well enough alone and enjoy what's cozy and familiar. Leos fume that Tauruses are resistant bores, while Tauruses smolder that Leos are pushy tyrants. When each feels the other is denying them what they want, a stubborn standoff ensues.

Tauruses' comfort zone gets usurped by Leos' drive for expansion, and they feel exhausted by the drama. They tire of Leos' need for applause and wish they would think of them more. Tauruses resent Leos' extravagant treating of themselves and others to opulent gifts and indulgences, thinking, *You'd be just as lovable if you stuck to a budget!*

Leos' sense of grandness gets deflated by Tauruses' security worries. They resent when Tauruses seem more loyal to their materialism than to them. Leos dismiss Tauruses' needs as selfish or shortsighted, and want to override them. Tauruses' predictable routines seem boring to Leos, who think, *You'd be more exciting if you took some action!*

Romantic problems arise if Tauruses resist Leos' need for indulging attention, or Leos resist Tauruses' need for tender wooing. When Tauruses lack the exciting passions of Leos' tastes, or if Leos' are too dramatic or intense for Tauruses', lovemaking can become frustrating for both.

Advice for the Taurus/Leo Relationship

Tauruses and Leos get along best when they capitalize on each other's strengths. When Tauruses allow room for Leos' creative risks, they'll not only recognize the savvy practicality Leos possess, they may discover the delights of their own spontaneous gumption. If Leos cooperate with Tauruses' conservative strategies, they'll not only benefit from their carefulness, they may discover how being more cautious helps direct their power even better.

Tauruses are most attractive to Leos when they're adventurous. When they shower Leos with applause, Leos will reciprocate with cooperative generosity. Tauruses better trust Leos' flamboyant risk taking by remembering that Leos rarely squander resources.

Leos appeal most to Tauruses by staying practical. Understanding how Tauruses show appreciation via practical actions and loyal support helps Leos let go of expectations of grander expressions. Tauruses are more cooperative with Leos' ideas when they introduce them patiently and show pragmatic ways they'll enrich Tauruses.

Romantic problems can better be resolved when Tauruses provide the glorious courtship Leos desire, while Leos provide the bighearted sweetness that melts Tauruses. Generous declarations of love ensure the bedroom will stay energized and satisfying.

The Taurus/Virgo Relationship ♥♥♥♥

Tauruses and Virgos can enjoy a terrifically warm, compatible, and productive relationship rich in satisfactions for both. They bond through their practical views, industrious resourcefulness, and love of physical pleasures. Their easy communication and shared values keep them interested. Tauruses and Virgos enjoy one another's company immensely as they work together to accomplish useful projects and provide a support foundation for all they love and serve.

Tauruses admire Virgos' reliable efficiency and take comfort in their excellent judgment. They find Virgos' analytical intelligence witty and entertaining, and they appreciate how Virgos help them expand ideas while still making them feel valued and secure. Tauruses enjoy Virgos' exquisite taste and worldly savvy. They trust that when Virgos promote change, it's for something better.

Virgos admire Tauruses' rock-solid strength and dependable practicality. They find Tauruses' simplicity refreshing and feel soothed by their patience. Tauruses' inner calm and sensuality help Virgos ease off their driving perfectionism and enjoy the splendors of life.

Romance comes naturally and easily between Tauruses and Virgos. Tauruses know how to tastefully awaken Virgos' sexuality, which they in turn lavish on Tauruses in a rich, trusting, take-all-of-me way.

Possible Taurus/Virgo Challenges

Although Tauruses and Virgos share Earth Sign compatibility, their individual focus and strategy for pursuing pleasures cause friction. Tauruses focus on activities that bring them comfort, but Virgos focus on activities that improve something. While Tauruses pursue material and sensual indulgences, Virgos receive pleasure from a job well done. Tauruses can find Virgos oddly pleasure-denying and think, *C'mon, Virgo! Relax and have some fun!* Virgos can believe that

Tauruses are selfishly hedonistic and think, *You'd accomplish even more if you'd apply yourself!*

Tauruses become exhausted by Virgos' incessant busyness. They resent Virgos' requests for help in attending to details and organizational chores. Virgos' sharp criticisms sting Tauruses, and their perfectionist expectations defeat their confidence.

Virgos feel thwarted by Tauruses' "It's fine the way it is—don't change it" stance. They wonder why Tauruses accept so much at face value instead of joining them in the mental explorations they enjoy. Virgos find Tauruses' predictable routines unimaginative and wish they'd be more zestful and adaptable.

Romantic problems arise if Tauruses believe Virgos value their work too much, or Virgos believe Tauruses value their own comforts more than their relationship. Or, should one or both make practical concerns more important that loving attentiveness, intimacy becomes just another duty.

Advice for the Taurus / Virgo Relationship

Tauruses and Virgos are happiest when they pursue things they both enjoy and humor each other's needs. When Tauruses understand that Virgos feel happiest while being productive, they'll not only better accept their busy schedules, they might discover the pleasurable rewards of organizing. If Virgos acknowledge Tauruses needn't strive for perfection in order to excel, they'll not only respect their strategies more, they may learn how being easier on themselves enhances their bodies, minds, and spirits.

Tauruses are most appealing to Virgos when they're alert and flexible. Letting Virgo in on their goals and aspirations is another way Taurus can attract them. If they simply listen to Virgos' critical observations without taking them personally, Tauruses will give Virgos what they want: the satisfaction of being heard and understood.

Virgos get the most out of Tauruses by being attentive and kind. When they show Tauruses appreciation through encouraging words, Tauruses melt. Knowing their efforts are valued makes Tauruses more enthusiastic about moving, growing, and changing to please Virgos.

Romantic problems can be minimized if Virgos show Tauruses affection and encouragement, and Tauruses give Virgos the adoring appreciation they need to feel loved. When Virgos shower Tauruses with their healing touch, and Tauruses caress Virgos with their tender strengths, lovemaking retains the luscious, earthy affection each craves.

The Taurus / Libra Relationship ♥♥

Tauruses and Libras can enjoy a loving, enriching, and creative relationship, especially when they accept that they each define those things differently. With both being ruled by Venus, they're bonded by the qualities she gives them: their love of love, appreciation of beauty, and urge for harmony. Yet, since each expresses different aspects of those qualities, they're great complements to one another: Libras learn from Tauruses the earthier side of love and beauty—the touching, feeling, and attainment of luxury. Tauruses learn from Libras the intellectual side—the ideal of love and beauty. They make a sensual and attractive pair, one that pursues the pleasures that satisfy them and offers stability to those they love.

Tauruses are captivated by Libras' beauty and enticed by their elegance. They enjoy how Libras can be so dynamic yet charming. With their initiative, Libras can heal Tauruses or help them better develop their life's work.

Libras are compelled by Tauruses' sensuality and drawn to their physicality. They respect Tauruses' practical ways and admire their loyalty and determination. Libras appreciate Tauruses' "say it like it is" approach, even if it ruffles feathers. Tauruses transform Libras, igniting their passions and helping them define their values.

Romance is swooning and delightful as Tauruses bring slow sensuality and Libras bring enticing wit. When Tauruses woo Libras with their physical prowess and Libras wow Tauruses with their gorgeous poise, lovemaking is special and satisfying.

Possible Taurus / Libra Challenges

The different ways Tauruses and Libras live in Venus's world of love can make them feel universes apart. Tauruses want to touch, possess, and be practically involved with all they love and adore. Libras, however, enjoy thinking and talking about what and who they adore, perhaps even from an objective distance. Libras' abstract aloofness frustrates Tauruses, who think they're all talk but little substance. Libras find Tauruses' earthiness too crude to be alluring.

Libra's indecisiveness frustrates Taurus to no end. They get confused when Libras say things indirectly or worry obsessively about keeping others happy. They think, *Just make a decision, say what you think, do what you want, and get it over with.*

Libras can find Tauruses too unrefined and overly concerned with physical pleasures. They cringe when Tauruses do what pleases them, especially if it means plowing over others' needs. Tauruses' insistence on sticking with decisions confines Libras. They wish Tauruses would use more finesse and entertain more interesting concepts.

Romantic problems arise if Tauruses feel abandoned by Libras' elusiveness, or Libras feel stifled by Tauruses' possessiveness. When Tauruses focus on the physicality of love and forget the charming wooing, or Libras indulge in too much flirting without enough physical affection, lovemaking disappoints both.

Advice for the Taurus / Libra Relationship

Tauruses and Libras get along best when they accept each other's unique gifts and strategies. When Tauruses see value in Libras' evaluations, they'll not only connect better with Libras, they may discover the benefits of their own negotiating ability. When Libras appreciate Tauruses' matter-of-fact directness, they'll not only feel more comfortable around Tauruses, they might discover how doing what's practical and saying what's on their minds maintains, rather than disrupts, peace.

Tauruses appeal to Libras by talking with them and being open to their ideas. Instead of pressuring Libras, Tauruses might patiently take refuge in knowing Libras stick to the decisions they eventually make. Tauruses needn't accompany Libras on their every social outing, but being charming and cooperative with others when they do elicits Libras' admiration.

Libras make Tauruses happiest by being practical and direct. They endear themselves to Tauruses by appreciating their interests. Libras prompt more of Tauruses' interest in their ideals and concepts by showing how they can be usefully applied.

Romantic problems can be solved if Tauruses flirt and Libras touch more. When Tauruses are communicative and creative, and Libras are physically indulgent, lovemaking has the "wow" that pleases both.

The Taurus/Scorpio Relationship ♥♥

Tauruses and Scorpios can enjoy an intensely compelling and deeply intimate relationship, especially when they remain considerate of one another. They are opposite signs, which means they're drawn to one another's complementary gifts: Tauruses provide the calm stability Scorpios take refuge in, while Scorpios ignite the emotional intensity and excitement Tauruses crave. Their many similarities—strength, loyalty, sensuality, and the urge to create stability—bond them.

Together Taurus and Scorpio make a powerful and determined pair, one that creates significant accomplishments that satisfy them and provide a pillar of strength to those they love and support.

Tauruses are spellbound by Scorpios' passion, power, and magnetic sexuality. Scorpios' depth, complexity, and worldly savvy fascinate them. Tauruses respect Scorpios' ambitions and admire their effective strategies for realizing them. They're honored to be included in Scorpios' inner circle.

Scorpios are magnetized by Tauruses' luscious sensuality and find their gentleness a sweet oasis. Scorpios relax around Tauruses and feel reassured by their pragmatism. They rely on Tauruses' steadfast loyalty and learn from them how to savor what they already possess.

Romance between Tauruses and Scorpios is legendarily sensual as each sign finds the other perhaps the most desirable person they've

ever met. Passions flair and lovemaking flourishes as these two celebrate their similarities and overcome their exquisite differences with
seductive rituals and affections.

Possible Taurus / Scorpio Challenges

Although Tauruses and Scorpios share a powerful attraction,
power struggles can ignite numerous fights. Control is a big issue.
Tauruses seek control by making themselves comfortable and securing
the status quo. Scorpios seek control by managing everything around
them and willingly overthrowing the status quo if it doesn't work well.

Tauruses' sense of security is threatened by Scorpios' penchant for crisis. Their whipping up of problems exhausts Tauruses, who believe they
create much of their unhappiness with suspicious and cynical thinking.
Scorpios' emotional passions overwhelm Tauruses, and their criticisms
hurt deeply. They wish Scorpios would just be nicer and happier.

Scorpios see Tauruses' maintaining security at any price as madden-
ing denial. Scorpios dismiss Tauruses' acceptance of life at face value
as naively superficial. They wish Tauruses would feel more, reach
deeper, and quit being so concerned with their physical comfort when
there are so many interesting problems to investigate and solve.

Romantic problems erupt if Tauruses don't trust that Scorpios are
loyal or considerate of their needs, or if Scorpios believe Tauruses are
withholding affection to manipulate them. When cold battles of will
develop and fights are harsh, lovemaking becomes scarce, indeed.

Advice for the Taurus/Scorpio Relationship

Tauruses and Scorpios get along best when they remain kind and flexibly cooperative. When Tauruses see value in Scorpios' urge to destroy what doesn't work as an avenue of creating even more security, they'll not only trust Scorpios more, they might take more transforming risks themselves. If Scorpios realize the power in Tauruses' conserving what's safe and secure, they'll not only appreciate Tauruses more, they might avert crises by building on what works.

Tauruses are smart to remember that it's their stability and sweetness that Scorpios need and want. Resolving power struggles by bringing in Scorpios' problem-solving skills is far more effective than using cold, willful resistance.

Scorpios appeal to Tauruses by treating them with a gentle hand and keeping criticism at a minimum. Knowing Tauruses don't need to probe every hidden truth to be savvy helps Scorpios appreciate the common sense they exude. Patiently presenting ways that change can be enacted without crisis better elicits Tauruses' trust.

Romantic problems are best resolved when Tauruses and Scorpios do what comes naturally: indulge their lusty desire for one another. When Scorpios remain sensual and giving, and Tauruses remain tender and available, their amazing chemistry prompts generous resolution.

The Taurus/Sagittarius Relationship ♥

Tauruses and Sagittarians can enjoy an interesting, unique, and even pleasure-filled relationship, especially when they understand they're nothing alike. They bond through a love of abundance and enjoying life's fine offerings. Even their differences can prove complementary: Tauruses help Sagittarians bring their inspired visions into a secured reality, while Sagittarians encourage Tauruses to stretch their know-how ever further. Together they make an ingenious pair, one that creates adventurous yet practical successes and provides encouragement to those who are drawn to them.

Tauruses feel inspired by Sagittarians' optimism and awakened by their antics. Sagittarians encourage Tauruses to develop more of their own potential, either by awakening their passions or by taking more risks. Tauruses' worlds expand as they explore the many philosophies and ideas Sagittarians bring.

Sagittarians respect Tauruses' strength and determination. They consider Tauruses' reliability as a solid foundation from which they can launch their many interests. Tauruses' love of simple pleasures quiets Sagittarians' wanderlust, helping them to be grateful for the people and things already present in their lives.

Romance between Tauruses and Sagittarians is unexpected, but it can be highly enjoyable. Sex is something both find highly interesting and valuable, and both deliver sensuality the other finds captivatingly unique.

Possible Taurus/Sagittarius Challenges

Although Tauruses and Sagittarians are both pleasure-seekers, what they find pleasurable and how they seek it are worlds apart. Tauruses desire the pleasure of a secure, predictable, paid-for life, while Sagittarians seek pleasure from adventure, variety, and the excitement that comes from pushing their limits. Tauruses wonder,

Why do Sagittarians resist commitments and insist on new challenges? Sagittarians wonder, *Why do Tauruses limit their options by hunkering down and committing so readily?*

Tauruses feel threatened by Sagittarian's risk taking, thinking they gamble way too much on luck and rely too little on practicality. They grow weary of Sagittarians' boastfulness and far-flung philosophies, and resist the discomfort of their overextended plans and expeditions. Tauruses grow suspicious of Sagittarians' need for variety.

Sagittarians feel confined and bored by Tauruses' predictable consistency. Tauruses' black-and-white thinking frustrates Sagittarians, who want them to be more curious and expansive. Sagittarians resent Tauruses' resistance to the changes and adventures they feel entitled to. Tauruses' careful pace seems oppressive to Sagittarians.

Romantic problems arise when Tauruses feel threatened by Sagittarians' flirting and reluctance to commit, or Sagittarians feel confined by Tauruses' need for reassurance and consistency. When Tauruses deal with misunderstanding by withholding, or Sagittarians becoming rebellious and aloof, both attraction and lovemaking disappear.

Advice for the Taurus/Sagittarius Relationship

When Tauruses and Sagittarians accept they'll have to work at getting along, doing so can prove invaluable. When Tauruses understand that Sagittarians' definition of security is freedom to roam, both physically and intellectually, they'll not only connect with them better, they may attain the valuable gifts their own expansiveness offers. When Sagittarians value Tauruses' practical philosophy, they'll not only appreciate them more, they may discover how pragmatism helps them avoid becoming overextended and wins them more success.

Tauruses are most appealing to Sagittarians when they're curious and enthusiastic. Tauruses needn't accompany Sagittarians on every expedition, but shouldn't try to keep Sagittarians from them either. Identifying the boundaries of what they can and cannot risk, then allowing Sagittarians to play with the rest, keeps Tauruses secure and Sagittarians fulfilled.

Sagittarians are most attractive to Tauruses when they're practical and reasonable. Quieting down their exuberance, pushing for less outrageous risks, and backing their declarations with solid actions work wonders to elicit Tauruses' trust. Plus, introducing ideas with tangible facts about how they'll work invites Tauruses' interest and support.

Romantic problems can better be resolved when Sagittarians show loyalty and thoughtfulness, and Tauruses show openness and flexibility. When each keeps their admiration singing and their playful sensuality flowing, satisfying lovemaking makes thornier issues disappear.

The Taurus / Capricorn Relationship ♥♥♥♥

Capricorns and Tauruses can enjoy a truly outstanding and compatible relationship that's rich in satisfaction and comfort. Both are earthy and reasonable and bond through a love of attaining abundance, an urge for stability, and an enjoyment of getting worthwhile things accomplished. Communication comes easily between Taurus and Capricorn as each adore the other's humor and speak practically without unnecessary drama. They make a solid pair, one that parlays resources into the successes they desire and provides support to all they love.

Tauruses are impressed by Capricorns' ambitions and admire their careful plans for achieving them. Capricorns' adherence to conservative traditions makes Tauruses feel wonderfully secure. Tauruses especially enjoy partaking of the prestigious fruits of Capricorns' labors.

Capricorns appreciate Tauruses' practicality and count on their steadfast loyalty. Tauruses' what-you-see-is-what-you-get bluntness helps Capricorns relax and trust. They especially admire Tauruses' determination to plow through obstacles and reach success. Capricorn's take refuge in Tauruses' ready sensuality, perhaps learning from them how to enjoy life's pleasures.

Romantically, Tauruses and Capricorns can enjoy a terrific love life. They rarely tell the world about their great sexual endeavors and the hours of pleasure they give one another, but they are definitely enjoying themselves. Their motto? "Take your time and do it right."

Possible Taurus/Capricorn Challenges

Although Tauruses and Capricorns usually understand each other, there are a few things each finds baffling. When one can't see why the other feels or wants something, they can dismiss it as unimportant. Or both might put feelings on the back burner in order to accomplish life's duties and forget the enjoyable kindnesses that keep them together. Both can suspect the other is withholding love, affection, attention, or money—and they might respond the same. Then a cold standoff takes place and bonding vulnerability is out of the question.

With their need to be touched and nurtured, Tauruses can interpret Capricorns' stoicism as cold and uncaring. They resent Capricorns' putting work or duty before them, suspecting that Capricorns value their ambitions more than them. With their urge for immediate gratification, Tauruses find Capricorns' delaying pleasures a needless, even cruel denial.

Capricorns find Tauruses' need for immediate gratification to be childishly indulgent. They wish Tauruses would think of their own needs less and consider them and what they're trying to accomplish more. Capricorns' minimalism dismisses Tauruses' need for cushy creature comforts, and they worry that Tauruses love their stuff more than them. Plus, Tauruses' stubborn resistance really irks Capricorns.

Romantic problems arise between Tauruses and Capricorns when affection is withheld or not given the way it's desired. When Tauruses pressure Capricorns to be more indulgently affectionate or Capricorns pressure Tauruses to accept what they give as enough, lovemaking loses its luster.

Advice for the Taurus/Capricorn Relationship

Tauruses and Capricorns enjoy each other most when they make clear efforts to support one another's needs. When Capricorns learn from Tauruses the value of being affectionate, tender, and considerate of another's needs, Capricorns will not only better connect to Tauruses, they might better connect with the world. When Tauruses see value in Capricorns' discipline, they'll not only relate better to Capricorns, they might learn how to achieve more of what they truly desire.

Tauruses are most attractive to Capricorns when they're flexible and motivated. Understanding that Capricorns aren't indulgent, even when they care deeply, helps Tauruses quit taking their stoicism or thriftiness personally. Capricorns are most responsive to Tauruses when they deliver the softness and caring they need.

Capricorns are most appealing to Tauruses when they're affectionate and encouraging. Remembering that Tauruses' needs and wants are much more immediate than their own helps Capricorns quit expecting them to wait for rewards. Tauruses are much easier satisfied and open to Capricorns' ideas when Capricorns show they're considering Taurus.

Romantic problems are better resolved when both signs give what each deeply desires: softness, affection, and encouragement. When Tauruses see Capricorns genuinely attempting to be more available, and Capricorns see Tauruses being supportive and admiring, each will return the favor with tender, loyal attentiveness, and sensuality.

The Taurus / Aquarius Relationship ♥♥

Tauruses and Aquarians can enjoy a fascinating and unusual relationship, especially when they understand that they're quite different. The similarities they do share bond them: loyalty, determination, and adherence to deeply held values. When they join forces, every base of success is covered: Tauruses ensure that personal needs are met and life remains comfortable, while Aquarians keep abreast of social concerns and worthwhile causes to contribute to. Together Taurus and Aquarius make an industrious and inventive pair, one that creates and maintains the important structures that satisfy them and provide direction for those they love.

Tauruses respect Aquarians' strength and admire their commitment to act on their ideals. Aquarians' big-picture vision widens Tauruses' world. They find it impressive that, although Aquarians' innovations seem quirky, ultimately they're extremely pragmatic. Aquarians encourage Tauruses to try new things, especially professionally.

Aquarians admire Tauruses' determination and appreciate their reliability. They take comfort in Tauruses' boiling this complicated world down to simple values. Tauruses' sensuality reminds Aquarians to receive the pleasures of the world and to consider more of their own needs.

Romance between Tauruses and Aquarians is unexpected but affectionate and loyal when it happens. With their natural sexuality, Tauruses delight and complement Aquarians' exotic tastes, as these two love experimenting with new pleasures.

Possible Taurus/Aquarius Challenges

Although Tauruses and Aquarians both possess strong ideas and desires, what they each think about and desire can cause alienating friction between them. Tauruses think mainly of themselves and make no apologies for desiring a life of comfort and abundance. Aquarians think of the world and want to make contributions that help humanity. Tauruses can find Aquarians' idealism too impersonal and far-fetched to connect with, while Aquarians consider Tauruses too selfish and limited in scope to be interesting.

Tauruses get annoyed when Aquarians' inventive tinkering upsets their comfortable status quo. They think that Aquarians' "brilliant" ideas are just kooky, and they feel put off by Aquarians' aloofness.

Tauruses flinch at Aquarians' unusual ways of expression, thinking, *Why be so rebellious?*

Aquarians feel thwarted by Tauruses' concern with tangible knowns. They dismiss Tauruses' materialism as unevolved if not boring. Aquarians fume when Tauruses resist changes that would obviously improve things, thinking, *Snap out of your comfort zone!*

Romantic problems arise if Tauruses want Aquarians to be more personally attentive and physically doting, or Aquarians need breathing room to socialize or time alone with their thoughts. When Aquarians talk too much, Tauruses talk too little, or both find the other stubborn or inconsiderate, a cold standoff makes lovemaking scarce.

Advice for the Taurus/Aquarius Relationship

Tauruses and Aquarians succeed best when they find ways to be enriched by their differences. When Aquarians learn from Tauruses that conservation can lead to progress and taking care of oneself is not selfish, they'll not only get along better with Tauruses, they may be more effective in creating the bright future they envision. When Tauruses learn from Aquarians the value of innovation and considering their larger community, they'll not only enjoy Aquarians more, they'll discover the profits that grander visions offer.

Tauruses are most appealing to Aquarians when they're open and curious. Understanding that Aquarians value uniqueness and social contributions above all else helps Tauruses to quit expecting Aquarians to be more mainstream and to start recognizing the gifts they bring. If Aquarians seem aloof, telling them, "I need some attention" is better than clamming up and feeling neglected.

Aquarians are most attractive to Tauruses when they're more practical and less shocking. Understanding that Tauruses open most by first tending to themselves helps Aquarians quit expecting them to be interested in matters that don't concern them and to join Tauruses in the valuable matters that do. If Aquarians seek Tauruses' loyalty and cooperation, they should be more personal and show tangible ways their ideas can be applied.

Romantic problems can easily be resolved when Aquarians stay affectionate and considerate of Tauruses' needs, and Tauruses give Aquarians the space to detach. When each keeps their sensuality and loyalty flowing, their sexy, unique connection kicks in.

The Taurus/Pisces Relationship ♥♥♥

Tauruses and Pisces can enjoy a wonderfully engaging and supportive relationship, especially when they combine their different worlds. Pisces are as dreamy as Tauruses are practical, yet somehow they click. They bond through their kindnesses, love of soft comforts, and urge to nurture whomever they love. Even their differences can prove complementary: Tauruses' solidity and strength makes Pisces feel secure, while Pisces' imaginative ways bring magic and texture to Tauruses' world. Together they pursue creative and helpful projects that satisfy them and lend understanding to the many they care for.

Tauruses relax in Pisces' compassion and feel bolstered by their admiration. Tauruses love how Pisces indulge their preferences and make them feel empowered. Pisces are fun friends to Tauruses, who accept them as they are and rarely push them any further than they're comfortable going.

Pisces love how Tauruses deftly navigate this world and batten down the hatches so things don't get too wacky. They appreciate Tauruses' tending to practical matters so they can relax and indulge their imaginations. Tauruses' humor makes Pisces giggle and their sweetness makes them melt.

Romance sizzles between Tauruses and Pisces as both adore love and all the affection, caressing, and exploring it invites. Tauruses dive into Pisces' sea of tender sexuality, and Pisces relish Tauruses' attentive, sensual courtship.

Possible Taurus / Pisces Challenges

Although Tauruses and Pisces usually enjoy good chemistry, their different ways of relating to reality can spark annoying misunderstandings. Pisces' fantasies are so vivid that sometimes they seem more real than what is actually happening. Tauruses are just the opposite: if they can't experience something through their five senses, it doesn't exist. Tauruses can feel Pisces are too out of touch to take seriously, while Pisces write Tauruses off as overly anchored in a boring reality.

Tauruses find Pisces' go-with-the-flow flexibility and relaxed schedules unreliable. Pisces' deep feelings and emotional dramas seem unnecessary to Tauruses, who believe they're indulgent. They wish that Pisces would invest less in their dreamworlds and more in reality.

Pisces can find Tauruses' bottom-line practicality harsh and hard to penetrate. They feel rebuffed and lonely when Tauruses refuse to let go of their feelings or boundaries. Plus, Pisces feel thwarted by Tauruses' insistence on maintaining the status quo, thinking, *Routines keep life so dreadfully ordinary!*

Romantic problems arise if Tauruses don't indulge Pisces with romantic, swooning flirtations, or Pisces resist making the commitments Tauruses need to feel loved. When Tauruses seem to love their material items too much, and Pisces seem to love their fantasies too much, their steamy courtship turns cold.

Advice for the Taurus / Pisces Relationship

Tauruses and Pisces get along best when they find ways their differences enrich them. When Tauruses see value in Pisces' creative and spiritual fluidity, they'll not only enjoy Pisces more, they may discover the rich pleasures that nonmaterial pursuits can bring. If Pisces respect Tauruses' security concerns and pragmatic views, they'll not only get along better with Tauruses, they may learn how to translate their fantasies into reality.

Tauruses are most attractive to Pisces when they're imaginative, flexible, and open. Releasing any expectation that Pisces should be reliable helps Tauruses get on with enjoying their muselike value. Tauruses entice Pisces to go along with their projects or ideas by showing them how rewarding or enchanting they would be.

Pisces appeal most to Tauruses by being practical, present, and a little less dramatic. Accepting that Tauruses' creativity is expressed by establishing stability and control helps Pisces quit hoping they'll be more adventurous and start appreciating the remarkable support they offer. Tauruses are most open to Pisces' ideas and projects when they're presented with a clear plan and the ways everyone will share responsibility.

Romantic problems can better be resolved when Tauruses stay tender, wooing Pisces with a little magic, and Pisces stay reliable, wooing Tauruses with sensual and emotional availability. When each frequently reminds the other how loved and valued they are, their lovemaking transports each to another world.

How Geminis Match Up

The Gemini/Aries Relationship

See *The Aries/Gemini Relationship* on page 292.

The Gemini/Taurus Relationship

See *The Taurus/Gemini Relationship* on page 324.

The Gemini/Gemini Relationship ♥♥

Two Geminis can enjoy a terrifically fun and fascinating relationship that's full of adventure and vibrant communication—especially when they stick around to enjoy it! Being the same sign gives each unique insight into the other's need for variety, stimulation, and action. They're bonded by their youthful, playful enjoyment of life wherein everything is exciting and promising. Geminis keep each other's interests piqued by investigating the novel ideas and activities that satisfy them, as well as entertaining and teaching the many interesting people they love.

Geminis like in each other what they like most about themselves: their cleverness, curiosity, and the ability to adapt to any situation. Their intelligence quickly captures the other's ideas and runs with them, leading to hours of satisfying conversations about anything and everything.

Geminis agree that matters shouldn't get too heavy or emotional. They don't bother diving into deep, dark feelings, or getting overly involved in complicated scenes. Instead, they encourage each other to resolve difficulties intellectually, or to look to the bright side of even the most challenging situation.

Geminis are so multifaceted they don't need or expect consistency from one another. They understand their Gemini companion is chock-full of different characteristics and interests, and they give each other plenty of space to explore them. After all, variety is the spice of life and relationships.

Romance between Geminis is playful and explorative. Courtship is a creative dance of fantasies, talking, and laughter, while lovemaking abounds with novelty and delightfulness. Why waste time being serious when there are so many pleasures to explore?

Possible Gemini/Gemini Challenges

As with all same-sign relationships, Geminis might be too much alike to stay interested, or in their case, stay around.

Since Geminis tend to be skittish about making commitments to anything, neither might insist on one. Fear of confinement can allow all sorts of distracting reasons to keep them from nailing matters down. Or, a chase ensues as one Gemini pleads for a commitment when the other won't, only for the situation to reverse when both change their minds. Since Geminis like to keep their options open, loyalty can sometimes be fleeting. There can also be a lot of talk with no action between two Geminis, or lots of starts and very few finishes because both get bored when things get too familiar.

With their youthful attitudes, Geminis can avoid making responsible decisions, or dealing with difficult feelings or issues, just because they're uncomfortable. That prevents the bonding that comes from deeply knowing themselves or each other.

Since Geminis know how easily they can break commitments, or say one thing and do another, a distrust over sincerity can develop. Or, Geminis' penchant for mind games can send such confusing signals that each wonders, *What's really going on here?*

Romantic problems between Geminis exist if they resist commitment or if their intellectual pursuits replace sensual explorations. Sometimes a siblinglike friendship takes the place of erotic attraction and exhilarating lovemaking fizzles into "let's just talk."

Advice for the Gemini/Gemini Relationship

Geminis' relationships are most successful when they exert as much effort to keep involved as they do to keep things interesting. Spending time together, taking the first steps to commitments, and expressing emotional availability are all good strategies for Geminis to stay connected.

Since emotional expression can be awkward between Geminis, each might have to put in extra effort to be forthcoming. Both need space to think emotions over, but eventually feelings need to be expressed. When each Gemini shows patience and understanding for the other's vulnerability, it gets easier and more natural to open up.

It's also helpful if Geminis encourage one another to see projects and relationships through to completion, rather than always enticing each other to start something new.

Romance between two Geminis stays saucy and exciting when each keeps their attention on pleasing and enticing the other. When the flirting, surprises, and gentleness keeps flowing, no one on earth is as interesting.

The Gemini / Cancer Relationship ♥♥

Geminis and Cancers can enjoy a delightfully playful and tender relationship, especially when they understand each other's needs. They're bonded through their young-hearted playfulness, curiosity, and agreement that life should be about satisfying personal desires. Even their differences can prove complementary: Geminis' intellectual and breezy nature keeps Cancers light and moving, while Cancers' tender emotional nature keeps Geminis soft and considerate. Together they make a sparkling and adorable pair, one that pursues interesting ideas that satisfy them and cooks up nurturing activities for the many they enjoy.

Geminis adore Cancers' bubbly natures and relish their tender nurturing. They're fascinated by how Cancers brim with ideas and adventures, yet bring an emotional depth that makes matters all the more interesting. Cancers' support makes Geminis feel secure and helps them capitalize on their resources.

Cancers delight in Geminis' intelligence and feel captivated by their youthful charm. They adore the way Geminis keep the surprises coming and encourage them to take risks that make life exciting. Cancers feel empowered around Geminis.

Romance between Geminis and Cancers is a playful, affectionate courtship full of innocent, first-time feelings. Hand-holding, light kisses, and passionate sensuality combine to make for an outstanding love.

Possible Gemini/Cancer Challenges

Although Geminis and Cancers share some delightful similarities, their different emotional natures can make it seem as if they have nothing in common. Cancers are intensely emotional and expect Geminis to understand and attend to all the feelings they express. But Geminis don't want or need to dig into deep feelings—their own or Cancers'.

Plus, whereas Cancers yearn for security that comes from commitments, a secure home and family, and reliable circumstances, Geminis crave the freedom that comes from taking risks, keeping options open, and surprises. Geminis can write Cancers off as too needy and reactive to have any fun, while Cancers find Geminis too unreliable and superficial to connect with.

Cancers are driven crazy by Geminis' unwillingness to be tied down and hurt by their reluctance to commit. They're threatened by Geminis' risk taking and exasperated by their restless search for novelty. Worse, Geminis don't seem to *feel*.

Geminis can become overwhelmed by Cancers' dramas and are put off by Cancers' insistence on exploring feelings. Cancers' nurturing can suffocate Geminis, who can find it possessive and clingy.

Romantic problems can arise when Geminis resist Cancers' yearning for commitment and emotive affection, or when Cancers refuse to go along with Geminis' playful novelties. Sexual fascination can wane into siblinglike adoration and lust goes out the window.

Advice for the Gemini/Cancer Relationship

Geminis and Cancers get along best when they learn from each other's differences. When Cancers value Geminis' intellectual approach, they'll not only enjoy Geminis more, they may discover how refreshing it can be to step away from feelings and look at matters objectively. When Geminis find Cancers' emotions interesting, they'll not only get along better with Cancers, they may discover the fascinating truths of their own feelings.

Cancers are most attractive to Geminis when they're curious and playful. Instead of expecting emotional breakthroughs, Cancers are better off being nurtured by the fun experiences Geminis bring them. When Cancers understand that Geminis are nourished by variety, adventure, and freedom, they'll more easily accept their roaming. They entice Geminis' cooperation by showing Geminis how they'll learn something or have some fun by doing so.

Geminis most appeal to Cancers by remaining soft, tender, and considerate. Geminis needn't join Cancers in every emotion, but not flying away when they're experiencing them helps Cancers trust and connect more easily. Geminis entice Cancers' interest in their ideas and projects when they show Cancers they'll be safe or nurtured in doing so.

Romantic problems are most easily resolved when Geminis demonstrate loyalty and consistency to Cancers, and Cancers keep an open mind regarding Geminis' interests. Striking a balance between affection, talking, and exploring keeps the lusty, playful sparks flying.

The Gemini / Leo Relationship ♥♥♥

Geminis and Leos can enjoy a wonderfully exciting and fascinating relationship brimming with sparkle and adventure. They bond through their playfulness, love of entertaining, and unbridled creative expression. Theirs is a mutual admiration society: Geminis' wit and charm thrills Leos, while Leos' regal drama send Geminis into a head spin. They'll spend hours telling stories, making each other laugh, and challenging one another to try the next intriguing thing. Never boring, always dynamic, Leos and Geminis can turn most anything into a delightful extravaganza for them and everyone around them.

Geminis adore Leos' flamboyance and are enchanted by their charisma. They're captivated by Leos' strength and enlivened by their creativity. In Leos, Geminis find fun friends whose generous style and confident encouragement keeps their interest perennially piqued. Geminis particularly love how Leos not only capture their ideas but make them a reality.

Leos applaud Geminis' amusing cleverness and become enthralled by their many talents. They love Geminis' classy companionship that mingles as much as they do. They delight in the surprises Geminis cook up and feel assured that if something is worth exploring, Geminis will bring it to them.

Romance between Geminis and Leos is a fiesta of flamboyant flirting and passionate sensuality. Shyness is unnecessary as these two fan each other's flames and captivate one another with countless creative ways to show affection, in and out of the bedroom.

Possible Gemini / Leo Challenges

Although Geminis' and Leos' personalities usually complement each other, their temperaments can spark annoyances. Leos are intense and want things to be done their way. They expect Geminis' complete attention and loyalty. But Geminis are more breezy and objective, preferring to take occasional breaks from Leos to explore other interests. Plus, Geminis don't need to bring every idea to completion and love doing things in a variety of ways. Leos can fume that Geminis are downright incorrigible, while Geminis complain that Leos are stubborn control freaks.

Leos get frustrated when Geminis talk but don't act on ideas. They wish that Geminis would be less flighty and express some passions they could get ahold of. Leos worry that Geminis' penchant for losing interest in matters makes them unreliable or disloyal. Geminis' active social life and versatility is admirable unless they disrupt Leos' plans.

Geminis can find Leos' intensity overwhelming. Their willful stubbornness irks Geminis, and their roaring temper turns them away. Geminis tire of Leos' demands for attention and don't agree that loyalty means Leos should always be put first. Plus, they wonder why Leos insist on orchestrating situations, thinking, *Let go of the reins and be truly spontaneous!*

Romantic problems arise when Geminis resist making a commitment or need time off from romantic passions, or if Leos feel Geminis aren't strong enough. Then their exotic fireworks turn into contentious ones.

Advice for the Gemini/Leo Relationship

Geminis and Leos get along best when they stick to the creativity and fun that makes them such good friends. When Leos give Geminis the space and variety they need in order to blossom, and Geminis cooperate with some of Leos' bottom-line control needs, they'll enjoy one another immensely.

Geminis are most attractive to Leos when they are expressive and available. Finding a playful way of telling Leos they're a bit overwhelming eases tensions and keeps both open and calm. If Geminis assure Leos that they adore them and love them—even when they roam—Leos will better accept their absences. Geminis can woo Leos into most anything by using their charm and letting Leos know they're special.

Leos get the most out of Geminis by remaining their fun, adventurous selves. When Leos understand that Geminis need experiences, not consistency, to feel fulfilled, they'll better accept Geminis' skipping around. Leos encourage Geminis' cooperation for their ideas and projects when they show them how interesting they'll be and give Geminis freedom to do things their way.

Romantic problems can most easily be remedied when Leos don't try to possess or manage Geminis, and Geminis demonstrate the loyalty and consideration Leos request. That keeps both happy and sets the stage for passions to resume.

The Gemini/Virgo Relationship ♥♥

Geminis and Virgos can enjoy a stimulating and active relationship that's intellectually vibrant, especially when they understand each other's perspective. Both are ruled by Mercury, the planet of thinking and communication, and can bond through the brilliance it gives them. Their curious minds and active natures stimulate and challenge each other to keep growing and discovering. Both are fast and adaptive and love nothing more than adding new talents and knowledge to their repertoire. Everything they endeavor has a resourceful ingeniousness to it that satisfies them and assists everyone around.

Virgos are fascinated by Geminis' quick wit and treasure being able to talk with them about anything. They admire Geminis' range of knowledge and love how they cleverly share it. Geminis' finesse also appeals to Virgos, who count on them to be as appropriate as they are. Geminis' influence helps Virgos develop authority or parlay their gifts into professional success.

Geminis admire Virgos' keen eye and are captivated by their analytical clarity. They appreciate how Virgos share their sharp intellect yet practically apply ideas with lightning-quick ease. They're impressed with Virgos' excellent taste and respect their refined style. Virgos' reliability offers Geminis security, and their understanding grounds them.

Romance between Geminis and Virgos is unexpected yet stimulating when it happens. Geminis encourage Virgos to loosen up and enjoy, while Virgos awaken physical pleasures that surprise and delight Geminis. Lovemaking is equal parts good conversation and explorative sensuality.

Possible Gemini/Virgo Challenges

Although Geminis and Virgos both possess bright intellects, their unique perspectives can spark annoyances. Geminis enjoy ideas for their own sake and don't necessarily need to apply them. But Virgos only consider ideas that have a purpose or can be used in some helpful way. Virgos complain that Geminis are too flighty to take seriously, while Geminis fume that Virgos are critically unimaginative.

Geminis' enthusiasm deflates in the face of Virgos' nitpicky focus on problems. They're annoyed by Virgos' analysis of inconsequential details and their blindness to exciting bigger pictures. Virgos' "work first" attitude squashes Geminis' playfulness, and their orderliness thwarts experimenting. Geminis wish that just once Virgos would accept their ideas without commenting on what should be improved.

Virgos find Geminis' changeable ideas and attitudes unreliable and hard to take seriously. They get exasperated when Geminis talk too much or don't act on their ideas. Geminis' gamesmanship keeps Virgos on the defensive, lest Geminis pull something tricky.

Romantic problems arise when Geminis find Virgos too critical or prudish to be fun or sexy, or if Virgos mistrust Geminis or find them too sexually experimental. Often, their intellectual spark eclipses their erotic charge, and lovemaking fizzles out.

Advice for the Gemini/Virgo Relationship

Geminis and Virgos get along best when they admire each other's intellectual gifts. When Geminis appreciate how Virgos' minds are wired to critically assess and apply ideas, they'll not only enjoy Virgos more, they may discover how practical analysis deepens their own understanding. When Virgos see the value of Geminis' learning things for the pure joy of learning, they'll not only respect Geminis more, they might discover the satisfaction of considering a wider range of subjects.

Geminis appeal to Virgos by talking about ideas with an eye toward how they can be used. Explaining how they got from point A to point B in their thinking and actions also helps Virgos recognize Geminis' reasonableness and sincerity. Want to gain Virgos' confidence? Keep agreements and make an effort to be more consistent, if not practical.

Virgos are most attractive to Geminis when they're open to their ideas and good-heartedly join in their interests. Seeing Geminis' minds as idea machines that spit out both good and bad ideas helps Virgos use their discernment to pick the ideas they like and capitalize on them. Virgos elicit Geminis' dependability and attentiveness by keeping their criticisms to a minimum and applauding what they find valuable.

Romantic problems can be resolved when Geminis demonstrate reliability and earthier affection, and Virgos show flexibility and adventurousness both in and out of the bedroom. That sparks their unique chemistry, which makes love blossom.

The Gemini / Libra Relationship ♥♥♥♥

Geminis and Libras can enjoy a remarkably fascinating and engaging relationship that's full of sparkling communication and social festivities. Both are bright and active creatures who bond through intellectual and creative pursuits and enjoyment of people. Their brilliant minds keep each other learning and growing while their quick wits keep them amused. Together they make a gracious and imaginative pair whose initiative and social skill accomplishes most anything and creates a delightful atmosphere that attracts most everyone.

Geminis adore Libras' loveliness and find their social graciousness enchanting. Their need for variety and stimulation is more than satisfied by Libras' many talents and interests. Geminis relish that Libras are not only attractive and charming companions, but that they're also smart enough to help them solve the Sunday crossword puzzle. Life is just more fun with Libras' creative and loving presence around.

Libras are captivated by Geminis' clever wit and compelled by their library of knowledge. They adore the delightful companionship that Geminis' good humor and storytelling provides. They appreciate how Geminis easily mix with their friends and count on their social finesse to never cause unsavory scenes. Geminis spark meaning in Libras' life by bringing expansive ideas to their doorsteps.

Romance between Geminis and Libras is as fascinating as it is lusty because both know that seduction begins with the mind. Good conversation combines with passionate, yet sensitive lovemaking as each uses finesse and creativity to deliver surprising delights.

Possible Gemini/Libra Challenges

*A*lthough Geminis and Libras bond through their intellects, it can be hard for them to emotionally connect. Since each feels more comfortable talking about emotions rather than feeling them, both can avoid expressing passions or vulnerability for fear the other would be turned off, which can result in each wondering about the other's true feelings. Libras might yearn for more consistency and commitment from Geminis but not ask for it or not get it if they do. Geminis can wonder if they are truly important to Libras when they act aloof or make others more important than them.

Geminis feel thwarted by Libras' indecisiveness. They lose patience when Libras weigh decisions a few hundred times or when Libras won't come out and say directly what they truly mean. Libras' insistence on being fair to everyone confines Geminis' choices, and they think, *Why try to keep the whole world happy? Why not please yourself?*

Libras can be disappointed that Geminis' scattered interests prevent them from reaching the potential they envision. They wish Geminis would demonstrate more fortitude and focus their powers on something truly worthwhile rather than just satisfying fleeting interests. Geminis' resistance to commitment really irks and scares Libras, who need clearly defined relationships. They wonder, *Why are you always looking around when all you need is right here?*

Romantic problems can arise over Geminis' resistance to commitment or Libras' indecisiveness about it. Sometimes their intellectual attraction is just more intriguing than their sexual one, and lovemaking takes a backseat to talking.

Advice for the Gemini/Libra Relationship

Geminis and Libras get along best when they maintain their natural friendship by keeping their communication stoked and lively.

Geminis are most attractive to Libras when they're focused and involved. When they declare their appreciation for Libras and assure them that they're thinking of them, even while off pursuing other interests, Libras can relax and not feel abandoned. When Geminis are open and communicative about their feelings, Libras are more forthcoming and direct about theirs.

Libras are most appealing to Geminis when they appreciate their many interests and are decisive about joining them in a few. Giving Geminis freedom to do things the way they choose, without pressuring them to take things further, also keeps them both happier. Libras entice Geminis' cooperation by showing them how much they'll gain and how little they'll lose.

Romantic problems are most easily resolved when Geminis show Libras how they treasure their relationship and honor the commitments they make, and Libras show Geminis openness and flexibility in and out of the bedroom. That keeps the other happy so their chemistry can do the rest.

The Gemini/Scorpio Relationship ♥

Geminis and Scorpios can enjoy an unusual and intriguing relationship, especially when they accept how different they are. They bond through their quick wits and savvy intelligence and ability to spot opportunities and subtleties others miss. Even their differences can prove complementary: Geminis discover more depth, complexity, and power by watching Scorpios, while Scorpios realize more levity, spontaneity, and adventure by joining Geminis. Together they investigate the delicious mysteries that satisfy them and provide fascinating insights to the friends their unique chemistry attracts.

Geminis' curiosity is piqued by Scorpios' penetrating insights. They love that no matter what they know, Scorpios add to it. They respect Scorpios' being keen to their tricks and their refusal to be controlled. Scorpios' insightfulness heals Geminis and helps them develop their abilities and life's work.

Scorpios find Geminis' wit compelling and their intelligence captivating. They admire Geminis' many talents, especially their ability to work and entertain a room. Scorpios respect that they can never fully understand or control Geminis, making them a mystery worth investigating. Geminis' influence transforms Scorpios, either by engaging their passions or redirecting their resources.

Romance between Geminis and Scorpios is unexpected yet steamy when it happens. Both relish seductive play to heighten desire, and then releasing every inhibition to try any and every pleasure imaginable.

Possible Gemini/Scorpio Challenges

Geminis and Scorpios are different in so many ways that each can find the other immensely frustrating. Whereas Geminis are changeable, intellectual, and need loads of freedom, Scorpios are consistent, emotional, and need stability. Geminis can complain that Scorpios are too deliberate and cautious to have any fun with, while Scorpios dismiss Geminis as too superficial or insincere to trust.

Geminis get overwhelmed by Scorpios' intensity and annoyed by their emotional probing. They get discouraged when Scorpios become negative and turned off by their tempers. Scorpios' suspicion of anything new and their refusal to change is especially frustrating to Geminis, as are Scorpios' attempts to control them. They wonder, *Why must every problem be inspected when there are so many fun things to investigate?*

Scorpios are disturbed by Geminis' "now you see me/now you don't" games. They mistrust Geminis' changeable personality and worry they might be fooled by it. Scorpios find Geminis difficult to understand because they don't seem to have much emotional or intellectual depth. Scorpios wish that Geminis would chat less, feel more, accomplish something solid, and quit buzzing around.

Romantic problems arise when Geminis skirt commitments or lack the emotional depth Scorpios desire, or Scorpios prevent the levity Geminis desire by becoming possessively jealous or focusing on problems. Misunderstandings and unfulfilled expectations can make both attraction and lovemaking disappear.

Advice for the Gemini/Scorpio Relationship

Geminis and Scorpios get along the best when they each appreciate what the other brings to the table. When Geminis validate Scorpios' emotions and deep analyses as worthwhile, they'll not only like Scorpios more, they may learn the satisfaction that comes from taking their own ideas and feelings deeper. When Scorpios acknowledge the brilliance of Geminis' many ideas, they'll not only enjoy

Geminis more, they may learn how stepping away from passions clarifies their insights.

Geminis are most attractive to Scorpios when they're sincere, involved, and emotionally available. Geminis needn't join Scorpios in their worries and suspicions, but showing patience and respect toward them elicits Scorpios' trust. Geminis invite Scorpios' interest in and cooperation with their ideas when they work with their need for control and take the time to consider Scorpios' input.

Scorpios appeal most to Geminis by being curious and flexible. Instead of expecting Geminis to be more emotionally deep or consistent, Scorpios remain happier by realizing that Geminis grow via variety and novelty. They might also encourage Geminis' wanderings and other interests, knowing Geminis aren't necessarily being unfaithful but rather refreshing themselves. Want to entice Geminis' cooperation or even commitment? Let them do things their way.

Romantic problems can better be resolved when Geminis demonstrate genuine loyalty and availability to Scorpios, and when Scorpios demonstrate flexibility and openness to Geminis. That satisfies each and encourages their lusty, inventive passions.

The Gemini/Sagittarius Relationship ♥♥

Geminis and Sagittarians can have a fascinating and exciting relationship, especially when they stick around to enjoy it. Their similarities bond them: both are bright thinkers, adore action, and keep boredom at bay by exploring whatever is new and promising. Being opposite signs, Geminis and Sagittarians complement each other's intellectual natures. Geminis keep fresh ideas rolling in, while Sagittarians bring meaning and purpose to them. Together they come up with tremendous insights and adventures, joking and telling stories the whole time.

Geminis love Sagittarians' bravado and are empowered by their confidence. They treasure how Sagittarians instinctively grasp their ideas and then use their fiery inspiration to take them a step further. Sagittarians' knack for initiating fascinating expeditions is especially appealing to Geminis, as are their gusto and optimism.

Sagittarians adore Geminis' quick wit and relish how they're ready for adventure in minutes flat. They're captivated by Geminis' vivid imaginations and enjoy how their social skills make anything they do more fascinating. Sagittarians respect Geminis' many talents, especially their ability to fit into any situation and make it fun.

Romance between Geminis and Sags alternates between them being passionate lovers one minute and playful sidekicks the next. Each gives the other the freedom they need to stay fresh and interested. Lovemaking is active, explorative, and very uninhibited.

Possible Gemini / Sagittarius Challenges

Although Geminis and Sagittarians' opposite-sign natures fascinate them, it can frustrate them as well. Whereas Geminis explore ideas for the joy of learning, Sagittarians study ideas to find meaning to live by. Geminis complain that Sags' philosophies make them agonizingly righteous, while Sagittarians fume that Geminis' knowledge stays too superficial to be transformative.

Since both are freedom-lovers who like to keep their options open, neither may ask for or be willing to make a commitment. Or, if neither wants to introduce the downer of a problem or initiate the discipline of difficult decisions, a superficiality can prevail that holds intimacy and maturity at bay.

Geminis can become bored with Sagittarians' windy lectures. They don't need to be philosophical or live by Sagittarians' ideals. And they resent Sagittarians insinuating they should. Sags' fiery energy and temper can overwhelm Geminis and turn them away.

Sagittarians can find Geminis too scattered or distracted to share meaningful things with. They wonder how Geminis can be so smart yet so naive. They wish Geminis would be less mental and more passionate once in a while. They wonder, *Why don't they read something of substance?*

Romantic problems can arise from Geminis or Sagittarians fearing the confinement and ordinariness of commitment. Vulnerability and tenderness might be laughed off or avoided as awkward. Both signs' flirting and wandering eyes don't help trust much, either.

Advice for the Gemini/Sagittarian Relationship

Geminis and Sagittarians get along best by learning from their unique perspectives. When Geminis consider the value Sagittarians' philosophies offer, they'll not only enjoy Sagittarians more, they may discover more meaning themselves. When Sagittarians acknowledge the intelligence in Geminis' ideas, they'll not only respect Geminis more, they'll be excited to discover even more paths to truth.

Geminis appeal most to Sags by remaining expansive and thoughtful. Geminis needn't adhere to Sagittarians' philosophies, but adding their own perspective is more endearing than just changing the subject. Should Sagittarians become verbose or fiery, use humor to remind them how levity is also a great avenue to enlightenment.

Sagittarians are most attractive to Geminis when they remain openly curious. Applauding the wit of the insights Geminis offer helps Sagittarians quit expecting them to go deeper. Geminis are most open to Sagittarians' ideas when they're presented as a "Here's an idea for you to consider" enticement rather than a lecture.

Romantic problems can be resolved when both Geminis and Sagittarians acknowledge their fear of commitment and entice each other to discover what making one might bring. When needs and feelings are treated as interesting subjects, intimacy and trust is solidified. Then their chemistry bonds them further.

The Gemini / Capricorn Relationship ♥

Geminis and Capricorns can enjoy a unique and interesting relationship, especially if they accept that they are nothing alike. They can connect through their initiative and urge to stay challenged by interesting projects. Their differences can prove compelling as each brings ideas and approaches the other rarely considers. Geminis show Capricorns easier, more innovative ways to accomplish things, while Capricorns show Geminis ways to discipline their ideas to make them more usefully applicable. Geminis and Capricorns come up with clever strategies and build great things from the simplest ideas.

Geminis can find Capricorns fascinating just because they are so utterly different from them. Their curiosity is piqued by Capricorns' considerable ambitions, and their respect is earned by Capricorns' steady resolve to overcome any obstacle in their path.

Capricorns respect Geminis' intelligence and admire their wide range of talents. They're intrigued by Geminis doing things so differently than they would, yet still getting good results. Capricorns wonder how Geminis come up with such clever ideas, seemingly with no preparation at all.

Romance between Geminis and Capricorns is unexpected yet delightful when it happens. Both agree public displays of affection are inappropriate, but behind closed doors they amaze each other with lusty, yet still refined lovemaking.

Possible Gemini/Capricorn Challenges

Geminis and Capricorns can find compatibility fleeting because their differences can spark gigantic frustrations. Geminis are playful, versatile, and intellectual, and enjoy spontaneity in life. Capricorns are serious, regimented and practical, and are intensely driven to build something solid. Geminis fume when Capricorns are too stodgy, while Capricorns dismiss Geminis as too flighty to take seriously.

Geminis' need for variety is squashed by Capricorns' exacting traditions and their spontaneity stifled by Capricorns' deliberateness. Capricorns' routines and order bore Geminis to tears. They wish that Capricorns would break loose and do something nutty just for the fun of it.

Capricorns feel disrupted by Geminis' darting around from place to place, idea to idea. They suspect that Geminis' inconsistency makes them unreliable, if not untrustworthy. Capricorns begrudge Geminis their playfulness, wishing they'd work harder. Worse, they resent it when Geminis drop the ball when things get rough or unappealing.

Romantic problems arise when Geminis find Capricorns too predictable or withholding, or Capricorns find Geminis too unreliable or elusive. When Capricorns' affection is too rigid or Geminis' is too airy, unmet expectations in and out of the bedroom turn them both off.

Advice for the Gemini/Capricorn Relationship

Geminis and Capricorns get along best by seeking ways their differences can be beneficial. When Geminis find Capricorns' carefulness and planning interesting, they'll not only enjoy Capricorns more, they may learn how focus and determination makes their own lives more interesting. When Capricorns see usefulness in Geminis' varied interests and breezy perspectives, they'll not only respect Geminis more, they may learn how levity and spontaneity make accomplishments even more satisfying.

Geminis are most appealing to Capricorns when they're focused, dependable, and practical. Although consistency is recommended, Geminis' versatility attracts Capricorns when they see how it leads to worthwhile outcomes. When Geminis show Capricorns the practicality of any idea or possible admiration they'll receive from it, Capricorns are more open and interested.

Capricorns are most attractive to Geminis when they're more open, curious, and flexible. If Capricorns consider Geminis muses rather than workers, they'll be more delighted in the clever things they do offer and less disappointed in what they don't. Capricorns engage more of Geminis' interest and cooperation with their ideas and projects by showing them how fun they'll be or how much they'll learn by doing them.

Romantic problems can be resolved if Geminis genuinely attempt to be committed and focused, while Capricorns show a willingness to be more experimental and playful. When each appreciates the other's affectionate style, both feel encouraged to get even better at it.

The Gemini / Aquarius Relationship ♥♥♥

Geminis and Aquarians can enjoy a delightfully fascinating and engaging relationship that's full of stimulating ideas and activities. Their similarities attract and bond them: each is bright, independent, and enjoys the surprise of discovery. Communication flows effortlessly in this relationship, as both love exploring the ideas and interests that keep life exciting and original. They make a sparkling and social pair whose creative and entertaining antics put them at the epicenter of any one of the many groups they're involved in.

Geminis adore Aquarians' progressive ideas and enjoy their social pursuits. They appreciate that, like themselves, Aquarians rarely let emotions make things sticky. Geminis also love how Aquarians discover innovative solutions to life's problems. Somehow, Aquarians inspire Geminis to reach for greater meaning.

Aquarians relish Geminis' quick wit and adore their curiosity. They're taken by Geminis' huge array of talents and love being a part of the adventures they instigate. Aquarians appreciate how Geminis make things simple without letting their emotions make them illogical. There's just something lovable about Geminis that make life fun.

Romance between Geminis and Aquarians is a delightful dance between exotic passions and best-friend talking. Each gives the freedom the other needs as well as the mental seduction they desire. Sexuality is playfully adventurous with plenty of inventive surprises to keep each other satisfied and invested.

Possible Gemini/Aquarius Challenges

Although Geminis and Aquarians' independence usually attracts them to each other, it can also keep them apart. One or both might fear the confinement of commitment and resist making one. Or, since Geminis and Aquarians both see themselves as free birds, each might expect the other to indulge their preferences but refuse to compromise themselves. Sometimes their styles clash as Geminis like open-ended spontaneity, while Aquarians like matters to be defined by boundaries or commitments (albeit unconventional ones). Geminis fume that Aquarians are stubborn and controlling, while Aquarians complain Geminis are too unreliable and uncontrolled.

Geminis resent Aquarians' belief that they and their ideas are more evolved, and therefore correct. Aquarians can seem overly involved with their social concerns and underinvolved with Geminis, who think, "Why does everything have to be about helping the world evolve?"

Aquarians find Geminis' thinking superficial and their drive for personal satisfaction selfishly unevolved. Geminis' talk seems inconsequential if they don't follow through with pragmatic actions. Aquarians suspect that Geminis will let them down. "Why do you use your gifts for personal gain when there's a world of important matters you could apply yourself to?"

And, since Geminis and Aquarians are more comfortable with ideas than emotions, each may withhold feelings for fear of appearing needy or mushy. That prevents the intimacy that vulnerability and deeper emotional expression creates.

Romantic problems arise when Geminis find Aquarians too detached to engage passionately, or when Aquarians find Geminis too inconsistent to trust. If feelings or emotional needs are avoided between them, lovemaking gets cold.

Advice for the Gemini/Aquarian Relationship

Geminis and Aquarians connect best when each makes an effort to do the things that satisfy the other. Plus, why not risk some emotional vulnerability? It'll be interesting.

Geminis are most appealing to Aquarians when they're good friends to them. Showing interest in their causes or research is always recommended. So is demonstrating loyalty, even if (and when) they're off exploring. If Aquarians seem too controlling, Geminis should remind them, "This is how I individually do things." They'll respect that.

Aquarians are most attractive to Geminis when they're engaged and consider Geminis' ideas as valid. Resisting pressuring Geminis to be more evolved helps Aquarians stay happily intrigued by the inventive brilliance Geminis' perspective offers. Aquarians encourage Geminis' cooperation with their ideas and projects when they show Geminis what they'll get out of them and then let them do things their way.

Romantic problems can more easily be resolved if both are forthcoming about their feelings and encouraging of the others'. When Geminis give Aquarians the consistency they need, and Aquarians give

Geminis the personal attention they desire, their friendship and chemistry take care of the rest.

The Gemini/Pisces Relationship ♥♥

Geminis and Pisces can enjoy a unique and enchanting relationship, especially when they make allowances for their different emotional natures. Their similarities bond them: each is inquisitive, changeable, and prefers spontaneity over the confines of a plan. Even their differences can prove compelling: Geminis' ability to learn by skimming along the surface of matters shows Pisces how to keep from getting overly involved with matters, while Pisces' depth invites Geminis into more profound understandings. They entice and entertain each other with inventive stories and artistic endeavors that make everything captivating, if not magical, for them and everyone around.

Geminis adores Pisces' mesmerizing world of fantasies. They enjoy how their unexpected surprises and drama keep matters eventful. Geminis are drawn to Pisces' mysterious, even spiritual, depth and look to them for insights. Pisces' influence helps Geminis build their authority or even their professional success.

Pisces become captivated by Geminis' clever talents and thrilled by their knack for keeping life exciting and shiny. They count on Geminis' keen intelligence to consider matters objectively and simply. Geminis' familylike connection to Pisces assists them in their personal lives.

Romance between Geminis and Pisces is beguiling and dramatic. Each specializes in the flirtations and fantasies that make courtship an affair worth dreaming about. Lovemaking is tender, yet richly explorative, as both love throwing inhibitions to the wind.

Possible Gemini/Pisces Challenges

*A*lthough Geminis and Pisces enjoy their creative expression, their other qualities can irk them to no end. While Geminis are more thinkers than feelers, Pisces are more feelers than thinkers. Geminis insist on space in relationships, but Pisces love merging into one boundaryless being with them. Geminis can't have that! They complain that Pisces are too drippy, needy, or indulgently emotional, while Pisces fume that Geminis are too elusive and distracted to connect with.

Geminis feel smothered by Pisces' insistent emotional dramas and needs. They wonder why Pisces allow themselves to lose control, and worse, try to take others along with them. Geminis tire of Pisces' hurt feelings and disrespect their self-sacrificing choices, wondering, *Why do you suffer so?*

Pisces feel a lonely dissatisfaction with Geminis. They wish Geminis would consider others' (and Pisces'!) feelings more. Pisces scratch their heads with wonder when Geminis ignore the insight empathy could provide, thinking, *Why can't Gemini have just one profound moment?*

Romantic problems arise if Geminis won't or can't reach the emotional depth Pisces require, or if Pisces infringe upon the space Geminis need. When Pisces want to merge and Geminis want to talk, unmet expectations make lovemaking awkward.

Advice for the Gemini/Pisces Relationship

Geminis and Pisces enjoy each other most by respecting the valuable perspective each offers. When Geminis accept that Pisces learn from their intense emotions, they'll not only relate better to Pisces, they may be encouraged to see what insights their own feelings offer. When Pisces notice the profoundness of Geminis' observations, they'll not only respect Geminis more, they may better uphold their boundaries by knowing they needn't merge with something to understand it.

Geminis are most attractive to Pisces when they remain emotionally available and tender. Geminis needn't join Pisces in every feeling, but acknowledging them as valid elicits more of Pisces' trust. Geminis invite Pisces' cooperation with ideas and projects by showing consideration for Pisces and everyone else involved.

Pisces appeal most to Geminis by staying alert and witty. Understanding that Geminis aren't emotional even when they care deeply helps Pisces enjoy the affections they do show through their ideas and actions. Sharing their emotions in shorter spurts keep Geminis less overwhelmed and more open. To entice Geminis' cooperation, Pisces need only to show them how entertaining or educational doing so will be.

Romantic problems can more easily be resolved if Geminis are the tender, understanding, emotionally involved lovers Pisces want them to be, and Pisces are the clever, communicative, composed companions Geminis want them to be. Then their deeper union can prevail.

How Cancers Match Up

The Cancer/Aries Relationship

See *The Aries/Cancer Relationship* on page 295.

The Cancer/Taurus Relationship

See *The Taurus/Cancer Relationship* on page 327.

The Cancer/Gemini Relationship

See *The Gemini/Cancer Relationship* on page 356.

The Cancer/Cancer Relationship ♥♥

Two Cancers can enjoy a snuggly and nurturing relationship, especially when they support each other's strengths. Being members of the same sign gives Cancers unique understanding of each other's drive for security, need for safety, and desire for home and family. Cancers know how important emotional availability, unflinching loyalty, and indulging consideration are to building trust and intimacy. The beauty of their relationship is they love giving those types of attentions as much as they do receiving them, so bonding is easy between Cancers.

When Cancers join forces to achieve ambitions, little deters them. They maximize opportunities and soldier on past every obstacle to realize their desires. All the while, they're baking cookies and throwing house parties so everyone around feels nourished and cozy.

Security is a central theme in a Cancer/Cancer alliance. They create their all-important emotional security by making sure each feels loved and cared for, protected, and safe to express their feelings. Financial security is also a must as each ensures resources are well tended to and poised to flourish.

Romance between two Cancers is loyal and tender, full of hopeful glances and gentle, lingering caresses. When the awkward, "Who's going to make the first move?" moment is overcome, love flows. Each knows to take their time and instinctively fulfills the other's desire.

Possible Cancer/Cancer Challenges

As with all same-sign relationships, two Cancers can be too alike to get along or to stay interested. Sometimes they just tire of each other's reactivity. Or, problems arise if each believes their needs and wants should be satisfied and feel tragically neglected when they're not.

Hurt feelings can also fester in a Cancer/Cancer relationship. With their incredible sensitivity, they're quick to take things as personal affronts, even if they weren't intended as such. Or, if one does lash out, the other can respond by clamming up or emotionally withholding, sometimes for long periods of time. Then it's miserable for both. Sometimes a dependent, parent/child dynamic plays out between Cancers. If one is always the caretaker, and the other always the cared for, neither grows like they could.

Cancers' security needs can deter each other's progress. The fear of lack of money or love can prompt a worry-laden conservatism between them. Instead of encouraging expansive risks, Cancers might pressure each other to remain in unsatisfying situations just to be safe.

Romantic problems arise when either Cancer feels hurt or improperly attended to and withholds attention. Or, lustiness can fall to the wayside if a parent/child dynamic takes over. Worse, if Cancers suspect disloyalty, there's not much action in the bedroom.

Advice for the Cancer/Cancer Relationship

A relationship between Cancers flourishes when each gives and receives in equal amounts. Kindness, caring, and supporting each other's security needs creates the womblike atmosphere Cancers take refuge in.

When differing needs arise, Cancers might use their respective resourcefulness to negotiate ways to satisfy what both desire, rather than rallying to win their own way. When one Cancer sees the other making a genuine effort to please, their hearts melt. They're moved to please the other in return. Sorting out actual needs from preferences also helps keep both clear about what they truly can and cannot live without.

Should Cancer's dark moods hit, reacting or taking it personally rarely helps. But gently assisting each other to remember how much they're loved and supported does. Saying things like "I care for you and I'll be here to talk about this when we're both more objective," helps Cancers sort out their own emotions without feeling abandoned.

Romantic problems can be resolved when both Cancers are generously affectionate and attentive, both in and out of the bedroom. When each creates an inviting atmosphere of safety and acceptance, Cancers readily open their hearts, give of their bodies, and resume their communion of sexual bonding.

The Cancer/Leo Relationship

Cancers and Leos can enjoy an adoring and affectionate relationship that's both tender and exciting. They're bonded by their mutual drive to give and receive the indulgences that make both life and relationships flourish. Kindness, creativity, and loyalty come easily between them. Leos and Cancers make affirming and appreciative audiences for one another and a bubbly, entertaining pair for others. Since each is highly motivated to create abundant security, their combined forces create a solid, yet flamboyant, lifestyle.

Cancers are awed by Leos' confidence and encouraged by their bighearted support. Leos create the excitement Cancers love but might be too timid to initiate. Leos build Cancers' self-esteem and other resources as well.

Leos love basking in Cancers' sweet admiration and feel reassured by their tenacious nurturing. Leos are grateful that Cancers' companionship is charming and fluid, yet they rarely try to steal their spotlight. Leos appreciate how Cancers express the sensitivities they value but are too assertive to take the time for themselves. Cancers help Leos access their deeper yearnings and their spirituality.

Romance between Leos and Cancers is a dance between passion and playfulness. Each thrives on the affection, intimacy, and doting the other exuberantly offers. Lovemaking is lustful, yet tender as each instinctively senses what turns the other on.

Possible Cancer/Leo Challenges

Although Cancers and Leos usually adore each other, their differences can make them steam. Leos' booming power overwhelms Cancers, while Cancers' emotional reactivity can deflate Leos' power. When Leos flex their dominating muscles, Cancers complain they're overpowering and bossy, then clam up and resist them. When Cancers control Leos by secretively revealing only bits and pieces of their plans, Leos fume they're frustratingly cagey and hard to trust, and override them. Both can feel the other is too self-involved and not paying them enough attention.

Cancers' feelings get singed by Leos' fiery temperament and inconsiderateness. They resent Leos mistaking their kindness or shyness as weakness and trying to take advantage of them. Leos' insistence on doing things their way makes Cancers feel discounted and that their creative input is thwarted.

Leos find Cancers' emotional demands whiny and wish they'd be stronger. They resent having to be careful lest they do something that offends Cancers. Cancers' coyness seems manipulative and Leos can't stand their expectation to be coddled, thinking, *Where's the dignity in that?*

Romantic problems can arise if Leos are too lustfully aggressive for Cancers' gentler tastes, or if Cancers are too soft or yielding for Leos' bold tastes. If each is too self-involved to focus on the other, resentments over unmet expectations makes lovemaking disappointing.

Advice for the Cancer/Leo Relationship

Cancers and Leos get along best when they support each other's needs. When Leos understand that Cancers need to have their feelings honored to uphold their dignity, they'll not only respect them, they may learn the dignity of honoring their own feelings more. When Cancers appreciate that underneath Leos' strength lies a vulnerability that craves reassurance, they'll not only relate better to Leos, they may learn how to step past fears and openly promote themselves.

Cancers appeal most to Leos by being strong, poised for action, and attentive. Understanding that Leos aren't wired to be as receptive as they are helps Cancers to recognize how they show caring via enthusiastic, appreciative encouragements. Cancers elicit Leos' cooperation when they're direct about their intentions. If Leos' dominance overwhelms Cancers, Cancers should know that clamming up is rarely as effective as confidently expressing themselves. That'll gain Leos' respect.

Leos are most attractive to Cancers when they're tender, purring, and encouraging. Leos needn't coddle Cancers' every hurt, but riding roughshod over them rarely works as well as being respectful. When Leos show Cancers they're genuinely considering their needs, Cancers are more likely to consider theirs.

Romantic problems can most easily be resolved when Leos woo Cancers by providing the intimacy and tenderness they desire, and Cancers entice Leos with the enthusiasm and drama that turns them on. Then each feels the security and adoration that sets their love-making singing.

The Cancer/Virgo Relationship ♥♥♥

Cancers and Virgos can enjoy a wonderfully warm and endearing relationship that brings out each other's best qualities. They're easily bonded through their enjoyment of the simple pleasures and duties of life, their love of helping others, and their desire to have life eventful but not overly so. Cancers offer the emotional tenderness that Virgos appreciate but feel embarrased about expressing, while Virgos bring a practicality and objectivity that Cancers need but might not work to exact. Communication flows as Virgos and Cancers innately understand and comfort each other. When they join their resourceful and caring gifts, matters big and small get accomplished in efficient and thoughtful ways.

Cancers feel reassured by Virgos' intelligent answers to every question and secure in knowing that Virgos do what's right. They admire Virgos' industriousness and love how their order and efficiency ensures stability. Virgos intrigue Cancers, and their humor tickles them. They cherish the siblinglike closeness they feel about Virgos.

Virgos' self-confidence is enhanced by Cancers' admiration, and their courage is bolstered by Cancers' nurturing. They relish that Cancers receive them with compassionate support, rather than criticism, and learn to be easier on themselves as a result. Cancers' emotional insights and vulnerability intrigue Virgos. They're grateful that Cancers' protectiveness rarely pushes them into anything they aren't ready for.

Romance between Virgos and Cancers is tender, affectionate, and appreciative. Each extends the loyalty, consideration, and safety the other needs to express their looser, lustier, explorative sexuality.

Possible Cancer/Virgo Challenges

Although Cancers and Virgos generally enjoy an oasis of simpatico, their differences can create a desert of misunderstandings. Virgos often dismiss Cancers as emotionally indulgent. They wish Cancers would reroute the energy they put into their feelings into accomplishing something useful. Cancers struggle with Virgos' hardlined factualness. They resent Virgos as callously pragmatic and wish Virgos would quit working and start feeling something.

Cancers find Virgos' criticisms cold and stinging. And their disapproving "Now what?" toward feelings and concerns they bring up makes Cancers feel discounted. Cancers resent being shelved while Virgos work and get bored by their attempts to perfect inconsequential tasks.

Virgos find Cancers' moodiness uncalled for and tiring. They're flustered when Cancers' emotions make things messy and squirm with discomfort when Cancers probe them about theirs. Cancers' indirect-ness or even secrecy seems unclear to Virgos.

Romantic problems can arise from Virgos being too unavailable, either physically or emotionally, or from Cancers being too needy or dependent. If either feels criticized or neglected, lovemaking becomes self-conscious and stilted.

Advice for the Cancer/Virgo Relationship

Cancers and Virgos get along best by being themselves, just a little less and a little more so. When Cancers are a little less emotional and a little more practical, Virgos remain comfortable and interested. When Virgos are a little less critically exacting and a little more emo-tionally available Cancers feel connected and appreciative. Those efforts not only enhance Cancers' and Virgos' compatibility, they might enhance their other relationships as well.

Cancers are most appealing to Virgos when they're productive and reasonable. Virgos are most comfortable and open toward Cancers' feelings when they're not overwhelmed by them, or when they can see how Cancers use them for practical results. Cancers needn't join Virgos in every analysis session, but they shouldn't belittle them. If Cancers instead offer their insight, Virgos will be grateful and adore them even more.

Virgos are most attractive to Cancers when they're flexible and con-siderate. Virgos appeal to Cancers by first connecting with them in the space they're in, then gently steering them toward whatever they're asking or suggesting. Virgos needn't join Cancers in every emotion, but they shouldn't dismiss them. Simply acknowledging them as important to Cancers is satisfying and endearing enough.

Romantic problems can be resolved when Virgos are spontaneous and available toward Cancers' needs for affection and indulgence, and Cancers allow their instincts to guide them to what pleases Virgos the most. When each feels safe and encouraged to express their caring, vulnerable selves, sexual desires are easily satisfied.

The Cancer/Libra Relationship ♥♥

Cancers and Libras can enjoy an adoring and delightful relationship, especially when they understand their unique emotional styles. They bond through their love of making loved ones happy and their homes beautiful, as well as their knack for whipping up enjoyable social activities. Cancers and Libras entertain each other with jokes and stories about people and things they find attractive. They make a sparkly and adorable yet surprisingly dynamic pair, one that creates beauty and refinements that satisfy them and please and nurture everyone in their social orbit.

Cancers are spellbound by Libras' outer beauty and enticed by their inner graciousness. They feel secure in the harmony Libras maintain, trusting they'll be fair to everyone, including them. Cancers appreciate Libras' ability to consider matters objectively yet remain caring. Cancers count on Libras' balanced advice that encourages them to take risks that promote them.

Libras are entertained by Cancers' bubbly personalities and soothed by their kindness. They appreciate Cancers' nurturing of everyone, including them, and count on Cancers being the emotional weather vane of their environment. Cancers' insights help Libras to better identify and understand their own needs or strategies for professional success.

Romance between Libras and Cancers is an indulgence of the seductive flirting and passionate affections that makes courtship a consuming affair. Lovemaking is tender, sensual, and communicative, as each truly wants to please the other and loves learning how.

Possible Cancer/Libra Challenges

Although Cancers and Libras are both caring and social creatures, their unique ways of expression can spark irksome problems. Although Cancers expect to connect with Libras' emotions in order to feel intimate, Libras are more intellectual and prefer to have a good conversation over a good cry. Libras might offer too little juice for Cancers to grab onto, while Cancers might be too mushy for Libras to understand.

Cancers can be exasperated by Libras' evasiveness. Although they want Libras to reveal the good, bad, and ugly truth about what they think and feel, Libras might remain noncommittal or keep things superficial with an "it's all good" gloss. Cancers are thwarted by Libras' indecisiveness.

Libras can be annoyed that Cancers' emotions disturb their peace and consider their reactivity unappealing. Cancers' clinginess suffocates Libras, while their probing seems invasive. They wish Cancers would consider themselves less and others more.

Romantic troubles arise when Cancers are too emotionally needy or passive for Libras' tastes or if Libras are too standoffish or noncommittal for Cancers. If neither feels comfortable revealing what truly pleases them, an unsatisfying "niceness" keeps sexual intimacy at bay.

Advice for the Cancer/Libra Relationship

Cancers and Libras get along best when they enjoy their differences. When Cancers appreciate the harmony Libras create by smoothing over conflicts and building consensus, they'll better understand Libras' reluctance to let their feelings flair. When Libras enjoy the cozy feelings that Cancers' nurturing creates, they'll see the value of their emotional outreach.

Cancers appeal most to Libras by being objective and communicative. Cancers woo Libras into considering their feelings and ideas by presenting them neutrally rather than emotionally exploding. They entice Libras into emotional revelation by allowing the appropriate space to do so. When Cancers show Libras their attempts to be fair and harmonious to everyone, Libras trust them even more.

Libras are most attractive to Cancers when they're emotionally available and expressive. Self-disclosure works wonders to help Cancers trust and open up to Libras. Libras needn't join Cancers in every feeling, but they'll keep more peace when they acknowledge them as valid. If Libras struggle to commit to something, letting Cancers in on the pain of their inner conflict helps Cancers be more patient and understanding.

Romantic troubles can most easily be resolved when Cancers understand that Libras needn't gush emotionally to care deeply, and Libras understand that Cancers can't help but emotionally gush when they do. When both are forthcoming about needs and preferences, each has a better chance at being genuinely satisfied. Openly treasuring one another is the key to making lovemaking rich and satisfying.

The Cancer / Scorpio Relationship ♥♥♥♥

Cancers and Scorpios can enjoy an incredibly enticing, compelling relationship wherein each feels deeply cared for and understood. Bonding comes easily as both are emotional, passionate, and loyal, and both value a safe environment. Diving to great depths of intimate sharing is their favorite pastime. Each respects the other's sensitivity and finds their insights fascinating. Scorpios and Cancers understand each other's concerns and help each other feel secure. They can create most anything together, especially when it involves building abundance or caring for others.

Cancers are captivated by Scorpios' power and drawn to their magnetism. They feel safe around their canny watchfulness and depend on their unwavering loyalty and protectiveness. Scorpios' intensity and intimacy not only satisfy Cancers' need for closeness, but challenges them to go deeper themselves. Their sex appeal is spellbinding!

Scorpios are drawn to Cancers' emotional depth and disarmed by their tenderness. They appreciate the intimacy they feel from sharing deep and subtle things with Cancers. Scorpios relax by watching Cancers nurture what's good in life. They find Cancers inspiring and helpful in creating a meaningful life.

Romance between Cancers and Scorpios is intimate and dramatic with captivating ups and compelling downs. Passion is their keyword as each expresses the seductive mystery, emotional depth, and tender loyalty the other needs to keep their hearts and bodies open.

Possible Cancer/Scorpio Challenges

*A*lthough Cancers' and Scorpios' sensitivity and intensity usually bond them, they also spark problems. Hurt feelings can ignite intense reactions wherein both say and do harmful things, knowing the pain they're causing. Those incidents are hard to recover from. Other times Cancers' and Scorpios' suspicious natures gang up and cause them to spend more time worrying about what's wrong with life than recognizing what's right.

Cancers become deeply wounded when Scorpios lash out. Scorpios' insisting they deal with matters they're not ready to gives Cancers a stomachache, while Scorpios' perfectionist demands deflate them. Cancers' power can be eclipsed by Scorpios' determination or their ability to beat Cancers at their own games.

Scorpios' control can be usurped by Cancers' unpredictable moods and actions. Scorpios disrespect Cancers' insistence on being coddled and resent them expecting others to make adjustments for their moods. When Cancers nurture only if their demands are met, Scorpios feel manipulated. Scorpios wish Cancers would wake up and take a look at the big picture.

Romantic problems can arise if suspicions of any kind, especially of betrayal, poison trust. If kindness or affection is withheld as a ploy to either gain control or protest a slight, Cancers' and Scorpios' consuming passions turn into consuming resentments.

Advice for the Cancer/Scorpio Relationship

Cancers and Scorpios' special, satisfying closeness flourishes when each sees the other as caring, trustworthy, and respectful. If emotional reactions flair, being responsible for dealing with their own feelings, and remembering how sensitive the other is, helps keep negative dramas to a minimum. Vulnerability is a far better strategy than anger for eliciting cooperation.

Cancers appeal most to Scorpios by remaining empowered, yet available and nurturing. Showing their loyalty and genuine concern helps Scorpios relax and trust. If Cancers want Scorpios to consider their ideas or requests, they can entice them by allowing their input. When Scorpios see Cancers hold no hidden agendas, they'll be more openly sensitive and caring.

Scorpios are most attractive to Cancers when they're tender, flexible, and encouraging. If Scorpios couple their insightfulness with compassion, Cancers trust and feel closer to them. Scorpios needn't hide their anger or cynicisms from Cancers. But it's easier for Cancers to hear if they're assured it won't be aimed at them. If it is, Scorpios would be wiser to soften the blow, lest they'll be left with clammed-up, defensive Cancers.

Romantic problems can best be resolved when both Cancers and Scorpios remain unquestionably attentive and loyal. Since withholding only backfires into painful separation, each is more likely to receive the affection and satisfaction they desire by offering generosity and compassion. That'll keep their fires kindled.

The Cancer/Sagittarius Relationship ♥

Cancers and Sagittarians can enjoy an unusual relationship that provides each with new approaches and perspectives. They're bonded by a mutual love of personal growth and stimulating experiences. Even their differences can prove complementary: Cancers' internal nature sparks Sagittarians to explore the richness of their inner life, while Sagittarians' love of the great outdoors awakens Cancers' adventurousness. When they connect, life becomes exciting and active yet also nurturing and tender. Unique things spring from their partnership.

Cancers feel empowered by Sagittarians' confidence and encouraged by their optimism to consider bigger possibilities. Sagittarians lift Cancers' spirits, and their cavalier attitude helps them overcome worries. Cancers learn directness from Sagittarians' frankness. Sagittarians' insightfulness heals Cancers and helps them succeed at work.

Sagittarians respect Cancers' nurturing world as a life-enhancing territory they'd like to explore. They're soothed by Cancers' tenderness and enjoy partaking of the insight their sensitivities offer. Sagittarians learn from Cancers how emotional availability, even vulnerability, doesn't negate strength but delivers it. In fact, Cancers help Sags to transform aspects of themselves or their lives into something more profound.

Romance between Cancers and Sagittarians is unexpected yet compelling. Cancers are awestruck by Sagittarians' skywriting courtship and robust sexuality. Sags love penetrating the mysteries of Cancers' interior world to discover and win the prize of their sensual, instinctive affections.

Possible Cancer/Sagittarius Challenges

Cancers and Sagittarians are different in so many ways, that it's easy for misunderstandings and frustrations to create distance between them. Whereas Cancers are personal, introverted, and emotional,

Sagittarians are social, extroverted, and intellectual. Cancers can consider Sagittarians' gregariousness overwhelming and their optimism too superficial to connect with. Sagittarians can consider Cancers to be too self-protective to have fun and too emotional to understand.

Cancers bristle around Sagittarians' fiery exuberance and are horrified by their frankness. Cancers wait in steamy resentment for Sags to quit dominating the conversation so they can get a word in edgewise. They wonder why Sagittarians always search foreign lands and study exotic philosophies when a rich home life could provide the satisfactions they seek.

Sagittarians find Cancers' worrisome feelings exasperating. They refuse to kowtow to Cancers' need for tender indulgences and expect them to toughen up more and react less. Sagittarians find Cancers' self-involvement boring and wish they would consider schemes grander than their personal lives.

Romantic problems arise if Cancers sulk because of Sags' thoughtlessness, or Sags become deflated by Cancers' moodiness. If Cancers feel distressed over Sagittarians' flirting or find them too sexually aggressive, or if Sagittarians feel suffocated by Cancers' clinginess or find them too sexually passive, lovemaking fizzles.

Advice for the Cancer / Sagittarius Relationship

Cancers and Sagittarians need to make some adjustments to get along, but the rewards can be worth the effort. Cancers' world blasts open when they ride the waves of Sagittarians' enthusiasm and take advantage of the opportunities they present. Sagittarians discover more of the enlightenment they seek by learning from Cancers' sensitivity.

Cancers appeal most to Sagittarians by staying open and curious good sports. Instead of expecting Sagittarians to be nurturing, Cancers might notice how they're supportive via encouragement and teaching. If Cancers feel hurt, simply telling Sagittarians about it works better than clamming up. Although Sagittarians will be surprised, they'll hopefully try to be more careful next time.

Sagittarians get the most out of Cancers when they are tender, attentive, and sensitive. Sagittarians needn't understand Cancers' every emotion. But if they would acknowledge them as okay, Cancers could relax and feel satisfied. Sagittarians endear themselves to Cancers by showing interest in their world and family. Cancers are most open to considering Sagittarians' projects and views when they see how they and those they love can benefit by them.

Romance flows most easily when Cancers trust Sagittarians' affection as sincere and Sagittarians accept Cancers' feelings as valuable avenues for intimacy. If Sagittarians approach Cancers with a bit more tenderness and gentle romance, and Cancers show more sexual adventurousness, lovemaking becomes all the more satisfying.

The Cancer/Capricorn Relationship ♥♥

Cancers and Capricorns can enjoy a rich and fulfilling relationship that comes from being opposite signs. They bond through their tenacious drive to create a life of security and abundance. Their unique gifts and perspectives are complementary: Cancers work to establish a warm and cozy personal life, while Capricorns work to create an impressive worldly life. Together, Cancers and Capricorns make a resourceful pair, one that achieves the personal and social distinctions that satisfies them and supports the many they care for.

Cancers feel supported by Capricorns' respectable capabilities. They love how Capricorns win prestigious trophies and tend to life's harsher realities so they don't have to. Cancers also appreciate how Capricorns hold life steady by refusing to allow passions to veer them off course. Capricorns may even act as parental figures who provide Cancers with realistic advice and disciplined direction.

Capricorns love how Cancers' admiration and support softens their world. They are grateful for Cancers' nurturing, and their genuine tenderness helps Capricorns let down their guard. They're awed by Cancers' instinctive ability to accomplish so much while caring for so many others as they do. Cancers' loyalty and support is the foundation from which Capricorns build their empire.

Romance between Cancers and Capricorns can be deliciously intimate as each feels grateful for the nurturing affection and sexual attentiveness the other provides. Lovemaking lingers with the rich exploring of delights. After all, when opposites attract, a feeling of wholeness ensues.

Possible Cancer/Capricorn Challenges

Although Cancers' and Capricorns' opposite natures attract them, they can also polarize them. Even when agreeing on goals, they go about achieving them in dramatically different ways. Cancers operate by making sure they and everyone around them are nurtured and personally tended to, while Capricorns operate by expecting themselves and others to attend to their pragmatic duties. Cancers pressure Capricorns to be more tender and sensitive, and they complain bitterly when Capricorns aren't. Capricorns wish Cancers would quit worrying about their feelings and dismiss them when they don't.

Cancers resent Capricorns' inflexible plans and rules. They're terribly hurt when Capricorns put business before their personal concerns, and they are deflated by Capricorns' perfectionism and criticism. Cancers think Capricorns' cautiousness keeps their and everyone's inner child from having any fun.

Capricorns can find Cancers' emotional demands and reactions as useless distractions. They roll their eyes as Cancers erupt with yet another emotional outburst, thinking, *Why can't you control yourself?* They wish Cancers would worry about their personal world less and their greater world and what should be achieved in it more.

Romantic problems can arise if Cancers feel shut out by Capricorns' stoicism, or if Capricorns feel exasperated by Cancers' emotions. Should one or both withhold affection or indulgence, their bedroom becomes a very cold place, indeed.

Advice for the Cancer/Capricorn Relationship

Cancers and Capricorns get along best by leveraging their differences. When Cancers respect Capricorns' practical strategies, they'll not only get along better with Capricorns, they may learn how stepping beyond distracting emotions helps them achieve even more. If Capricorns value Cancers' sensitivity, they'll not only connect better with Cancers, they may learn how to connect better with everyone and be more satisfied by their achievements.

Cancers are most appealing to Capricorns when they're practical, reasonable, and productive. Instead of expecting Capricorns to be cushy, Cancers are happier when realizing that Capricorns show caring by doing and accomplishing things that provide. Capricorns are most interested in Cancers' requests when Cancers do what nurtures them most: show them respect and admiration.

Capricorns are most attractive to Cancers when they let their hair down and make an attempt to consider their feelings and concerns. Instead of expecting Cancers to be less sensitive, Capricorns might use them as emotional weather vanes of the environment. Cancers feel more willing to consider Capricorns' requests when they're presented with tenderness and flexibility.

Romance flows most easily when Cancers and Capricorns keep their affection and desirous attentiveness flowing. When both feel loved for who they are, both open their vulnerable and giving natures. That makes their luscious, captivating sexuality last.

The Cancer/Aquarius Relationship ♥

Cancers and Aquarians enjoy an unusual relationship that awakens one another to innovative ideas and approaches—especially when they accept they're nothing alike. They can bond through their mutual love and concern for others and their drive to create a better world. Their differences can be intriguing complements: Cancers' ease with emotions reminds Aquarians to connect with others' feelings when trying to introduce new ideas while Aquarians' logic shows Cancers how to look at matters objectively in order to better recognize what others truly need. When they join forces, Cancers and Aquarians spark unique ideas and creations that combine global vision with a personal touch.

Cancers respect Aquarians' social vision, which treats the world as one big family. They're fascinated by Aquarians' knack for emotional resistance, which helps them take a useful, rational stance. Aquarians stir Cancers to transform, awaken, or use their resources in a new way.

Aquarians appreciate the goodness of Cancers' nurturing and respect their efforts to care for others. Cancers' emotional promptings help Aquarians take better care of themselves, and their satisfying personal lives remind Aquarians to create one of their own. Cancers heal Aquarians and help them succeed at work.

Romance between Cancers and Aquarians is unexpected yet interesting. Cancers feel honored that Aquarians show them special interest and indulge them with affectionate thoughtfulness. Aquarians relish Cancers showing them unusual intimacy by satisfying their every sexual desire.

Possible Cancer/Aquarius Challenges

Cancers' and Aquarians' many differences can make it hard for them to understand each other, much less get along. While Cancers focus on their personal lives, and the emotions and dramas involved, Aquarians focus on their community and the inventive ways it could be improved. Cancers seek intimate, family-type relationships, while Aquarians enjoy friendly relationships with many people, including strangers. Cancers complain that Aquarians are too logical and distracted with causes to share any intimacies, while Aquarians complain that Cancers are too self-involved and needy to have a rational conversation.

Cancers feel lonely due to Aquarians' detached stance and shiver around their cold reason. They consider Aquarians too remote or uncaring, especially when they turn a deaf ear toward others' (and their) emotional pleas and requests. They wish Aquarians would reveal the person behind all their concepts and inventions.

Aquarians find Cancers' emotions illogical and their need for indulgence to be annoyingly selfish. Aquarians don't want to hear about Cancers' private concerns, and they cringe when Cancers ask them about theirs.

Romantic problems arise if Cancers feel hurt by Aquarians' aloofness or independence, or Aquarians are turned off by Cancers' moodiness and clingy possessiveness. When misunderstandings or unmet needs erupt, attraction and lovemaking both fade out.

Advice for the Cancer/Aquarius Relationship

Undoubtedly, Cancers and Aquarians need to make adjustments in order to get along. But each teaches something so unique, they're worth it! When Cancers see how supportive Aquarians' logic can be, they'll not only get along better with Aquarians, they'll discover how sticking to the facts can lend them greater emotional freedom. When Aquarians learn from Cancers that acknowledging emotions and personal needs solidifies friendships, they'll not only connect better with Cancers, they'll more effectively build the community they envision.

Cancers are most attractive to Aquarians when they're logical and neutral. Accepting that Aquarians aren't wired to be emotionally gushy or personal helps Cancers realize how they show deep affection via friendship and sharing ideas. Aquarians are most interested in Cancers' ideas and requests when Cancers show them how they'll help make the world a better place.

Aquarians get the most out of Cancers when they are more expressive and personally available with them. Instead of expecting Cancers to be less reactive, Aquarians are happier when they see Cancers' sensitivity as an evolved gift. Cancers are most open to Aquarians' innovations when they see how they and others will be nourished by them.

Romance between Cancers and Aquarians flows most easily when Aquarians show special attention to Cancers, and Cancers give Aquarians space to be with friends and to think and talk about ideas. When Cancers snap Aquarians out of aloofness by wooing them with creative flattery, and Aquarians entice Cancers with tender indulgences, their uniqueness sparks remarkable satisfaction.

The Cancer/Pisces Relationship ♥♥♥♥

Pisces and Cancers can enjoy a wonderfully rich and harmonious relationship wherein each feels deeply understood and cared for. Their similarities bond them: both are emotional and sensitive and love caring for others. Each functions best when the atmosphere is safe and tender, so they'll gently smooth over any problems that arise. Communication comes easily between Pisces and Cancers as they love using their insights, feelings, and creativity to make life more textured and interesting. They especially enjoy combining their caring forces to attend to anyone and everyone who has a need they could fulfill.

Cancers love the safe and soft world Pisces create. They enjoy getting lost in Pisces' imaginative ideas and thrill to their creative surprises. Cancers especially appreciate how Pisces yield their own preferences to create a loving harmony with them and others. Plus, Pisces help Cancers feel in control and safe.

Pisces enjoy the tender pampering Cancers provide them and others. They appreciate Cancers' vulnerability and take refuge in their sensitivity. Cancers' adoration sparks Pisces' confidence and creativity. They love impressing Cancers with their insights and relish giggling thanks to Cancers' kooky humor. Importantly, Cancers understand Pisces' complexity and sufferings.

Romance between Cancers and Pisces is a lush, dreamy affair. Each thrives on the affectionate and imaginative courtship the other provides. Lovemaking is incredibly intimate and tender, and it communicates the depth and spirituality they share.

Possible Cancer / Pisces Challenges

Although Cancers and Pisces usually take refuge in each other's emotional sensitivities, they can also find them troubling. Each might feel hurt or imagine slights the other never intended. Or, instead of encouraging each other to see what's good in life, they can reinforce a belief that life is painful or discouraging. Then, feeling sorry for themselves gets in the way of feeling empowered.

Cancers find Pisces' disinterest in the material world threateningly irresponsible. They're distressed when Pisces break agreements and fume when Pisces neglect practical concerns. Cancers feel invisible when Pisces get lost in their own feelings and imaginative scenarios.

Pisces find Cancers' concern about themselves to be selfish. They want Cancers to worry about meeting their own needs less and worry more about the plight of needy others. The bubble of Pisces' magic gets popped when Cancers insist on discussing security concerns, like how the mortgage will be paid. They wish Cancers would quit controlling and start trusting life's magical flow.

Romantic problems arise if Cancers feel Pisces are more in love with their fantasies than they are with them, or if Pisces feel Cancers are more concerned with security than with romance. Hurt feelings make each turn silent and withdrawn. When neither trusts the other's loyalty or genuine concern, their bedroom magic goes poof.

Advice for the Cancer/Pisces Relationship

Cancers and Pisces get along best when they clearly support and nurture each other. When Pisces value attending to Cancers' security needs, they'll not only win Cancers' trust and openness, they might learn how to secure more of their own desires. When Cancers support Pisces' creative fantasies, Pisces not only remain interested and available, it might also help Cancers better tend to their own creativity.

Cancers are most attractive to Pisces when they're tender and imaginative. When they indulge Pisces' romanticism, Pisces find anything, even paying the mortgage, more compelling. It also helps if Cancers clearly yet gently identify what they need from Pisces to feel safe. That gives Pisces boundaries they can work with.

Pisces get the most out of Cancers when they remain attentive. Cancers will be more open and cooperative with Pisces' needs when they see they won't lose anything by indulging them. Cancers find Pisces' imaginations captivating, but resent being eclipsed by them.

Pisces might reassure Cancers that they are included and considered, even if they seem miles away.

Romantic problems can most easily be resolved when Pisces remain the attentive and trustworthy creatures Cancers need them to be, and when Cancers remain the understanding, romantic souls Pisces seek. That allows both to fully immerse themselves in a glorious sea of intimacy.

How Leos Match Up

The Leo / Aries Relationship

See *The Aries/Leo Relationship* on page 298.

The Leo / Taurus Relationship

See *The Taurus/Leo Relationship* on page 330.

The Leo / Gemini Relationship

See *The Gemini/Leo Relationship* on page 359.

The Leo/Cancer Relationship

See *The Cancer/Leo Relationship* on page 386.

The Leo/Leo Relationship ♥♥

Leos can enjoy a flamboyant, powerful, and adoring relationship that's wonderfully rich in affection and drama. Being the same sign gives each Leo unique insight into the other's need for excitement, indulgence, and being exalted as special. They'll lavish that and plenty more on each other like few others can. Leos' shared passion to live a fabulous life helps them support each other's considerable ambitions. Their love of creating an admirable image sparks each to look and act their best. Everything a pair of Leos endeavor in is delivered with grand leadership and creativity. With their humor and bighearted showmanship, they provide endless entertainment for themselves and the crowds of admiring others who want to be a part of their circle.

Leos love the exciting extravaganzas other Leos stir. They feel honored to be with fellow powerful creatures who make them shine. Leos also understand that behind their companions' bellowing, expressive confidence is a desire to be loved and reassured. Each provides the encouragement and bolstering neither would ever ask for directly but needs and deeply appreciates nevertheless.

Romance between Leos is a sight to behold! Glamorous dates, lavish gifts, and doting attentions all create a gloriously festive courtship. Lovemaking is earth-shattering as both adore showing off and giving full rein to their lusty passions.

Possible Leo/Leo Challenges

*A*s with all same-sign relationships, Leos can be too much alike to get along or keep each other interested. Leos' wills are so powerful and their determination is so strong that huge control clashes can erupt between them. Both are driven to direct matters in the superior way they envision. If they should (erroneously) assume the other will follow, a defiant standoff will ensue. Since Leos see compromise as weakness, cooperation can be hard to achieve. Competition over anything can complicate Leos' relationships. Vying for the spotlight is a common challenge. Both want the attention and resent it if the other gets it.

Sometimes in their attempt to maintain a good image, Leos can pressure each other to parade appealing, but false, fronts. Or, they can get so caught up in their fantasies about their relationship that Leos can ignore what's truly happening. That makes both feel lonely.

Leos have passionate, fiery temperaments. When tempers blow, hurtful things can be said. Posturing requests for respect go something like this, "Do you know who you're talking to?" or, "I should be treated better than this!"

Romantic problems arise between Leos if they feel they don't get the adoration or affection they deserve or if either suspects disloyalty. If they fall in love with their image of the other and ignore their true selves, it's disappointing for both. When arguments take the place of affection, the fireworks happen outside rather than in the bedroom.

Advice for the Leo/Leo Relationship

Leos get along best when they treat each other the way they like to be treated. Showering each other with applause, listening with encouragement, and purring about each other's wonderfulness works wonders to bring out their best. When Leos feel appreciated, they can't help but generously return the favor.

Leos are happiest when they make loving a stronger priority than maintaining control, image, or pride. What reminds Leos to choose love? By watching the other Leos do so. That's the dignity and class Leos love best in each other.

When stubborn standoffs take over, showing clear respect for one another and each taking a step toward flexibility (even if it's a tiny one) help diffuse willfulness. Offering understanding, support, and a joke or two works wonders to encourage Leos to see each other's point of view. Leos remembering that the spotlight is big enough for both of them keeps them from begrudging the other's time in it.

Romantic problems can be resolved when each Leo keeps the courtship job one. Never taking each other for granted and always showing admiration is the key to keeping Leos' love affairs burning. Making their Leo feel like the sexiest lover alive keeps the enthusiasm and creativity burning in the bedroom.

The Leo/Virgo Relationship ♥♥

Leos and Virgos can enjoy an interesting and dynamic relationship, full of satisfying ideas and projects. They're bonded by their industrious urges, intelligent perspectives, and interest in others. Their gifts can be most complementary: Leos appreciate how deftly Virgos handle the details so they can attend to grander visions, while Virgos love how Leos whip up exciting adventures they might be too humble to initiate on their own. Whatever Virgos and Leos endeavor in comes off with the flair and effectiveness that satisfies them and attracts admiration from the many they appeal to.

Virgos feel encouraged by Leos' confidence and inspired by their big-picture ambitions. They count on Leos' leadership to makes things happen with gusto and flair while retaining a solid practicality they feel secure in. Virgos appreciate how Leos show them how they can work against themselves less and apply their talents toward significant success more. Leos' applause reminds Virgos they needn't be perfect to be lovable.

Leos love that Virgos are classy, refined companions whose discerning brilliance and concern gives support they can rely on. Leos appreciate how Virgos offer realistic advice yet never steal their thunder or try to take over control. Virgos bolster Leos' self-esteem and perhaps their bank accounts!

Romance between Virgos and Leos is celebratory yet refined. Each offers the loyalty and respect the other needs to expose their loving hearts and desires. Their love life is supported by a natural affection that teeters into the occasional wild "Wow! That was awesome!"

Possible Leo/Virgo Challenges

Since Leos are fiery and boisterous, and Virgos are earthy and subtle, their different styles can spark clashes. Virgos' knack for focusing on details rather than getting excited over the big picture deflates and annoys Leos, while Virgos become overwhelmed and suspicious when Leos' plans seem too outrageous or ambitious to be realistic. Both can believe the other's perspective is way off.

Leos' pride gets hurt when Virgos criticize rather than applaud them. Their worries over possible problems or mistakes cause Leos' optimism to plummet. Leos resent Virgos' eye-rolling insinuations that their egos are overblown. Their urge to make life a party gets drowned out by Virgos making life a job.

Virgos see Leos' self-congratulating as egomaniacal. They cringe around Leos' chest-pounding pronouncements of greatness, thinking they should work harder to become as great as they claim they are. They resent that Leos are clueless but don't know it.

Romantic problems can arise when Virgos' fastidious propriety and Leos' lusty spontaneity clash. If Virgos aren't exuberant enough or Leos subtle enough to woo each other, their courtship and lovemaking become disappointing.

Advice for the Leo/Virgo Relationship

Leos and Virgos get along best by leveraging their differences. When Leos understand that Virgos' care and creativity are expressed through their detailed, helpful critiques, they'll realize how special they are for receiving them. When Virgos understand that Leos' job is to be a strong leader, they can get on with appreciating what they do best: promoting what's good. If Virgos use Leos' exuberance and Leos use Virgos' analysis more, both could be more effective in realizing their dreams.

Virgos appeal most to Leos when they are enthusiastic and

confident. Showing Leos they're considering their ideas with optimism and respect helps Leos be more open to Virgos' concerns. Leos
respect Virgos' smart insights, they just don't want their visions or
their pride clobbered by them. Virgos can entice Leos' cooperation
when they make it seem fun and admirable to do so.

Leos are most attractive to Virgos when they demonstrate finesse
and levelheaded practicality. They entice their playfulness by assuring
Virgos it won't mess things up. Showing Virgos they're considering
subtle truths, about themselves and others as well as their projects,
makes Virgos want to join them even more.

Romance works best when Leos do those little nuanced acts that turn
Virgos on, and when Virgos do those expressive big shows that turn
Leos on. Leos: subtlety and attention to detail is Virgos' delight! Virgos:
be enthusiastic! Let Leos know how much you like what they do right!

The Leo / Libra Relationship ♥♥♥

Leos and Libras can enjoy a wonderfully delightful relationship
that's rich in creativity and interesting social adventures. Their similarities attract and bond them: both have a flair for initiating fun and
gracious activities, pursuing the finer things in life and creating beauty.
Each cherishes their relationships and devotes themselves to making
them sing. Libras and Leos also find it easy to understand each other
and enjoy promoting each other's dreams. They make a sparkling,
glamorous pair, one that entertains the many in their wide social circle
with clever repartee and worthwhile contributions. Everything they
endeavor is done with elegance and style.

Leos are enchanted by Libras' outer beauty and captivated by their inner graciousness. They adore how Libras' charm and elegant companionship makes them shine. Leos especially appreciate how Libras support them with fair and diplomatic advice while never trying to overtly control them.

Libras are moved by Leos' power and honored to be part of their glamorous show. They respect Leos' leadership and are grateful for their loyalty. Libras love how Leos' creative surprises make life zesty and posh. Leos make natural friends to Libras, who help them realize hopes and dreams through savvy advice and influential connections.

Romance between Libras and Leos is full of the glamorous dates, indulgent affections, and the "I can't live without you" moments that make courtship thrilling. Sexuality is a dance between lusty ravishing and enticing conversations about delights still to come.

Possible Leo/Libra Challenges

Although Leos and Libras are compatible, they do have some traits that drive the other nuts. Since Libras approach things intellectually and Leos are more instinctive, decision making can be problematic. Libras' strategy of intellectually weighing options differs from Leos', who make gut-level decisions in seconds flat. Leos feel thwarted by Libras' indecisiveness, while Leos' insistence that their ideas are the best seems controlling and inconsiderate to Libras. Leos wish Libras would spend less time considering and more time acting, while Libras wish Leos would spend less time selling themselves and more time genuinely considering others.

Leos see Libras' indecisiveness as weak. They wonder if Libras and their resolve are strong enough to handle them or to keep them loyal.

Plus, Libras' constant concern over being appropriate exasperates Leos. They wish Libras would quit worrying about offending others and just say what's on their minds.

Libras can find Leos' expression too dominating. They resent when Leos try to push decisions they aren't ready to make or seem distracted when they want to talk ideas out. And why do bossy Leos have to bellow out commands when a simple "Would you mind" would be more gracious?

Romantic problems can arise if Leos find Libras too yielding to stand up to their sexual power, or if Libras find Leos too vigorous to woo them. If Libras shun Leos' lustiness, or Leos aren't sensitive to Libras' need for finesse, lovemaking is full of disappointments.

Advice for the Leo/Libra Relationship

It's pretty easy for Leos and Libras to get along when they make simple adjustments for each other's temperament. If Libras accept Leos' dominating power as fair in its own right, and Leos understand Libras' evaluations as a form of strength, admiration and peace can flourish between them.

Leos get along best with Libras when they remain creative and expressive. And remember to ask about them. Libras love Leos' dynamism, they just don't like when it creates imbalanced social scenes. Libras also relax and enjoy Leos when they show consideration to all in Libras' orbit.

Libras get the most out of Leos when they remain charming and expressive, yet direct and decisive. Leos like powerful companions, and find Libras most attractive when they show confidence and poise. If

Libras are indecisive, no apologies! Instead, they should let Leos know that's how they make up their minds. Leos respect that.

Romantic problems between Libras and Leos are resolved when Leos add refinement and Libras add power to their lust. When each reassures the other how loved and desired they truly are, issues are easily overcome and their relationship is filled with laughter and togetherness.

The Leo / Scorpio Relationship ♥♥

Leos and Scorpios can enjoy an intense and compelling relationship, especially when they forget trying to control each other. Their similarities can bond them: both are strong, determined, and ambitious and agree that life should be stable and consistent. Each places a high value on loyalty and sticks to commitments they make. Even their differences prove complementary: Scorpios count on Leos' extroversion to capitalize on and promote opportunities their own private natures may shun, while Leos count on Scorpios' strategic insights to draw them past appearances to notice the deeper workings of the world and themselves. When they combine their considerable forces, Leos and Scorpios realize grand ambitions with strategic brilliance and motivate throngs of others.

Leos are seduced by Scorpios' power and enthralled by their magnetism. They love that Scorpios not only stand up to their power but challenge them to reach for more! Leos respect Scorpios' deep insights and learn from their psychological savvy. Scorpios encourage Leos to achieve more earnest successes by helping them step away from simply glamour-based ones.

Scorpios are struck by Leos' confidence and intrigued by their charisma. They admire how Leos openly parade who they are and what they want for all the world to see. Scorpios are encouraged by Leos' warmhearted assurances, especially since Leos are remarkably capable. Leos support Scorpios' authority and professional success.

Romance between Leos and Scorpios is an explosion of the seductions and lusty sexuality each lives for. Intensity is their keyword as each enchants the other to forget about inhibitions and try anything, even if it's a little naughty. Arguments? Guaranteed. But the lovemaking afterward is fantastic.

Possible Leo / Scorpio Challenges

Clashing of wills is expected between Leos and Scorpios, as each uses their power and determination toward different ends. Leos are fiery and open and want to make everything fun and celebratory. Scorpios are more emotional and secretive and love piercing through images to discover hidden issues. Leos write off Scorpios as negative and obsessed with problems. Scorpios dismiss Leos as superficial and naive. When both stubbornly adhere to their vision while resisting the other's input, their power struggles reach mythic proportions.

Leos drown in Scorpios' suspicions and deflate due to Scorpios' cutting remarks. Scorpios' perfectionism and micromanagement frustrates big-picture Leos. They wish Scorpios would quit imagining the worst and start imagining happier possibilities.

Scorpios feel usurped by Leos' antics. They cringe when Leos brush off their concerns as pessimistic. Scorpios find Leos' boastful self-satisfaction particularly objectionable, thinking, "How can they be so proud of themselves when their lack of introspection leaves them so clueless?"

Romantic problems can arise from Leos being too brash and showy, or Scorpios being too subtle. If Scorpios deny the fanfare and applause Leos need, or Leos avoid the deep, merging intimacy Scorpios crave, no amount of makeup sex overcomes the frustrations.

Advice for the Leo/Scorpio Relationship

Leos and Scorpios certainly need to bend a bit to each other's wills in order to get along. The good news? Their determined resolve can be used to overcome problems and get on with enjoying the assets each offers.

Leos appeal most to Scorpios when they're thoughtful and deep. Instead of expecting Scorpios to be sunnier, Leos might value the deeper insights Scorpios offer. That not only helps Scorpios trust and take Leos seriously, it helps Leos notice complexities that can promote them. Plus, toning down their self-promotion and tuning up their sensitivity motivates Scorpios to support rather than sting Leos.

Scorpios are most attractive to Leos when they remain good sports. Scorpios elicit more cooperation and support from Leos when they support their egos rather than belittle them. Instead of expecting Leos to go any deeper, Scorpios might look to see the savvy intelligence they do express. When Scorpios ride Leos' optimism, they not only appeal more to Leos, they might find life itself becomes more appealing.

Romantic problems can better be overcome when Leos bring the depth and explorative rhythm Scorpios desire, and when Scorpios rev up the playful demonstrativeness Leos adore. That'll release a tidal wave of satisfaction that washes misunderstandings to sea.

The Leo/Sagittarius Relationship ♥♥♥♥

Leos and Sags can enjoy a wonderfully exciting and passionate relationship that's rich in inspiring ideas and joyful adventures. Their similarities make relating and bonding natural: both have excitable, confident, and extroverted natures and relish living life to its fullest. Their mutual admiration inspires one another to take risks and be the best they can be. Leos and Sagittarians each love using their dynamism and leadership skills to create grand, extraordinary scenes. Whatever they do together is sure to be fun for them and impressive to others.

Leos love Sagittarians' nonstop action and excitement. They adore that Sagittarians never flinch from their power but rather fan its flames by applauding their ideas and running with their projects. Leos respect Sagittarians' confident thinking and ride on their optimistic philosophies. Sagittarians make Leos' lives more fun and expressive by awakening their hearts and encouraging their childlike zest.

Sagittarians thrive on Leos' positive encouragements and adore their entertaining antics. They appreciate how Leos never shrink from their risky or grand ideas, but rather initiate strategies to make them a reality. Sagittarians find Leos' regal dignity admirable and rely on their glamorous savvy to guide them. Leos' bighearted loving and generosity brings even greater meaning to Sagittarians' lives.

Romance between Leos and Sagittarians is an extravaganza of overt, lusty passions and playful adventures. The exciting dates and effusive adorations make courtship a consuming affair. Sexuality is intense and passionate with loads of laughter.

Possible Leo/Sagittarius Challenges

Since Leos and Sagittarians are such fiery creatures, their powers occasionally combust. When they compete for dominance or drive toward different goals, tempers flair. And monumental battles ensue if both feel the other isn't exalting them as they should.

Leos find Sagittarians' restless wanderings threatening. They might want more commitment from Sagittarians but not get it, then resent Sagittarians doing what they please as selfish and uncontrollable. Sags' expansive ambitions can seem too pie-in-the-sky for pragmatic Leos.

Sagittarians can find Leos' control confining and dismiss their need to maintain a good image in others' eyes as a waste of time. They resent Leos' need for stability as limiting and their drive to have their own way as annoyingly dominating. Sagittarians lose patience with Leos' need for applause and wish they would be inspired by something other than themselves.

Romantic problems can arise when Leos become jealous and try to corral Sagittarians' wandering eyes, or when Sagittarians rebel from Leos' control, making them feel insecure. When consuming passions turn into consuming resentment, the raging bonfires of the bedroom quickly turn into cold cinders.

Advice for the Leo / Sagittarius Relationship

Leos and Sagittarians get along best when they enjoy each other's power without trying to direct or improve it. Then they can get on with the inspiration and admiration that attracted them in the first place.

Leos are most attractive to Sagittarians when they're flexible and inspired. Instead of expecting Sagittarians to be more pragmatic, Leos remain happier by understanding that Sagittarians love ideas just for their own expansive sake. Leos entice Sagittarians' commitments by showing how much they'll gain and how little they'll lose by making them. After all, no one can be as captivating to Sagittarians as Leos, especially when they're happily in control.

Sagittarians appeal most to Leos by being loyal and attentive. Instead of rebelling from Leos' control, Sags might appease them by negotiating some basic things they need to feel secure. As long as Leos feel special and adored, they'll be most flexible and accommodating.

Romantic problems can be resolved when Sagittarians make Leos feel special by lavishing attention on them, and when Leos make Sagittarians feel free by good-naturedly letting them explore. When both remain their confident, indulgent selves, they remain irresistibly enticed inside and outside the bedroom.

The Leo / Capricorn Relationship ♥

Leos and Capricorns can enjoy an intriguing and powerful relationship, especially when they respect each other's leadership. Much can bond them: both are strong, determined creatures who love partaking of life's best offerings and orchestrating big and important events. Even their differences can prove complementary: Leos' flamboyance brings the glamour and excitement Capricorns enjoy but might be too cautious to create, while Capricorns' careful regimens create the sound structures Leos admire but are too expansive to adhere to. They inspire each other to attain the achievements that satisfy them and attract throngs of admirers who want to be part of their success.

Leos love that Capricorns are as powerful as they are and think as big as they do. They admire Capricorns' political savvy and respect how they overcome tough obstacles. Leos are most attracted to the prestige and honor Capricorns' success creates. They especially adore Capricorns' humor. Capricorns heal Leos and influence their professional success.

Capricorns respect how Leos' regal presence ushers them to the head of any line. They admire Leos' magnetism and respect how their gutsy leadership "shoots from the hip" yet still realizes remarkable success. Leos' joviality lifts Capricorns' spirits and their flattery encourages them. Leos transform Capricorns by enticing their sexuality or guiding their resources to greater aims.

Romance between Leos and Capricorns is unexpected, yet compelling. Since each finds the other's power and influence an aphrodisiac, courtship is a parade of impressive dates and prestigious activities. Sexuality is a surprisingly lusty melding of Leos' fiery passions and Capricorns' earthy sensuality.

Possible Leo/Capricorn Challenges

Since Leos and Capricorns use completely different strategies to lead, power struggles over control are likely. Whereas Leos command with flamboyance, trumpet blows of self-promotion, and glamorous enticements for others to join in their fun, Capricorns direct with careful regimens and plans and expect others to respect their position of authority. Leos consider Capricorns' adherence to duty oppressive and unimaginative, while Capricorns think Leos are all sizzle and no substance.

Leos feel stifled around Capricorns' cautiousness and confined by their stuffy decorum. Capricorns' stoicism deflates them, and they feel sorry Capricorns have to take themselves and life so seriously. Worse, Leos feel hurt when Capricorns focus on responsibilities rather than on them.

Capricorns resent Leos' sense of entitlement for power they don't pay dues for. They dismiss Leos' confidence as brash arrogance that's naively unaware of important things. Capricorns wish that Leos would quit preening, stop congratulating themselves, and do something substantive.

Romantic problems can arise when Capricorns' stoicism or criticism hurt Leos, or when Leos' overt sexuality embarrasses Capricorns. Leos' passions may be deflated while waiting for Capricorns to find their right time and place, while Capricorns are turned off when Leos insist on showy public displays of affection.

Advice for the Leo/Capricorn Relationship

Leos and Capricorns get along best when they show admiration for one another by supporting rather than complaining about the other's style of control. If Leos admit that Capricorns' dutiful decorum has respectable merit, and Capricorns get excited over Leos' glamorous inspirations, both are more generous and cooperative with each other. Who knows? They might even learn something from each other.

Leos appeal most to Capricorns by toning down their flamboyance and turning up their practicality. Capricorns are more interested in Leos' suggestions when they're presented with logical plans Capricorns can feel secure about. Leos endear themselves to Capricorns by admiring their accomplishments and downright melt them with sincere flattery.

Capricorns are most attractive to Leos when they're spontaneous and creative. Leos will consider Capricorns' plans and concerns when they show how exciting they'll be to create. Leos glow when Capricorns applaud them and stop at nothing to help them when they praise their efforts as marvelous.

Romantic problems can better be resolved when Capricorns indulge Leos' need for applause and flattery, and when Leos indulge Capricorns' need to be respected and revered. Leos get to see Capricorns' sexiest selves by patiently awaiting for the appropriate setting. Capricorns arouse the wildcat in Leos when they surprise them with creative seductions.

The Leo/Aquarius Relationship ♥♥

Leos and Aquarians can enjoy a wonderfully interesting and intriguing relationship, especially if they accept their different styles of showing caring. They're opposite signs, which means each expresses a different side of the same coin. Leos express regal distinctiveness with a personal warmth Aquarians adore but might be too cool to display, while Aquarians wow with zany individuality and impersonal objectivity Leos might respect but not always display. They bond through their inventiveness, strong wills, and desire to make a positive impact on their community. Their endeavors have an attention-grabbing, liberating, and awakening effect that makes the world a better place.

Leos respect Aquarians' global concerns and progressive thinking. They admire that Aquarians devote themselves to worthy causes and become inspired by them to make a contribution of their own. Plus, Aquarians' surprising unconventionality and interesting ideas entertain Leos to no end.

Aquarians adore Leos' irrepressible confidence and creativity. They respect Leos' ability to motivate and entertain others and enjoy being part of their social celebrations. Aquarians admire Leos' bighearted loyalty and learn from them how to openly encourage others' greatness. They appreciate Leos' wholehearted investments in who and what they love.

Romance between Aquarians and Leos is an enticing dance of sensual experimenting and playful talking. When Aquarians' surprising creativity meets Leos' dramatic passions, inhibitions fly away and their lovemaking is filled with satisfaction.

Possible Leo/Aquarius Challenges

Leos' and Aquarians opposite sign qualities can make them too different and yet ironically too alike to get along. They can whip up serious power struggles if each is determined to achieve different things. Or, Leos and Aquarians often stubbornly resist each other's control for fear of compromising their individuality.

Whereas Leos express individuality through a sense of being

special, Aquarians express it through uniqueness. Leos want and need to be exalted, while Aquarians believe they and every creature in the world is of equal importance. Each can feel they aren't important enough in the other's world.

Leos can find Aquarians' detached, logical ways alienating. They get hurt that Aquarians don't applaud or fuss over them, especially when they make huge fusses over members of the world they've never met. Leos' enthusiasm deflates around Aquarians' unemotional pragmatism. They wish Aquarians would quit being so aloof and start being more passionate.

Aquarians get overwhelmed by Leos' intensity and personal demands, and they feel exasperated by Leos' requests for personal attention, thinking "What makes *you* so special?" They resist catering to Leos' ego when the world needs so much attention.

Romantic problems can arise when Leos feel rejected by aloof Aquarians, or when Aquarians feel suffocated by Leos' pressures to be romantic. If one or both feels the other is stubbornly dismissing their requests or needs, lovemaking becomes scarce.

Advice for the Leo/Aquarius Relationship

Leos and Aquarians thrive when Leos understand that Aquarians show caring by being objective, and Aquarians accept that when Leos care, their passions make them anything but objective. If Leos think more impersonally and Aquarians think more personally, they'll not only get along better, they'll each gain a greater perspective for themselves.

Leos appeal most to Aquarians by being creative yet equal members of their group. Understanding that Aquarians show affection by being loyal, interesting friends, rather than applauding fans, helps Leos quit expecting them to be warmer. Leos entice Aquarians' support for their ideas by showing them how many people can benefit by them.

Aquarians get the most out of Leos when they are more indulging and warm toward them. They elicit more of Leos' enthusiasm and support by applauding them, rather than acting like they're no one special. After all, Leos want to make worldly contributions, too; they just want to be important and glamorous as they do so.

Romantic problems can more easily be resolved if Leos use their confidence and creativity to woo detached Aquarians back into the sexual game, and when Aquarians let Leos know how very special they are even when they're feeling detached. When Leos open Aquarians' hearts by being their friends, and Aquarians awaken Leos' hearts by being their lovers, their opposite natures keep them together.

The Leo/Pisces Relationship ♥

Leos and Pisces can enjoy an unusual and dramatic relationship, especially when they understand how very different they are. They can bond through their rich imaginations and knack for making life creative and romantic. Even their differences can prove enticing: Leos' confidence and ego-strength compels Pisces to stand up and promote themselves more, while Pisces' sensitivity and yielding awakens Leos to the power of their compassion. With their combined imaginations and visionary skills, Leo and Pisces invent marvelous projects that delight them and entertain the others they attract.

Leos are captivated by Pisces' mystery and enthralled by their fantasies. They love Pisces' creativity and all the romantic glamour it sparks. Their curiosity is piqued by how Pisces can be so tender and accepting yet still make important impacts. Pisces transform Leos, either by awakening their feelings or enriching their resources.

Pisces are awed by Leos' dynamic prowess and charmed by their magnetic charisma. Leos' bighearted heroism thrills Pisces, and their confidence makes Pisces feel uplifted. Pisces especially love the excitements Leos stir up, and they feel amazed by how Leos see their grand visions turn into reality. Leos heal Pisces and support their work.

Romance between Leos and Pisces is a grand stream of the glorious fantasies, delicious seductions, and enticing playfulness that creates the romance both dream about. Sexuality is fiery and deeply sensual as both adore losing themselves in consuming sensual pleasures.

Possible Leo/Pisces Challenges

Leos and Pisces are different in many essential ways, so frustrations and misunderstandings are likely between them. Whereas Leos are extroverted and use their egos to single themselves out, Pisces are more introverted and dissolve their egos' boundaries to merge with others. Leos can find Pisces maddeningly passive and impossible to pin down. Pisces can find Leos overwhelming and impossible to connect deeply with.

Leos interpret Pisces' knack for yielding to others as weak. They feel usurped by Pisces' easily interrupted schedules or their wandering from commitments they don't find interesting. Leos are suspicious that Pisces are hiding something and want them to have firmer convictions.

Pisces find Leos' outward focus boorish and lacking refinement.

Leos' temper singes Pisces' tender feelings to the core. Pisces see Leos' self-promotion as immature and misdirected, and they feel lonely when Leos don't listen to them. Pisces wish Leos would acknowledge pain and suffering, and find more (needed) depth and insightfulness.

Romantic problems can flair if Pisces aren't powerful enough for Leos, or if Leos aren't sensitive enough for Pisces. Leos can find Pisces too passive and resent being eclipsed by their emotions and fantasies. Pisces wish that Leos would be more gentle and try to connect with their feelings.

Advice for the Leo/Pisces Relationship

Leos and Pisces relate best when they direct their drama and creativity toward useful projects. If Leos understand that Pisces become empowered by the occasional painful feeling or merging with others, it not only helps them respect Pisces, it might show them how their own vulnerability makes them more accessible. When Pisces see how Leos' promoting their own egos enriches them so they feel capable of enriching others, they'll not only understand Leos better, they may learn how taking care of themselves helps them take better care of others.

Leos are most attractive to Pisces when they're considerate and flexible. Pisces trust and express more when they're wooed by Leos' strength, not overridden by it. Leos entice Pisces to adhere to their requests by showing Pisces how they would genuinely appreciate it or be helped by it.

Pisces are most appealing to Leos when they're powerful and involved. Leos respect Pisces' dreams and fantasies, but they need to be expressed in practical ways and include Leos. Want to entice Leos' support? Show them how heroic they'll be!

Romantic problems can be resolved when Pisces show the aggressive gusto and Leos show the sensitivity that each woo the other. When both feel assured and loved, their sexual powers are unstoppable.

How Virgos Match Up

The Virgo/Aries Relationship

See *The Aries/Virgo Relationship* on page 300.

The Virgo/Taurus Relationship

See *The Taurus/Virgo Relationship* on page 332.

The Virgo/Gemini Relationship

See *The Gemini/Virgo Relationship* on page 362.

The Virgo/Cancer Relationship

See *The Cancer/Virgo Relationship* on page 389.

The Virgo/Leo Relationship

See *The Leo/Virgo Relationship* on page 414.

The Virgo/Virgo Relationship ♥♥

Two Virgos can enjoy a fascinating and productive relationship, especially when they focus on what works. Their keen intelligence bonds them, as does their appreciation of fine details and love of service. They enjoy talking for hours about their analysis of matters great and small and how all things can be improved. Since Virgos love nothing more than a job well done, their combined industriousness tackles even the most difficult challenges to making life good for each other and great for those they love and serve.

Virgos see in each other what they most adore about themselves. They love the brilliant insights, respect their many accomplishments, and applaud their striving for excellence. Virgos cherish being able to depend on each other to complete tasks with refinement and zeal. They laugh about their pickiness and are eternally grateful to share their drive for order and cleanliness with someone who considers it as important as they do.

Virgos' unique understanding of each other's qualities helps them comfort and support each other. They know how satisfying, yet also challenging, their perfectionism and self-criticism can be, and how fears of inadequacy pop up because of it. Virgos bolster each other by pointing out what they do well, if not spectacularly. Virgos also understand how gratifying it is to be dedicated to work and rarely begrudge each other's busy schedules.

Romance between Virgos is a dance of subtleties: knowing glances, witty seductions, and surprisingly affectionate touches. Virgos respect the other's need for purity and genuineness, and extend countless little considerations that relax and open the other to sharing their natural sensuality.

Possible Virgo/Virgo Challenges

As with all same-sign relationships, two Virgos can be too alike to get along or keep each other interested. Sometimes Virgos' critical natures get the best of them. They can go overboard in finding what's wrong in life, lose sight of what's right, and become disheartened. Since Virgos are intensely aware of what needs to be improved about themselves, they don't appreciate their companion chiming in with more stinging analyses, even if they are offered as simply "helpful feedback."

Virgos' mutual perfectionism can make them overly concerned about little details while blinding them to bigger pictures. Instead of taking giant steps they're capable of, two Virgos stay sidetracked trying to get the littler ones right.

Virgos' humility can also keep them stuck as neither has the confidence that asks for or expects big wins. Instead of egging each other on to wild success, they can get caught worrying about what might not work or where they might make a mistake.

Romantic problems can arise from Virgos being too self-conscious to be passionate. Stilted routines or polite advances might make each wish for a partner who makes them feel more adventurous and lusty.

Advice for the Virgo/Virgo Relationship

Virgos get along best when they turn up the adoration and support for one another and keep their criticism to a minimum. When Virgos exchange affirming feedback about what they see as excellent and worthwhile, both in each other and in the world, both feel appreciated.

Virgos flourish when they urge each other to expand. Instead of getting caught in the order of the familiar, Virgos are more helpful when they challenge each other to break into new territory. Then they can use each other's practical savvy to create doable, step-by-step strategies that help them realize more success. When ambitions seem daunting, Virgos are most helpful when they remind each other that they gain confidence by doing, not analyzing, a task.

Virgos relationships sing when they take a compassionate and humorous approach toward those pesky traits they struggle with in themselves. Being sensitive and understanding toward the other's issues and challenges may even help Virgos become more accepting and easier on themselves.

Romantic problems can better be resolved when Virgos are more confident and expressive about their sexuality. Letting their instincts lead the way can deliver powerful satisfaction.

The Virgo/Libra Relationship ♥♥

Virgos and Libras can enjoy a delightful and satisfying relationship that's full of admiration and respect. They bond easily through their intelligence, caring thoughtfulness, and love of all things refined. Both hate crass, love class, and adore each other's knack for looking and acting just right. Shared interests and perspectives that include others make communication easy and fluid between them. Whatever Libras and Virgos endeavor shines with a tasteful graciousness and orderly elegance that attracts admiration from all they touch.

Virgos love the polished finesse of Libras' sophisticated atmosphere and respect how Libras do the fair and just thing. Virgos enjoy the exciting social activities Libras stir up and especially appreciate how they maintain an appealing orderliness. Virgos admire Libras' excellent taste and applaud their elegantly appropriate style. Libras enhance Virgos' security or even their finances.

Libras adore how Virgos' thoughtful and giving ways sustain harmony and balance. They appreciate the intelligence of Virgos' observations and enjoy the elegance of their streamlined style. Libras count on Virgos to carry things off in a smart and efficient way, and they love that they're never uncouth or disturbing. Virgos help Libras understand themselves better and awaken their spirituality.

Romance between Virgos and Libras is a flow of understated yet delightful enchantments. Always appropriate, each woos the other through the wit, consideration, and subtle seductiveness each savors. Sexuality is a mingling of the gentle touches, attentive giving, and beautiful pronouncements that make both feel special and intimate.

Possible Virgo/Libra Challenges

Although Virgos and Libras both relish refinement, their different strategies for creating it can cause frustrations. Virgos' knack for creating refinement through precise orderliness comes off as overly stiff or structured to Libras, while Libras' urge to create refinement via beauty and harmony seems impractical to Virgos.

Virgos can see Libras as lazy. Their socializing seems indulgent to Virgos, especially when it distracts everyone from getting things done. With their black-and-white clarity, Virgos don't seem to respect Libras' indecisive nature. They wish Libras would declare beautiful ideals less and take practical actions to achieve them more.

Libras can find Virgos' work ethic unappealingly harsh. Their perfectionism creates drudgery and distracts from the beauty that exists. Libras don't share Virgos' practical concerns and find their critical observations hurtful.

Romantic problems can arise if both Virgos and Libras guard themselves from expressing their lustier natures. When Libras' need for indulgent romance and extravagance is discouraged by Virgos' focus on practicality, or Virgos' desire for earthier affection sees Libras as too ethereal or detached, lovemaking becomes awkward.

Advice for the Virgo/Libra Relationship

Virgos and Libras get along best when they use, rather than resist, each other's assets. When Libras apply Virgos' practical suggestions, their visions can more easily become a reality. Virgos can enjoy more support from others by employing Libras' social finesse.

Virgos can enjoy Libras most by remembering their job is to create beauty and sustain relationships, rather than do any dirty work. Then they'll appreciate the intelligence and opportunities Libras deliver without expecting them to be more pragmatic. Virgos invite Libras' consideration of their ideas by showing how they and others will benefit by them. Virgos needn't hide their critical observations from Libras, but expressing them with wit makes them easier for Libras to accept.

Libras appeal most to Virgos when they are industrious and practical. They encourage Virgos' support of their relationships and artfulness when they show how they make a useful contribution. When Libras acknowledge the things Virgos want to achieve are important, Virgos relax and become the delightful companions Libras adore.

Romantic problems can be resolved when Virgos are creatively romantic for Libras, and when Libras are more earthy and physical for Virgos. When each releases inhibitions to reveal more natural sensuality, a wonderfully satisfying harmony and intimacy connects them both.

The Virgo/Scorpio Relationship ♥♥♥

Virgos and Scorpios can enjoy a truly rewarding and fascinating relationship that's rich in affection and admiration as well as in satisfying endeavors. They easily bond through their astute observations, drive to make things perfect, and urge to fix others. Nothing escapes their canny intelligence as each loves analyzing situations and solving any problems that might exist. Virgos and Scorpios fascinate each other with subtle humor, worthwhile projects, and an ability to look past the obvious to deeper truths. Together they make an intelligent and productive pair, one that savors their own company as they try to make this world a better place.

Virgos are thrilled that Scorpios analyze life with as much gusto as they do. Scorpios' power and strategic gifts amaze Virgos, who admire their ability to pull off impressive feats. Scorpios encourage Virgos to develop and express their brightest ideas.

Scorpios respect Virgos' intelligence and adore that they love fixing problems, too. With their helpful intentions and life-ordering ingenuity, Virgos earn Scorpios' trust and reliance. Virgos are natural friends to Scorpios and help them realize their ambitions.

Romance between Scorpios and Virgos is steamy and intense. Initially attracted to each others' minds, physical chemistry quickly takes over as they begin to please each other in countless ways. Satisfaction comes easily as intimate depth and loyalty are givens.

Possible Virgo/Scorpio Challenges

Although Virgos' and Scorpios' penchant for analysis and drive for perfection attracts them, it also drives them nuts. Whereas Virgos analyze practical concerns so matters can run more smoothly, Scorpios analyze the emotions and motivations that make people tick. Virgos can find Scorpios too suspicious and meddling in their and others' feelings, while Scorpios can find Virgos too narrow in their scope and obsessed with things that don't matter. Or, both can get so focused on problems they forget to have any fun!

Virgos can find Scorpios' directing others as controlling and manipulative. They don't want to go to the intense emotional depths Scorpios do, often finding it distracting or negative.

Scorpios become frustrated by Virgos' busy schedules, suspecting they are avoiding them. They dismiss the detailed physical order Virgos are driven to achieve as inconsequential. Scorpios wish Virgos would be less obsessed about their physical health and more interested in something important, like their and the rest of the world's emotional health.

Romantic problems can arise if Scorpios seem too sexually raw and naughty for Virgos' tastes, or if Virgos seem too uptight or prissy for Scorpios' tastes. Both can become so distracted over worries and obsessions they keep intimacy at bay or forget to bring playfulness or enjoyment to their relationship.

Advice for the Virgo/Scorpio Relationship

Virgos and Scorpios get along best when they use their insightfulness to encourage each other's best. When both remember to laugh it up a little while they're analyzing, no one is as interesting or entertaining a companion.

Virgos enjoy Scorpios most when they understand it's their job to pierce into others' psyches and situations. That helps Virgos appreciate Scorpios' emotional scenes as avenues for healing. Virgos elicit Scorpios' trust and intimacy by revealing, not hiding, their feelings. Virgos should remember: Scorpios are not only fascinated with their perfection, but with their imperfections, as well.

Scorpios get further with Virgos when they are less emotionally intense. Virgos want to hear Scorpios' insights, but they're uncomfortable if there isn't something positive attached to them. Scorpios better gain Virgos' trust and cooperation when they reveal how their intentions are designed to serve and uplift others as well as them.

Romantic problems can better be resolved when Scorpios use support and encouragement to woo Virgos, and Virgos release inhibitions and let themselves feel and express what comes naturally. When each opens their body and mind, few others can be as pleasing or enticing.

The Virgo/Sagittarius Relationship ♥♥

Virgos and Sagittarians can enjoy a stimulating and adventurous relationship, especially when they respect each other's perspective. They can bond through their love of learning and teaching, their interest in personal growth, and their urge to live a meaningful life. Even their differences can prove fascinating: Virgos help Sagittarians' inspired ideas come to life by providing the practical advice Sagittarians need, but might be too unrestrained to consider, while Sagittarians broaden Virgos' world and possibilities with the expansive optimism Virgos need, but might be too careful to employ. Together they make an inquisitive and helpful pair, one that loves exploring progressive ways of making life better for them and the many who are attracted to their ingenuity.

Virgos applaud Sagittarians' quick minds and respect their expansive knowledge. They love talking with Sagittarians about life's greater implications and gain confidence from their cavalier attitude that everything is good just as it is. Sagittarians help Virgos to dig deeper into themselves and make the most of what they've inherited.

Sagittarians delight in Virgos' keen intelligence and enjoy their analytical wit. They respect Virgos' intention to live a life of service and the meaning they find in doing so. Sags especially enjoy how Virgos' attending to details frees them up to focus on bigger scenes. Virgos help Sagittarians build authority and/or professional success.

Romance between Virgos and Sagittarians is unexpected yet interesting. Their wits attract them, and then their sensual surprises delight them. Virgos are amazed by Sags' uninhibited sexual gusto, and Sags are enticed by Virgos' gift for subtle pleasures. Sexuality is a mingling of seductive conversation and intimate exploration.

Possible Virgo/Saggitarius Challenges

Although Virgos and Sagittarians are both bright and curious, their different perspectives can really irk them! Virgos zero in on the details of matters and enjoy practical ideas. Sagittarians look at the broad picture and seek inspiring ideals. Virgos can consider Sagittarians' thoughts as too grandiose to materialize, while Sagittarians can dismiss Virgos as too stuck in meaningless minutia.

Virgos fume over Sagittarians' penchant for professing one thing but doing another. They're frustrated by Sagittarians' optimism that everything is okay while overlooking problems galore. They wish that Sagittarians would preach grand pronouncements less and apply themselves to producing something useful. Plus, Sagittarians' passionate gusto can overwhelm cautious Virgo.

Sagittarians get deflated by Virgos' insistence or harping about what's wrong. They're frustrated when Virgos' pickiness blinds them to what's great about life. Sagittarians wish that Virgos would stop analyzing and listen to their gut passions.

Romantic problems can arise if Virgos feel Sagittarians are too aggressive in their lovemaking, or if Sagittarians think Virgos are too prudish in theirs. Virgos don't appreciate Sagittarians' anytime-anywhere openness to lovemaking, and Sagittarians find Virgos' proper decorum limits the fun of lustiness.

Advice for the Virgo/Sagittarius Relationship

Virgos and Sagittarians get along best when they capitalize upon, and resist judging, each other's point of view. When Sagittarians understand the fascination Virgos find in analyzing and solving problems, they'll not only support them, they might enjoy the insights critical thinking offers them. If Virgos recognize how Sagittarians' enthusiastic ideals inspire them to reach for more success, they might indulge their own inner optimist more often.

Virgos appeal most to Sagittarians by being confidently explorative and good sports. Keeping sight of the big picture and holding criticisms to a minimum are also helpful. Virgos rarely win Sagittarians' attention with a "That won't work" attitude. Instead, enticing Sags to consider matters with a curious "What do you think about this?" piques their interest.

Sagittarians are most attractive to Virgos when they are practical and focused. They win Virgos' attention and cooperation when they demonstrate the useful ways their ideas can be applied. Sagittarians needn't analyze everything with Virgos, but genuinely considering their concerns endears them to Virgos and elicits their respect and trust.

Romance flows most smoothly when Virgos show adventurous sexuality and Sagittarians show subtlety and propriety. When each accepts the other's rhythms and needs, plenty of intimacies excite and satisfy them both.

The Virgo/Capricorn Relationship ♥♥♥♥

Virgos and Capricorns can enjoy an outstandingly compatible relationship that's full of warmth, understanding, and mutual support. They easily bond through their love of useful projects, enjoyment of developing practical skills, and interest in becoming the best of the best. Their differences complement their industrious natures: Virgos count on Capricorns' big-picture planning to pave the way to greater success, while Capricorns count on Virgos to deftly organize and handle the important details they're both sticklers for. Whatever they endeavor together possesses a high quality and refinement that satisfies them and contributes to the world around them.

Virgos admire Capricorns' ambitions and adore their sure-footed way of achieving respectable goals. They rely on Capricorns' solid advice that's neither too indulgent nor too unachievable. Virgos feel assured by Capricorns' foresight and dependability. Their subtle jokes and inner sweetness all work to open Virgos' hearts.

Capricorns are fascinated by Virgos' intelligence and impressed with their discerning tastes. They adore Virgos' industriousness and admire their good-service attitude. Capricorns especially appreciate Virgos' loyal, efficient support that allows them to concentrate on grander ambitions. They love that, like themselves, Virgos strive for excellence yet are never gauche or boastful. Virgos help Capricorns seek greater meaning in life.

Romance between Capricorns and Virgos is subtle but extremely satisfying. Each offers the discreet seductions, admiration, and loyalty the other needs to feel loved and adored. Their natural comfort with each other's physical expression melts inhibitions and leads to sensual, earthy, sexual exploration and satisfaction.

Possible Virgo/Capricorn Challenges

Although Virgos' and Capricorns' perfectionism attracts them to each other, it can also annoy them. Both get discouraged when each other's critical observations work overtime and convince them that what they do isn't good enough. Plus, Virgos' focus on details can seem too limited in scope for Capricorns' grander intentions, while Capricorns' ambitions can seem overly calculated. Capricorns wonder why Virgos let picayune concerns deter them, while Virgos wonder if Capricorns are truly serving others or just their image.

Virgos can feel thwarted by Capricorns' regimens, while their need for variety is starved by Capricorns' routines. Virgos get hurt when Capricorns dismiss even their best ideas and insist on their own way. They wish that Capricorns would be more curious in their thinking and less cautious in their actions. *And why are they so bossy?* they wonder.

Capricorns get distracted when Virgos insist on obsessing over tiny details. They wish that Virgos would be less timid and more secure so they could admire them more. Virgos' critical comments deflate Capricorns' need to be applauded and admired. They wish that Virgos would complain less and just get with their program more.

Romantic problems can arise if Capricorns are too mechanical or careful to entice Virgos, or if Virgos' need to have things just right deflates Capricorns' confidence. When both are more devoted to their work than their courtship, their affection and relationship cool off.

Advice for the Virgo/Capricorn Relationship

Virgos and Capricorns relate best when they work as a well-oiled machine to achieve things both value. When each is made to feel important, no companion is as interesting or supportive.

Virgos enjoy Capricorns the most when they understand it's their job to create and adhere to structures. Then they'll appreciate Capricorns' purposefulness without seeing it as too rigid or bossy. Virgos' ideas appeal most to Capricorns when they show Capricorns how important they are to their overall visions. Plus, kindness and thoughtfulness work better at capturing Capricorns' attention than criticism does. When Virgos extend genuine admiration, Capricorns will move mountains to support them.

Capricorns get the most out of Virgos when they are gently supportive. They elicit Virgos' cooperation by applauding them and doling out expectations respectfully. Capricorns earn Virgos' trust by showing how their plans genuinely benefit everyone, and they win Virgos' affection with humor and flexibility.

Romantic problems can more easily be resolved when Capricorns show affection with more refinement and delicacy, and when Virgos encourage Capricorns about what they do right. When each showers the other with adoration and acceptance, both will give deeply of themselves and more than satisfy the other.

The Virgo/Aquarius Relationship ♥

Virgos and Aquarians can enjoy an unusual and fascinating relationship, especially when they respect their drastically different perspectives. They bond through their intelligence, interest in useful innovations, and love of helping others. They love talking about matters they find curious or amazing and sharing ideas about how to make anything and everything work better. Even their differences can prove fascinating: Virgos' attention to practical details helps bring Aquarians' ideas into refined form, and Aquarians' global concerns can show Virgos where they can make a greater contribution. Whatever they endeavor has a quality of ingenious originality that interests them and improves the world around them.

Virgos admire Aquarians' brilliance and respect their devotion to worthy causes. They appreciate that, like themselves, Aquarians use cool logic to see and do the right thing while avoiding unnecessary emoting. Virgos are especially impressed that Aquarians can be zany individuals, yet still remain respectably solid and dependable. Aquarians help Virgos' work and even heal them.

Aquarians relish Virgos' keen insights and admire their service to others. They respect Virgos' industriousness and discerning tastes. They especially enjoy how Virgos give unselfishly of themselves and act with excellence, yet don't demand special treatment. Virgos stir Aquarians' passions and spark their transformations.

Romance between Aquarians and Virgos is unexpected, yet interesting. Each offers the attentive wooing, mental seductions, and thoughtfulness the other needs to feel loved and appreciated. Lovemaking is a mingling of gentle, yet creative sensuality and clever conversation.

Possible Virgo/Aquarius Challenges

*A*lthough Virgos and Aquarians find each other's brilliance fascinating, the ways they apply it can annoy them to no end. Virgos devote their cleverness to practically analyzing issues they can fix or have an immediate impact on. Aquarians love to consider progressive innovations that impact the future. Virgos can consider Aquarians wild cards who are caught in nutty, impractical thoughts. Aquarians can write Virgos off as no-vision complainers.

Virgos consider Aquarians' rebelliousness as disruptive and their radical individualism as weird. They steam over Aquarians' stubbornness or insistence that their ways and ideas are right. Virgos feel isolated by Aquarians' mental aloofness.

Aquarians can find Virgos' manicured orderliness maddeningly unimaginative. They cringe at Virgos' obsession with details, thinking they're missing the wonders of the bigger world. Aquarians get particularly irked when Virgos dismiss their inventions and ideals as unworkable.

Romantic problems can arise if Virgos are too modest or routine for Aquarians' experimental sexual tastes, or if Aquarians seem too disconnected or peculiar for Virgos' tastes. Or, both may act so cool and detached neither knows how much the other cares.

Advice for the Virgo/Aquarius Relationship

*V*irgos and Aquarians usually have to make adjustments in order to get along, but it can be worth it. When Aquarians consider the practical details Virgos bring up, they not only endear themselves to

Virgos, they might realize how detailed analysis sharpens their ideas even more. If Virgos are more tolerant of Aquarians' innovative expression and concepts, they'll not only gain friendship, their whole world might get bigger.

Virgos are most attractive to Aquarians when they are innovative and big-thinking. Realizing it's Aquarians' job to evolve situations by inventively tinkering with them helps Virgos enjoy Aquarians' radical nature and recognize the pragmatism they actually offer. Virgos pique Aquarians' interest by showing how their ideas are cutting edge or contribute to the greater whole. And, Virgos, remember—Aquarians are aloof. Don't take it personally.

Aquarians appeal most to Virgos when they are practical and more conservative. They win Virgos' consideration and support by showing them how their ideas can be usefully applied right now. It also helps if Aquarians show warmth and are okay with a little give and take on who's right.

Romantic problems can better be resolved when Aquarians and Virgos extend warmth and special consideration toward each other. Openly expressing needs and desires helps satisfy the other. Openhearted tenderness and respectful friendship also lead the way to the uniquely precious sensuality they share.

The Virgo/Pisces Relationship ♥♥

Virgos and Pisces can enjoy a uniquely sweet and supportive relationship that comes as a result of being opposite signs. Since each expresses a different side of the same healer/server coin, they can bond through their love of helping others. Virgos heal by analyzing and serve by fixing problems, while Pisces heal through compassion and serve by emotional sensitivity. Even their differences can complete them: Virgos help Pisces turn their dreams into workable realities, while Pisces awaken Virgos to grander objectives. They make a fluid and adaptable pair, one in which each intrigues the other and attracts many who admire the contributions they gladly offer.

Virgos appreciate Pisces' kind humility and respect their selfless giving. Pisces remind Virgos about the magical "rightness" of life and prompt Virgos to be easier and less exacting on themselves and others. Pisces boost Virgos' confidence and let them know how excellently they do things.

Pisces admire Virgos' keen insightfulness and are impressed by their ability to accomplish so much. Virgos comfort Pisces, and their handling of all things practical gives Pisces freedom to get lost in more interesting endeavors.

Romance between Pisces and Virgos is unexpected yet tenderly romantic. Pisces' romantic creativity woos Virgos' sensuality, while Virgos' tender appreciation makes Pisces feel loved and supported. Both offer the flexibility, thoughtful giving, and kindness that make courtship graceful and sweet.

Possible Virgo/Pisces Challenges

As with all opposite signs, Virgos' and Pisces' differences can spark intense frustrations between them. Virgos can discount Pisces' imaginativeness and dismiss their flowing ways as unreliable. Pisces get hurt by Virgos' criticism and discouraged by their insistence that everything must be practical. Virgos wish Pisces would quit dreaming and get to work, while Pisces wish Virgos would be less hard-driving and more compassionate.

Virgos become disoriented around Pisces' creative tangents and feel upset when Pisces shun tasks that aren't interesting. Virgos don't see value in Pisces' emotional yearnings, roll their eyes at their dramas, and resent their fantasies. Pisces' vulnerability and urge to connect can seem needy and clingy to independent Virgos.

Pisces' magical visions are deflated around Virgos and their focus on details, and they feel confined by Virgos' rigid routines. Pisces are devastated when Virgos overlook all that's wondrous only to focus on problems. Virgos' cutting observations seem harsh and thoughtless to Pisces.

Romantic problems can arise when Virgos lack the romantic flair Pisces need, or when Pisces lack the stability Virgos need. Or, if Virgos make work more important than courtship, or if Pisces make fantasy more important than reality, both can be left frustrated and lonely in the bedroom.

Advice for the Virgo/Pisces Relationship

Virgos and Pisces get along best when they use their opposite natures to fulfill them.

When Virgos see value in Pisces' emotional sensitivities, they'll not only connect better with Pisces, but they also might awaken their own compassionate understanding and feel more connected to themselves and the world. When Pisces use Virgos' analytical discernment, they'll not only appease Virgos, and they might gain a clarity that helps them realize what and who truly serves their higher purpose.

Virgos are most appealing to Pisces when they are imaginative and emotionally thoughtful. Understanding that it's Pisces' job to dream, feel, and be imaginative about reality helps Virgos to take advantage of Pisces' inventive ideas and value their compassion. Virgos entice Pisces' interest and cooperation by requesting their creative input on anything they request of them.

Pisces get the most out of Virgos when they are practical and focused. Understanding that Virgos find deep meaning in their analytical pursuits helps Pisces have compassion for their demands and driving schedules. Want to spark Virgos' interest and cooperation? Show them how usefully helpful they'll be in doing so!

Romantic problems can best be solved when Virgos woo Pisces with tenderness and creativity, and Pisces woo Virgos by doing thoughtful things they appreciate. When each adores the other's uniqueness, their opposite natures will keep their love vibrant and their relationship strong.

How Libras Match Up

The Libra/Aries Relationship

See *The Aries/Libra Relationship* on page 303.

The Libra/Taurus Relationship

See *The Taurus/Libra Relationship* on page 335.

The Libra/Gemini Relationship

See *The Gemini/Libra Relationship* on page 365.

The Libra/Cancer Relationship

See *The Cancer/Libra Relationship* on page 392.

The Libra/Leo Relationship

See *The Leo/Libra Relationship* on page 417.

The Libra/Virgo Relationship

See *The Virgo/Libra Relationship* on page 439.

The Libra/Libra Relationship ♥♥

A pair of Libras can enjoy a satisfying and engaging relationship that's rich in creativity and refined pursuits. They bond through their love of beauty, social interests, and urge to create justice. Communication flows easily between Libras as each loves exploring ways to make everything attractive and trying to understand why people act the way they do. Libras make an enchanting and intelligent pair who fascinate each other and attract loads of admirers who enjoy their charming ways.

Libras see in each other what they most love about themselves: their sense of fair play, exquisite elegance, and flair for being dynamic without causing a scene. Libras especially enjoy exchanging ideas about how this world could be a better place if everyone would just get along.

Two Libras can be quite active and industrious, yet everything is done with such ease and grace that no one sees how hard they work to make things perfect. Their dedication to improving whatever they're involved in, especially their relationships and creative projects, keeps life fresh and interesting. They agree that distressful emotions should be kept to a minimum and behaving with class kept at a premium.

Romance between two Libras is something to behold. Each thrives on the glamorous dates, declarations of admiration, and attentive togetherness their all-consuming courtship ignites. Sexuality is a satisfying combination of tasteful, yet luscious affections mingled with enticing pillow talk and joyful giggles.

Possible Libra/Libra Challenges

As with all same-sign relationships, two Libras can be so alike they can annoy or bore each other to distraction. Ironically, it's usually Libras' indecisiveness that's so frustrating or prompts each to yearn for a stronger, more directive partner.

Libras' sense of decorum can cause them to maintain a surface pleasantness that blocks juicier intimacy. Their fear of rocking the boat, or worse, appearing selfish can prompt each to avoid deep feelings or truths they suspect might be unpleasant. Or, they may smooth over arguments before anything gets truly resolved. Libras' urge to maintain a pleasant image might make them evasively dart from situations that could reveal something they don't want to show. All of which can lead to Libras wondering, *What's really going on in that (attractive) head of yours?*

Plus, Libras' reluctance over making decisions creates a limbo wherein no one decides which movie to see, much rather whether or not to get married.

Libras' determination, albeit indirectly pursued, can also cause problems. Each might feel manipulated by the other's roundabout, yet insistent, way of guiding matters to the way they see fit. And, if both Libras want something different, each can resent the other's not giving in as unfair.

Romantic problems arise if neither Libra feels sure about making a commitment, or a "nice" passivity prevents excitements both need. Sometimes their need to maintain harmony keeps passions too polite for any fire to develop in the boudoir.

Advice for the Libra/Libra Relationship

Libras get along best with each other when they blend a touch of spicy honesty into their relationship to keep both challenged and satisfied.

Libras get the most out of one another by being direct. After all, Libras appreciate knowing where others stand: it's not only interesting, it helps them to clarify where *they* stand. If both Libras are forthcoming about what they need and want, both have a better chance of truly pleasing and being pleased.

Because expressing intense feelings can seem awkward for two Libras, when one finally does reveal their deep feelings, it's heroic. Such an act paves the way for both to demonstrate their understanding natures and reveal deeper passions that build trust and intimacy.

Romantic problems can be resolved when both Libras stay juicy and enthusiastic. Being passionate with abandon, as well as vulnerable and thoughtful, enhances Libras' connections. Then their lovemaking becomes the magical and profound union each dreams about.

The Libra/Scorpio Relationship ♥♥

Libras and Scorpios can enjoy a passionate and captivating relationship that's rich in intriguing insights and pleasing endeavors. They bond through their love of intelligent conversation, urge to improve matters, and desire to positively impact others' lives. Even their differences prove complementary: Libras count on Scorpios to point out problems with people and situations they also see, but hate expressing themselves, while Scorpios admire Libras' negotiating and peacekeeping skills they're too passionate to exhibit themselves. Together they make a charming, yet powerful pair whose magnetism and worldly savvy satisfies them and attracts admiration from the many others they know.

Libras swoon around Scorpios' power and are in awe of their raw sexuality. Scorpios thrill Libras with their wit, and their emotional insightfulness satisfies Libras' urge to understand others. Scorpios support Libras' self-confidence and sense of security, and maybe even their bank accounts.

Scorpios are captivated by Libras' beauty and stimulated by their intellect. Libras entice Scorpios to discover the mysteries beneath their elusive charm. Scorpios are intrigued by Libras' nature, one that's sometimes passive, but other times fights for things they believe in. Libras calm Scorpios, and their insightfulness prompts Scorpios to better understand their own motivations and awakens their spirituality.

Romance between Scorpios and Libras is a dance of refined and naughty passions. Libras' allure drives Scorpios to distraction, while Scorpios' prowess makes Libras weak in the knees. Sexuality can be so exciting, each might believe they can't live without the other.

Possible Libra/Scorpio Challenges

Although Libras and Scorpios initially find one another attractive, their differences spark disappointments that can drive them apart. Libras cringe when Scorpios stir up problems or spoil the fun with intense or dark feelings. Scorpios resent when Libras polish things up to look good, while avoiding feelings or unpleasant truths. Libras wish Scorpios would be nicer and quit making others uncomfortable with their probing and negative observations. Scorpios can wish Libras would quit being so superficial and reveal something of consequence.

Libras resent Scorpios' dominating control, and with their ability to see everyone's side of the story, they're horrified by Scorpios' intolerance and vengefulness. Libras dismiss Scorpios' worries as obsessive and consider their intense feelings indulgent.

Scorpios get bored around Libras' detached niceness. Their love of meaty probing is unfulfilled by Libras' adherence to surface acceptance or intellectual ideals. Scorpios fume around Libras' reluctance to commit and especially resent their holding themselves hostage to other people's opinions.

Romantic problems arise if Scorpios are too possessive or controlling for Libras' tastes, or if Libras are too aloof or uncommitted for Scorpios'. Scorpios might find Libras too standoffish or delicate, while Libras might find Scorpios too invasive or intense.

Advice for the Libra/Scorpio Relationship

Libras and Scorpios get along best when they forget about correcting and get on with capitalizing on each other's expression.

Libras get the most out of Scorpios when they are emotionally available and decisive. Instead of expecting Scorpios to accept things the way they are, Libras might relax and trust that Scorpios' pushing others' buttons eventually leads to a more solid peace. Libras entice Scorpios to consider and cooperate with their ideas when they show how they'll work to transform matters into something better. Remember: indirectness makes Scorpios suspicious. Just say it.

Scorpios enjoy Libras most when they notice the intelligence of Libras' tactics. Then they'll realize how Libras' social savvy makes them appear gracious and fair, even while they're stirring up as much action as Scorpios would. Scorpios needn't hide their negative thoughts and observations from Libras, but Libras accept them more easily when they're packaged with wit.

Romantic problems can be resolved when Libras reveal more emotional and physical rawness to satisfy Scorpios, and when Scorpios include more glamorous courtship to delight Libras. When Scorpios give Libras breathing room and Libras are clearly loyal to Scorpios, their chemistry takes care of the rest.

The Libra/Sagittarius Relationship ♥♥♥

Libras and Sagittarians can enjoy a truly delightful and interesting relationship that's full of fun adventures and shared interests. They bond through their love of inspiring subjects, social interests, and pursuit of the "good life." Each complements the other's nature: Libras enjoy how Sagittarians' bravado makes life exciting, while Sagittarians love how Libras' social grace brings an interesting elegance and class. Together they make a sunny and intelligent pair, one that explores whatever's new and promising. Their enthusiasm and charisma keeps them happily involved and attracts throngs of others who enjoy being included in their endeavors.

Libras love riding the powerful waves of Sagittarians' optimistic confidence and enjoy the hours they spend talking about meaningful subjects. They adore Sagittarians' puppylike charm and applaud their ability to work a room and win hearts just like they do. Sagittarians inspire Libras to reach for greater achievements.

Sagittarians are soothed by Libras' intelligent peacefulness and captivated by their mysterious allure. They love the easy companionship Libras offer, which flows and adapts to any new situation Sagittarians dream up. Sagittarians love how Libras applaud their heroism and laugh at their jokes. They especially respect how Libras' panache makes everything dazzle.

Romance between Libras and Sagittarians is a parade of exciting dates, enthusiastic declarations of love, and tantalizing seductions that create a wonderfully dramatic courtship. Lovemaking is festive and intimate as both feel so comfortable that they're both the other's lover and best friend.

Possible Libra/Saggittarius Challenges

Although Libras and Sagittarians usually make fast friends, their differences can be alienating. Libras are logical and like to maintain an air of detachment so as to remain balanced and objective. But Sagittarians are passionate and love consuming and being consumed by whatever or whoever interests them. Libras can find Sagittarians' intensity overwhelming, possibly even distasteful, while Sagittarians can find Libras too aloof or middle-of-the-road to be juicy. Or, if both feel awkward expressing deep or troublesome feelings, a superficiality prevails wherein genuine understanding or intimacy is held at bay.

Libras get distressed when Sagittarians' tell-it-like-it-is honesty comes off as a thoughtless foot-in-mouth faux pas. Their sense of balance is thrown by Sagittarians' extremes, and they feel lonely when Sagittarians wander. Libras resent when Sagittarians do what pleases them without considering others.

Sagittarians feel thwarted by Libras' seemingly endless indecisive weighing of choices. Libras' indirectness confuses Sagittarians and makes them wish Libras would just come out and say what they think. Sagittarians especially resent having to edit themselves to please Libras. Sagittarians get irked when Libras always manage to have the last word.

Romantic problems can arise if Sagittarians are too lusty or unpolished to woo Libras, or Libras are too distant or refined to woo

Sagittarians. Libras might need more commitment or togetherness than Sagittarians do, while Sagittarians might be hurt by Libras aloofness. Sometimes, it's just more natural to be friends than lovers.

Advice for the Libra/Sagittarius Relationship

Libras and Sagittarians get along best when they capitalize on their friendship and apply humor, and perhaps vulnerability, to matters that irk them.

Libras get the most out of Sagittarians by being decisive and impassioned. When they let Sagittarians know directly and honestly what's on their minds and what they want, Sagittarians are more comfortable and cooperative. Libras encourage Sagittarians' greater consideration of others when they remind them how classy doing so makes them. And, why not let Sagittarians be totally right once in a while?

Sagittarians are most appealing to Libras when they are gracious and use finesse. Libras love Sagittarians' bravado, especially when it doesn't ruffle their or others' feathers. Sagittarians entice Libras' cooperation with ideas and projects by showing Libras the companionship they'll enjoy while doing it. And, if Sagittarians really want to appeal to Libras, just tell them they're right!

Romantic problems can better be resolved when Sagittarians demonstrate loyalty toward Libras, and Libras extend admiration toward Sagittarians. When each feel sure the other loves and desires them, they'll give their all and love doing it.

The Libra/Capricorn Relationship ♥♥

Libras and Capricorns can enjoy an interesting and dynamic relationship, especially when they accept that different things please them. They can bond through their appreciation of the fineries of life, love of initiating important projects, and social concerns. Even their differences can prove complementary: Libras bring the social finesse and elegance that Capricorns admire but might not take time for, and Capricorns deliver the disciplined leadership that Libras respect but might not feel comfortable exhibiting. Together they make a classy and ambitious pair, one that enjoys pursuing the best of life's offerings and contributing something worthwhile to their community.

Libras are impressed by Capricorns' grand ambitions and respect how they achieve considerable things. Libras especially admire how no-nonsense Capricorns do what's needed without getting sidetracked with pleasing others. Capricorns empower Libras' leadership and help them professionally.

Capricorns admire the refined beauty and gracefulness that comes so easily to Libras. They respect Libras' ability to win the hearts and happy cooperation of others. Libras' equanimity soothes Capricorns and their flattery appeases them. Libras' insightfulness helps Capricorns access deeper feelings of what's truly meaningful to them.

Romance between Capricorns and Libras is unexpected yet dynamic. Libras love the prestigious dates and social activities Capricorns take them on and Capricorns enjoy having such an appealing companion. Lovemaking is surprisingly sensual and satisfying, as each considers it a worthy mission to be a great lover.

Possible Libra/Capricorn Challenges

Libras' and Capricorns' different intentions often cause problems between them.

Libras intend to please people and create a lovely harmony, whereas Capricorns intend to get things accomplished. Libras consider Capricorns too harsh and driven, and they feel hurt by Capricorns' callousness. Capricorns dismiss Libras' need to make things attractive as an unnecessary distraction, and they think their considering everyone's point of view is ineffective. Both can fume that the other has their values wrong.

Libras bristle around Capricorns' dry pragmatism and feel offended when Capricorns use others or hurt feelings on the way to achieving ambitions. Libras get bored by Capricorns' stiff regimens and feel stifled by their routines and yearn for more graciousness from them. They think Capricorns are stingy with both their compliments and their pocketbook.

Capricorns feel usurped by Libras' creative tangents. They resent that Libras expect them to be fair when life really isn't fair. Libras' use of charm to get their way makes Capricorns suspicious, and they lose patience when Libras demand extravagance or expect others to do their dirty work. Libras seem to value packaging over substance; Capricorns wish they'd be less pleasant and more productive.

Romantic problems can arise if Capricorns don't indulge Libras' need for romance or creativity, or Libras overlook the thoughtful little things that make Capricorns feel loved. When neither tries to understand the other's needs, much less try to satisfy them, the bedroom becomes awfully cold.

Advice for the Libra/Capricorn Relationship

Libras and Capricorns get along best when Capricorns use more of Libras' flair and considerateness, and Libras employ more of Capricorns' practical strategies. That not only makes them more appealing to each other, it might make each more effective in achieving what they desire out of life.

Libras enjoy Capricorns most when they quit expecting them to be more upbeat and instead notice the artistry of their strategies and the clever humor of their stoicism. Libras entice Capricorns' attention and cooperation when they show Capricorns their practicality or ways they'll promote Capricorns' agenda. Want more generosity? Show Capricorns how it'll enhance their prestige.

Capricorns enjoy Libras most when they respect how Libras excel at the social and refined tasks, and quit expecting them to attend to the mundane ones. Capricorns attract Libras' attention and cooperation when they present tasks in a charming light or show Libras how classy their results will be. After all, Libras love being part of Capricorns' winning goals—they just hate being enslaved by them.

Romantic problems can better be resolved when Capricorns are creative and attentive, and Libras are thoughtful and practical. When each tells the other how important they are and shows admiration for their style, their affections become even more enthusiastic and delightful.

The Libra/Aquarius Relationship ♥♥♥♥

Libras and Aquarians can enjoy a truly fascinating and engaging relationship that's rich in exciting ideas and enjoyable activities. They bond through their wide range of interests, intellectual acumen, and social awareness. They talk for hours about anything and everything, especially about ways to bring people together to make the world a better place. They make a bright and inventive pair whose knack for being on the cutting edge of whatever's new and promising satisfies them and attracts throngs of others to their interesting world.

Libras delight in Aquarians' brilliance and adore their uncompromising respect of their own and other's individuality. They applaud Aquarians' community-minded values and admire their urge to make a positive impact on the world. Libras find it especially intriguing that Aquarians express both free-spirited unpredictability as well as loyal dependability. Aquarians awaken Libras' hearts and support their creative expression.

Aquarians admire Libras' quick wit and sharp intellect, which is open enough to consider matters from countless points of view. They love how Libras offer terrific companionship without ever being needy or clingy. Aquarians appreciate the peaceful social harmony Libras create and enjoy being part of their interesting circle of friends. Libras inspire Aquarians to find even greater meaning in life.

Romance between Aquarians and Libras is a wonderful dance of impassioned lovers one minute and best friends the next. Each appreciates how the other is clever enough to seduce with their minds as well as their bodies. Sexuality is intimate and creative as each loves surprising the other with unexpected delights.

Possible Libra/Aquarius Challenges

Although Libras and Aquarians enjoy loads of traits that connect them, they also possess traits that can set them apart.

Libras get disappointed when Aquarians include their whole group in their activities. They become discouraged if Aquarians treat others with the same interest and thoughtfulness as they treat them. Aquarians' air of detachment can prompt Libras to wonder if they truly care.

Aquarians can feel confined by Libras' zeroing in on them when there is a world of people to connect with. They wince at Libras' molding themselves to meet other's expectations or hiding truths to keep the peace. Aquarians wish Libras would spend less energy being obsessed with their personal relationships and more energy being concerned about the world.

Romantic problems arise if Libras feel hurt by Aquarians' detached aloofness, or if Aquarians feel pressured by Libras' insistence on togetherness. Both can avoid expressing the vulnerable, deep emotions that create intimacy, leaving each wondering what the other truly wants and feels.

Advice for the Libra/Aquarius Relationship

Libras and Aquarians enjoy each other the most when Aquarians acknowledge the special tie they feel with Libras, and when Libras give Aquarians plenty of freedom to spend time with their community.

Libras get the most out of Aquarians when they are social and curious. Aquarians especially love Libras' companionship when they accompany them in investigating quirky ideas and enjoying unusual acquaintances. Libras entice Aquarians to consider their ideas when they see how they benefit many others and give Aquarians latitude to fulfill their request in their own way.

Aquarians are most attracted to Libras when they are attentive and personal. They elicit Libras' giving friendship and cooperation by including them in their varied interests and doing things that make them feel special. After all, Libras enjoy Aquarians' interests, they just don't want to play second fiddle. And, if Aquarians can be a bit more flexible and compromising, and a little less provocatively shocking around Libras' friends, Libras will be satisfied that all is fair between them.

Romantic problems can better be resolved when Aquarians woo Libras with warmth and personal thoughtfulness, and when Libras woo Aquarians with inventiveness and friendship. When both are more emotionally expressive, each feels more secure and loved. That helps them swing from great friends to intimate lovers.

The Libra/Pisces Relationship ♥

Libras and Pisces can enjoy a unique and captivating relationship, especially when they accept how different they truly are. They can bond through their creativity, love of making life beautiful, and their satisfaction in helping others. Even their differences can be satisfying: Libras bring a social finesse Pisces admire and create gorgeous designs and ambiance Pisces delight in. Pisces deliver the tender sweetness Libras crave and their imaginations create the dramatic worlds that transport Libras. Together they make an inventive and giving pair, one that creates an enchanting atmosphere that they and the many who are drawn to their dramatic magnetism love getting lost in.

Libras adore Pisces' gentle kindnesses and admire how their selflessness creates peace. Libras find Pisces' emotional depth compelling and their complexity intriguing. Libras love how Pisces' clever input makes even mundane tasks seem exotic. Pisces' understanding heals Libras and guides them to satisfying work.

Pisces love lingering in the elegant and beautiful world that Libras create. They respect how Libras aren't swayed by emotions but measure the facts to identify what's most fair and right. They appreciate Libras' considerateness and respect that they, too, sacrifice themselves to maintain harmony. Libras ignite Pisces' passions and transform them.

Romance between Pisces and Libras is unexpected yet very dramatic. Each relishes the exciting and enchanting courtship the other dreams about and yearns for. Sexuality is beautiful and rich as each wants nothing more than to please the other.

Possible Libra/Pisces Challenges

Although Libras and Pisces are both creative and caring types, their unique ways of demonstrating that can cause problems between them. Pisces love delving into feelings and connecting so deeply with others that they merge into one. Libras don't. They're more intellectual and prefer to maintain breathing room in their relationships. Pisces feel frustrated that Libras offer few juicy feelings to connect with. Libras get dismayed when Pisces get so consumed by their emotions and fantasies that they're impossible to logically relate to.

Libras can feel overwhelmed by Pisces' intense emotional needs and dramas. They don't like sharing deep feelings, especially the painful ones, which Pisces find so interesting. Libras are put off by Pisces allowing others to take advantage of them and then wallowing in self-pity.

Pisces feel rebuffed by Libras' "everything's fine" attitude and are lonely when Libras refuse to join them in their empathies. Pisces wish Libras would be less interested in appearing attractive and nice, and more intrigued with their own and other's feelings.

Romantic problems arise when Libras are too detached or independent for Pisces' tastes, or if Pisces are too clingy or needy for Libras'. Sexuality can become awkward due to different rhythms or needs. Both can be disappointed that the relationship or the lovemaking doesn't measure up to the fantasy they envisioned.

Advice for the Libra/Pisces Relationship

Libras and Pisces get along best when they learn from each other's gifts. When Pisces use Libras' objectivity, they'll not only appeal more to Libras, they'll learn how avoiding being overtaken by feelings makes them more effective. If Libras employ Pisces' empathetic skills, they'll not only connect better with Pisces, they'll awaken a greater compassion within that connects better with everyone. Both entice cooperation and support from each other by showing how interesting and helpful they'll be in doing so.

Libras get the most out of Pisces by being emotionally available. Instead of losing patience with Pisces' feelings, Libras might see them as emotional guides or muses. This helps them recognize the brilliant insight Pisces' instincts offer.

Pisces are most appealing to Libras when they are clear and focused. Libras adore Pisces' sensitivity and imagination, but fume when their reality is eclipsed by them. Understanding that Libras aren't wired to express loads of emotions and instead show their deep caring through knowing and thoughtfulness helps Pisces feel less isolated around them.

Romantic problems can better be resolved when Pisces are communicative and allow breathing space for Libras, and Libras show feelings and consideration to Pisces. Then they're freer to indulge in the glorious affections each finds so satisfying.

How Scorpios Match Up

The Scorpio/Aries Relationship

See *The Aries/Scorpio Relationship* on page 306.

The Scorpio/Taurus Relationship

See *The Taurus/Scorpio Relationship* on page 338.

The Scorpio/Gemini Relationship

See *The Gemini/Scorpio Relationship* on page 367.

The Scorpio/Cancer Relationship

See *The Cancer/Scorpio Relationship* on page 395.

The Scorpio/Leo Relationship

See *The Leo/Scorpio Relationship* on page 420.

The Scorpio/Virgo Relationship

See *The Virgo/Scorpio Relationship* on page 441.

The Scorpio/Libra Relationship

See *The Libra/Scorpio Relationship* on page 461.

The Scorpio/Scorpio Relationship ♥♥

Two Scorpios can enjoy a deeply compelling and intimate relationship that's rich in emotional exchanges, insights, and intrigue. Their matching power and intensity creates a satisfying dynamic wherein each feels understood and challenged. Bonding is easy for Scorpios because, perhaps more than anyone else, they appreciate one another's need for control as well as their emotional complexity, which demands loyalty and depth. When Scorpios join forces, they are so effective, little stops them from realizing their considerable desires and ambitions.

Scorpios see special things in one another. Each relishes the other's magnetism and feels weak in the knees around their raw sexuality. Scorpios respect one another's sensitivity and intelligence as well as their strategies for accomplishing goals. They agree that, instead of broadcasting intentions or abilities, it's smarter to quietly wield power from behind the scenes. Hence, when Scorpios are together, their mysteriousness doubles. Scorpios are especially captivated by each other's subtle, piercing insights. They appreciate how neither insists on an "Everything is fine" stance, and instead acknowledge the problems they see. Scorpios treasure exchanging knowing glances that say, "Did you see that?" "Oh, yes, I did. Let's talk about it in private."

Romance between Scorpios is extremely intense and satisfying. Both specialize in the seductiveness, intimate exchanges, and unbridled sexuality the other craves. Love and sex are so encompassing, each might believe they have met their perfect match.

Possible Scorpio/Scorpio Challenges

As with all same-sign relationships, Scorpios can be so alike they can drive each other crazy. Their mutual power and intensity can turn negative and make life miserable for both. Sometimes Scorpios' suspicions work overtime and blind them to what's positive. Or, emotions can boil over and make them mean, even destructive toward one another. Although Scorpios understand why the other stings, it's hard for them to forgive and even harder to forget when they do.

Scorpios' urge to control matters can ignite explosive power struggles between them. If each wants something different, a fight to the very finish can ensue. They stubbornly take an "I'd rather die than let you control me!" stance wherein they're willing to sacrifice all that's good between them just to avoid the humiliation of giving in.

Moreover, Scorpios are keen to each other's knack for manipulation, and they slam on the brakes if they even suspect the other is trying to pull their strings. Sometimes Scorpios fear the other is cooking up plots or betrayals against them because they know they're capable of it.

Romantic problems can arise if Scorpios suspect disloyalty or believe the other isn't protecting the sanctity of their intimacy. Power struggles or hurt feelings can cause a standoff that makes the bedroom uncharacteristically cold. Withholding lovemaking is agonizing to both, but it's a protest strategy nevertheless.

Advice for the Scorpio/Scorpio Relationship

Scorpios get along best when each makes it absolutely clear that they are completely loyal and have the other's best interests at heart. Directing their combined powers toward projects of consequence, like fixing problems, handling crises, and making matters more functional, also ensures that Scorpios' powers are used in positive ways. Their tenacious resolve to have honest, loving communication also helps Scorpios overcome thorny issues and keeps their unique intimacy flourishing.

If differences arise, mutual respect is a necessity. When Scorpios acknowledge the validity of one another's viewpoint, they create the trust that leads to cooperation.

When emotions flair, Scorpios might do their best to remember the other is as sensitive as they are. When Scorpios consider how difficult it is for them to forgive a hurt, or worse, a betrayal, they're more likely to think twice before lobbing one toward the other. That said, Scorpios understanding how hard it is to disarm their own attacks while feeling hostile can make it easier to understand when their companion fails to disarm theirs.

Romantic problems can better be resolved when Scorpios clearly demonstrate the loyalty and consideration the other needs to feel cherished and loved. Keeping the fires stoked in the bedroom works wonders to heal and maintain Scorpios' uniquely satisfying connection.

The Scorpio/Sagittarius Relationship ♥♥

Scorpios and Sagittarians can enjoy a dynamic and intriguing relationship, especially when they accept their different attitudes. They bond through their interest in exploring unknown territories, love of creating grand schemes, and urge to make significant contributions. Even their differences can prove satisfying: Sagittarians lift and inspire Scorpios, while Scorpios bring depth to Sagittarians' philosophies. Together they make an insightful and savvy pair who pursue the ambitions of consequence that satisfy them and capture the respect of the many others their good deeds impact.

Scorpios are impressed by Sagittarians' fiery confidence and admire their ability to communicate knowledge. Sagittarians' relentless positive nature piques Scorpios' interest; they're amazed how Sagittarians trust that matters will turn out well. Sagittarians' influence builds Scorpios' security and even their bank accounts.

Sagittarians are enticed by Scorpios' magnetism and compelled by their sexual prowess. They respect Scorpios' power and unwavering allegiance to whatever and whomever they're committed to. They especially enjoy Scorpios' wit and canny intelligence. Scorpios help Sagittarians better understand their own motivations and spark their spirituality.

Romance between Sagittarians and Scorpios is intensely sensual and compelling. Each provides the power, sexuality, and intellectual challenge the other craves. Sagittarians' courting gusto sweeps away Scorpios' caution and ignites their passions, while Scorpios' deep nature is territory Sagittarians are compelled to explore.

Possible Scorpio/Sagittarius Challenges

Although Scorpios and Sagittarians are neighbors in the zodiac, their different attitudes make it seem as if they're living in different worlds. For starters, Sagittarians are optimistic and trusting, and live life with flexibility, while Scorpios are more suspicious and problem-oriented, and prefer matters to be predictable. Sagittarians wonder why Scorpios insist on looking at the dark side of matters and write them off as negative brooders. Scorpios think Sagittarians are blind to any truths that don't make them happy and dismiss them as superficial blowhards.

Scorpios get overwhelmed by Sagittarians' boisterousness and hurt by their thoughtlessness. Sagittarians' restlessness and changeability, both in lifestyle and philosophy, make Scorpios suspicious of their sincerity or commitment. They cringe when Sagittarians pronounce ideas as truths, thinking they're arrogant, if not poorly researched.

Scorpios don't believe that life is always as grand as Sagittarians insist it is.

Sagittarians become discouraged around Scorpios' cynicism and feel thwarted when Scorpios block risks that make life exciting. Sagittarians especially resent Scorpios' control, as well as their refusal to change, and rebel against it. They're baffled when Scorpios get insulted over innocent things they say.

Romantic problems arise if Sagittarians' wandering eyes stir Scorpios' jealousy, or if Scorpios' possessiveness suffocates Sagittarians. When Scorpios yearn for more depth, or Sagittarians yearn for more fun, the passion in the bedroom fades away.

Advice for the Scorpio/Sagittarius Relationship

Scorpios and Sagittarians get along best when they respect each other's point of view and stop expecting the other to be more like them. When Scorpios use Sagittarians' encouraging optimism, and Sagittarians use Scorpios' insightful analysis, they'll not only appreciate each other more, they'll likely create more of what they want in life.

Scorpios appeal to Sagittarians most when they are open and good sports. Instead of expecting them to be more analytical or careful, Scorpios might rely on Sagittarians' cavalier advice to provide keys to freedom and grander possibilities. Rather than putting the kibosh on Sagittarians' philosophies or risky endeavors, Scorpios more effectively entice Sagittarians with a "What's your approach toward this possible challenge?"

Sagittarians are most attractive to Scorpios when they display thoughtfulness toward them and their concerns. They fare better by recognizing that deeper, even darker considerations are integral to Scorpios' philosophies and resist overriding them as negative. Instead of expecting Scorpios to stay happy and perked up, Sagittarians might accept how Scorpios value and enjoy their moods and suspicious perspectives and look to discover the meaty realizations they offer.

Romantic problems can better be resolved when Sagittarians are clearly loyal to Scorpios, and when Scorpios give Sagittarians room to roam. When each works to discover and respect what the other wants to feel cared for, their natural chemistry kicks into gear, bonding them with love.

The Scorpio/Capricorn Relationship ♥♥♥

Scorpios and Capricorns can enjoy a compatible and compelling relationship, as their power and intensity are well matched. They bond through their broad ambitions, love of solving problems, and subtle humor. Trust and appreciation are easily earned as each is capable of the deliberate thinking, loyalty, and discipline the other respects. Whatever Capricorns and Scorpios endeavor has a strategic vision and calculated carefulness that satisfies them and creates a considerable impact on the world around them.

Scorpios love Capricorns' accountability and determination, and admire their authority. They're comforted by Capricorns' sober and cautious natures, especially appreciating that Capricorns don't pressure them to "act happier." Scorpios count on Capricorns' sound advice to steer them toward their most practical and productive choices. They enjoy a welcoming ease of communication with Capricorns wherein most anything can be said and understood.

Capricorns are thrilled by Scorpios' intriguing prowess and compelled by their canny insights. They appreciate that, like themselves, Scorpios envision great possibilities and work cleverly to realize them, bringing their passionate intensity to bear. Scorpios are natural friends to Capricorns, whose insights and loyalty help them achieve their dreams.

Romance between Scorpios and Capricorns is rich in the subtle seductions, thoughtfulness, and loyalty each needs to feel loved and enticed. Lovemaking is lingering, explorative, and unusually satisfying.

Possible Scorpio/Capricorn Challenges

Problems can spring up as a result of Scorpios' and Capricorns' cautious, controlling natures. When each vies for power or dominance, a cold, cunning fight to the finish can ensue. Life can become dour if each lets their perfectionism, suspicions, or even jealousies become stronger than their acknowledgment of what's good.

Scorpios can feel emotionally isolated by Capricorns' stoicism. They're hurt, if not resentful, when Capricorns refuse to reveal their own feelings or lack compassion. Scorpios get frustrated when Capricorns show allegiance to traditions, rather than to their passions.

Capricorns mistrust Scorpios' emotionality as something they can't control. They're suspicious of Scorpios' secretiveness, wondering if what Scorpios are hiding might hurt them. Capricorns feel threatened by Scorpios' knack for shaking things up and are exasperated by their crises.

Romantic problems can arise if Capricorns are too cautious or unresponsive to satisfy Scorpios, or if Scorpios' intensity overwhelms Capricorns. If Scorpios find Capricorns cold, or Capricorns feel violated by Scorpios, their sexual splendor turns into a mechanical duty.

Advice for the Scorpio/Capricorn Relationship

Scorpios and Capricorns get along best when they respect one another's power and leadership, and remember that levity is effective and important. If Capricorns honor the wisdom of Scorpios' feelings, they'll not only connect more deeply with Scorpios, they may discover the insights their own emotions provide. When Scorpios acknowledge the power in Capricorns' decorum and traditions, they'll gain Capricorns' trust and learn even more about political strategies.

Scorpios are most appealing to Capricorns when they're direct and pragmatic. Instead of expecting Capricorns to express their passions emotionally, Scorpios are wiser to recognize them through their devotion and actions. Scorpios woo Capricorns by being patient and consistent, offering their corrective suggestions with respect and gentleness.

Capricorns win Scorpios' affection and trust when they are self-disclosing and expressive. They elicit Scorpios' support when they show how their plans protect and include Scorpios. After all, Scorpios want to be part of Capricorns' goals; they just don't want to be sidelined by them. If Scorpios get too intense for Capricorns, a simple, "That's too much for me" is better than a cold brush-off.

Romantic problems can better be resolved when Capricorns learn specific ways to satisfy Scorpios' emotions and lusts, and when Scorpios honor Capricorns' needs for appropriateness. That builds trust for the magic and intimacy to flourish in and out of the bedroom.

The Scorpio/Aquarius Relationship ♥♥

Scorpios and Aquarians can enjoy a fascinating and dynamic relationship, especially when they accept their different emotional natures. They can bond through their interest in global and social issues, and an urge to improve whatever they're involved in. Even their differences can prove compelling: Scorpios appreciate how Aquarians' intellectual clarity steers passions toward constructive outlets, while Aquarians appreciate how Scorpios' emotional instincts help build meaningful connections. Together they make a powerful and visionary pair that tackles significant projects that satisfy them and make a worthwhile contribution to their world.

Scorpios admire Aquarians' humanitarian concerns and count on their strength and loyalty. They're fascinated by Aquarians' ability to step away from distracting feelings to do what's logical and useful. Aquarians' intelligence elicits Scorpios' self-understanding and influences their personal lives.

Aquarians respect Scorpios' prowess and treasure their mental acuity. They find Scorpios' depth and mysteriousness curiosities worth investigating. Aquarians appreciate that, like themselves, Scorpios put themselves on the line for principles they believe in, yet bring a passionate intensity that stirs excitement. Scorpios help

Aquarians develop their authority and direct them toward professional success.

Romance between Aquarians and Scorpios is unexpected, yet powerful. Scorpios love being the ones Aquarians reveal their tender, emotional sides to, while Aquarians are thrilled by the challenge of exploring Scorpios' intimate depth. Sexuality is surprisingly creative, even explosive, as each loves to ravish and be ravished.

Possible Scorpio / Aquarius Challenges

Scorpios and Aquarians have such different emotional natures that huge clashes can occur between them. Scorpios are intensely emotional and become deeply involved with whomever interests them. Aquarians are logical and prefer to remain objectively detached. Scorpios use instincts, while Aquarians look to the facts. Scorpios fume that Aquarians are cold and out of touch, while Aquarians dismiss Scorpios as blinded by passions. Since both are confident their ideas are right, and neither is prone to compromise, stubborn standoffs ensue if each wants something different.

Scorpios can get hurt and resentful over Aquarians' impersonal stance. They feel thwarted by Aquarians' logical, mental approach. Scorpios wish Aquarians would be more grounded and personally revealing. Aquarians' quirkiness is hard to understand or to control.

Aquarians get exasperated by Scorpios' emotional reactivity and become disappointed when they strike out against them or others. They wish Scorpios would be less concerned about who's trying to usurp their power and more concerned with making the world a better place.

Romantic problems erupt when Scorpios feel isolated due to

Aquarians being unresponsive to their feelings, or when Aquarians feel overwhelmed by Scorpios' possessiveness. If Scorpios feel Aquarians are too distant or Aquarians feel Scorpios are too invasive, lovemaking becomes rare and unsatisfying.

Advice for the Scorpio/Aquarius Relationship

Scorpios and Aquarians relate best by capitalizing on the visions and goals they share. When Scorpios appreciate Aquarians' reason, they'll not only admire them more, they may discover how objectivity helps overcome baser reactions. When Aquarians acknowledge the valuable insights Scorpios provide, they'll not only connect better with Scorpios, they may connect better to the insights their own feelings provide. That, plus their strong resolve to maintain commitments, helps them work together.

Scorpios get the most out of Aquarians when they are objective and neutral. Instead of trying to connect with Aquarians via emotions, Scorpios are more effective engaging them with mental wit. Scorpios woo Aquarians out of aloofness by eliciting their advice or friendship.

Aquarians connect best with Scorpios by being open and attentive. Letting Scorpios know how deeply they feel about things draws more of their support. If Scorpios become too intense, a simple request for a bit of time to consider their thoughts works better than being aloof.

Romantic problems can better be resolved when Aquarians are attentive and reveal their feelings more, and when Scorpios talk more and give Aquarians time to themselves. Showing respect for one another's needs and wants sparks a fascination that keeps their affection alive.

The Scorpio / Pisces Relationship ♥♥♥♥

Scorpios and Pisces can enjoy a truly wonderful touching relationship that's full of intimacies, magic, and spark. They easily bond through their emotional sensitivity, creativity, and concern for others. Each possesses qualities the other seeks and admires: both love to deeply connect and possess intuitive awareness of emotions. They captivate each other's interest by exploring the hidden dynamics and possibilities of life. Whatever Scorpio and Pisces endeavor has a sensitivity and depth that satisfies them and supports the many who love them.

Scorpios are beguiled by Pisces' imaginative, romantic ways. They relax in Pisces' softness and revel in their compassionate tenderness. Scorpios enjoy that Pisces yield to their leadership yet retain a mysteriousness that keeps them intrigued. Pisces stir Scorpios and spark their creativity.

Pisces are downright spellbound by Scorpios' power and drawn to their charisma. They rely on Scorpios' loyalty and determination to see matters through and appreciate how they handle harsher realities so they can linger in more pleasant endeavors. Scorpios' influence keeps Pisces inspired to reach for life's greater meaning.

Romance between Pisces and Scorpios is rich in the seductions, intimacies, and affections each craves. Inhibitions evaporate as each lives for the enthralling lovemaking the other provides. Terrific!

Possible Scorpio / Pisces Challenges

Although Scorpios and Pisces are basically compatible, problems still pop up between them. Usually it's over trust: both are so mysterious and complex, each can find the other hard to pin down. Pisces' need for change and Scorpios' need for predictability can cause annoying clashes, too. Pisces can consider Scorpios control freaks, while Scorpios consider Pisces irresponsible dreamers.

Scorpios lose patience when Pisces see the world the way they imagine it to be rather than the way it is. They especially resent it when Pisces escape difficult realities. They fume that Pisces let themselves be used or insist on suffering when taking a stand could remedy their situation. Pisces' elusiveness sparks Scorpios' suspicions.

Pisces feel overwhelmed by Scorpios' dominant natures and confined by their control. They don't understand Scorpios' perfectionism and need to expose every truth. Scorpios' criticisms wound Pisces to the core. Their defensiveness or knack for revenge seems scarily harsh to Pisces.

Romantic problems arise if either's seductiveness seems to be aimed at someone else. If each gets consumed by their own emotional dramas or behaves insensitively to the other's feelings and needs, their lovemaking becomes dull and empty.

Advice for the Scorpio/Pisces Relationship

Scorpios and Pisces get along best when they demonstrate trust, sensitivity, and loyalty. Then their natural compatibility takes care of the rest.

Scorpios get the most out of Pisces when they are tender and imaginative with them. Instead of expecting Pisces to look at reality with the same piercing analysis they use, Scorpios are smarter to join Pisces in their world. Then Pisces feel safe and valued enough to open more to Scorpios. When bringing up problems or corrective feedback, Pisces are most receptive when it's presented gently. And, Scorpios—let life be a little surprising.

Pisces are most appealing to Scorpios when they stay present and involved. Scorpios love Pisces' imaginativeness but hate being eclipsed by it. Instead of being threatened by Scorpios' critical eye, Pisces might have compassion for it. Then, instead of evading the difficult issues Scorpios bring up, Pisces can offer their wise council to help them deal with it. A little elusiveness and chaos are intriguing to Scorpios, but too much tortures them.

Romantic problems can better be resolved when Scorpios and Pisces demonstrate clear focus and loyalty toward each other. Vulnerability works wonders to open and soften both, creating sacredness in the bedroom.

How Sagittarians Match Up

The Sagittarius / Aries Relationship

See *The Aries/Sagittarius Relationship* on page 309.

The Sagittarius / Taurus Relationship

See *The Taurus/Sagittarius Relationship* on page 340.

The Sagittarius / Gemini Relationship

See *The Gemini/Sagittarius Relationship* on page 370.

The Sagittarius / Cancer Relationship

See *The Cancer/Sagittarius Relationship* on page 397.

The Sagittarius / Leo Relationship

See *The Leo/Sagittarius Relationship* on page 423.

The Sagittarius / Virgo Relationship

See *The Virgo/Sagittarius Relationship* on page 444.

The Sagittarius / Libra Relationship

See *The Libra/Sagittarius Relationship* on page 464.

The Sagittarius / Scorpio Relationship

See *The Scorpio/Sagittarius Relationship* on page 481.

The Sagittarius/Sagittarius Relationship ♥♥

*T*wo Sagittarians can enjoy a fun and fascinating relationship that's full of exciting adventures and ideas, especially when they stick around to experience it. They bond through their love of philosophy, an urge to explore new vistas, and the search for whatever's promising. Sagittarians spend hours exchanging views and sharing pointers about all they've learned and everywhere they've traveled. Since they live by the principle "If it isn't fun, don't do it!" Sagittarians' relationships are joyful and joke-filled. Whatever they endeavor has a zesty expansiveness that satisfies them and inspires all those who are drawn to their gregarious ways.

Sagittarians are attracted to what they love most about themselves in each other: their independence, optimism, and adventurous search for meaning. Each knows to give the other the freedom of thought and action they desire for themselves. Sagittarians also adore the levity each delivers and their refusal to see any glass as half empty.

Communication between Sagittarians comes easily as both love teaching and learning. Their enthusiasm satisfies and uplifts each other. Sagittarians don't mind a little exaggeration—it makes stories more exciting. And, these free spirits agree: nothing should fence them in. If something loses its luster? Move on!

Romance between Sagittarians is erotically sensual one minute, playfully buddylike the next. Since both are lustily passionate yet love freedom, they enjoy a dance between intimacy and space. When fights occur? Sex or laughter (preferably both) quickly smooth things over.

Possible Sagittarius/Sagittarius Challenges

*A*s with all same-sign relationships, Sagittarians can be too much alike to stay attracted or even get along.

Sagittarians' skittishness around commitment can make long-term connectedness hard. Sags might maintain a breezy informality in their relationship even when they're terrifically interested.

Sagittarians' sense of entitlement to live exactly the way they want can also pull them apart. They may not be willing to compromise on much of anything—from their goals to their lifestyles—thinking that would mean they're not being true to themselves. Since Sagittarians hate to consider negative thoughts, they can prompt each other to take overly big risks or do nutty things, counting more on luck than genuine preparation. And, since Sags' "truths" are so important, serious problems can arise when they don't agree. Both believe they're right and refuse to back down.

Romantic problems arise if Sagittarians avoid commitment or they continue flirting after they do commit. Sagittarian lovers aren't possessive, but they are proud: if they're not treated like royalty, they're out of there! Sometimes the buddy aspect of Sagittarians' relationship just gets stronger and their erotic attraction fades away.

Advice for the Sagittarius/Saggitarius Relationship

*S*agittarians get along best when they continue to applaud the intelligence, values, and fun the other delivers.

When Sagittarians consider conceding to each other's requests and needs as heroic as rallying for what they want and need, they will be more inspired to make the compromises that keep their relationship afloat. For that matter, why not try more vulnerability? Not the gushy-needy kind, but the "I respect you enough to be completely honest with you" kind.

If there's a clash over whose truths are right, Sags might try a "Tell me why you see it that way" approach, or even make a pact to leave contentious views out of the conversation. Also, Sagittarians should remember it's possible to be both encouraging and pragmatic.

Romantic problems can better be resolved when both Sagittarians are clear with themselves and each other about their intentions. It might be okay if someone won't commit; it's the not knowing that's tough. And, emotional disclosure and vulnerability work as aphrodisiacs to ignite even greater sexual passion.

The Sagittarius / Capricorn Relationship ♥♥

Sagittarians and Capricorns can enjoy an inspiring relationship, especially when they respect their different styles of seeking fulfillment. They bond through their worldly interests, love of making meaningful impacts, and admiration of integrity. Even their differences can prove compelling: Sagittarians admire how Capricorns achieve success through the disciplined regimens they admire but are too freedom-loving themselves to practice, while Capricorns appreciate the rewarding lives Sagittarians lead by seeking the meaningful subjects and activities Capricorns enjoy but are too practical to pursue. They make a thoughtful and capable pair who work and play hard and prompt one another to make worthwhile contributions to the world around them.

Sagittarians admire Capricorns' heroic ambitions and respect their effectiveness in achieving them. Sagittarians especially relish Capricorns' subtle humor and love the playfulness that emerges after goals are accomplished. Capricorns' advice strengthens Sagittarians' self-value and even their bank accounts.

Capricorns are amazed by Sagittarians' accomplishments, especially when they succeed despite having goofed off. They respect how Sagittarians live according to their principles and find their optimism something they would like more of themselves. Sagittarians prompt Capricorns to understand their motivations and even awaken their spirituality.

Romance between Sagittarians and Capricorns is lusty, deep, and compelling. Both have strong natures that challenge each to stay on their toes and take nothing for granted. Lovemaking can be surprisingly inventive, close, and intimately satisfying.

Possible Sagittarius/Capricorn Challenges

Although Sagittarians and Capricorns are zodiac neighbors, their differences make them seem worlds apart. For starters, Sagittarians view life as an adventure to enjoy, while Capricorns view life as a serious situation. Sagittarians are optimistic and rely on the luck that blesses them. Capricorns are more worrisome and count on obstacles to plague them.

Sagittarians lose patience with Capricorns' cautiousness and wonder why they insist on being so controlling. Capricorns' thriftiness irks

Sagittarians, as do their structured regimens. Sagittarians dismiss Capricorns' concerns as negative and wish they'd loosen up.

Capricorns panic over Sagittarians' ill-conceived risk taking and consider their ideas unrealistic. They cringe when Sagittarians boast knowledge about things they've taken little time to truly master. Capricorns especially hate when Sagittarians tell them to be positive when there are so many important things to worry about.

Romantic problems can arise when Sagittarians are too brash or overtly affectionate for Capricorns, or when Capricorns are too careful or prim for Sagittarians. When Sagittarians' amorous enthusiasm clashes with Capricorns' sense of propriety, negotiating over what's acceptable to both makes lovemaking fizzle.

Advice for the Sagittarius/Capricorn Relationship

Sagittarians and Capricorns get along best when they respect each other's lifestyle and strategies. When Sagittarians acknowledge Capricorns' cautious thinking and planning as worthwhile, they'll not only be more successful with Capricorns, they might apply it toward their own success. If Capricorns accept Sagittarians' trusting expansiveness as a viable strategy, they'll not only connect better with Sagittarians, they might recognize the wisdom their own optimism offers.

Sagittarians are most appealing to Capricorns when they stay grounded and reasonable. Understanding that Capricorns' philosophy involves being serious and working hard allows Sagittarians to quit expecting Capricorns to be looser and to start enjoying the integrity of their natures. Sagittarians entice Capricorns' interest and support when they show evidence of their preparation and forethought, and keep jokes to a minimum until success is imminent.

Capricorns get the most out of Sagittarians when they are more spontaneous and expansive. When Capricorns accept that living freely is Sagittarians' definition of prestige, Capricorns will quit expecting them to shape up and instead enjoy the refreshing lift their views provide. Sagittarians will be more cooperative with Capricorns' strategies when they package them with enthusiasm. Jokes are always welcome.

Romantic problems can better be resolved when Sagittarians show the sincerity and commitment that elicit Capricorns' trust, and Capricorns show the spontaneity and zest that thrill Sagittarians. When affection is more important than differences, the satisfaction they feel in the bedroom can conquer disputes.

The Sagittarius / Aquarius Relationship ♥♥♥

Sagittarians and Aquarians can enjoy a wonderfully interesting and satisfying relationship that's full of exploration, fun, and admiration. They bond through their love of new ideas, their quest for freedom, and their search for inspiration. Communication flows easily between them, as does friendship and trust. Since both Sagittarians and Aquarians see themselves as free spirits, they enjoy an atmosphere of openness between them. Together they make a bright and innovative pair that whips up loads of adventure and sparks adoration from the many whose lives they inspire.

Sagittarians are captivated by Aquarians' brilliant minds and inspired by their social and moral ideals. They adore Aquarians' uniqueness and applaud their independent, inventive ways. Sagittarians count on Aquarians' loyalty and their resolve to do what's good for them and others. Sags especially love how they can say or do most anything around Aquarians and feel understood.

Aquarians relish the adventure that Sagittarians deliver and adore how their expansive philosophy urges them to keep growing. They love Sagittarians' enthusiasm and appreciate the surprise of never knowing what Sagittarians will pull off next. Sagittarians bring to Aquarians what they value the most: natural friendship.

Romance between Sagittarians and Aquarians is deliciously rewarding as they enjoy a wonderful sexual compatibility. Their adoration of each other's individuality and respect for one another' freedom sparks an attraction that keeps things sexy and enticing. Lovemaking is explorative, with plenty of captivating surprises.

Possible Sagittarius/Aquarius Challenges

Although Sagittarians and Aquarians are compatible, the very qualities that attract them can also pull them apart.

Since both signs are determined individualists, commitment can be fleeting. Sometimes it's because neither wants to endure the confinement that commitments demand. Other times it's because both are ambivalent about the ordinariness that comes from doing the same thing over and over, which they fear commitment entails.

Aquarians' and Sagittarians' individualism can also be troublesome if they hold differing ideals. Since neither feels they should back down one iota from principles they believe in, contests over who's right can become so contentious that both lose sight of what they like about each other. Or, they can refuse to cooperate or concede for fear that would make them disloyal to their principles.

Sagittarians can find Aquarians' stubbornness unappealingly difficult. They're stunned to discover that their free-bird companions are also quite set in their ways.

Aquarians are disappointed when Sagittarians' self-promoting philosophies allow them to get ahead without carrying others along, as Aquarians believe they should.

Romantic problems arise when Sagittarians and Aquarians refuse to make a commitment or show loyalty the way the other needs or expects. Sagittarians' flirting and Aquarians' focus on friends can make each other feel unimportant. Sometimes their friendship overrides their love affair and sexuality gives way to "just talking."

Advice for the Sagittarius/Aquarius Relationship

Sagittarians and Aquarians get along best when both approach loyalty to their relationship as an act of freedom. Then they'll appreciate being together as a great choice rather than a "have-to." That, plus keeping their common interests charged, keeps both excited and involved.

Sagittarians maximize their appeal to Aquarians when they acknowledge the importance of Aquarius's friends and causes. Instead of arguing over who's right, extending a curious "Tell me more about your thoughts on . . ." helps Aquarians return the favor and be more open to them. Sagittarians should accept that Aquarians are carefree about some matters but really do need consistency in others.

Aquarians win Sagittarians' affection the most when they are expansive and flexible. Instead of expecting Sagittarians to devote themselves to making the worldly contributions they see fit, Aquarians fare better when they appreciate Sags' inspiration. Knowing that Sagittarians don't need the consistency they do helps Aquarians better accept their comings and goings.

Romantic problems between Aquarians and Sagittarians can best be resolved when both seek the greater possibilities commitment offers them instead of focusing on what they might lose. When each acknowledges the pleasurable surprises in connecting deeply, their respective heroism easily overcomes fear and chooses love.

The Sagittarius / Pisces Relationship ♥♥

Sagittarians and Pisces can enjoy a dynamic and creative relationship, especially when they understand their different emotional needs. They can bond through visions of possibilities, a love of the fantastic, and their quest to live large. Even their differences can prove enticing: Sags discover from Pisces how not always knowing the answers to life's questions can create magic and deeper spirituality, while Pisces gain objectivity and courage from Sagittarians' positive nature. Together they make a thoughtful and adaptable pair, one that explores the meaningful aspects of life and contributes understanding to the many attracted to their fascinating ways.

Sagittarians are intrigued by Pisces' spirituality and fascinated by their love of serving others. They enjoy the enchanting world of

Pisces' fantasies and applaud their flowing creativity. Pisces prompt Sagittarians to understand their deeper, gut-level yearnings and truths.

Pisces love riding the waves of excitement and inspiration that Sagittarians offer. They respect Sagittarians' leadership and ability to make any situation worthwhile and fun. Sagittarians help Pisces gain greater personal authority and promote their careers.

Romance between Pisces and Sagittarians is active and dreamy as each lives for the swooning, hopefulness, and abandon that courtship provides. Inhibitions are unnecessary as both relish satisfying the other's every fantasy.

Possible Sagittarius/Pisces Challenges

Although Sagittarians and Pisces are both adaptable, their differences can nevertheless make them fume. Sagittarians are fiery, positive, and extroverted. They value winning and dominating. Pisces are emotional and internal. They suffer and surrender so others can prevail. Sagittarians can consider Pisces as overly sensitive, and dismiss their yielding as wimpy. Pisces can view Sagittarians as harshly uncaring or arrogant.

Sagittarians get frustrated with Pisces' emotional indulgences, especially their feelings of pain. Pisces' belief that they or others are victims really annoys Sagittarians, who think, *Stand up for yourself and make yourself happy!*

Pisces get hurt when Sagittarians override or laugh off their feelings. They think Sagittarians lack an acceptance of pain and miss the poignancy of life. Pisces wish Sagittarians would spend less time spouting out heady "truths" and more time being truly sympathetic.

Romantic problems arise when Sagittarians dip too infrequently into tender vulnerability, and Pisces dip too often. When Sagittarians feel confined by Pisces' clinginess or unchallenged by their passivity, or when Pisces feel abandoned by Sagittarians' wandering or unimportant in lieu of their many inspirations, intimacy becomes unsatisfying.

Advice for the Sagittarius/Pisces Relationship

Sagittarians and Pisces get along best when they respect each other as different sides of the same spiritual/inspirational coin. When Sagittarians acknowledge the valuable insights Pisces' sympathies offer, they'll not only relate better with Pisces, they might rev up their compassion and relate better to others in general. If Pisces use more of Sagittarians' confident outlook and heroism, they'll not only win Sagittarians' respect, they might win more of the world's.

Sagittarians enjoy Pisces the most when they understand that Pisces value the gamut of emotions, including pain. Knowing that Pisces are uplifted by yielding to and supporting others allows Sags to appreciate the strength and wisdom of their doing so. Sagittarians elicit Pisces' support of their ideas when they tell Pisces how helpful they'll be to them or the others who'll be served.

Pisces are most attractive to Sagittarians when they are inspired and confident. When they understand that Sagittarians don't need to feel as much as they do to understand life, Pisces will better accept Sagittarians' ways. Pisces encourage Sagittarians' involvement with their goals when they show them how heroic doing so would be.

Romantic problems can better be resolved when Sagittarians are more attuned toward Pisces' feelings, and when Pisces show more initiative toward Sagittarians. When both use their creativity, the fireworks of their love remind them why they're such a special pair.

How Capricorns Match Up

The Capricorn/Aries Relationship

See *The Aries/Capricorn Relationship* on page 311.

The Capricorn/Taurus Relationship

See *The Taurus/Capricorn Relationship* on page 343.

The Capricorn/Gemini Relationship

See *The Gemini/Capricorn Relationship* on page 373.

The Capricorn/Cancer Relationship

See *The Cancer/Capricorn Relationship* on page 400.

The Capricorn/Leo Relationship

See *The Leo/Capricorn Relationship* on page 425.

The Capricorn/Virgo Relationship

See *The Virgo/Capricorn Relationship* on page 447.

The Capricorn/Libra Relationship

See *The Libra/Capricorn Relationship* on page 467.

The Capricorn/Scorpio Relationship

See *The Scorpio/Capricorn Relationship* on page 484.

The Capricorn/Sagittarius Relationship

See *The Sagittarius/Capricorn Relationship* on page 497.

The Capricorn/Capricorn Relationship ♥♥

*T*wo Capricorns can enjoy a solid and satisfying relationship that's full of admiration and impressive accomplishments. They bond through their prestigious ambitions, sense of duty, and appreciation of life's best offerings. Capricorns adore each other's reliable approach to matters and love being able to count on each other's good sense. They make a powerful pair, one that pursues respectable goals that satisfy them and make significant contributions to the world.

Capricorns find attractive in each other what they most like about themselves: their big-picture visions, strategic planning, and subtle but acerbic humor. They're relived to feel understood by another who knows the sacrifices they've made and the disappointments they've endured along the way to achieving their goals.

Capricorns also appreciate one another's no-nonsense attitude. They count on each other to do what they say they will and admire their class in foregoing self-congratulations, even when they're at the top of their game. Capricorns respect each other's refusal to bow to unnecessary displays of emotions. Working hard together is especially satisfying. But fun is done with excellence as well.

Romance between two Capricorns is sweet and gentle, especially when they've gotten past their initial shyness. Love is extremely special to them, and they guard it with respect. Lovemaking is wonderfully earthy, affectionate, and satisfying.

Possible Capricorn/Capricorn Challenges

*A*s with all same-sign relationships, Capricorns can sometimes be too alike to stay attracted or even get along.

Capricorns' serious, sometimes worrisome natures can get the best of them. Their protective shells can keep them from exuding vulnerability that invites closeness. Or their perfectionism or pessimism can keep them from recognizing what's good about their relationship or what they have done. Capricorns' suspicions can go into overdrive, convincing them that others are plotting to undermine what they've achieved. Sometimes Capricorns just find each other too "heavy" and seek companions who offer levity.

Capricorns' ambitions can also pull them apart. If each puts their work or duties ahead of their relationship, it suffers. Or, if a competition erupts over whose job or plans are more important, neither gets the support or respect they crave.

Capricorns' cautiousness and need for propriety can keep them from taking the risks that make life interesting. They might discourage each other from exploring new adventures for fear of enduring failure. Or, in the name of being appropriate or respectable, Capricorns might pressure the other into routines that aren't truly satisfying.

Romantic problems can arise from Capricorns being too mistrustful of being hurt and hesitating to take steps toward deeper intimacy. Stoicism can mask deeper interest and affection, leaving each wondering if the other truly cares.

Advice for the Capricorn/Capricorn Relationship

When Capricorns capitalize on their innate understanding of one another, few companions can be as powerful or trusted.

Putting themselves on the line and showing how interested they are keeps Capricorns' relationships moving. Instead of waiting for the other to make the first move, reaching out helps each put the other at ease. Doing specific things that demonstrate "You can trust me!" are always endearing to Capricorns.

Incorporating levity—not the goof-off type, but the kind that shows irony and insight—also helps Capricorns stay interested. Remembering to notice the goodness in things prevents them from feeling deflated over how poorly things around them are run.

Romantic problems between Capricorns can better be resolved when each does their best to show warmth, appreciation, and tenderness. Instead of letting disappointments lead to distance, Capricorns are smarter to openly express needs and hurts so each has clues into the other's sensitive psyche. This keeps their relationship rewardingly intimate.

The Capricorn/Aquarius Relationship ♥♥

Capricorns and Aquarians can enjoy a dynamic and engaging relationship that's rich in respect and ingenuity. They can bond through their worldly concerns, a need to make significant impact, and their love of progress. Aquarians and Capricorns are both visionary thinkers who keep each other captivated with their pragmatic ideas for making everything better. They make a powerful and productive pair, one that tackles worthwhile projects and makes the world a better place for the many they love and support.

Capricorns enjoy Aquarians' brilliance and respect how they serve humanity. They admire how Aquarians not only envision possibilities, but they work to bring them into reality. Capricorns also appreciate how Aquarians care deeply yet don't complicate matters with gushy emotions. Aquarians build Capricorns' self-value and even their bank accounts.

Aquarians respect Capricorns' many accomplishments and practical sense. They enjoy Capricorns' adherence to respectable principles and willingness to make sacrifices to serve greater causes. Capricorns' subtle humor tickles Aquarians and their stoicism is refreshingly reasonable. Capricorns help Aquarians better understand their deeper motivations.

Romance between Aquarians and Capricorns is unexpected yet powerful. Each one's strength and wit provides the challenge and interest the other needs to stay enticed. Lovemaking brings out a tender softness they rarely express.

Possible Capricorn/Aquarius Challenges

Although both Capricorns and Aquarians are visionaries, what they have visions about and what they envision as useful strategies can cause problems.

Whereas Capricorns respect social order and like to work along well-established lines, Aquarians don't mind upsetting the status quo. Capricorns can consider Aquarians' shocking, zany ways too outlandish to trust or take seriously and write them off as loose cannons. Aquarians can dismiss Capricorns as uptight conservatives.

Capricorns feel threatened by Aquarians' unconventionality, which makes them nervous and seems disrespectful. They cringe over Aquarians' progressive ideals, thinking they're too radical to work. Capricorns wish that Aquarians would invest less time tinkering with innovations and more time recognizing the usefulness of traditions.

Aquarians feel thwarted by Capricorns' adherence to rules and protocols. They wish that Capricorns would be more willing to try new things and less concerned about what others think. They also wish Capricorns would be more creative and free.

Romantic problems can arise from both Capricorns and Aquarians feeling awkward about emotional expression or being too detached to show love. Aquarians might be disappointed by Capricorns' resistance to variety in lovemaking, while Capricorns are put off by Aquarians' taste for it.

Advice for the Capricorn/Aquarius Relationship

Capricorns and Aquarians get along best when they respect each other's unique lifestyles. Showing interest and loyalty works wonders to keep their relationship lively and engaged.

Capricorns are most appealing to Aquarians when they are creative and spontaneous. Instead of expecting Aquarians' ideas to be pragmatic, Capricorns are smarter to look for the potential genius in their unconventional viewpoints. Capricorns entice Aquarians' cooperation with their strategies when they show Aquarians how others will benefit by them and how unique they are.

Aquarians enjoy Capricorns best when they understand that they express their individuality by being respectable members of society. Then, instead of expecting Capricorns to be more unique, they'll respect the creativity with which they achieve their status. Aquarians ignite Capricorns' interest in their ideas and projects when they show them how respectable they'll be and how practically they can be attained.

Romantic problems between Aquarians and Capricorns can better be resolved when Capricorns are more spontaneous and Aquarians are more earthy in their lovemaking. When each does what the other needs to feel valued and engaged, sexuality is rewardingly satisfying.

The Capricorn/Pisces Relationship ♥♥♥

Capricorns and Pisces can enjoy a sweet and satisfying relationship rich in adoration and magic. They bond through their care for others, an interest in worldly concerns, and even a shared melancholy about the harshness of this world. Their differences can prove complementary: Pisces love that Capricorns take charge of practical realities they need but find unappealing, while Pisces' compassion provides the gentle understanding Capricorns crave but might be too stoic to request. Together, they're a concerned and giving pair, one that pursues important projects and provides a foundation of support for the many they include in their circle.

Capricorns feel reassured by Pisces' kindness. Pisces' romanticism provides a respite to Capricorns, who'll take time out to linger in their relaxing dreams. Capricorns appreciate how Pisces provide encouragement and support for their ambitions, but rarely compete with them. They love saying anything to Pisces and feeling understood.

Pisces feel assured by Capricorns' savvy and protected by their competency. They love being able to count on Capricorns' solid advice. Pisces enjoy looking past Capricorns' cautious exteriors to find the precious soul few others see. Capricorns make a natural friend to Pisces, who help them realize their hopes and dreams.

Romance between Capricorns and Pisces can be endearing and sacred as each opens the other's romantic nature. Capricorns relish the creative abandon Pisces woo them with, while Pisces are awed by Capricorns' special attentiveness. Lovemaking is luscious and intimate.

Possible Capricorn / Pisces Challenges

Although Capricorns and Pisces usually enjoy a sanctuary of compatibility, their differences can ignite a war zone of frustrations. Whereas Capricorns are stoic, practical, and reality-based, Pisces are vulnerable, emotional, and imaginative. Capricorns are worldly, but Pisces escape into imagination. Capricorns can dismiss Pisces as sentimental dreamers of little consequence, while Pisces fume that Capricorns are insensitive grumps.

Capricorns become frustrated when Pisces fail to adhere to important rules. They resent Pisces' floating away from situations or "forgetting" to keep agreements that they lose interest in. Capricorns find Pisces' fantasies a waste of time and their escapism dishonorable. Their emotional dramas exasperate Capricorns, and their belief that they and others are victims seems irresponsible.

Pisces feel shut out by Capricorns' stoicism and hurt by their dismissal of everyone's feelings. Pisces feel confined by Capricorns' regimens, and their need for creative chaos is squelched by Capricorns' perfection-seeking order. Pisces feel disappointed that Capricorns value accomplishment over connection.

Romantic problems arise when Capricorns refuse to express the tender intimacies Pisces need for love, or when Pisces get so wrapped up in theirs that Capricorns feel eclipsed by them. When Capricorns' ambitions or Pisces' escapism seems more important than their relationship, lovemaking peters out.

Advice for the Capricorn / Pisces Relationship

Capricorns and Pisces get along best when they value one another's natures. When Capricorns honor Pisces' sensitivity as a worthwhile contribution, they not only connect better with Pisces, they may connect more to their own and others' feelings. When Pisces respect Capricorns' practical strategies they not only endear themselves to Capricorns, they might learn how to translate their dreams into this reality.

Capricorns enjoy Pisces most when they understand that their highest ambition is to bring compassion and creativity into this world. Capricorns inspire Pisces' interest in their ideas when they show Pisces the adventure of them and how they'll help others.

Pisces capture Capricorns' attention by being practical. Instead of expecting Capricorns to show caring emotionally, Pisces are wise to look for it through their actions. Pisces command Capricorns' interest and support for their ideas and requests when they show Capricorns how admirable and useful they'll be.

Romantic problems can be resolved when Capricorns extend the softness and vulnerability Pisces need, and Pisces show the loyalty and involvement Capricorns need. When each sees the other putting in effort, both melt and the magic of their lovemaking thrives.

How Aquarians Match Up

The Aquarius/Aries Relationship

See *The Aries/Aquarius Relationship* on page 314.

The Aquarius/Taurus Relationship

See *The Taurus/Aquarius Relationship* on page 346.

The Aquarius/Gemini Relationship

See *The Gemini/Aquarius Relationship* on page 376.

The Aquarius / Cancer Relationship

See *The Cancer/Aquarius Relationship* on page 403.

The Aquarius / Leo Relationship

See *The Leo/Aquarius Relationship* on page 428.

The Aquarius / Virgo Relationship

See *The Virgo/Aquarius Relationship* on page 450.

The Aquarius / Libra Relationship

See *The Libra/Aquarius Relationship* on page 470.

The Aquarius / Scorpio Relationship

See *The Scorpio/Aquarius Relationship* on page 487.

The Aquarius / Sagittarius Relationship

See *The Sagittarius/Aquarius Relationship* on page 500.

The Aquarius/Capricorn Relationship

See *The Capricorn/Aquarius Relationship* on page 511.

The Aquarius/Aquarius Relationship ♥♥

*T*wo Aquarians can enjoy a fascinating and inventive relationship that's rich in adventure and mental stimulation. They bond through their search for whatever's new and progressive, an interest in worldly causes, and their love of being unique. Aquarians captivate each other's canny intelligence with shared interests and ideas about how to make any and everything better. Together they make an interesting and outstanding pair, one that explores the progressive subjects that satisfy them and makes significant contributions to the wide social world they care intensely about.

Aquarians adore in each other what they like most about themselves: their brilliance, rebelliousness, and striking individuality are all wonderfully attractive. Aquarians are thrilled to discover another who lives life as creatively and unexpectedly as they do. They adore each other's zaniness and good-hearted devotion to making the world better.

Aquarians find each other's logic and detachment a refreshing respite from others' needlessly emotional ways. They appreciate each other's loyalty—to their own calling as well as to each other. Aquarians applaud each other's refusal to cooperate with anyone or anything that encroaches on the values and ideals they hold so high.

Importantly, Aquarians value each other's friendship. They enjoy the freedom their Aquarian companion extends as well as the open acceptance of their quirky ways. Aquarians sometime feel like a lonely stranger in a strange land, and they treasure the rare fellowship another Aquarians' understanding provides.

Romance between two Aquarians is an erotic friendship. Their strong individualities provide the stimulation and challenge each needs to stay interested. Plus, the freedom and surprises each extends ensures their lovemaking remains creative.

Possible Aquarius/Aquarius Challenges

As with all same-sign relationships, Aquarians can sometimes be too much alike to stay interested or even get along.

Aquarians' determined individuality can sometimes cause problems between them. Each might expect the other to go along with their preferences while being unwilling to compromise themselves. Or, both consider their calling as more important than the other's, and a bitter standoff takes place. And, since Aquarians tend to believe they're "right," neither considers the other's differing viewpoint as valid.

Aquarians' aloofness can also make it hard for them to connect. Awkwardness with emotional expression can make Aquarians hesitant to reveal the feelings that secure friendship and intimacy, even if they're quite interested.

Aquarians' need for freedom can also interfere with their relationship. Each might hesitate to ask much of the other for fear of seeming too needy. Or, if one Aquarian expects more freedom or freedom in different ways than the other, feelings of abandonment can prevail.

Romantic problems can arise from neither Aquarian being comfortable with the emotional intimacy or commitments typical courtship requires. Both might find the other too independent or aloof to feel close. Sometimes Aquarians' friendship is so strong that erotic feelings dissolve.

Advice for the Aquarius/Aquarius Relationship

Two Aquarians get along best when they capitalize on their unique fellowship and use their strong resolve to remain committed.

When Aquarians remember how important their ideals and freedom are to them, they'll better understand how important they are to their Aquarian companion. Then, instead of defending their ways, they'll be great friends and show tolerance.

Risking emotional expression also helps Aquarians stay connected. Aquarians don't like being fenced in, but they hate being abandoned. They need to show one another they care deeply and won't disappear.

When Aquarians do bump heads over ideas or preferences, instead of arguing over who's right, respectfully honoring one another's individuality and agreeing to disagree keeps their relationship alive.

Romantic problems can better be resolved when both make a special effort to be attuned with each other's needs. Showing consideration, interest, and vulnerability works wonders to keep Aquarians' hearts open and their lovemaking uniquely magical.

The Aquarius / Pisces Relationship ♥♥

*A*quarians and Pisces can enjoy a captivating and enriching relationship, especially when they understand their different emotional dispositions. They can bond through their interest in the unusual and fantastic, worldly visions, and love of humanity. Even their differences can prove complementary: Aquarians count on Pisces to fluidly express the emotions and compassion they might feel but hesitate to express, while Pisces count on Aquarians to maintain the cool logic they admire but can't always stick to. Together they make an involved and creative pair, one that pursues the social projects that satisfy them and assists the people they care deeply about.

Aquarians respect how Pisces genuinely help others and find their harmlessness endearing. Aquarians admire that, like themselves, Pisces are unpredictably unique and devote themselves to making worthwhile differences in the world. Pisces' understanding helps Aquarians feel secure and might help them develop their resources.

Pisces admire Aquarians' advanced thinking and are captivated by their surprising individuality. They appreciate that Aquarians also look at the big picture and want to make the world a good place. Aquarians awaken Pisces to their deeper motivations and spark their spirituality.

Romance between Pisces and Aquarians is unexpected yet compelling. Both deliver the creativity and wonder that keeps each intrigued and involved. When Pisces woo Aquarians with their spellbinding romanticism, and Aquarians beguile Pisces with their unique attentiveness, lovemaking is magical.

Possible Aquarius/Pisces Challenges

Although Aquarians and Pisces share global concerns and innovative visions, the way they pursue them can cause a world of frustrations between them.

Aquarians love being logical and resist gushy emotional scenes, while Pisces specialize in expressing the gamut of feelings and live for emotional dramas. Aquarians uphold their individuality, while Pisces love losing themselves to whomever or whatever interests them. Aquarians can write Pisces off as sentimental clingers, while Pisces dismiss Aquarians as cold fish.

Aquarians become uncomfortable around Pisces' emotional natures, especially their penchant for painful feelings. Aquarians wish Pisces would replace their sympathy with logical actions and their fantasies with productive efforts.

Pisces become hurt over Aquarians' dismissal of their and others' feelings and feel discouraged with their insistently logical stance. They're lonely when Aquarians eschew connectedness. Pisces wish Aquarians would snap out of their aloof worldly idealism long enough to recognize the plight of the person in front of them.

Romantic problems arise if Aquarians resist the tender, sentimental intimacies that draw Pisces close, or when Pisces express too much of them and suffocate Aquarians. When Pisces demand more merging or Aquarians demand more space, lovemaking becomes unsatisfying.

Advice for the Aquarius/Pisces Relationship

$\mathcal{A}$quarians and Pisces get along best when they capitalize on their unique assets. When Aquarians acknowledge the brilliant insights Pisces' sensitivities offer, they'll not only better connect with Pisces, they'll discover how their own compassion helps them feel closer to the world. When Pisces recognize the caring in Aquarians' objectivity, they'll not only relate more effectively with Aquarians, they'll discover how stepping away from consuming emotions makes them more clear and effective in relating to others, including themselves!

Aquarians are most captivating to Pisces when they are passionate and emotionally available. Respecting Pisces' ability to feel and merge with others as evolutionary helps Aquarians to quit expecting them to be logical and start delighting in the unique artistry and mysticism Pisces do contribute. Aquarians entice Pisces' cooperation with ideas and projects by reminding them how emotionally satisfying or helpful their contributions will be.

Pisces get the most out of Aquarians when they are logical. Instead of expecting Aquarians to show love or concern emotionally, Pisces are smarter to notice it through their actions. Pisces capture Aquarians' interest and cooperation with their ideas and requests when they present them with facts or challenge them to figure out how they could work.

Romantic differences can be smoothed over when Aquarians keep up the affection and attentiveness Pisces need, and Pisces maintain the surprises and openness Aquarians need. Then their lovemaking reminds them why differences are delicious.

How Pisces Match Up

The Pisces / Aries Relationship

See *The Aries/Pisces Relationship* on page 317.

The Pisces / Taurus Relationship

See *The Taurus/Pisces Relationship* on page 349.

The Pisces / Gemini Relationship

See *The Gemini/Pisces Relationship* on page 379.

The Pisces / Cancer Relationship

See *The Cancer/Pisces Relationship* on page 406.

The Pisces / Leo Relationship

See *The Leo/Pisces Relationship* on page 431.

The Pisces / Virgo Relationship

See *The Virgo/Pisces Relationship* on page 452.

The Pisces / Libra Relationship

See *The Libra/Pisces Relationship* on page 472.

The Pisces / Scorpio Relationship

See *The Scorpio/Pisces Relationship* on page 490.

The Pisces / Sagittarius Relationship

See *The Sagittarius/Pisces Relationship* on page 503.

The Pisces/Capricorn Relationship

See *The Capricorn/Pisces Relationship* on page 514.

The Pisces/Aquarius Relationship

See *The Aquarius/Pisces Relationship* on page 524.

The Pisces/Pisces Relationship ♥♥

*T*wo Pisces can enjoy an enchanting and precious relationship that's richly intimate and creative, especially when they support each other's strengths. They bond through their sensitive awareness, love of exploring intriguing subjects, and an urge to assist or rescue others. Pisces love the gentle understanding the other's sympathetic nature offers and relish each other's magical fantasies and spiritual depth. They especially appreciate how the other's fluid boundaries allow a connectedness between them. Together Pisces make an imaginative and giving pair, one that pursues the dreams that satisfy them and contributes supportive understanding to the many they love and serve.

Pisces love in each other what they most like about themselves: their ageless wisdom, kindness, and emotional depth. Pisces respect one another's complexity and appreciate how they compassionately reach out to others, even if it's uncomfortable or painful.

Pisces are also relieved to be with someone who focuses on the yearnings of their soul rather than worldly titles or demands. They agree love and creativity are the most important pursuits. Escaping together is delicious, be it through service, creativity, spirituality, or other consciousness-altering activities.

Romance between Pisces is an indulgent stream of surrendering to the throes of love, breathless visions of merging, tender thoughtfulness, and giving that creates the dreamy courtship they crave.

Possible Pisces/Pisces Challenges

*A*s with all same-sign relationships, two Pisces can be too much alike to stay interested or even get along. Sometimes their complexity causes problems between them. Pisces' tendency to simultaneously want something and not want it can create confusion or ambivalence in their relationship. Each might broadcast mixed signals that make understanding each other confusing. Or, Pisces might mask feelings or hide truths for fear of being hurt or too vulnerable. Ironically, Pisces might bolt just when the closeness they crave starts to happen.

Sometimes two Pisces can become so consumed with their fantasies, they miss what is actually happening. Each can be so enthralled with the potential they imagine for their relationship that they might forget to look to see if it is actually taking place. Or, if both get lost in the throes of emotions, neither might have enough objectivity to see clearly.

Pisces' belief that they or others are victims can also get the best of their relationship. Spending time feeling sorry for themselves or the world can make them miss the goodness of life or take steps to remedy matters.

And, Pisces' knack for whipping up dramatic chaos and their penchant for escaping can sometimes distract them from tending to the ordinary responsibilities or routines that make life work. Agreements and commitments might be missed as Pisces get lost in more compelling matters.

Romantic problems can arise from Pisces' ambivalence or conflicting feelings about what they want. If one wants more of a commitment than the other or defines it differently, or if neither are forthcoming about genuine feelings and expectations, mistrust can make lovemaking disappointing and distant.

Advice for the Pisces/Pisces Relationship

Pisces get along best when they show one another they can be trusted to be emotionally safe, honest, and loyal. That sets a foundation of security and understanding so both can open up.

Remembering to maintain healthy boundaries as they connect helps prevent Pisces from getting lost in or confused by the other's feelings and issues. Looking for the opportunities or lessons their challenges offer helps Pisces maintain the clarity that's genuinely supportive of each awakening to their rare wisdom.

Creative endeavors are always captivating for Pisces, as is exploring all things fascinating and spiritual. Agreeing to workable time frames and respecting each other's commitments helps Pisces enjoy their adventures while still satisfying life's practical demands.

Romantic problems can be better addressed when Pisces are direct and honest about how they feel and what they need. When each acts to make the other feel loved, secure, and trusting, their compassion overcomes differences and returns them to the magical intimacies they find so satisfying.

Also from
Phyllis F. Mitz

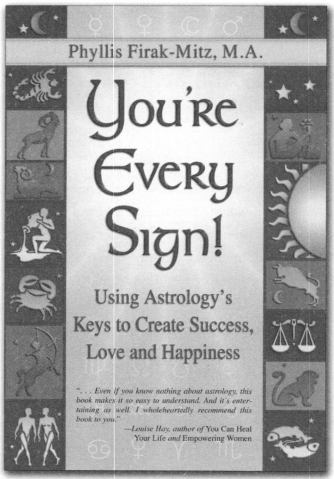